PERSONALITY DEVELOPMENT

Theoretical, Empirical, and Clinical
Investigations of Loevinger's
Conception of Ego Development

PERSONALITY DEVELOPMENT

Theoretical, Empirical, and Clinical Investigations of Loevinger's Conception of Ego Development

Edited by

P. Michiel Westenberg
Leiden University—The Netherlands

Augusto Blasi
University of Massachusetts—Boston

Lawrence D. Cohn
The University of Texas at El Paso

Psychology Press
Taylor & Francis Group

New York   London

First Published by
Lawrence Erlbaum Associates, Inc., Publishers
10 Industrial Avenue
Mahwah, New Jersey 07430

Published 2009 by Psychology Press
711 Third Avenue, New York, NY 10017
27 Church Road, Hove, East Sussex, BN3 2FA

First issued in paperback 2014

Psychology Press is an imprint of the Taylor & Francis Group, an informa business

Cover design by Kathryn Houghtaling Lacey

Library of Congress Cataloging-in-Publication Data

Personality development : theoretical, empirical, and clinical
  investigations of Loevinger's conception of ego development / edited
  by P. Michiel Westenberg, Augusto Blasi, Lawrence D. Cohn.
      p.   cm.
  includes bibliographical references and indexes.
  ISBN 0-8058-1649-6 (alk. paper)
  1. Ego (Psychology) 2. Developmental psychology.   I. Westenberg,
P. Michiel.   II. Blasi, Augusto.   III. Cohn, Lawrence.
BF175.5.E35P47 1998
155.2—dc21   97-41407
                                                              CIP

ISBN 13: 978-0-8058-1649-5 (hbk)
ISBN 13: 978-1-138-01232-5 (pbk)

Publisher's Note
The publisher has gone to great lengths to ensure the quality of this reprint
but points out that some imperfections in the original may be apparent.

Contents

Introduction:
Contributions and
Controversies

Personality theories often lack an appreciation of development, and developmental theories often lack an appreciation of individual differences. Jane Loevinger's work on ego development bridges the gap between these two domains. "Individual differences in character," she noted (1976), "have interested men for centuries. Interest in how character is formed in childhood and youth is also ancient. But to see those two phenomena as manifestations of a single developmental continuum is a modern twist. That insight is the origin of ego development as a formal discipline" (p. 3). Loevinger regards ego development as the central dimension of personality, second only to intelligence in its pervasiveness and influence. Her empirically based descriptions of the stages of ego development must be counted amongst the most important achievements of personality and developmental psychology (see Appendix for an overview of the stages of ego development).

Until recently, personality and developmental psychology pursued seemingly incompatible goals. Personality research sought to identify individual differences in polar variables, a goal that could not meaningfully incorporate evidence of qualitative changes in personality growth. In contrast, developmental psychology sought to identify age related qualitative changes, a goal that could not meaningfully incorporate evidence of individual differences within age cohorts. The theory and measurement of ego development addresses both goals simultaneously.

Loevinger's measurement strategy provides investigators with a method for converting qualitative data into psychometrically sound quantitative data. More importantly, it permits a continual exchange between data and theory, leading to progressive refinements of theory

1

(Loevinger, 1993a). Her solution to the problem of converting qualitative material (sentence completions) into quantitative data (ego level ratings) avoids the excesses of positivism while also avoiding the temptation to force theoretical interpretations on data. In this regard, her strategy of "micro-validation" provides a way of interweaving test construction with concept refinement; that is, it provides a means for using objective tests as instruments of psychological theory (Loevinger, 1957).

Loevinger's innovative research methodology, psychometric rigor, and theoretical scope have attracted the widespread attention of scholars and researchers around the globe. Empirical investigations employing the Washington University Sentence Completion Test of Ego Development (WUSCT) appear with increasing frequency and total more than 300 studies. The first comprehensive revision of the WUSCT scoring manual appeared (Hy & Loevinger, 1996), and the time seems ripe for reflecting on the strengths and limitations of Loevinger's developmental model.

The first 19 chapters in this volume are grouped into four sections corresponding to four broad questions one can raise about Loevinger's conception of ego development:

1. What is its scope and intellectual tradition?
2. What evidence is there for construct validity?
3. What are its relations with other social-developmental models?
4. What are its clinical implications?

This quadripartite grouping provides a framework for organizing the present material, but the questions raised in one section are often addressed in other sections.

In the final chapter Loevinger addresses several issues raised in the current volume by recounting the history of the WUSCT and the construct it seeks to measure.

PART I: THE NATURE OF EGO DEVELOPMENT

Chapters in Part I address several questions left unanswered in Loevinger's original formulation of the theory: What is the nature of the stage sequence? What mechanisms underlie development? Where should Loevinger's theory be located within the field of developmental theories? Loevinger argues that ego development must be distinguished from intelligence on the one hand and psychosexual development on the other hand. She has resisted pressure, however, to further define ego development as a psychological construct. From her perspective, ego development is too encompassing and too fluctuating in its manifestations to pin down its abstract nature. Instead of providing a formal definition, Loevinger offers a pointing definition, providing empirically based descriptions of each developmental level. Yet a more formal definition of ego development may be necessary for resolving a number of theoretical issues, including (a) deciding what determines the constitutive elements of each stage, (b) identifying principles that explain the coherence of each stage, and (c) proposing a mechanism that drives development.

Two misconceptions frequently arise over Loevinger's work. First, her stage sequence is often located within a Piagetian framework, leading many investigators to regard ego development as an index of cognitive growth or, more generally, an index of intelligence. Attempts to link Loevinger's developmental model to early psychoanalytic theory reflects a second misconception. Blasi (chap. 1) argues that Loevinger's conception of ego development cannot be understood within the context either of cognitive-developmentalism or of psychoanalysis. He details how the cognitive component within ego development is qualitatively different from the cognitive component within Piagetian theory and its offshoots. Westen (chap. 4) also argues that Loevinger's theory of ego development is not an outgrowth of psychoanalysis and has little overlap with the four classical psychoanalytic models. Despite the conceptual independence of ego development and psychoanalytic theory, Westen notes that Loevinger's work anticipated many contemporary currents in psychoanalysis, particularly psychoanalysis' current emphasis on interpersonal relationships (see also Josselson in this volume).

What are the central features of ego development if they are neither cognitive nor psychosexual in nature? Stated more concretely: What changes during the course of ego development, and why? Blasi (chap. 1) suggests that ego development reflects the evolution of a motivation for mastery. McAdams (chap. 2), using James' distinction between "I" and "Me," argues that ego development would be the I that progressively constructs the Me, eventually by constructing one's life story. Kegan, Lahey, and Souvaine (chap. 3) define the central organizing tendency of ego development as the progressive differentiation between "subject" and "object"—the aspects of self one controls and those one is controlled by. All of these authors share the view that ego development, however defined, reflects an underlying unity in personality (see Westen's chap. 4 for a contrary opinion).

All stage models face the problem of explaining why growth occurs. Holt (chap. 5) proposes that General Systems Theory provides important insights into this issue. In so doing, he demonstrates that the central principles of ego development theory are found in other domains of science, ranging from astronomy to biology. The issue of developmental pacers is addressed by several other authors (e.g., Cohn; Josselson; Borders, this volume).

PART II: CONSTRUCT VALIDITY

Chapters in Part II present empirical findings that, directly or indirectly, address issues of construct validity. Are stage descriptions generally valid, regardless of age and gender? What is the course of development during adolescence and adulthood? Two comprehensive reviews of early research with the WUSCT have been published (Hauser, 1976; Loevinger, 1979a), but an overview of more recent findings is not available. The present volume attempts to fill that gap, partially, by presenting chapters that include elaborate reviews of research in a particular area. Pals and John (chap. 7), for example, review evidence in support of the premise that developmental maturity is related to individual differences in personality. Chapters throughout the book present novel findings pertaining to the validity of the ego development construct and measure.

Westenberg, Jonckheer, Treffers, and Drewes (chap. 6) examine the extent to which Loevinger's stage descriptions and scoring categories are applicable to children and adolescents. Their study of more than 2,500 Dutch respondents support the cross-national and cross-age validity of Loevinger's developmental model. Their findings also suggest a need for revising descriptions of the earliest developmental stages, at least when applied to children and adolescents. Such findings rekindle a question Loevinger considered answered: Does age-contingent scoring permit more precise assessments of ego development?

Pals and John (chap. 7) examine the link between ego development and personality traits and typologies. Their findings suggest that developmental maturity is related to individual differences in personality types. However, they found that subtle distinctions among ego development stages could not be captured by objective personality measures.

Employing a meta-analysis of findings obtained from cross-sectional and longitudinal studies, Cohn (chap. 8) examines the course of ego development across adulthood. His analysis supports Loevinger's expectation that development tapers off by early adulthood. Knowing the trajectory of development may provide some insight into the factors that promote or inhibit growth. Rogers (chap. 9) examines whether gender-related experiences differentially affect ego development. She proposes that certain types of experiences, such as conflict over social conventions, may inhibit or even reverse the course of ego development in girls.

PART III: RELATED DEVELOPMENTAL MODELS

Chapters in Part III examine the empirical relations between ego development and several related constructs, including moral development, the development of interpersonal understanding, and attachment classifications. Contrary to Loevinger's assumption that the edge of growth may occur in any domain (Loevinger, 1983), some authors in this section suggest that growth in one domain is a necessary but not sufficient condition for growth in another domain. Snarey (chap. 10) examines the link between moral and ego development, investigating whether ego development is a necessary, but not sufficient, condition for moral development. Despite the strong correlation between ego and moral development, Snarey argues that the two constructs are far from interchangeable, and their relationship depends on one's age and gender.

Schultz and Selman (chap. 11) link ego development to an increasing capacity for coordinating perspectives of oneself and other people. Such coordination involves an understanding of relationships, affective meaning, and interpersonal action. The authors argue that ego development is most closely aligned with the cognitive component in this process (i.e., understanding relationships), and is a necessary but not sufficient condition for mature real-life relationships. A related theme is raised by Hauser, Gerber, and Allen (chap. 12), who examine the association between ego level and attachment status. Their research suggests that adolescent ego level predicts security of attachment in young adulthood. The authors argue that ego development may function as a necessary, but not sufficient, condition for secure attachment in adolescence and adulthood. Labouvie-Vief and Diehl (chap. 13), in contrast, propose that ego development is more closely aligned with cognitive rather than affective aspects of personality growth, and would thus be unrelated to attachment styles.

Many authors throughout the volume (e.g., Blasi; McAdams, Noam, Westen) raise a central question about the nature of ego development: Does Loevinger's conception of ego development only capture the cognitive component of personality and personality growth? The evidence thus far does not support this interpretation. Indeed, Loevinger's scoring manual and stage descriptions emphasize the affective and motivational aspects of personality growth, such as impulse control, conscious preoccupations, interpersonal orientation, and character development. Loevinger (e.g., 1976) considers *cognitive style* (sometimes referred to as *cognitive complexity*) as one of several strands of ego development. However, it is not clear that Loevinger and some of the authors in this volume attach the same meaning to these terms. Should cognitive complexity, however it is defined, be regarded as a central component of ego development or should it be seen as only an important correlate? Can the affective-motivational components of ego development be split, theoretically or practically, from the cognitive components of personality, implying the existence of two separate developmental strands? Such questions can be explored empirically. The ideas proposed by several authors in this volume provide a useful context for pursuing this investigation.

PART IV: CLINICAL IMPLICATIONS

Chapters in Part IV examine the clinical implications of Loevinger's developmental model. Several issues are addressed, including the link between ego development and psychopathology, the necessity of tailoring psychotherapy to the developmental level of the patient, the link between ego development and clients' representations of psychotherapy, and the relations between ego level and counseling skills. Loevinger (1968) maintained that ". . . every stage has its weaknesses, its problems, and its paradoxes, which provide both a potential for maladjustment and a potential for growth" (p. 169). She suggested that some psychopathologies are probably more common at certain developmental stages, but she also emphasizes that the relation between ego level and mental health can only be accurately assessed when the two constructs are defined independently of each other (Loevinger, 1968).

Rierdan (chap. 15) accepts Loevinger's conceptual distinction between ego level and mental health, while Noam (chap. 16) explicitly rejects it, arguing that mental health indicators are woven into Loevinger's developmental model. Rierdan approaches this general issue by examining the link between ego level, depression, and pubertal timing in girls. Noam examines the issue of ego level and mental health within the context of his research program with clinical populations, linking ego level and adolescent psychopathology. Taken together, both chapters provide an extensive review of the empirical relations between ego level and symptomatology, a topic the authors locate within their more general discussion of developmental psychopathology. Both authors conclude that ego level influences the presence, severity, and specific form of psychopathology. However, the extent to which ego development and mental health are conceptually distinct remains unresolved. Findings obtained by Westenberg et al. (chap. 6) touch on the latter issue. Much of the malignancy that is typically associated with Impulsive and Self-protective adults was missing from the SCT responses of Impulsive and

Self-protective children and adolescents. Such findings must be incorporated into models linking ego level and mental health.

Horowitz (chap. 17) discusses development from the standpoint of an individual's increasing capacity for supraordinate organization of self and other schemas. He suggests that healthy adjustment accompanies the capacity for supraordinate organization, and he illustrates how therapeutic strategies could be tailored for different developmental levels. His discussion is not specifically tied to Loevinger's model of ego development and thus provides readers with an alternative framework for conceptualizing the link between mental health and development. Young-Eisendrath and Foltz (chap. 18) return to Loevinger's model and examine how ego level influences patients' understanding and expectations of psychotherapy. Their findings suggest that clients at low ego levels perceive psychotherapy as a concrete service provided by therapists who are responsible for the outcome; at higher developmental levels psychotherapy is conceived of as a personal process of internal discovery for which the patient is primarily responsible.

Borders (chap. 19) shifts the focus of discussion and examines how counselors' ego level influences the perception of patients, in-session cognitions, and counseling ability. She hypothesizes that one's ego level restricts the attainable level of counseling skills, although counseling training itself may promote ego development.

POSTSCRIPT

Loevinger recounts the history of the WUSCT and the empirical basis of her developmental model. It was data analysis, not psychoanalysis, that shaped the evolution of her stage theory. Several additional issues are addressed in her chapter, including the relationship between ego development and intelligence, and the limits of computerized scoring of WUSCT protocols. Although seemingly disparate in focus, both topics are concerned with predicting ego development scores. Loevinger cautions, however, that the WUSCT was not developed for the sole purpose of calculating a total protocol rating. Rather, the WUSCT was designed to reveal insights into the nature of personality growth, a goal that could be eclipsed by focusing solely on the prediction.

The contributions to this volume attest to the pervasive influence of Loevinger's theory and the lively state of work in the field of ego development. Important questions remain unanswered and there is disagreement over some central issues. But such debate reflects the normal development of any theory. We hope the present chapters succeed in clarifying important theoretical and empirical questions underlying this debate and, in so doing, stimulate further inquiry into the nature of ego development as a psychological dimension.

P. Michiel Westenberg
Augusto Blasi
Lawrence D. Cohn

APPENDIX

SOME CHARACTERISTICS OF LEVEL OF EGO DEVELOPMENT

Level	Code[a]	Characteristics		
		Impulse Control	Interpersonal Mode	Conscious Preoccupations
Impulsive	E2 (I-2)	Impulsive	Egocentric, dependent	Bodily feelings
Self-Protective	E3 (Delta)	Opportunistic	Manipulative, wary	"Trouble," control
Conformist	E4 (I-3)	Respect for rules	Cooperative, loyal	Appearances, behavior
Self-Aware	E5 (I-3/4)	Exceptions allowable	Helpful, self-aware	Feelings, problems, adjustment
Conscientious	E6 (I-4)	Self-evaluated standards, self-critical	Intense, responsible	Motives, traits, achievements
Individualistic	E7 (I-4/5)	Tolerant	Mutual	Individuality, development, roles
Autonomous	E8 (I-5)	Coping with conflict	Interdependent	Self-fulfillment, psychological causation
Integrated	E9 (I-6)		Cherishing individuality	Identity

[a]The previous versions of the scoring manual for the WUSCT used I-level and Delta codes and distinguished between full stages and transitional levels (Loevinger & Wessler, 1970; Redmore, Loevinger, & Tamashiro, 1978); the current version of the scoring manual uses E-level codes and does not distinguish between stages and transitions (Hy & Loevinger, 1996).
Note. From *Measuring Ego Development* (p. 4), by L. X. Hy and J. Loevinger, 1996. Mahwah, NJ: Lawrence Erlbaum Associates. Copyright (1996) by Lawrence Erlbaum Associates, Inc.

9

I

THE NATURE OF EGO DEVELOPMENT

1

Loevinger's Theory of Ego Development and Its Relationship to the Cognitive–Developmental Approach

Augusto Blasi
Department of Psychology
University of Massachusetts—Boston

Even though Loevinger consistently places her work within the cognitive–developmental approach (e.g., Loevinger, 1987b), her theory of ego development does not fit neatly with the assumptions and methods of that tradition. In fact, her continuing interest in psychoanalysis, her use of the term *ego*, and her reliance on both psychoanalytic and cognitive concepts led some writers (e.g., Langer, 1969) to interpret her theory as one recent version of ego psychoanalysis.

In this chapter, I argue that Loevinger's theory of ego development is not a variant of the cognitive–developmental approach, as this approach is usually understood. There is nothing magical or absolute about the distinctions on which I rely. A "lumping" strategy may indeed bring out interesting aspects of ego development theory. Here I adopt a "splitting" strategy, hoping to highlight those unique aspects of Loevinger's thinking that cannot be reduced to either cognitive–developmentalism or psychoanalysis.

As used here, the term *cognitive–developmentalism* refers to the body of work begun in the late 1950s and early 1960s, mainly by a group of researchers in the United States. These researchers recognized their distant and more recent roots in the ideas of J. M. Baldwin, G. H. Mead, and J. Piaget, but extended these ideas into the domain of social and personality development. As it turned out, this branch of the cognitive–developmental approach came to be overwhelmingly guided by Piaget's theory. Perhaps one important factor in this theoretical turn was Kohlberg's early work on moral development and his codification of the basic theoretical principles in *Stage and Sequence* (Kohlberg, 1969).

As applied to personality, cognitive–developmentalism found its inspiration in Piaget's early work, including among its topics morality and interpersonal communication and having its unifying idea in egocentrism and perspective taking. However, its theoretical principles were borrowed, literally and without adaptation, from Piaget's later theoretical formulations concerning the development of intelligence and logic.

This orientation came to be characterized by a number of pivotal ideas:

1. The concept of *operations*, namely, of mental strategies, abstracted from interactions with objects and people.

2. The concept of stage as an operational structure, namely, a structure that is characterized by rigorous compensatory transformations.

3. The idea of equilibrated interactions with the environment, out of which a series of increasingly adapted, broad, and stable structures are successively constructed. These structures would be related to each other according to a logic of implication and integration and, therefore, would be increasingly adequate.

4. The idea of universal development, deriving from the stages' logical hierarchy and from the fact that the most basic features of objects and interactions are universal.

5. A final idea, not found in Piaget, but frequently used by Kohlberg and his collaborators (e.g., Snarey, Kohlberg, & Noam, 1983), concerns the necessary but not sufficient relations among several developmental dimensions.

Cognitive–developmentalism, in the sense described here, originated from and thrived on the expectation that logical operations, logic-like structures, and the principle of equilibration would give us the key to understand and explain the development of personality, that is, of social and interpersonal behavior, of interests and values, of self-control, and similar characteristics. After more than 30 years of work we can begin to assess this expectation. It cannot be denied that the cognitive–developmental approach contributed enormously to our knowledge of the ways people come to grasp a variety of concepts and ideas, including those of person and friendship, justice and altruism, religion, emotion and defense, normality and deviance. However, all of this may be related to, but is not yet, personality development. We hoped that personality could be found behind concepts and reasoning strategies, but behind concepts we found other, perhaps more sophisticated and complex, concepts.

Loevinger avoided this problem of bridging the gap between cognition and personality, because she entered cognitive–developmentalism with an already well-developed set of research questions and a series of observations. These had relatively little to do with concepts and reasoning, but concerned impulses and methods for controlling impulses, personal preoccupations and ambitions, interpersonal attitudes and social values—what psychologists normally call *personality*. Throughout her career she remained faithful to these matters and selected from Piagetian theory (or from psychoanalysis) what best suited her. On the other hand, what makes her theory a genuine theory of personality also makes it less of a cognitive–developmental theory. In what follows I build my argument by comparing Loevinger's theory and the cognitive–developmental approach on three issues: the content of stages, the nature of structures, and the explanation of development. In a final section I sketch a theoretical interpretation of Loevinger's stages centering on the motivation for mastery. This interpretation, although fully located within the domain of personality and personality development, involves certain features that make ego development similar in some respects to cognitive development.

THE CONTENT OF STAGES

One difficulty of extending cognitive–developmental theories to issues of personality and personality development is the difference betweeen the abstract nature of Piagetian operations and the essential concreteness of emotional and motivational processes. The former seem to be ill-suited to represent the latter.

But there is another, perhaps related difference between ego development and cognitive–developmentalism, concerning the perspective through which the content of the stages is approached. In all cognitive theories, Piagetian or otherwise, the focus is on the relations among objects (including people, relationships, personality traits, etc.): for example, two different beakers filled with water, different interactions among friends, an act of revenge and an act of justice. In all instances of cognitive grasp, one understands an aspect of reality by relating it to a set of similar and contrasting aspects. Of course, all these relations occur in a mind and are established by it. According to some theories, the mind (or the computer program) determines and limits the kind of relations that can be established among objects and the kind of objects that can be assimilated. But the mind is conceived as an impersonal ground, a "field," on which these object-to-object relations occur. To indicate the combination of the assimilatory quality of the mind and its impersonality and objectivity, Piaget devised the concept of the *epistemic subject* which, in the ordinary sense of the term, is not a subject at all.

It is important for my argument to emphasize that this objective perspective is a characteristic of cognition as cognition. Whatever specific topic one may wish to study, the interest is in understanding objective reality—the relations among objects—even when these objects are our own actions, traits, and thoughts. Although it is normally accepted that personality frequently influences cognition, it is also taken for granted that the effect of personality characteristics can in principle be sorted out or compensated, so as to recover the impersonal structure of the world.

In ego development, by contrast, objects, people, and also the person's own characteristics are approached specifically for the relations they have with the subject, namely, with the person's needs, anxieties, interests, goals, and so on. Here the mind is not a field on which relations among objects are established, but a necessary pole of relations with every object. For instance, a person at the Conformist stage does not simply understand, in the manner of a dispassionate observer, that friends tend to trust each other and expect reciprocity from each other. Loevinger's Conformist person is also able to transcend insecurity and selfish impulses in order to actually experience and value mutual trust.

There is no doubt that Loevinger's ego developmental stages have these subject-to-object or subject-to-subject relations as elementary units or components. In her study of the Authoritarian Family Ideology, before she explicitly focused on ego development, Loevinger (1962) empirically derived three qualitatively different clusters of psychological characteristics, that could be considered (as she did) as her first rudimentary descriptions of ego stages. The traits comprising these clusters have little to do with cognition, but concern personal orientations and attitudes toward people and events. For instance, the middle cluster included fear of impulses, anxiety produced by instinctual material, and repressive strategies to deal with anxiety. Loevinger maintained this interpretation even after she rejected the psychoanalytic explanation of development in favor of a cognitive–developmental account.

As for her final version of ego development (e.g., Loevinger, 1976), Loevinger frequently organizes the characteristics of the stages along four dimensions, all dealing with personal orientations and investments. The first concerns impulse control and character development (which, incidentally, is not the same as moral reasoning, even though Loevinger tended to place Kohlberg's work within this dimension); the second, interpersonal style, includes such traits as independence, manipulativeness, need to belong, and autonomy; the third dimension has to do with conscious preoccupations, where the emphasis is on "preoccupations." Even the last one, cognitive style, is in fact less cognitive than its label may suggest, as it includes traits like tolerance of ambiguity and tendency (i.e., interest, motivation) toward objectivity.

One reason Loevinger located her stages within the cognitive–developmental tradition may be that they, like Piaget's or Kohlberg's, are defined in terms of basic meanings. In fact, striving for meaning may be the closest to a definition of ego development that Loevinger ever offered. But "meaning" is a highly analogical concept needing to be specified and clarified by its context. Piagetian or cognitive meanings and the meanings of ego stages do not differ so much for their content as for the type of relations that are established with their content.

The distinction between *meaning* and *significance* may be useful in clarifying the differences. Meaning (whether semantic, logical, physical, or psychological) is purely cognitive and, once more, consists of the relations between an object or event and other objects or events, as represented in concepts and theories. Significance is an entirely different matter and can only be established subjectively, namely, by the relations objects and events have with people's interests, needs, values, in sum, with people's lives. For instance, for a person at the Conscientious stage the manipulativeness and opportunistic tendencies of the Self-Protective individual is a meaningful behavior pattern, which, however, has little or no significance in his or her life.

This distinction is illustrated when comparing Piaget's concept of object permanence and the concept of object constancy in psychoanalytic and object relations theories. Both concepts refer to the early differentiation of self and other. The former, however, is frequently seen in terms of the child's organization of the spatial field and the coordination of his or her movements (e.g., Piaget, 1954). The latter is understood as a child's affective relations to his or her internal representations of the loved parent, representations that are inevitably tied to conflicts, defenses, and distortions. Object constancy, as described by object relations theory, and not the Piagetian object permanence (at least not directly), is related to the child's ability to develop beyond the Symbiotic stage of ego development.

Of course, personal significance and cognitive meaning are frequently related to each other in concrete individuals. Object constancy seems to require some kind of object permanence. A trusting participation in friendship most likely coexists with a similar understanding of friendship, whichever of the two achievements may precede and facilitate the other. However, even so, these two aspects of human functioning—cognitive understanding and personal significance—can be differentiated at an abstract conceptual level and, at times, also at the level of concrete behavior. Because of their conceptual differences, it makes sense to ask in what way the development of cognitive understanding influences ego development, or vice-versa.

Loevinger's stages, like psychoanalytic stages, refer to certain kinds of significance. Even though the significance emphasized in psychoanalysis is different from the significance characterizing ego development, neither can be reduced to cognitive meanings. Because meaning and significance are distinct and irreducible to each other, we can ask about the significance of pursuing cognitive projects; and a psychologist, taking an objective perspective, can also ask about the meaning of ego development.

THE NATURE OF STRUCTURE

A different approach to the elements or units of a psychological organization also implies a different understanding of what a structure is. In elaborating his understanding of structure, frequently in contrast with the kind of mental organization that is described in psychoanalysis, Piaget (1970, 1985) relied on the structures of logic as real, and not simply analogical, models. He defined psychological cognitive structures, then, in terms of the sort of equilibrium that allows for rigorously equivalent compensatory transformations. This model was adopted by and became the trademark of cognitive–developmentalism, also in its extension to personality. Kohlberg's notion of *hard stage* (Kohlberg, Levine, & Hewer, 1983) corresponds to it.

Other kinds of mental organizations (e.g., those described by psychoanalysis or other personality theories), although not fitting the Piagetian concept of structure, do include compensatory processes and certain forms of equilibrium. Any theory postulating clusters of traits and a minimal degree of dynamic stability also needs to postulate some compensatory processes. According to psychoanalysis, compensations are achieved through defense mechanisms.

There would be two main differences between personality (e.g., psychoanalytic) structures and the Piagetian ones. In the former, transformations could not be represented in rigorous logical terms. Moreover, and this is crucial, the principle of transformation and the criterion of equilibrium would not be cognitive, but perhaps would have to do with affective and motivational states, for instance, the satisfaction of impulses, the management of anxiety, or the maintainance of self-esteem.

In my view, Loevinger's structures could theoretically be located somewhere between the cognitive–developmentalist and the psychoanalytic extremes. Therefore, Kohlberg was probably correct in considering Loevinger's stages as "soft," according to the meaning he gave to the hard–soft distinction. It would be a mistake, however, to take this label, as he did, as an evaluative criterion. The value of a theory depends, among other things, on whether it fits the nature of what it attempts to explain. This is precisely the point of my argument: Personality is a different kind of reality than the subject matter of cognitive theories.

Another important difference should be mentioned, specifically between ego developmental and cognitive structures, whether hard or soft. If it is true that the content of ego development consists of relations between the person–subject and the person's emotions, interests, needs, values, and so on, rather than of object-to-object relations, then the structuring of ego developmental units is guided by self-consistency and not necessarily by logical coherence. Of course, there can be different principles of self-consistency as there can be different kinds of logic. Piaget understood the structures of cognitive stages as reflecting basically different logical principles. In an analogous way, one can try to understand the stages described by Loevinger by attempting to formulate, for each stage, the special principle of self-consistency that would maintain the same significance across its various manifestations.

THE EXPLANATION OF DEVELOPMENT

Like many others in the field of developmental psychology, Loevinger gave relatively little attention to the topic of what she called "trans-stage theory" (Loevinger, 1976, p. 418). In her 1976 book (especially pp. 418–425), taking a detached perspective, Loevinger briefly reviewed five different kinds of explanation given by various theorists and then argued that they are not mutually exclusive. However, a close reading reveals clear preferences, although perhaps not a theoretical commitment. In my view, her preferences are not congruent with a cognitive–developmental approach.

First of all, not only is equilibration presented as one of several possible explanations, but what is said about it is relatively brief and unspecific. Second, the main focus of Loevinger's discussion is on two other principles. She labels the first *dialectic of personal growth* and relates it to the formulations of J. M. Baldwin, G. H. Mead, and S. Freud. According to this principle, the relationships one has with people are internalized and become parts of one's personality or serve as models for one's internal differentiation. The other explanation, expressed as the reversal of passive to active voice (see also Loevinger, 1966b), is derived from psychoanalytic theory: it suggests that mastery and self-control are achieved by the impulse to actively repeat what one had to tolerate passively. This barely sketched explanation for stage transitions and for the transformation of motives is

less eclectic than it seems at first: Its center is occupied by the motivation
for mastery, whereas Piagetian equilibration plays a minor role.

By contrast, cognitive–developmentalism in general, and not only
Kohlberg, followed Piaget in adopting equilibration as the only central
principle of development. As understood by Piaget, this principle seems
to be uniquely suited to explain cognitive development. According to it,
changes in one's conceptual structure are motivated by contradictions
between one's present understanding and actual experience with reality
and are guided by the twin requirement of achieving consistency with
external reality and maintaining the logical coherence of the structure.
Equilibration, therefore, makes the development of knowledge exclusively
sensitive to its convergence with or divergence from reality and logical
consistency—our two basic epistemological criteria.

In summary, I argue so far that Loevinger's theory does not fit the
cognitive–developmental mold by discussing their different understanding
of the contents of the stages, the nature of structure, and the nature of
development. Of course, this negative conclusion does not clarify the
nature of the theory Loevinger seems to propose with her stages. In the
last section of this chapter I will try to sketch a positive answer, or to suggest
a direction for working out an answer. First, I take seriously Loevinger's
claim that ego development has important cognitive features, at least in
some sense of "cognitive." Second, I think it would be important to
distinguish Loevinger's theory not only from cognitive–developmental
theories, but also from those theories that look at personality and the ego
as systems aimed at achieving the best possible compromise between need
satisfaction and social adjustment. I suspect that Loevinger's genuine
contribution to a theoretical understanding of personality development
lies in her having pointed to the necessity for a coherent explanation that
is independent of the cognitive and the psychoanalytic extremes.

COGNITION AND MASTERY MOTIVATION

In attempting to relate ego development to cognition, one route would be
to search, once again, for a strict structuralist solution, namely, to try to
relate to each other all developmental threads—from the purely cognitive
to the social, motivational, and emotional—by rules of rigorous
compensatory transformations. This seems to be the solution attempted
by Kegan (1982). In my view, this solution is improbable for both empirical
and theoretical reasons. Empirically, this kind of solution, even more than
Piaget's theory, would be beset by intractable problems of decalage.
Human personality, as we know it, does not function according to the
harmonious totality such a theory would have to postulate. Theoretically,

an all-encompassing structuralism would have to confront a serious dilemma from which it is difficult to see an exit. It would either lead to the subordination of cognition to personal needs, interest, and motives; or it would arrive at a rationalistic view of personality. The first is the typical risk of psychoanalysis; the latter is the risk of cognitive–developmentalism. Kegan (1982) may avoid these risks by treating the structural parallels among developmental domains in a metaphorical rather than literal way.

Perhaps an answer to the question posed by Loevinger's theory may begin to appear when one focuses on the motivation for mastery. I already pointed out how important is mastery in Loevinger's explanation of ego development. As she put it, "The striving to master, to integrate, and make sense of experience is not one ego function among many but the essence of the ego" (Loevinger, 1976, p. 59). What needs to be emphasized, in addition, is that mastery has a special relation to cognitive development. Already White (1959) had understood this point, when he reinterpreted Piaget's stages—the type of interactions with the environment and the developmental dynamics they imply—in terms of mastery motivation. Kohlberg (1969) made a similar move when he presented mastery and the need for self-esteem that it establishes as the theoretical bridge between cognitive and personality development.

The fact is that mastery, probably alone among the motives, has the interesting feature of being simultaneously oriented toward the self and toward the external world of objects and people. Its focus is the self, namely, self-control, coping, self-esteem, the modification of personality according to ego ideals, and so forth. And yet all of this can only be achieved by working on the objects in ways that respect the properties of those objects and activities one attempts to master. As for cognition, the touchstone of mastery is reality.

But mastery, being defined in terms of its relation to reality, can equally apply to different categories of reality and can take as many different shapes as are the forms of reality. Thus, White (1959, 1960) was able to interpret from the perspective of mastery not only cognitive development, but also the different sets of behaviors that psychoanalysts classify under the oral, anal, and phallic stages. In sum, what mastery concretely means to a person as well as its special domains may well change from ego stage to ego stage, determining the special type of significance of each stage. One could also hypothesize that mastery's successive orientations would form a hierarchical sequence. In their comprehensiveness, Loevinger's ego development stages, like Erikson's (1950) psychosocial stages, are landmarks in the development of mastery. The hierarchy, however, would not be based on the logic of implication, differentiation, and integration, as in cognitive development, but it would be based on the ordering of psychological requirements. That a person should achieve a reasonable degree of impulse control before mastering mutuality in interpersonal relationships is not a matter of logic but of human psychology.

Of course, one domain of mastery is the cognitive domain. Because mastery, by definition, must respect the properties of the activities one attempts to master, the desire to possess the world cognitively would not interfere with, but instead would adopt and use the intrinsic laws of cognition. In other words, cognitive development in all its branches would become the object of ego development mastery. This is one sense in which ego development can be considered to be cognitive and by which it can be differentiated from psychoanalysis.

Moreover, the relation of ego development to cognition and cognitive development may also change from stage to stage. Not in the sense that ego structures would determine cognitive principles, but that they would determine the significance of knowing and knowledge for the person and therefore the specific *uses* that a person would find for knowledge. The distinction between knowing and the use of knowledge (cf. Blasi, 1982) is a crucial one for maintaining the respective autonomy of cognition and personality. For example, a certain degree of conceptual development and knowledge of social reality (e.g., the understanding of "trait" and the nonegocentric grasp of others' needs) seems to be required for a person to focus one's mastery motivation on interpersonal relationships. And yet interpersonal relationships and not cognition establish the central principle of significance of the Conformist stage. Therefore, it would be self-consistent for a conformist person to subordinate cognition to relationships and even to distort his or her knowledge in order to maintain an important friendship. Because of the partial independence of different developmental strands, this person may be perfectly capable of understanding and appreciating objective reality—for instance, the domain of mathematics and physics—and to enjoy the intellectual grasp of these fields and the sense of accomplishment it provides. But this type of understanding would not be centrally significant in this person's life, and could be used for social rather than cognitive purposes.

At higher ego developmental stages, as it seems, cognition, objectivity, and respect for reality acquire a high priority in the desire for mastery (see Loevinger & Wessler, 1970, chap. 4). This may be a *second sense* in which ego development is cognitive: What one knows to be true and real becomes affectively and practically more significant, a quasi-telos of the ego developmental sequence. Even so, this ideal integration of cognition and personality is not a given, a more or less automatic result of structuring processes, but a largely conscious and forever fragile personal achievement.

CONCLUSION

Loevinger did not formulate a set of explanatory statements that would amount to a theory of ego development. Certain issues were not addressed, others were touched on in a fragmentary and tentative way. Temperamentally she tended to shy away from proposing answers for which she could not find support or clarification in empirical data. In this respect, her intellectual style represents a dramatic contrast with the all-ordering, monistic attempts of many cognitive–developmental theorists.

However, it is possible to gather in her description of ego stages, from occasional explanatory hints, and particularly from the overall spirit pervading her work, if not a theory or a sketch of a theory, at least a theoretical direction, a broad framework that would constrain further attempts at theory construction. In my view, this framework cannot be easily accommodated by most of the existing personality theories—either those that rely on logic, rationality, and cognitive disequilibrium as basic principles; or those (like Freudian psychoanalysis) that find in the satisfaction of elementary needs the main explanation for adaptation and change; or those (including several versions of ego psychoanalysis) that look for inspiration at biological–evolutionary processes.

That human functioning involves and requires all these aspects—environmental adaptation and survival, need satisfaction, sensitivity to reality and to the logical constraints of its representations—is obvious. It is because of the seeming heterogeneity of these aspects that psychological theories, at least those that are responsive to the organismic features of personality, hypothesize some sort of synthesizing function, something like what came to be known as ego in the psychoanalytic tradition. The role assigned to this function is crucial and the way it is defined—its nature, aims, and modes of operating—determine the basic character of a theory.

Frequently the synthesizing function is conceived unilaterally from the perspective of one of the main psychological dimensions; the result is a monolithic (and not simply organized) portrait of personality, in which its multifarious aspects are reductionistically transformed. Extreme examples of a reductionistic ego can be found in Freud's psychoanalysis and in Hullian approaches to personality.

By contrast, a central characteristic of Loevinger's understanding of ego development, it seems to me, is just the opposite of a reductionistic tendency, and derives from her deep respect for psychological reality in all its variety and keen sensitivity to the complexities of human functioning. Thus, in her hands, all human issues become material for the construction of ego stages: eating and drinking, feelings about one's body and sexuality, pregnancy and fatherhood, financial needs and health, social roles and social stereotypes, education and career, abilities and accomplishments, morality and self-control, individuality and independence, and also unconscious desires and the pull toward self-deception. No human concern is rejected as irrelevant to ego stages, which, therefore, become reflections of the meaning people give to life as a whole.

What is more important, human concerns are approached for their surface meaning, namely, for the reality with which one is confronted at the experiential level. At this level, reality is grasped in its multiple aspects, but also acquires a special significance to one's life as a whole. For each one of us, education can be many things at the same time: boring, a way to eventually get a remunerative job, an attempt to fit in and respond to social expectations, an expression of love for parents and teachers, a stimulus for self improvement. Similarly, sex can be a way to satisfy immediate impulses, a tool for manipulating other people, a means to boost our self-esteem, or a special way to achieve intimacy. Which events become important, which aspects become salient and acquire central significance, depends on what the world and our life in it mean for us at the ego developmental level we have reached.

This approach is miles away from the reductive theorizing of psychoanalysis, learning theories, or sociobiology. Of course, in assigning significance to events and in constructing life meanings from the events they encounter, people select and interpret, and in some sense "reduce" their world to what is significant to them, whether or not they can verbally articulate their principle of significance. However, Loevinger attempts to interpret each person's significance as the person himself or herself sees it. In so doing, she affirms her belief that a genuine theoretical explanation of development is possible at the level of subjective meanings, regardless of the relations these meanings may have to evolutionary adaptive processes, physiological determinants, or unconscious motivation.

Here probably lies the profoundest analogy between ego development and cognitive development. Like cognition and the development of knowledge and understanding, ego development is open to the widest range of objects. There is no limit to the kinds of information and experience people can rely on in constructing the meanings that are embodied in ego stages. In addition, events and experiences are approached nonegocentrically, in the sense that ego developmental meanings are not constructed capriciously, as a way of satisfying immediate impulses, but respond to a pull toward the general and the suprapersonal. Thus, the exploitiveness that characterizes the Self-Protective stage differs from the occasional exploitiveness at higher stages, because it derives from a perhaps inarticulated world view, in which the satisfaction of one's needs has a general and ultimate validity.

However, the parallelism between ego development and cognitive development is only analogical. The meanings constituting ego developmental stages, though nonegocentric in the sense just indicated, have the person with all of his or her affects and investments at their center. Because ego development concerns what is central to the person as person, moving from one stage to the next, could be more like a personal conversion than a progression in conceptual differentiation or logical rigor.

CHAPTER

2

Ego, Trait, Identity

Dan P. McAdams
Department of Psychology
Northwestern University

In 1977, I completed the first assignment for a desultory course on contemporary personality research by doing a paper on Jane Loevinger's concept of ego development. Those familiar with the history of personality psychology as an academic discipline will know that 1977 was not an especially good year in my field. As a second-year graduate student, I was all too aware of the conventional wisdom of the day: Behavior is situationally specific rather than consistent across situations; personality dispositions do not predict behavior; personality resides more in the eyes of the observer than in the lives and behavior of people observed (Magnusson & Endler, 1977; Mischel, 1968, 1973; Sechrest, 1976; Shweder, 1975). If there is such a thing as personality, we learned in that class, its influence is small and variable, and it can only be studied by employing the humblest constructs (Mischel, 1977) and the most circumscribed measures (Fiske, 1974), and we must do so with the greatest caution and defensiveness.

In reading Loevinger's (1976) *Ego Development*, I decided she was either blissfully unaware of the gloom that I, as a fledgling personality psychologist, saw everywhere around me, or she had chosen to ignore it all. In either case, Loevinger had forged ahead with a tremendously creative research program that operationalized just about the biggest and most influential personality construct one could think of—the ego itself—and presented a full theory of personality development that was elegant and integrative enough to buoy my enthusiasm for the enterprise of studying whole persons (Murray, 1938; White, 1964) in a scientifically responsible way. My subsequent class report on Loevinger failed to convince my colleagues (and, alas, the professor) that I had happened upon a promising approach for personality studies. It all seemed too vague and mushy to them. But outside this rather unenlightened coterie in 1977, psychologists were beginning to see how Loevinger's cognitive–developmental perspective could provide a compelling framework for personality theory and research (Hauser, 1976; Rosznafszky, 1981). Looking back now at the many years since I wrote that paper, I can say something I virtually never get to say: I was right in 1977.

But I think I was right for the wrong reasons. In my class paper, I concluded that ego development might be profitably employed by personality psychologists as a moderator variable in the prediction of behavior (e.g., Bem & Allen, 1974). If personality measures do not predict behavior particularly well, as was the common belief in 1977, it is partly because, I argued, trait X behavior relationships were different for each ego stage. For example, neuroticism might be associated with one set of behaviors at, say, the Impulsive (I–2)[1] stage of ego development and quite another, even contrary, set of behaviors at, say, the Conformist (I–3) stage. By taking into consideration a person's ego stage, the personality psychologist could improve his or her predictive efficacy in research. Reflecting my own developing interest in human motivation, I argued that an especially illuminating research strategy might involve predicting behaviors (dependent variables) from scores on power (Winter, 1973) and intimacy (McAdams, 1980) motivation (independent variables) within particular ego-stage cohorts (moderator variable).

From the beginning, however, I was never able and perhaps never all that willing to predict "behavior"—observable, public action—by combining motive and ego scores. Following instead the research lead of Candee (1974), I found that what I could predict from ego development and social motives was human meanings. In a study of the development of religious identity, for example, I found that religiously oriented college students who scored at the Conscientious (I–4) and above levels of ego development tended to construe their own faith development in terms of a personal journey or quest involving difficult decisions and dramatic transformations in value and belief. By contrast, those scoring at lower stages (I–3/4 and below) tended to deny their beliefs and values had changed much since childhood, or they described a developmental pathway along which they first rejected and then came to reaccept their

[1]The notation for ego levels used in this chapter corresponds to the notation of the first edition of the scoring manual for the WUSCT (Loevinger & Wessler, 1970; Redmore, Loevinger, & Tamashiro, 1978). The current edition of the scoring manual (Hy & Loevinger, 1996) introduced several changes. See the Appendix to the introductory chapter of this volume for a comparison between the previous and the current system.

initial religious perspectives (McAdams, Booth, & Selvik, 1981). In *Power, Intimacy, and the Life Story*, I described a series of studies showing that being high in ego development is associated with the construction of a more complex life story (McAdams, 1985). The self-defining life narratives fashioned by men and women high in ego development tend to incorporate a large and varied collection of plots, conflicting characters, critical scenes of transformation rather than continuity, and the hint of "much more to come" in the future chapters of the story (see also McAdams, Ruetzel, & Foley, 1986).

From my own perspective, a major unit of meaning in an adult's life is his or her internalized *life story*—an integrative narrative that seeks to provide a life with unity and purpose (McAdams, 1985, 1990, 1993). Ego stage is a good predictor of the *structural complexity* of the narrative, whereas social motives of power and intimacy are good predictors of the story's *thematic content*. A woman with high power motivation and a Conformist (I–3) ego stage, for example, will likely construe her life as a rather undifferentiated and simple story (structure) in which she strives for power, impact, or control (content). The story *is her identity*—the evolving pattern of self providing her life with unity and purpose. Methodologically speaking, ego development may be employed as a "predictor" of identity.

But the relation between ego and identity involves more than a statement about research methodology. In viewing ego development in 1977 as a useful moderator variable in the prediction of behavior, and in reconceiving it in 1985 as a valuable predictor of the structure of a person's life story, I consistently placed Loevinger's concept of ego on the "left side" of my functional propositions. Reading a standard proposition from left to right, as we do in English, we typically encounter the subject and then the predicate. In the propositions I have in mind, the ego always seems to be the subject. The predicate, by contrast, may be many different things, for it may include any and all aspects of the self as an object—all that the person considers to be what William James (1892/1963) called the *Me*. In Jamesian terms, the ego is best conceived as the *I*—the self-as-subject. Linguistically and psychologically, the I-as-subject precedes the Me-as-predicate: I —> Me. Loevinger (1976) stated: "The ego [the I] is above all else a process, not a thing" (p. 58)—the process of synthesizing experience as an agential and self-contained subject in the world (Blasi, 1988). The ego, or I, is the process of "selfing," of apprehending subjective experience and making something out of it. The most cherished thing selfing makes is the Me, the self-as-object, the concept of the self that is recognized and reflected upon by the I. Thus, as James suggested, the *duplex* self is both I (process) and Me (product). The ego is the I part. The ego reflects upon the Me. The ego knows the Me. The ego synthesizes the Me out of experience. The ego makes the Me. Putting the ego on the left side of a series of Jamesian propositions about the self positions Loevinger's seminal work in a singularly crucial place on the contemporary scene of personality studies, a scene that has changed dramatically since the dismal days of 1977. Furthermore, positioning the ego in this way sheds considerable light on both the structure of personality and its development over time.

THE SELF-AS-OBJECT:
THREE LEVELS OF PERSONALITY

In my field of personality psychology, about the worst thing you could be called in 1977 was a "trait psychologist." Around that time, Jackson and Paunonen (1980) wryly observed that trait psychologists were viewed "like witches of 300 years ago . . . [T]here is confidence in their existence, and even possibly their sinister properties, although one is hard pressed to find one in the flesh or even meet someone who has" (p. 523). Beginning with Mischel (1968), the situationist critique in personality argued that behavior was too specific to the exigencies of situational demands to be guided by traits or to be predictable from trait scores. Traits were no more than figments in the minds of psychologists.

Things changed dramatically, however, since then. Today, the field of personality embraces the concept of trait as never before (Digman, 1990; McCrae & Costa, 1990). Well-designed studies from the 1980s showed conclusively that individual differences in personality traits predict general trends in behavior aggregated across situations and over time. Longitudinal studies documented the stability of individual differences over the adult life course. Twin studies suggested substantial heritabilities for many traits. A consensus is emerging that the vast universe of possible trait attributions may be reduced to five or so basic categories called the Big Five trait taxonomy (John, 1990). Factor analytic studies suggest that most all personality traits may be grouped into the five fundamental categories of extraversion, neuroticism, openness to experience, agreeableness, and conscientiousness.

Methodologically, trait estimates are typically derived from self-report questionnaires. People have little trouble rating themselves on linear, bipolar, and implicitly comparative trait dimensions. Furthermore, the ratings are typically valid in that they usually correlate highly with peer ratings of the same dimensions and they tend to predict trait-relevant behavior aggregated across situations (Funder & Colvin, 1991). Beyond our responses on structured questionnaires, we all make trait ratings about ourselves and others in daily living. Implicit trait attributions are important parts of the self-concept—the self-as-object. In the process of living, people gather a great deal of information on their own behavior and experience and draw conclusions about their own general "standing" on a series of broad, linear, comparative dimensions. Like a good trait psychologist, the I synthesizes subjective experience into trait attributions in creating the Me. As a result, the Me is a trait profile.

But the I does more. And the Me is more than my traits. James suggested that the Me is all that I can call mine, encompassing the material, social, and spiritual realms. Beyond my own traits, therefore, I may appropriate my house and my clothing, my friendships and my feelings about my wife, my deepest convictions and my religious beliefs, as elements of the Me. The I puts these things together (the ego's prime function of synthesis, as Loevinger says) to fashion a self-as-object. The self contains many things. It is multiple, encompassing a host of features and facets, coming in many different versions, differently displayed to various social tribunals, as James remarked. Among the elements of the Me are included those psychological features identifying and explaining my characteristic adaptation as a social being. These are features of personality as appropriated by the I into the Me. They include my standing on various implicit trait dimensions. I know that I am, say, generally outgoing, socially very dominant, highly gregarious, impulsive, mildly anxious, tending toward hypochondriasis, hard-working, dogmatic, and not very altruistic. Let us call this trait profile a *dispositional signature* that might characterize one particular person's self-as-object. Beyond the dispositional signature, what else might I include to specify my characteristic adaptation to social life?

I would likely add to my trait profile those motivational, developmental, and strategic personality features contextualizing my life in time, place, and role, so that the Me may be known in more specific and intimate terms (McAdams, 1994a, 1995). Trait attributions give nothing more than a "psychology of the stranger" (McAdams, 1992, 1994a, 1994b) in that they provide information on those most general, comparative, nonconditional, and decontextualized dimensions of the self that are the products of the social perceptions and interpretations strangers make of each other upon an initial encounter. Trait information provides a crucial but ultimately superficial first read on the self. Therefore, in order to know Me well, you must have access to (and I must articulate) such things as my plans and goals for the future, my characteristic ways of coping with challenge and stress, the life tasks I set for myself at this point in my development, my domain-specific skills, my tactics and strategies, my roles, and so on. Beyond my traits, therefore, the Me might include: "I am planning to take over my father's business when he retires"; "I am striving to lose weight"; "I strongly desire power at the workplace but not among my friends"; "I tend to intellectualize my problems"; "I play the piano beautifully but I cannot sing"; "I am very coy with members of the opposite sex"; "I am a good mother"; "I am not a good Christian." These statements about the self cannot be derived from the dispositional signature. They are not mere instances of traits. Instead, goals, plans, strategies, and so on specify a second domain of self-description, which we may call the realm of personal concerns (McAdams, 1994a, 1995).

Dispositional traits and personal concerns represent two separable domains of self-knowledge—two areas in the Me—and they correspond to two independent levels of personality structure(McAdams, 1994a, 1995). By making traits, the I provides the Me with a succinct personological summary, identifying where the Me stands on a series of broad, comparative dimensions of social functioning. In assessing traits, the personality psychologist obtains an economic dispositional profile of a stranger, a person who can now be compared to other strangers on a series of nomothetic and consensually defined dimensions. Beyond traits, the I fashions and organizes a vast collection of plans, goals, values, skills, tasks, styles, and so on within the Me to give the Me greater definition and articulation and to contextualize the Me in a temporal and spatial nexus and with respect to self-defining social roles. To go beyond a psychology of the stranger, the personality psychologist must garner information on personal concerns. These typically specify what persons want, often during particular periods in their lives or within particular domains of action, and what life methods people use (strategies, plans, defenses, and so on) in order to get what they want or avoid getting what they do not want over time, in particular places, or with respect to particular roles. For the Me and for the personality psychologist, traits are not enough.

But ultimately in our society, personal concerns are not enough either. Erikson (1959) was one of the first to point out that modern life in Western societies typically demands more of the adult self than the articulation of dispositional traits and personal concerns. No matter how complex and intricately articulated the Me becomes, the modern adult Me in the West cannot claim a mature and integrated status until it is endowed with the Me-quality of *identity* (Baumeister, 1986; Breger, 1974; Erikson, 1959; McAdams, 1985). Identity provides the Me with unity and purpose in a world prizing the individuation of the self but offering no consensually agreed upon formulas for achieving it. Identity functions as an aesthetically appealing, psychologically integrating, morally vivifying, and socially activating pattern or arrangement of the Me that tells the adult who he or she is and how he or she fits into the adult world.

Beginning in late adolescence and young adulthood, the I is challenged to create identity within the Me, to make the Me unified and purposeful. Many contemporary Westerners believe the Me should be constructed and told in a manner that synthesizes the disparate roles they play, incorporates their many different values and skills, calls upon their self-ascribed traits, and organizes into a meaningful temporal pattern their reconstructed past, perceived present, and anticipated future. The challenge of identity demands that the I synthesize synchronic and diachronic elements of the Me to suggest that (a) despite its many facets the Me is coherent and unified, and (b) despite the many changes attending the passage of time, the Me of the past led up to or set the stage for the Me of the present, which in turn will lead up to or set the stage for the Me of the future (McAdams, 1993, 1996).

How does the I effect its grandest synthesis of all? What form does the Me take when the Me is endowed by the I with identity? As I suggested, the I confers unity and purpose upon the Me by fashioning an internalized and evolving life story, or "personal myth." A growing number of theorists believe the only conceivable form for a unified and purposeful telling of a life is *the story* (Bruner, 1990; Charme, 1984; Cohler, 1982; Hermans & Kempen, 1993; Howard, 1991; MacIntyre, 1984; Polkinghorne, 1988). Contemporary adults create identity in their lives to the extent that the I can tell the Me as a coherent and vivifying narrative that integrates the person into society in a productive and generative way and provides the person with a purposeful self-history explaining how the Me of yesterday became the Me of today and will become the Me of tomorrow. Beyond traits and personal concerns, therefore, lies the Me-realm of identity-as-a-life-story. In a parallel manner, this third realm of the Me corresponds to the third level of personality description to be explored by the personality psychologist. When the psychologist's subject is a contemporary Western adult, a full description of personality requires a systematic exploration of the three levels of traits, personal concerns, and life narrative.

THE SELF-AS-SUBJECT:
THE FUNCTION OF THE I

Let me summarize the argument to this point. I began with James's distinction between the I as subjective self and the Me as self-as-object. Loevinger's conception of the ego is James's I, the process of synthesizing subjective experience. As one product of the I's synthesizing power, the Me consists of all those things, qualities, and phenomena the I attributes to the self. Among the Me's constituents are those psychological features identifying a person's unique adaptation to the social world, psychological features that were traditionally viewed as aspects of personality. If personality, therefore, may be described on three independent levels (McAdams, 1994a, 1995), then the Me, too, may contain at least three different genres of psychological meanings the I makes to define the self. At the first level are dispositional traits, which provide a "rough-and-ready" summary, especially useful for comparative purposes, of broad behavioral tendencies in social life. The second level contains goals, values, tasks, strivings, defenses, strategies, tactics, and other motivational, developmental, and strategic features of the self (personal concerns) contextualized in time, place, or role. Although personal concerns provide detail and texture to the self, they are unable to confer upon life that sense of unity and purpose—that is, identity—that Western adults typically demand for their lives. At the third level of personality, therefore, adults fashion identities by constructing integrative life stories. The I makes identity by narrating a coherent life story integrating disparate elements of the Me.

As the agent responsible for creating the Me, the I (ego) is the fundamental meaning-making process in human life. To experience life from the standpoint of a self (the I) is to apprehend one's actions, thoughts, and feelings as "mine" and "mine alone." Thus, subjective selfhood is experienced most clearly in intentional action when one feels that one "owns" or "authors" one's experience. Blasi (1988) wrote: "In every intentional action that we perform, in fact in every experience that we undergo, we experience ourselves, in the process of acting and experiencing, as related to our actions and experiences" (p. 228). Therefore, the self-as-subject is responsible for our feelings of agency, or "the degree to which an action is unreflectively grasped as one's own and oneself is grasped as its source" (p. 229). The I is also responsible for our fundamental sense of otherness (Blasi, 1988; Hart, 1988). I am I; you are the other. Regardless of the intimacy between us, rarely would I come to feel that I am you in the same way that you are you. There is a certain solidity and integrity to the self-as-subject, perhaps from the first year of life onwards (Stern, 1985). Rarely do we mix things up. As James (1892/1963) observed, rarely does Peter go to bed and wake up the next morning thinking he is Paul. Whether or not Peter knows precisely who he is, Peter virtually never forgets that he is. To do so would be to suffer a dramatic disturbance in the I.

There is a great deal of confusion s in psychology because of the failure of many researchers and theorists to distinguish clearly between the self-as-subject and the self-as-object. A large number of contemporary "self-theories" speak variously of "self-schemata," "possible selves," "actual and ideal selves," "subselves," "self-systems," and the like, but few are clear as to whether they are talking about the I or the Me. In many cases, they are talking a bit about both. For example, *self-schemata* are defined by many personality and social psychologists as knowledge structures about the self (self-as-Me, product) operating as filters or frameworks for processing self-relevant information (self-as-I, process; e.g., Fiske & Taylor, 1984). By contrast, Loevinger (1969, 1976, 1984, 1987b) focused unswervingly upon the self-as-subject since she introduced the concept of ego development in the 1960s. She wrote (1976): "The organization or the synthetic function is not just another thing the ego does, it is what the ego is" (p. 5). And, in 1969, "The striving to master, to integrate, to make sense of experience is not one ego function among many but the essence of the ego" (p. 85).

Although differing on the details, a variety of theories converge on the notion that the ego emerges in the first 18 months of life or so as an agential or "existential" I that ideally receives sustenance and support from an attentive and caring interpersonal milieu (Bowlby, 1969; Harter, 1983; Kohut, 1977; Lewis & Brooks-Gunn, 1979; Mahler, Pine, & Bergman, 1975; Stern, 1985). Attachment bonds (Bowlby), mirroring relationships (Kohut), experiences of affective attunement (Stern), and the like provide the interpersonal support to strengthen and consolidate the infant's developing sense that it exists as "an active, causal agent, a source and controller of actions, separate from other persons and objects in the world" (Harter, 1983, p. 279). Picking up the I at this point, Loevinger's theory of ego development specifies what happens to the ego once it arrives on the scene to stay. Thus, the process of selfing—the I itself—begins with the establishment of an existential base—"I exist"; "I am the source of my experience"—and then evolves over time along the lines described in Loevinger's stage scheme, from the early impulsive stage, through conformity, and ideally toward the more mature and complex modes of meaning-making characteristic of the higher stages of I development.

PERSONALITY DEVELOPMENT

A full theory of personality must seek to describe the content and function, the biological and cultural determinants, and the developmental course of a comprehensive set of constructs residing at three independent levels of analysis: dispositional traits, personal concerns, and life narratives (McAdams, 1995). Each of the three levels requires its own descriptive taxonomies and explanatory principles. Within such a theory, Loevinger's ego should function as the master orchestrator of traits, concerns, and narrations. The ego is a part of personality, but not in the same sense that traits, concerns, and narrations are. The ego's relation to the three levels of personality is that of the I to the Me: It is the authorial process, the synthetic selfing function that stands outside the three levels, the orienting perspective from which the three levels are subjectively viewed.

Personality development encompasses ego development, as Loevinger as shown, but it also includes meaningful and orderly change in the realms of traits, concerns, and identity. In other words, a full understanding of personality development would require knowing how four very different kinds of constructs change over the life course and how their developmental trajectories interrelate.

Loevinger spelled out a structural model of hierarchical ego stages wherein subsequent stages, which are broad and complex, build upon and ultimately subsume earlier, simple stages. As the ego develops according to Loevinger's scheme, other aspects of personality are developing, too. One's unique genetic endowment lays the groundwork for the broad temperament traits of early childhood, which may evolve into the trait dispositions ultimately comprising the Big Five (McCrae & Costa, 1996). By early adulthood, individual differences in traits are remarkably stable, and development at the level of traits seems virtually to cease (McCrae & Costa, 1990). Personal concerns follow a more variegated course, ebbing and flowing over the life span in response to shifting developmental, motivational, and role demands (Cantor & Zirkel, 1990; McAdams, 1994a). Life stories begin to take form in late adolescence and young adulthood, and their development through the middle-adult years is a matter of narrative revision in the direction of *story goodness,* as expressed in greater coherence, credibility, openness, differentiation, reconciliation, and generative integration over time (McAdams, 1993, 1994a). As the orchestrator of personality, the ego monitors personality development at the levels of traits, concerns, and narrations and synthesizes subjective experience in ways that reflect the changes occurring in each of the three realms. In addition, certain ego stages may relate to particular kinds of personality features in predictable ways. For example, the concept of "trait" seems to become a progressively more salient idea in meaning-making as one moves from the most primitive ego positions through the Conscientious stage (I–4). Self-descriptions at the Impulsive (I–2) and Self-Protective (Delta) stages seem too global and psychologically deprived to provide descriptive trait attributions. In addition, the immature ego is too egocentric to comprehend the comparative nature of trait information—how one's standing on a given trait dimension is relative to those others in one's social world. As Blasi (1988) pointed out, simple trait attributions begin to appear in the Conformist (I-3) stage (e.g., "I am considerate"; "I am gentle") as the individual begins to evaluate the self according to conventional standards of goodness, making simple comparisons of one's action trends to those of others. Trait attributions move beyond simple action trends during the Conscientious–

Conformist (I–3/4) transition to specify inner psychological qualities, and they reach a zenith in complexity and salience during the Conscientious (I–4) stage. Loevinger (1976) wrote:

> A rich and differentiated inner life characterizes the Conscientious person. He experiences in himself and observes in others a variety of cognitively shaded emotions. Behavior is seen not just in terms of action but in terms of patterns, hence of traits and motives. (p. 21)

A hallmark of Loevinger's Conscientious stage of ego development is the remarkable clarity with which individuals are able to understand the world and the self. Having separated their Me-conceptions from the dictates of social convention, Conscientious individuals have internalized principles and standards for ethical behavior, they have articulated precise goals and aspirations to guide their behavior over time, and they have formulated a clear picture of where they stand vis-a-vis others. Trait attributions are ideal for providing concise and clear-cut information on how the self stands in comparison to others. A differentiated trait profile provides an intricately detailed and yet efficient organizational scheme for making sense of the Me. The Conscientious person's preoccupation with striving to accomplish life goals in accord with inner standards may grow out of the confidence and clarity that attend meaning-making from the Conscientious perspective. In that it is couched in consensually defined categories and grounded in comparative observations made across situations and over time, trait language is well designed to foster confidence and clarity.

By contrast, stories are often ambiguous and open-ended. Although good narratives should be more or less coherent, stories function more to entertain, inspire, and integrate than to define specific terms and set clear agendas (Bruner, 1990). Some of the best stories in life and in literature are subject to multiple and even contradictory interpretations. Therefore, as one moves beyond the Conscientious stage in Loevinger's ego scheme, one encounters I-perspectives that become increasingly hospitable to the fashioning of life stories. At the Individualistic (I–4/5) level, the ego adopts a thorough "developmental" perspective on life, opening the door to narrative constructions whose beginning–middle–ending sequences mirror the past–present–future organization of developmental thinking. The Autonomous (I–5) stage brings an increasing tolerance for ambiguity and conflict, a strong focus on self-fulfillment over personal achievement, and a deeper understanding of and appreciation for psychological causation in human life. The "new element" in the final Integrated (I–6) stage is what Loevinger (1976) calls "the consolidation of identity" (p. 26). As I argued earlier, life stories are the psychological structures that consolidate identity, providing life with unity and purpose. Stories thrive on ambiguity and conflict (McAdams, 1985). They provide the most satisfying explanations of psychological causation by telling how early events lead to later events (Polkinghorne, 1988). Self-fulfillment is perhaps best characterized as living the most enriching or noble or satisfying story one can reasonably construct (MacIntyre, 1984).

In conclusion, ego, trait, and identity play off one another in intriguing ways in the development of personality. As the ego develops from the early to the middle stages in Loevinger's scheme, the meaning-making process becomes more and more suitable for the articulation of dispositional traits. The Conscientious I fashions an intricately traited Me to establish exactly where the Me stands in relation to others and to support the I's striving for personal goals and individual accomplishments. From the Impulsive to the Conscientious stages, therefore, the developmental move in personality is toward the clear and logical organization of a trait system. As one moves beyond the Conscientious stage, however, meaning-making seems to become progressively more amenable to the development of life stories. Ambiguity, conflict, development, and personal fulfillment are not well captured in the language of traits, but require a narrative mode of expression.

Over the idealized course of ego development, therefore, as the ego moves away from traits it moves in the direction of identity. However, traits do not erase identity in the early stages, and identity does not replace traits in the later ones. The many adults who do not get beyond the Conscientious stage in Loevinger's scheme are not bereft of identity-giving life stories, and the few who do move into the higher stages do not lose their traits as they do so. It is, rather, a matter of relative focus and articulation in the Me. The ego is especially well-suited for making meaning in dispositional trait terms at the Conscientious stage. This is likely to be the apex of the trait's influence in the self-concept. At the same time, the problem of unity and purpose in adult life challenges the Conscientious person to fashion a life story to provide the Me with identity. As one moves beyond the Conscientious stage, the process of selfing becomes more expertly equipped for meeting the storytelling challenge of identity in an especially appealing way. In the post-Conscientious stages, traits recede into the Me's background. A clear dispositional signature becomes less and less influential in defining the self. Thus, the ultimate psychosocial demand becomes the consolidation of identity for the storytelling I.

ACKNOWLEDGMENT

Preparation of this manuscript was aided by a grant from The Spencer Foundation.

3

From Taxonomy to Ontogeny: Thoughts on Loevinger's Theory in Relation to Subject–Object Psychology

Robert Kegan
Harvard University and
Massachusetts School of Professional Psychology

Lisa Lahey
Emily Souvaine
Harvard University

In the 1970s, when I (Kegan) was a doctoral student at Harvard in Lawrence Kohlberg's shop, Jane Loevinger's visits were anticipated with something like the eagerness, curiosity, and trepidation a family might have awaiting the arrival of an outspoken, stern but loving aunt whose tough-minded integrity concealed a sympathetic heart. Ordinary colleagues say highly critical things about your work behind your back and respectful things to your face. Loevinger was just the opposite. She would leave a trail of overturned vanity in her wake, and then months later you would hear from a colleague how highly she spoke of what you were up to.

I remember one visit when, after beating us all up for several days with her unerring eye for weak links in someone's thinking or method, she joined Carol Gilligan and me as we accompanied Kohlberg to a talk he was going to give to a local psychoanalytic institute. While Kohlberg spoke, amid the dark Victorian woods and high ceilings of the institute, the analysts grew more and more restless (and no doubt "interpretive") with what they took to be his preoccupation with the superego. Loevinger, Gilligan, and I watched as they proceeded to actively misunderstand and demean his life project in the kindest terms. We departed with a crestfallen Kohlberg (but not before one analyst had sniffingly asked Jane if she was "the Loevinger of the scales" as if there were something slightly fishy about her). In the ride home, though, it was Loevinger, much more than his closer colleagues, who shrewdly and sensitively found ways to restore Kohlberg's diminished spirits.

In this essay we try to honor Loevinger's style by emulating it. We begin with a little tough talk, what we take to be a central limitation to the progress of her theory. We then proceed to suggest how our own work— in the generation that has elapsed since those nervously anticipated visits from Aunt Jane—might constitute a sympathetic support to hers, a program of work we respect and admire. In particular, we organize the essay around the status of a fundamental tenet in Loevinger's thinking, the idea that there exists in personality, at any given time, a holism or "central tendency" in one's meaning-organizing. This concept is widely challenged today, although it is quite central to the idea of an "ego." It is a concept we share with Loevinger, and we hope to suggest here how our work lends further credence to it.

FROM TAXONOMY TO ONTOGENY:
THE NEXT STEP IN THE EVOLUTION
OF A THEORY OF EGO DEVELOPMENT

According to Wells (1972), the maturation of a line of scientific thought often involves a shift from attending to entities to attending to processes. The first step is nearly always one of classification. Botany and biology, for example, spent hundreds of years in taxonomic attention to plants and animals. But the next step is ontogeny: Attention turns to the origins, development, underlying processes, and direction of the phenomenon. Mature theories of personality development need to provide us with both a taxonomy (e.g., the stages of development) and an ontogeny (e.g., the structures underlying the stages, and the processes of reconstruction). Although Loevinger clearly locates her work within the ambitions of the study of personality development (Loevinger, 1976), her methods and measure have equipped her only to do an excellent job at taxonomy. They also perhaps blocked the growth of her project from taxonomy to ontogeny. Loevinger's Sentence Completion Test (SCT) yields data that, at best, "signals" a given stage of ego development. The inferential leap from data to stage assignment is a large one, because by her own admission her method includes "classify[ing] responses having no obvious relation to ego development" (Loevinger, 1986, p. 189). In contrast to a "sign" approach to interpretation, a "symbolic" or "representative" approach (Hewer, 1982; Kohlberg, 1979) seeks to minimize the inferential space from datum to interpretation by generating data that actually demonstrate (rather than "point to" or "associate with") the phenomenon under investigation. This approach is far more cumbersome than the efficient SCT because it involves talking with subjects; providing them opportunities to clarify the meanings of their responses; refining the data by reducing, or optimally, eliminating the variety of possible interpretations one could draw.

Although an interviewing approach to data gathering is more cumbersome, the data it generates permits just the sort of ontogenetic exploration Loevinger's more taxonomic method does not. It permits the researcher to observe a mental structure at work. Used longitudinally, it permits the researcher to trace the evolution of a mental structure. Applied to a variety of life contexts, it permits a researcher to test the central hypothesis that Loevinger holds for the ego, namely that there exists a "central tendency" in one's meaning organizing at any given time, commonly reflected across a wide range of personal domains.

We agree with Loevinger's view that there exists at any moment in personality development a central organizing tendency, and that this principle of meaning coherence gradually becomes more complex throughout development. Underlying the forms of physical–cognitive meaning-making Piaget described (1952), or the social–cognitive meaning-making Kohlberg (1984) or Selman (1980) described, or the broader systems of meaning-making that Loevinger described, we hold that there exists a common process giving rise to these entities. But in order to test a particular conception of what these underlying structures or processes are, we had to develop the more cumbersome method of data gathering in which mental structures are actually demonstrated. The result of this work, we believe, can be taken as a further step in the evolution of a cognitive–developmental theory of ego development, a process so well begun by Loevinger. Not only does this work constitute a corroboration of Loevinger's stage "classification" (by providing the underlying logic explaining why the various features of her given stages do in fact go together), but it also advances her central claim for a holism to meaning organizing, further clarifying what sorts of "consistency" can and cannot be expected in the forms of our meaning-organizing.

The particular conception of the underlying form and process of ego development we have explored since the 1970s (Henderson & Kegan, 1989; Kegan, 1976, 1982, 1985, 1986, 1994; Kegan, Broderick,& Popp, 1992; Kegan & Lahey, 1983; Kegan, Noam, & Rogers, 1982; Lahey, 1986; Rogers & Kegan, 1990; Souvaine, Lahey, & Kegan, 1990; Noam & Kegan, 1982) is reflected in our research instrument which identifies the level of complexity of an individual's prevailing *epistemological structure*. The Subject–Object Interview (Lahey, Souvaine, Kegan, Goodman, & Felix, 1988) clarifies what aspects of meaning-organizing one has control over, can make use of, reflect upon (what is "object" in one's meaning-making), and what aspects control one, what aspects one is captive of, identified with (what one is "subject" to in one's meaning-making). Longitudinal study shows that if people change the underlying structure of their meaning-making, they do so in a developmental direction, that is, they differentiate from structures to which they were subject, thus making those structures into objects; and integrate these structures into a more complex organizational principle to which they are newly subject (Kegan, 1994).

Piaget (1952) often wrote about development along these lines, seeing development as a process of successive *decentrations* or triumphs over egocentrism. So, for example, Piaget's stage of equilibrium in early childhood, which he called *preoperational thinking*, is a balance of subject and object in which the structure of "perception" is subject in the sense that one is not able to distinguish one's perception of a thing from the thing itself. Preoperational thinkers may be unable to see that the same amount of liquid has gotten no greater for being poured into a thinner, taller glass because they lack the structural ability to coordinate their two perceptions of the water in each glass. What Piaget called *reversibility* would require a system or logic that can take perceptions as elements or objects to be coordinated by a new system or subject, rather than perceptions being themselves the subject, system, or logic.

Fellow genetic epistemologist Heinz Werner made even more explicit use of the language of subject and object to describe mental development. He said that his *orthogenetic principle*—that "wherever development occurs it proceeds from a state of relative globality and lack of differentiation to a state of increasing differentiation, articulation, and hierarchic integration"—generates two propositions (Werner, 1957):

1. A state involving a relative lack of differentiation between subject and object is developmentally prior to one in which there is a polarity of subject and object.
2. This increasing subject–object differentiation involves the corollary that the organism becomes increasingly less dominated by the immediate concrete situation; the person is less stimulus bound and less impelled by his own affective states. (pp. 126–127)

By way of example, let us consider some well-known developmental descriptions of regularities in meaning-making to demonstrate the single subject–object principle that may underlie all of them. Consider, for example, some widely agreed upon cognitive (Piaget, 1952), sociocognitive (Kohlberg, 1984; Selman, 1980) and intrapersonal (Kegan, 1982; Selman, 1980) capacities commonly emerging in latency (see Table 3.1).

First Principle (Roughly 2 to 6 years)	Second Principle (Roughly 6 years to teens)	Third Principle (Teenage years and beyond)
Cognitive Organizing		
Can: recognize that objects exist independent of own sensing of them (object permanence)	*Can:* grant to objects their own properties irrespective of one's perceptions; reason consequentially, i.e., according to cause and effect; construct a narrative sequence of events; relate one point in time to another; construct fixed categories and classes into which things can be mentally placed	*Can:* reason abstractly, that is, reason about reasoning; think hypothetically and deductively; form negative classes (e.g., the class of all not-crows); see relations as simultaneously reciprocal
Cannot: distinguish own perception of an object from actual properties of the object; construct a logical relation between cause and effect	*Cannot:* reason abstractly; subordinate concrete actuality to possibility; make generalizations; discern overall patterns; form hypotheses; construct ideals	*Cannot:* systematically produce all possible combinations of relations; systematically isolate variables to test hypotheses
Social-Cognitive Organizing		
Can: recognize that persons exist separate from oneself	*Can:* construct own point of view and grant to others their distinct point of view; take the role of another person; manipulate others on behalf of own goals; make deals, plans, and strategies	*Can:* be aware of shared feelings, agreements, and expectations that take primacy over individual interests
Cannot: recognize that other persons have their own purpose independent of oneself; take another person's point of view as distinct from one's own	*Cannot:* take own point of view and another's simultaneously; construct obligations and expectations to maintain mutual interpersonal relationships	*Cannot:* construct a generalized system regulative of interpersonal relationships and relationships between relationships
Intrapersonal Organizing		
Can: distinguish between inner sensation and outside stimulation	*Can:* drive, regulate, or organize impulses to produce enduring dispositions, needs, goals; delay immediate gratification; identify enduring	*Can:* internalize another's point of view in what becomes the coconstruction of personal experience, thus creating new capacity for empathy and

(continued)

TABLE 3.1
(CONTINUED)

	qualities of self according to outer social or behavioral manifestations (abilities—"fast runner"; preferences—"hate liver"; habits—"always oversleep")	sharing at an internal rather than merely transactive level; coordinate more than one point of view internally, thus creating emotions experienced as internal subjective states rather than social transactions
Cannot: distinguish one's impulses from oneself, that is, is embedded in or driven by one's impulses	*Cannot:* internally coordinate more than one point of view or need organization; distinguish one's needs from oneself; identify enduring qualities of the self according to inner psychological manifestations (inner motivations—"feel conflicted"; self attributions—"I have low self-esteem"; biographical sources—"My mother's worrying has influenced the way I parent")	*Cannot:* organize own states or internal parts of self into systematic whole; distinguish self from one's relationship; see the self as the author (rather than merely the theater) of one's inner psychological life

The question naturally now arises: Are these descriptions of developmental attainments in three independent spheres, or are these the expression, in three different spheres, of a single development? This is actually a complicated and controversial question for the field of mind-oriented developmental psychology, especially when it appears in this form: Should we conceive of individual mental development as the gradual evolution of a single process of increasing complexity, or as consisting in the gradual evolution of a number of relatively independent processes of increasing complexity? At some level this becomes a wave–particle kind of question. Both views have merit. The field of developmental psychology is in far greater danger of losing the wisdom in the *common mental enterprise* view than the *multiple mental adventures view.* But if there is a wisdom to be found in the former view it must address a prior question: How does it make sense even conceptually to speak of a single order of mind or order of consciousness that is organizing a person's experience across such an array of domains? Or, if we stay with our current example (looking at developments in later childhood) the question becomes: What common order of consciousness is being expressed in the apparently disparate capacities to construct a concrete world, to see that others have a point of view distinct from one's own, and to conceive of the self as consisting of durable (rather than moment-to-moment) preferences, abilities, intentions?

In each of the three spheres, what is being demonstrated is the ability to construct a mental *set, class or category*, the ability to order the things of one's experience—whether physical objects, other people, oneself or one's desires—as property-containing phenomena. Consider these not intuitively comparable discoveries: (a) the quantity of liquid is not changed by its being poured into a smaller glass; (b) a person who could have no way of knowing you would be made unhappy by his actions cannot be said to be "mean"; and (c) when I tell you "I don't like spinach," or think to myself, "I'm a Catholic girl," I mean that these are things that are ongoing about me, not just how I feel or think now— these are how I am or tend to be. Now as different as these three discoveries are (they are about one's understanding of the physical, social and personal world), it is the same, single epistemological principle or way of knowing that makes these discoveries possible.

In each case, the discovery arises out of the same, single ability to see that the phenomenon being considered (things, others, the self) has its own properties, which are elements of a class to which these properties belong, and that the phenomenon (thing, other, self) is itself known as this class (which, like all classes, has durable, ongoing rules that create the idea of class membership and regulate that membership). *Liquid* is now a class having as a member the property of quantity, and that property is not regulated by my perception; *other person* is now a class that has as a member the property of intention, and that property is not determined by my wishes; *self* is now a class that has as members the properties of preference, habit, and ability, and—the self now being a class, something that has properties—these are things about me in some ongoing way, as opposed to just what I want to eat now, for example. Hence new ways of knowing in such disparate domains as the inanimate, the social, and the introspective may all be occasioned by a single transformation of mind.

At some point after childhood, usually in adolescence, we expect people to transcend what Loevinger would call this Self-protective stage, and be able to think more abstractly, identify a complex internal psychological life, orient to the welfare of a human relationship, construct values and ideals self-consciously known as such, and subordinate one's own interests on behalf of one's greater loyalty to maintaining bonds of association or group participation. All these capacities, largely reflective of Loevinger's Conformist stage, reflect the same underlying epistemology. As "durable categories" move from subject to object, a more complex general structure evolves that can coordinate or subordinate durable categories. Thus, for example, cognitively, our thinking can now take the concrete as figure rather

DURABLE CATEGORIES
(Second Order of Consciousness)

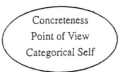

CROSS-CATEGORICAL MEANING MAKING
(Third Order of Consciousness)

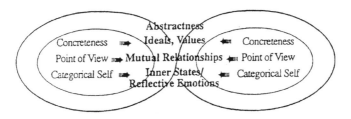

FIG. 3.1. The transformation from durable categories to cross-categorical meaning-making (and its products in the cognitive, sociocognitive, and intrapersonal–affective domains).

than ground and we think more abstractly; or, interpersonally, we can now simultaneously hold our point of view with another's point of view and create a more reciprocal or mutual frame on human relationships. "I used to worry that I would mess up," as one newly cross-categorical adolescent told us, "and that others would make me pay for it. Now I worry that if I mess up, others will worry." Both the "I" and the "others" moved from categorical phenomena (defined by their own properties of intention and need) to cross-categorical phenomena (defined by the link between the categories). Figure 3.1 illustrates this link. In fact, our approach identifies a succession of such epistemologies—successive differentiations of subject and object— that can be taken as a more ontogenetic approach to Loevinger's taxonomy of ego development (see Fig. 3.2).

SUBJECT	OBJECT	UNDERLYING STRUCTURE
1 PERCEPTIONS *Fantasy* SOCIAL PERCEPTIONS IMPULSES	Movement Sensation	Single Point/ Immediate/ Atomistic •

	LINES OF DEVELOPMENT
K	COGNITIVE
E	INTERPERSONAL
Y	INTRAPERSONAL

SUBJECT	OBJECT	UNDERLYING STRUCTURE

2 CONCRETE
  Actuality
  Data, Cause-and-Effect
POINT OF VIEW
  Role-Concept
  Simple Reciprocity (tit-for-tat)
ENDURING DISPOSITIONS
  Needs, Preferences
  Self Concept
	Perceptions
	
	Social Perceptions
	
	Impulses
		Durable Category

TRADITIONALISM **3** ABSTRACTIONS
  Ideality
  Inference, Generalization
  Hypothesis, Proposition
  Ideals, Values
MUTUALITY/INTERPERSONALISM
  Role Consciousness
  Mutual Reciprocity
INNER STATES
  Subjectivity, Self-Consciousness
	Concrete
	
	Point of View
	
	Enduring Dispositions
	Needs, Preferences
		Cross-Categorical
		Trans-Categorical

MODERNISM **4** ABSTRACT SYSTEMS
  Ideology
  Formulation, Authorization
  Relations between Abstractions
INSTITUTION
  Relationship-Regulating Forms
  Multiple-Role Consciousness
SELF-AUTHORSHIP
  Self-Regulation, Self-Formation
  Identity, Autonomy, Individuation
	Abstractions
	
	Mutuality
	Interpersonalism
	
	Inner States
	Subjectivity
	Self-Consciousness
		System/Complex

POST-MODERNISM **5** DIALECTICAL
  Trans-Ideological/Post-Ideological
  Testing Formulation, Paradox
  Contradiction, Oppositeness
INTER-INSTITUTIONAL
  Relationship between Forms
  Interpenetration of Self and Other
SELF-TRANSFORMATION
  Interpenetration of Selves
  Inter-Individuation
	Abstract System
	Ideology
	
	Institution
	Relationship-
	Regulating Forms
	Self-Authorship
	Self-Regulation
	Self-Formation
		Trans-System
		Trans-Complex

FIG. 3.2. Five orders of consciousness (from Kegan, 1994).

EXPLORING THE ONTOGENETIC
APPROACH TO EGO DEVELOPMENT

The Subject–Object Interview (SOI) has served as a tool not only to assess "stage of ego development," but specifically to explore our particular conception of the underlying structure and process that gives rise to stages of ego development. The interview procedure is in the tradition of the Piagetian semiclinical interview in which the experimenter asks questions to determine how a given "content" (e.g., the same quantity of water in two differently shaped glasses) is construed. The chief innovations of the SOI are that the contents are generated from the real-life experience of the interviewee; and the interview involves emotional, cognitive, intrapersonal and intrapersonal aspects of psychological organization. Real-life situations are elicited from a series of 10 uniform probes (e.g., "Can you tell me of a recent experience of being quite angry about something . . .?"), which the interviewer then explores at the level of discerning its underlying epistemology.

Interviews are transcribed and those portions of the interview where structure is clarified are the units of analysis. A typical interview may have from 8 to 15 such units. Each unit is scored independently. Interviews are usually scored by two raters to determine interrater reliability, at least one of the raters having previously demonstrated reliability. The psychological theory, as Fig. 3.2 illustrates, distinguishes five broad, increasingly complicated epistemological equilibria believed to evolve in sequence, each successive epistemology containing the last. But additionally, the assessment procedure is able to reliably distinguish four transitional gradations between each equilibrated epistemology, so over 20 distinctions, each a slightly different principle for meaning-organization than the last, can be made. (The formal research procedure for generating and analyzing the data of the interview is described in detail in Lahey et al., 1988.)

In comparison with the SCT, it is important to see, for example, that the SOI does not simply make a quantitatively larger number of between-stage discriminations (4 vs. 1), but that each between-stage designation actually represents a qualitatively and describably different structure in the gradual transformation from one stage to the next. Between the third and the fourth underlying structures, for example, it distinguishes between a way of organizing in which:

1. Only the cross-categorical structure is in evidence (designated 3);
2. The cross-categorical structures begin to be reflected on, but the next underlying structure (the "general system") is not yet constructed (designated 3(4));
3. Both structures are in evidence, but the cross-categorical predominates (designated 3/4);
4. Both structures are in evidence, but the general system predominates (designated 4/3);
5. The general system is the governing principle but it must work at keeping the cross-categorical structure integrated as object (designated 4(3)); and
6. The general system is securely established (designated 4).

Thus, the scores on the SOI, unlike the scores on the SCT, do not only name "entities"; taken in sequence, they depict a developmental process.

Consider, for example, the following excerpt from a SOI.[1]

> I've been just doing some of the things I like to do by myself rather than either not go or try to get Randy to go with me. He really prefers to sit at home and watch TV, and I used to just sit there with him or not go out. But now I realize that he really doesn't mind just doing that by himself and that he really feels better if I go off to an art museum by myself, because then he doesn't feel as if he's depriving me of going or as if he really should go. Before, it really was a strain between us because we didn't get to go as much as I'd want or we'd go and he really wouldn't like it and I'd feel guilty for making him come. Going by myself occasionally makes both of us happier and even makes things between us a lot smoother.

The speaker talks about a change in her own behavior. She used to stay at home with her husband, even though she wanted to go out and do things she enjoyed but he did not. Now she is going out, even if it has to be by herself, and doing a little more of what she likes. Although this is a change in her behavior, it is not necessarily a change in her subject–object development.

Although she is able now to go out alone where before she could not, and to pursue some of her interests without her husband's companionship, the change in behavior is being constructed in such a way that preserves rather than alters her existing (cross-categorical) subject–object organization. She internalizes her husband's point of view and continues to be made up by it. Although the husband is not physically going with her, he is still psychologically accompanying her because it is his not minding or actually preferring she go that allows her to go (e.g., "I used to just sit there with him or not go out. But now I realize that he . . . really feels better if I go off to an art museum by myself"). She is separating a little from her husband physically, but she is not separating either herself or him from his internalized point of view as a co-determiner of her own meaning. Evolution between Stage 3 and Stage 4 is the story of gradually separating internalized points of view from their original sources in others and making the self itself a coherent system for their generation and correlation. When that has happened, for example, we stop making others responsible for our own feelings, and experience it as a kind of violation when others make us responsible for theirs.

---

[1]This section is drawn largely from Lahey et al., 1988, pp. 46-71.

Now consider only slightly different versions of the same speech, each of which represents a further move of cross-categorical structuring from subject to object.

> But now I just go out more on my own if that's what I want to do. [How does that work?] It's not good for me to be so dependent on Randy. Randy helps me to see that. He keeps saying I have to do more what I want to do and I really do feel that it's important for me to decide myself. [Why is that important to you—deciding for yourself?] I'm an adult, and I think it *is* time that I started making my own decisions, don't you think?

Here she also takes responsibility for his point of view, but it is a new point of view, that she should decide for herself. "Deciding for oneself," however, is more than just another internalized point of view; it is about how to regard internalized points of view. That is, the particular point of view she has internalized here is about how she is to listen to, or regard, her husband's internalized points of view. The particular message is something like "Pay attention to what you (the speaker) want to do and don't be dependent on me (the husband)." Structurally, a slight change has taken place because there is a slight change in the distance between the self and its internalized points of view. She is now "further" in a structural sense, from all internalized points of view except the one giving her permission to pay less heed to those. She is as subject to that point of view as our previous Stage 3 speaker was to her husband's feeling unhappy when she goes out. However, it is her operating out of her subjectivity to this particular internalized point of view that allows for the new possibility that the self's choices might not be mediated by the perspectives of others it internalizes.

This describes the slight "4ish" element of the excerpt. Note however, that this 4ish element (that she decides for herself) is essentially being governed or run by a Stage 3 structure: The structure of "deciding for self" is being co-constructed by the speaker and the husband. Thus, as (a) the husband is centrally implicated in her ability to maintain this distance, (b) she is not responsible for it independent of him, and (c) they are together constructing a structure within which she can be self-determining, the developmental position is primarily Stage 3 with the appearance of Stage 4 bent to Stage 3's purposes. For coding purposes we call this 3(4). Development will entail the increasing ability to take full responsibility for the viewpoint that she decides for herself.

Now I just go out more by myself and don't wait around for him. When I want to go to a new art exhibit I'll tell him about it and say, "Honey, I'd like you to come if you want to. I'm going to go." Of course he doesn't come and I'd enjoy it more if he did, but at least I get to go. To tell you the truth, though, sometimes I wonder if doing it this way is much better than not going, because even though he doesn't say that much I can see that it hurts his feelings that I just go out without him and I feel like I'm being a bad wife. "Why don't I just stay here with him and watch TV? It's not so bad and he works so hard." But then I get mad and think, "Don't I have the right to do some things I like to do? It isn't fair of him to make me feel guilty." And so I go, but I end up feeling guilty about it.

Consider here the relationship being constructed between the speaker's self, the other's point of view which the self internalizes (hence, at least Stage 3), and the other person (her husband) whose point of view is being internalized. It is these three elements—self, other's point of view, and other—that are being increasingly differentiated and newly associated as the cross-categorical structure moves from subject to object. At Stage 3, it is not possible to distinguish the other from his or her internalized points of view.

In the last version, 3(4), the possibility emerged that the self's choices might not have to be mediated by the perspectives of others it internalizes, that there could be some differentiation between the self and the points of view it internalizes. This was only an emergent possibility, because this "differentiation" was actually being co-constructed with the other; its very source was in the nondifferentiated internalization of the other's point of view. In the present version, the emergent possibility has taken another qualitative step toward realization, because the speaker is generating the decision to go by herself, distinguishing between the other's point of view, which she still holds, and her own.

What also makes this version further along in the 3–4 transition is the speaker's ability to take responsibility for the decision (to go) which can lead to her husband's unhappy feelings. In the earlier constructions, Stages 3 and 3(4), the speaker is not solely responsible for her decisions because she is making them in one sort of mental partnership with her husband or another. So this version is clearly beyond 3(4); the question as to how far beyond, directs us to consider just how the self, the views it internalizes, and the other are not differentiated. She continues to hold herself responsible for his bad feelings ("I feel like I'm being a bad wife") and to hold him responsible for her bad feelings ("he's making me feel guilty"). Having begun to distinguish the self from its internalized perspectives (the 4ish structure present in this version), the consequences of doing so are still constructed in the "3ish" way; she is unable to release him as a source for her own feelings or to release herself from being (in her experience) a source of his feelings. It would be one thing for her to regret not deciding in line with his view, to feel badly for him or even for herself in not being able to satisfy him. That would be a more Stage 4 construction. But to feel guilty, self-blaming, in default of what is then constructed as an obligation to be determined by the views one can internalize, is to be subject to the process of internalization, hence, Stage 3.

Data units demonstrating two simultaneous structures get scored X / Y or Y / X depending on which structure seems to be ruling. The evidence for scoring this bit 3 / 4 rather than 4 / 3 is best found in the way the speaker seems to hold the other responsible for her negative feelings associated with simultaneously exercising her own judgment and continuing to take in his point of view. "It isn't fair of him to make me feel guilty," in this context, seems at once to reflect on the process by which her feelings get determined by his internalized points of view, and to make herself the helpless victim of this process.

> I just go by myself now. I feel guilty about it sometimes because I know he'd rather I didn't go and that I'd just stay home with him. I can see him there feeling sad or mad about my decision and I feel myself changing my mind, right on the spot, that it's not right for me to go and I can just get stopped in my tracks. (So what happens?) Sometimes I don't go and sometimes I go. (How are you able to go?) I remind myself that it doesn't make sense to stay because then I only end up punishing him for my decision to not go. We both end up unhappy then.

Like the previous version (3 / 4), this speaker is (a) able to empathically hold the other's point of view (i.e., it matters to the self not because of its consequences to the self's preconstructed point of view—(Stage 2)—but actually influences what the self's own view shall be, hence, minimally Stage 3); (b) able, at least some of the time, to differentiate itself from this empathic process (i.e, this kind of empathy is a structural capacity or element of the self, but is not the very structure determinative of the self— empathy here need not mean identification, hence minimally post-3; (c) susceptible to the loss of the Stage 4 structure, especially when its exercise leads to actions contrary to the empathically derived wishes of the other; in these instances, we gather, there are times when the other's view becomes determining (hence, not fully Stage 4). Were she to tell us this is what always happens when she picks up his negative feelings, and that she always "can feel myself changing my mind" this version might be structurally identical to the prior version (3 / 4): In the "feeling myself changing my mind" we can see both the ability to take a perspective on the self-determining qualities of the other's point of view, and the "caughtness" in that determination.

But what is structurally different here is that however powerful the determining hold of internalized views still may be (the 3ish structure), she is not only able to look to herself for decisions contrary to the other's views which she internalizes, but she is also able to look to herself as the source of the feelings she has about deciding contrary to his views. That is, she is responsible not only for decisions which may lead to his bad feelings (3/4), but she takes responsibility for making the decision (e.g., "it's my decision to not go"), as well as for punishing him. Notice that punishing her husband is the consequence of a Stage 3 construction, where she punishes him because she blames him for her not going. However, she also takes responsibility for this 3ish structure, which is still present but modified by (rather than itself modifying, as in the previous version) the 4ish structure, hence 4/3.

> I just go by myself now. He doesn't like it a lot of the time but I think it's not only better for me but better for us. I've just had to accept the fact that there are some things I'm not going to get from him and he has to do the same thing. He's married to a woman who likes to go on nature hikes and see art exhibits and though he doesn't like to do either of those and doesn't have to do them, he does have to understand that I do and that sometimes I'm going to do these things rather than be with him. I know he doesn't like it but I try not to dwell on that. And I'm aware that there's this part of me that doesn't want him to dwell on it either—I find it much easier when he doesn't dwell on his not liking my going out. (What makes it hard if he does dwell on that?) Well, I just have to work hard to remember that although I can be sad about his not liking it, I do think it's very important for me to honor my own interests. (It's very important?) Yes, because I'm not me if I don't.

The content of this version seems largely to have to do with someone wanting to keep a certain kind of distance from another person: She doesn't want either of them to dwell on his feelings about what she does. It may be helpful in understanding this version, however, to see that this distance is fundamentally about keeping the self separate from its internalized points of view. This version evinces no less an ability to "empathize" in the sense of taking in and registering the other's point of view, but in a way qualitatively different than the previous versions in that it differentiates the self (its particular decisions and its overall character) from the points of view it internalizes. The self is now itself a generator of its own points of view; it has become itself a whole system; the speaker can articulate a kind of theory of how the self is, which can be compared and contrasted with other selves, which are also whole systems. Other selves are let out of the job of providing self-determining points of view and can now be related to as persons whose views and feelings can be cared for, thought about, weighed or related to, from the perspective of one's own system of meaning. This speaker not only expresses a kind of respect for both "how she is" and "how he is" (she's a person who likes such-and-such; he, however, prefers to spend time in such-and-such a way); she also does not make him responsible for "how she is," either in terms of having caused her to be this way or having to do anything about it now that she is; nor does she make herself responsible for how he is or his reactions to her choices (she can support, sympathize and regret his bad feelings about some of her choices, but she does not feel guilty over them; they are his feelings, his choices, and she is not responsible for them). All of this is expressive of a Stage 4, "general systems" structure, in which internalized points of view are no longer determinative of the self's organization but mediated by the self's organization.

However, her last three sentences of this version indicate that the ability to distinguish the self from the views it internalizes is quite tenuous. In saying it is better for her not to have either of them focus too much on his negative feelings, she is saying something like, "It is only with difficulty that I can maintain the differentiation between my self and the views I internalize; if he presses this view too strongly I feel vulnerable to losing the boundary I prefer to maintain." To the extent she must actually avoid considering the other's negative reactions to her choices or work hard to continue honoring her own interests or get the other to keep this distance for her, the psychological evolution from Stage 3 to Stage 4 is not quite complete. When she can distinguish both herself and the other from his feelings on a matter, then he can press his views as much and as emphatically as he likes and she will not have to feel in danger either of losing her ability to care for herself or thinking that the only way to continue caring for him is to be responsible for his feelings. The speaker seems to fear she may not be able to keep herself from identifying with his feelings or identifying him with his feelings, or both. More than just a "less confident Stage 4," this is a structurally different subject–object position precisely because the source of the "less confidence" is the structural circumstance of not yet fully integrating the Stage 3 organization as element of a new system. This subject–object position is the last qualitative distinction we are able to reliably make in our data analysis before the appearance of the fully evolved new balance, and, for coding purposes, it is designated 4(3). Thus we have illustrated the gradual evolution from a Stage 3 epistemology (which gives rise to Loevinger's Confornist stage) to a Stage 4 epistemology (which gives rise to Loevinger's Conscientious stage.

THE CLAIM FOR HOLISM REVISITED

This ontogenetic (as opposed to taxonomic) view of ego development allows us to revisit and perhaps to clarify the nature of Loevinger's most fundamental claim, namely that there exists, at any given moment in personality, a central organizing tendency, or a meaning-making whole organizing the parts. This is a claim lately out of favor (Basseches, 1989; Noam, 1988a; Schweder, 1977) but one we join Loevinger in making, so long as we understand what the claim for "holism" or "consistency" really does and does not entail.

First, the consistency we speak of at any given moment in the self's development is a consistency in the structure, or order of complexity, of one's meaning-making (i.e., *how* one thinks). We are certainly not speaking about a consistency in behavior, and we are not even speaking about a consistency in the content of one's meaning-making (i.e., *what* one thinks). One's behavior can change without any change in one's epistemological structure. One's preoccupying concerns or position on an issue can change without any change in one's epistemological structure. The idea of consistency or holism means that the epistemological shape or form of one's meaning-making, at any given time in one's development, comes under the influence of a commonly exercised epistemological structure. Describing that structure more precisely, as we try to do, makes this claim both clearer and more explorable. Lahey (1986), for example, explored the widely held, commonsense notion that people do not construct their love lives the same way they construct their work lives. Despite how differently people may say they feel about love conflicts and work conflicts; despite how differently they do feel; despite the clinical literature's understanding of how much more "primitive," "undefended," "unbounded," or even "immature" we experience ourselves to be in our private, intimate relations, what Lahey found was an extraordinary degree of epistemological consistency within subjects across these domains.

Our approach also makes it possible to conduct a more refined exploration of the consistency hypothesis across psychological domains, such as cognitive, sociocognitive, or moral meaning-making. As examples, Carroll (1986), studying children; Villegas (1988), studying high school-age adolescents; Walker (1995), studying college-age adolescents; and Dixon (1986), studying adults, all using the SOI, found support for the hypothesis that subject–object structures form the underlying basis for cognitive or social–cognitive stages.

The subject–object approach also clarifies how a "mix of epistemologies" may not violate the holistic or consistency hypothesis, if the subject is consistently using the same mix. The ontogenetic view allows us to see that what gets called a "mix of epistemologies" may actually be a transitional place in an evolutionary process where older and newer epistemological structures are simultaneously operating.

Still, a frequent and sensible family of questions that often comes up when people consider the consistency claim goes something like this: "Do you really think people tend to use the same epistemology (or "order of consciousness") across all the different domains of their living, or even in the same domain all the time? I mean, isn't it possible, or even likely, that I use one structure in my work life and another with my children? Isn't it possible that although I usually use the `fourth order,' say, with my children that, once in a while, on a bad day, I may revert to a simpler order of consciousness? Might not people, under stress, use a simpler order of consciousness? When we evolve to a higher order principle of meaning-organization, isn't it possible that some aspects of our experiencing do not `go along' with the transformation, but get `split off' or dissociated from the whole, and go on being organized according to earlier principles?"

Our answer to these questions—drawn from our vantage points as clinicians, consultants, researchers, and incurable observers of ourselves, family members, friends and associates—is "Yes, we think all these things are possible, but they do not necessarily violate `the consistency assumption'." In other words, we hold to a consistency assumption, but not a simple-minded one. We believe the self does seek for the coherence of its organizing according to its most complex principle of organization, and of course it does not always succeed. But, even when it does not succeed, forms of consistency or holism are still in evidence. How can this be?

Perhaps a few examples will suggest what we mean. Let us take a commonly posited form of inconsistency, the idea of temporary regression, in response to stress, for example, or a disconfirming context. We travel to our parents' home, say, for the holidays. As the airplane touches down we say to ourselves, "This time it's going to be different. This time I will not feel regressed (or depressed or enervated) after 3 days with my parent(s)." But, alas, it is to no avail, and we do find ourselves feeling regressed. Perhaps we would say we feel like a child, or just "not ourselves," but the main internal experience is negative: We do not like the way we feel. Or perhaps we are grown people who go back to school. We now find ourselves in a context where we have less control over our work lives, less authority; instead of people coming to us for consultation we are seeking out hard-to-find faculty. The experience may feel to us quite regressive. We may feel "juvenilized." It may actually be that aspects of our thinking or feeling in this context are younger or simpler than we now know ourselves normally to be. Above all, we, again, do not like the way we feel. If we in fact are organizing our experiencing in these examples according to less complex principles, then how can we say a form of structural consistency is also present?

It may be true that we are organizing aspects of our experiencing according to a principle inconsistent with our current, most complex capacity. But it is also true that we do not like the way we feel. The way we are thinking does not feel to us acceptable or syntonic; we do not feel like ourselves. *Now who or what is doing this evaluating?* We do not feel unhappy in our juvenilized state because we were unhappy when juveniles. We feel unhappy because our current, most complex, adult way of organizing is *still* at work, here evaluating this whole experience, finding it dystonic, even lamenting that we are not able to "put into play" our fullest selves. If regression refers to an actual process of "devolution," of losing a more complex order for a simpler one, then these are not experiences of regression because the most complex structure is still present and at work, however confined it may at the moment be. To the extent in such situations we are unable to be fully consistent it costs us something; we do not like it. But even in such situations of inconsistency a form of consistency continues to exist. The overall way we feel about, think about, or evaluate the situation is expressive of, and consistent with, our most complex principle of organization.

Let us consider the phenomenon of "losing it." As parents of fourth order consciousness, say, we generally try not to make our children responsible for our own feelings, but, occasionally, we may lose it, and yell at them when we are really angry with someone else. Is such behavior a violation of the holism hypothesis? Not at all. It would be a violation if we did not construct it as losing it! That is, the term is evidence that however inconsistent we may temporarily have been with our most complex way of organizing, we are so identified with this way that when we deviate from it we construct the phenomenon as a deviation, consistent with our most complex principle of organization.

Finally, let us consider those more chronic phenomenon of split off, encapsulated, or dissociated aspects of our experiencing that fail to be transformed by the new, more complex principle of organization and continue to be organized according to earlier, simpler principles (Noam, 1988a). The fact that such situations always take a toll on psychic life (cognitively, they can cause distortions; affectively, they can generate painful symptoms; biologically, they drain off energy that goes into keeping the parts separate) is a demonstration that the self seeks consistency even if it cannot always achieve it. But even in situations like these there is also a form of consistency that is being demonstrated.

Once again, if we look at the totality of the self's organizing—at the whole system rather than just at the dissociated parts—what we see is a self that, besides organizing different domains according to different organizational principles (an expression of inconsistency), is also "keeping out" or "holding back" these aspects of the self's organizing from coming under the influence of the most complex organizational principle. Now who or what is doing this "keeping out" or "holding back"? What principle of organizing is expressed in the defenses that sustain the lack of integration within the self? It would be counterintuitive on logical grounds alone to consider that defenses sustaining this relationship could be less complicated than our most complex way of organizing. But we also see clinically demonstrated that the defensive structures maintaining the dissociation bear the mark of (i.e., are consistent with) the self's most complex way of organizing. This is really another way of speaking to the two-sided nature of increasing psychological complexity. Development creates a potential resource for enhanced self-observation, but increased complexity can also be put to the purpose of creating ever more elaborate ways to hold off unintegrated parts of the self's meaning-making.

It would be too simple to suggest that one's most complex epistemological principle is the only way one organizes experience all the time, across all domains. But it may also be too simple to suggest that phenomena like regression, "losing it," or even chronic encapsulations necessarily contradict the consistency hypothesis. In all such phenomena, the expression of one's most complex epistemological principle—the central tendency—can still be seen.

Thus Loevinger's most fundamental claim, however widely contested, may nonetheless receive considerable support from this more ontogenetic approach to ego development.

Loevinger's Theory of Ego Development in the Context of Contemporary Psychoanalytic Theory

Drew Westen
Department of Psychiatry
Harvard Medical School and
The Cambridge Hospital

When Loevinger began her work on ego development, psychoanalysis was a very different discipline. In contrast to its contemporary pluralistic state (Wallerstein, 1988), psychoanalysis was a somewhat monolithic, authoritarian guild, where dissent was cause for excommunication, particularly if that dissent questioned the centrality of Freud's theory of psychosexual development. Many analysts were ardently antiempirical, for a number of reasons. The one good reason was that empirical data too seldom had a fraction of the depth of clinical data. The other reasons were less commendable. For one, data challenge hierarchy, and the institutes were organized in a hierarchical fashion in which gray-haired, bearded men were the keepers of the faith and the ultimate arbiters of what was or was not "analytic"—which was too often confused with what was or was not true. To the extent that psychoanalysis had an epistemology, it was a somewhat medieval epistemology of authority. To make a new theoretical argument, an analytic author had to show that Freud had already said the same thing in some footnote, so that the potential heretic was really just explicating—literally making explicit—what was in the *Standard Edition*. Perhaps, then, it is no surprise that Loevinger has had little, if any, impact on psychoanalysis, much like Bowlby and, to a lesser degree, Erikson (who is rarely cited in psychoanalytic journals).

Although vestiges of this medieval state of affairs still remain in some psychoanalytic institutes, the situation is markedly different today, as are the theories that dominate psychoanalysis. Ideas once anathema to mainstream psychoanalysts—the centrality of relational needs, the importance of strivings for self-esteem, the importance of empathy as a curative element in the analytic situation, among others—are now an integral part of psychoanalytic discourse in even the most conservative journals. And attitudes toward empiricism have changed, or at least grown less polarized, as evidenced by the enthusiastic reception of Stern's (1985) work on infant development in psychoanalytic circles.

Categorization is always, at some level, reification, and I have undoubtedly done an injustice to an earlier era of psychoanalysis—which, after all, spawned object relations theory, ego psychology, Bowlby's marriage of ethology and psychoanalysis, Eriksonian developmental theory, and the experimental work constituting the New Look in perception. I have perhaps also underplayed the continuing tensions in contemporary psychoanalysis among the keepers of the faith, the Luthers (or perhaps Pilates) who seem at times too ready to cast off important insights of the past, and "moderate" reformationists trying to grapple with what they see in their patients, themselves, and relevant empirical literatures. So perhaps this parable of the development and organization of psychoanalytic thinking is analogous to the parable Loevinger tells of the development and organization of the ego. Psychoanalysis was never impulsive, but it was certainly self-protective. One could certainly read the way thousands of sentence stems were completed in the pages of the major psychoanalytic journals to demonstrate that point empirically. So, too, could one document the growing appreciation for ambiguity and internal dissent, signaling the field's move toward toleration of conflict and complexity and heralding a higher form of collective "ego" organization.

In this chapter, I briefly outline the major contemporary currents in psychoanalytic thinking. I then try to address the question of how Loevinger's work relates to this tradition. The chapter concludes with some thoughts about what Loevinger has added and what remains to be done.

CURRENTS IN CONTEMPORARY
PSYCHOANALYTIC THEORY

Psychoanalytic theorizing has passed through a number of "stages," although the stage analogy is imperfect, because the different models proposed by Freud and later psychoanalysts continue in many respects to compete with each other, rather than to show a pattern in which each model integrates and transcends its predecessor. Classical psychoanalytic theory is a theory of drives, psychosexual stages, unconscious conflicts and compromises, and interactions among enduring sets of internal processes Freud called *structures.*

According to the first of Freud's classical models, his *drive model*, all human motivation ultimately springs from the wells of libido (broadly speaking, pleasure-seeking, and narrowly speaking, sexual pleasure-seeking) and aggression that is converted into various forms. The virtue of this model lies in its linkage of motivation to the body: Freud never forgot, as many of his successors in psychoanalysis and personality psychology appear to have, that humans are fundamentally housed in bodies, and that the human hypothalamus remains, in its essentials, more like than unlike the hypothalamus of other mammals. Thus, humans compete for mates, care for their young, seek sexual gratification, and so forth. They also gratify aggressive and sadistic fantasies and wishes in ways that elicit social reinforcement (aggressive sports, corporate or scholastic competition, mildly aggressive sexual acts such as biting), as well as those that do not (such as the 20,000-plus murders committed annually in the United States). Indeed, the most persuasive data—from Bosnia, Ruanda, Somalia, and wherever the rule of law gives way—seem to support Freud's theory of aggression: Freed from social constraints, many people (or, to modify Freud's view somewhat, many males) will rape, kill, steal, torture, and show little evidence of any functioning superego whatsoever under the right conditions, a point to which we shall return. Whether this is true of *most* males is an empirical question, but the historical recored is certainly suggestive.

The second classical model, Freud's psychosexual model, is a set of hypotheses about the way children develop in their pleasure-seeking. It provides a model of development Loevinger's in many respects supplements, because her theory of ego development describes the way children, adolescents, and adults move beyond pleasure-seeking as their primary orientation to the world. The psychosexual theory was near and dear to Freud and became the article of faith distinguishing the loyal from the disloyal. Much about the theory seems objectionable or peculiar to anyone who has not done clinical work or reared children, although the latter vantage points provide some fascinating corroborative data. A colleague, for example, recently told me how his oedipal-age son said to his wife, "I want daddy to go away." "Why?" she asked innocently. "Because he has a bigger penis than I do." I have trouble imagining an explanation for this statement in terms of the Five Factor Model. Similarly, a woman came to my office for a consultation complaining that she could not talk to the female therapist she had just begun seeing because "she's too attractive—I just can't talk to a woman who's so perfect." The crucial question about Freud's psychosexual theory is not whether it captures aspects of reality—which the empirical evidence suggests that it does, albeit very imperfectly (Fisher & Greenberg, 1996)—but whether its place should be as central as Freud presumed (and whether a number of the details, for example, about the centrality of penis envy in the development of all females, are accurate). Loevinger thought not, and many contemporary psychoanalysts agree with her.

The third classical psychoanalytic model—aside from Freud's drive and developmental models—is the topographic model, which distinguishes conscious, preconscious, and unconscious processes. Freud argued that much of mental life is unconscious, including affects and motives, and this aspect of his theory has now been amply confirmed by laboratory research (see Westen, 1990a, in press). Freud viewed thoughts, feelings, wishes, and fears as organized along unconscious networks of association, and used free association, among other techniques, to gain access to those networks. Central to this model was the notion of conflict and compromise—that people have multiple motives that may be active simultaneously and may seek expression in ways unavailable to conscious introspection. The concept of compromise-formations—thoughts, behaviors, or other psychological processes that integrate competing or collaborating motives—is one of the most important contributions of Freud's theory of psychic conflict that continues to evolve in more classical analytic circles (Brenner, 1982). Loevinger's theory is less concerned with the specific conflicts people experience than with the capacity to tolerate conflicts consciously, which emerges at her higher ego levels.

Freud's fourth classical model was his structural model (id, ego, superego). In his earliest writings, Freud focused on what he came to dub the "it," translated as the *id*—that nasty, bestial side of human nature that makes life interesting, even if not comfortable. Living in society, however, requires constraints on self-interest, which become internalized from parents in the form of the superego. Much of Loevinger's theory and measurement strategy focus on what psychoanalysts would call superego development. Although psychoanalytic theory has focused most on the years from age 3 to 5 in the development of internalized morality, Loevinger, like Kohlberg, offers a more extended view of moral development, from an initial completely self-interested stage, characterized by minimal little or no concern for others or for moral rules, through later stages in which morality means conformity and, if the person achieves higher stages of ego development, a capacity to reflect on one's own internalizations and make conscious choices about values. The third structure in Freud's triumvirate was what he called the "I," translated as *ego*—that part of the mind whose functions include perception, thought, decision making, managing affective states, finding a way to satisfy often conflicting motives, and maintaining a sense of coherence in the midst of a constant internal civil war.

This initial description of the ego in the structural model led to the first of three contemporary psychodynamic models coexisting today alongside the more classical models (although these recent approaches have roots in Freud's writings circa 1915 and began developing considerably in the 1930s and 1940s.) The first is psychoanalytic ego psychology, which flourished in the 1950s through 1970s and is now essentially taken for granted among many psychoanalytic theorists. The ego psychologists were influenced by the cognitive–developmental theories of Werner and Piaget, and one of their major accomplishments was to contextualize the motivational strivings Freud had described within a mind capable of progressively more efficient thought and self-regulation. Loevinger (1976) makes clear that she is not primarily an ego psychologist in this tradition, although her model taps some of the central features of psychoanalytic theories of ego development, such as the child's growing capacity for complex thought about the self and others, regulation of impulses, self-reflection, insight, and what analysts described as the "synthetic function" of the ego.

Perhaps the major contemporary perspective in psychoanalysis is object relations theory, which continues to coexist uneasily with the classical drive, psychosexual, topographic, and structural models (see Greenberg & Mitchell, 1983; Mitchell, 1988). Fairbairn (1952) perhaps stated most succinctly the difference between classical Freudian theory and object-relational (or, simply, relational) approaches when he asserted that libido is object-seeking, not pleasure-seeking. In other words, people need people (there is a song in that), not just bodily satisfaction, and they do not pursue relationships primarily to get sexual gratification in more or less sublimated forms. Fairbairn proposed a developmental movement from immature dependence to mature dependence, which in many ways parallels what Loevinger describes as the shift from impulsive and self-protective levels of ego functioning to more mature modes of relating in which others are valued for who they are, not what they offer. A central point of agreement among developmental object relations theorists of various sorts is that once children become clear on the boundaries between self and others, they move from relatively simple, one-dimensional representations of others (e.g., people are either good or bad) and a tendency to treat others as objects of gratification, to more complex, integrated representations and a capacity to love others in a deep, mutual way (see Westen, 1991).

A final, and related model in contemporary psychoanalysis is self psychology, initiated by Heinz Kohut (1971, 1977). Self psychology is a mixture of good ideas and sometimes fuzzy conceptualizations. The good ideas include the notion that people need to feel good about themselves and that they are likely to have unstable self-representations and low or highly variable self-esteem if they lack appropriate mirroring or empathic resonance in childhood from their caretakers. Like many other self theorists in the history of psychology, however, Kohut and other psychoanalytic self psychologists have had difficulty coherently defining and delimiting the domain of the "self," which sometimes refers to representations of self, sometimes means a particular hypothesized theoretical structure, and sometimes just means whatever a clinician who cannot be bothered to think clearly wants it to mean (e.g., "the patient suffers from deficits in the self"—translation: the person has a problem). At its most coherent, self psychology addresses the way people with certain personality disorders (notably narcissistic) alternate between grandiosity and self-loathing, have difficulty treating others as independent entities with their own needs and interests, and have difficulty empathizing with other people. As such, self psychology has added an important dimension to psychoanalytic theory.

THE RELATION BETWEEN LOEVINGER'S THEORY OF EGO DEVELOPMENT AND PSYCHOANALYTIC THEORY

Loevinger's theory has little overlap with the four classical Freudian models. She is not particularly interested in taxonomies of motives, in the biological basis of developmental transitions, in sexuality or its development, or in the content of conflicts. Rather, she is interested in the development of *character*, of the capacity to rein in impulses when necessary; to think complexly about oneself, others, and one's environment; and to treat others as ends rather than means. These are the central concerns of psychoanalytic ego psychology, object relations theory, and self psychology. What Loevinger offers is an approach bridging these three more contemporary psychoanalytic approaches.

Indeed, although Loevinger used the term *ego* to describe what is developing (somewhat reluctantly, as she would rather describe its general developmental course than to define ego in a way leading to reification), she also used the term *self* at times as a synonym (Loevinger, 1976, 1987a), and was equally explicit in describing ego development as the changing organization of an individual's "frame of reference for . . . perceptions and conceptions of the interpersonal world" (Loevinger, 1984, p. 49). Elsewhere (1979) she argued that ego development "encompasses the complexity of moral judgment, the nature of interpersonal relations, and the framework within which one perceives oneself and others as people" (p. 3). Loevinger derived this notion of ego or self as a frame of reference or map for understanding oneself and the interpersonal world largely from Sullivan's (1953) description of the self-system as a filtering process people use to maintain some stability to their self-representations and to their moods. This process filters out information that is too threatening or discrepant, and provides an organization to perceptions of the self and others.

Loevinger (1976) was vehement that her theory of ego development is not the same as psychoanalytic ego developmental theory, which was derived primarily from clinical experience rather than from research, and includes many more functions (such as perception and defense). Within psychoanalysis, the concept coming closest to ego as Loevinger intended it is Kernberg's (1975, 1984) concept of *personality organization.* Personality organization refers to an individual's overall level of impulse control, reality testing, capacity for representing the self and others in complex and differentiated ways, and relational capacity. Kernberg described three levels of personality organization—psychotic, borderline, and neurotic—which correspond to developmental junctures (infancy, toddlerhood, and the oedipal age and beyond) at which a person's character structure can be arrested or centered. Like Loevinger's concept of ego, Kernberg had in mind an organization of perception, cognition, impulse control, and orientation toward the self and others.

Kernberg's model differs from Loevinger's, however, in four major respects. First, Loevinger's theory and method begin with a person who is verbal, whereas Kernberg aimed to chart the evolution of personality structure from the earliest days of life. Second, Kernberg tied his model of psychopathology to a model of personality development derived from object relations theories that locate fixation points in the first 3 to 4 years of life. Loevinger, in contrast, made no assumptions about the earliest years and was more interested in tracing character development through adolescence and beyond. Third, Kernberg is a clinician, who wants to account for the range of clinical phenomena, from the psychotic to the neurotic. For example, a central aspect of personality structure is capacity for reality testing. Although the person with a psychotic personality organization can confuse inner and outer and self and other, the individual with borderline structure has weakened reality testing and experiences occasional brief lapses into disordered thinking but does not typically live in a psychotic world. Loevinger, in contrast, is most interested in people whose functioning is at least in the character-disordered range, and only rarely does she mention reality testing as a central aspect of ego development (e.g., 1976, p. 16, where she suggested that at the Impulsive stage, "[s]uperstitious ideas are probably common"). Finally, whereas Kernberg's source of data was exclusively clinical and qualitative, Loevinger used a sophisticated quasiclinical method to transform qualitative into quantitative data. Thus, she did not tend to make assertions about development that she could not test.

THE PROMISE AND LIMITS OF LOEVINGER'S
APPROACH TO EGO DEVELOPMENT FOR
PSYCHOANALYTIC THEORY

The comparison with Kernberg's concept of personality organization provides a useful way of considering what Loevinger's approach has to offer psychoanalysis. In many ways, Kernberg's theory is more comprehensive, beginning earlier and taking into account a wider range of psychopathology. But the breadth of Kernberg's theory comes at the cost of accuracy. Where testable, some of the developmental hypotheses are wrong, and where not testable, the hypotheses often have power as metaphors but not as explanations. For example, Kernberg's linkage of infancy and psychosis is untenable; infants resemble psychotics in that they both eat and breathe, and to some degree in their lack of conscious control over their thought processes, but the structural similarity of the two states probably does not extend much further. Infants do not, as far as anyone can tell, hallucinate. Similarly, Kernberg attributes to oedipal-age children (i.e., age 5) the capacity to integrate ambivalent views of the self and others, which research shows is not generally normative until age 12 or 13 (Harter, 1986; Westen, 1990b). He needs to do this in order to link borderline pathology with the toddler years, because splitting of representations is supposed to reflect an arrest around age 2.

As these comments suggest, although Kernberg's model of personality structure is extremely useful clinically, his model of development is much more problematic. Loevinger's is not, for the simple reason that it arose from, was tested against, and was revised on the basis of empirical data. What Loevinger offers psychoanalysis is a developmental approach to personality organization informed by data that can falsify and refine it. Unlike developmental models of object relations, self, and personality structure in psychoanalysis, Loevinger's model does not have the luxury of drifting too far afield from the realities of development because quantitative data cannot be as easily explained away as clinical data. Beyond the extraordinary depth and breadth of conceptualization manifest to anyone who reads her 1976 volume, Loevinger brings to psychoanalytic thinking something it desperately needs: a sophisticated empiricism. And to date, no researcher who is as fluent in, and has wrestled as much with, psychoanalytic ideas has had the combination of psychometric and theoretical sophistication of Jane Loevinger.

So should Kernberg, Kohut, Fairbairn, and Winnicott renounce their place in the psychoanalytic pantheon to make room for Loevinger? Loevinger's impressive rendering of the development of character should certainly become a more prominent feature of the psychoanalytic landscape alongside the terrain charted by Kernberg and Kohut. As Loevinger herself has repeatedly noted (e.g., 1976, 1987a), however, theories are Vaihingerian fictions, imperfect depictions of aspects of reality that are always flawed and incomplete. Loevinger does not offer a personality theory, only a developmental model of a central aspect of personality development. She does not offer a theory of motivation, cognition, affect, or their interaction, or a theory of consciousness. These were not her intentions.

But there is another way in which Loevinger's approach is, like all approaches, contextualized by the thinking of the times—by, we might say in her terms, the organization or frame of reference of an era. Loevinger developed her theory and method in an era of grand, unidimensional stage theories. Freud, Piaget, and to some extent Werner and Sullivan had each offered his own dazzling depiction of the developing child, and Loevinger had the genius to pull together their insights with the new research of Kohlberg and a dozen other theorists who were all tracking what seemed like the same animal. And to a great extent they were.

Since the 1970s, however, the limitations of holistic theories like that of Piaget have become more clear, as researchers increasingly challenged the notion that stages apply across all domains (e.g., Case, 1992; Fischer, 1980) and focused attention on the microprocesses that lead, in aggregate, to changes at the macro level. For example, the progressive decentration Piaget described, in which children learn to see others' perspectives more clearly, depends in part on factors such as the ability to hold increasingly larger amounts of information in working memory and the progressive development of strategies (such as home-grown mnemonic devices) allowing greater control over information.

Loevinger (1976) once schematized ego development as including domains of impulse control, interpersonal relations, conscious preoccupations, and cognitive complexity (p. 26), but she insisted, based in part on years of careful attention to data, that "There is just one dimension." Hauser (1993) discerned three central themes in Loevinger's conceptualization of ego development: psychological-mindedness, synthesis and coherence of perceptions and cognitions, and agency. To some extent, whether one focuses on the micro or the macro probably depends on the current Zeitgeist as well as on personality variables such as cognitive style and, perhaps, derivitives of early toilet training.

Thus, at a global level, the concept of ego development, and the strategy Loevinger has devised for measuring it, has proven useful and robust. But theories have an unfortunate tendency to obscure as well as to elucidate, and the time may have come to unpack some of what may be too tightly wrapped into a single construct. The issue is both theoretical and methodological (and can ultimately only be decided by data).

Consider, for example, Loevinger's description of the Impulsive stage (citations from Loevinger, 1976, p. 16), which includes Eriksonian autonomous strivings (the "emphatic 'No!' and the later 'Do it by self'"), a need-gratifying orientation toward relationships ("others are seen and valued in terms of what they can give"), a tendency toward splitting and simplistic representations ("tends to class people as good or bad"), a primitive morality and an anal psychosexual orientation ("Good and bad at times are confounded with 'nice-to-me' versus 'mean-to-me' or even with clean and pure versus dirty and nasty"), externalizing defenses ("likely to see his troubles as located in a place rather than in a situation, much less in himself"), and mild deficits in reality testing ("superstitious thinking"). Many of these phenomena are indeed likely to covary, at least in most people whose personality is organized at this level, but clinical experience, as well as some research evidence (see Westen, 1990b), challenges their inherent inseparability. In our own research, we found high correlations between some dimensions of object relations that would be subsumed under Loevinger's construct, but moderate to zero correlations among others. To the extent that the construct of ego development encompasses psychological-mindedness (which is highly correlated with social–cognitive complexity), moral development, and the person's cognitive–affective "frame of reference" in thinking about the self and others (such as whether the person expects relationships to be pleasurable or threatening), the fact that these three variables are only imperfectly correlated (see, e.g., Westen, 1991) poses a challenge to the notion of a unified dimension.

I suspect, further, that decalage is to be expected across and within subdomains. Consider the narcissistic therapist, who can understand people extraordinarily well, respond empathically to his patients, and show considerable generativity toward supervisees. When others are in a nonthreatening, subordinate role, the narcissistic therapist shows the highest level ego development. But place the same person at a case conference, and colleagues will roll their eyes at the person's displays and thinly veiled efforts to defend against threats to self-esteem. When a different set of representations is active—for example, representations of self-in-competition instead of self in a caring, authoritative role (or Oz-like grandeur, depending on the individual's degree of narcissistic disturbance)—the individual may be more properly classified as Self-Protective. Or consider the way this person may behave in romantic encounters. Again, depending on his degree of disturbance (or level of personality organization, in Kernberg's model), he (we shall use the masculine pronoun, because the shoe more often fits) may be capable of deep love toward others but only insofar as they are experienced as part of self (such as his children), may be sexually exploitative, or may need others to mirror his grandiosity so that he can avoid slipping into the feeling states that engender a shift toward a more self-protective stance.

These final thoughts suggest directions for future theory and research, but they should not obscure the tremendous contribution Loevinger's work has to offer psychoanalysis, even if many psychoanalysts do not recognize its relevance. If integrating theoretical with methodological sophistication constitutes a high level of "scientific ego development," Loevinger has few peers whose sentences can serve as prototypes to flesh out the upper stages.

ACKNOWLEDGMENTS

The author thanks the editors of this volume and Stuart Pizer for their very useful comments on an earlier draft.

5

Loevinger's Conception of Ego Development and General Systems Theory

Robert R. Holt
Department of Psychology, Emeritus
New York University

Jane Loevinger was right to distinguish the conception of ego development (ED) from theories thereof, and insightful in grasping the likelihood that the conception might outlast the theories. In this chapter, I propose that the conception implies general systems theory (GST) and might profit from being explicitly grounded in it.

Why GST? What is it and what does it have to offer? GST does not resemble a specific, elaborated theory like, say, Newtonian statics or Skinnerian learning theory, as much as it does the evolutionary theory of Darwin: It is a set of assumptions, definitions, and working approaches within which particular working theories are developed. GST postulates that it is fruitful to look at almost all phenomena as occurring in *self-organized assemblies of interacting entities* (natural systems), which are themselves components of superordinate systems. Their component entities or subsystems usually also have systemic properties. The result is a hierarchical view extending from subatomic particles to the entire cosmos, and comprising living and nonliving systems, concrete and conceptual or ideational systems, though the latter, being artificial systems, are not fully self-organizing. A person is a system, within larger systems like the family and organizations, and comprising a body and a mental–emotional–behavioral subsystem, a personality. GST looks for homologies and common laws across diverse types of systems.

I proceed by outlining Loevinger's major propositions about development, looking for parallels or homologies in other sciences. Then comes a brief review of relevant principles and findings of (GST), Miller's (1978) theory of living systems, and Thelen and Smith's (1994) dynamic systems approach to development. Finally, I discuss the relevance of these theories to Loevinger's conception, sketching some implications for ED research.

PRINCIPLES OF EGO DEVELOPMENT
AND THEIR GENERALITY

1. Development is Twofold: It Proceeds not Only by Incremental, Additive Change (Polar Variables), but by Phasic Change (Qualitative Milestones)

The predominant theory of development in U.S. psychology was, for many years, linear and incremental. The type case was intelligence, conceived and measured in ways that produced the assumed additive growth. The assumption of no qualitative change, only quantitative growth, was shared by people who emphasized a general factor (g) as well as those who emphasized a multifactorial approach.

In the long era when behaviorism dominated mainstream U.S. psychology, even personality was defined as a summative whole. Its development, accordingly, was a linear matter of simple accretion of habits, traits, or other such units.

From the perspective of Holton (1973), this point of view embodied the thema of atomism and a methodology that gave priority to analysis, the preference for approaching the solution of problems by breaking them down into small separate components accompanied by the (often implicit) assumption that constructs had to have similar properties. Going a step further, one can see here the influence of a set of still deeper, indeed metaphysical, assumptions, those called *mechanism* (Pepper, 1942).

Nevertheless, as early as the middle of the 1800s, intellectual pioneers were setting forth the alternative, phasic conception of development. It surfaced in the realms of moral development and philosophy (Loevinger, 1976), but the most significant impact on psychology came from the work of Piaget. He was the first to pose a clear alternative to the incremental, linear view of the growth of intelligence in his scheme of distinct, qualitative stages of intellectual development.

Loevinger and her students showed that traits like conforming to rules gradually increased in early childhood but then would make a sudden advance, a nonlinear or phasic change. Moreover, conforming became part of a new configuration of interrelated kinds of behavior she described as the I–3,[1] Conformist stage. Similarly, steeply inflected growth curves and change in an organized pattern of behavior were said to characterize the transitions between each pair of successive stages of ED.

Analogies From Other Sciences. Let us see, now, to what extent there are similarities in the scientific conceptualization of other kinds of growth, starting with the largest possible frame of reference, that of *cosmology.* The predominant contemporary theory of how the entire universe originated and developed is popularly known as the Big Bang theory. It has linear, incremental aspects: At the beginning, everything was concentrated in one almost infinitely small and dense point at an unimaginably high temperature. Since then, the universe has been continually expanding and shows no sign of stopping. Meanwhile, its average temperature has been rather steadily dropping. So, there is a place for the polar variables of time, mass, extension (in space's three dimensions), and temperature in the description of how the universe has developed.

Far more striking, however, are the phase changes and emergents. (The following brief account mentions only a few examples.) The basic constituents of matter first appeared as a cloud of quarks, then a plasma of subatomic particles, and finally the first atomic nuclei, those of hydrogen. Each of these marks the emergence of qualitatively new phenomena, constituting developmental milestones. As the vague swarms of matter coalesced, small random variations in what may have been an almost homogeneous distribution in space were exaggerated by gravitational attraction, and proto-galaxies appeared—again, a qualitatively new emergent.

At this point, it is convenient to switch disciplines to *physics,* and trace the development of atoms. As gravity drew the hydrogen atoms together into dense clouds (protostars), they encountered one another more forcibly and the temperature rose, and with it, the energy of the impacts. At first, the force of such impacts could not surpass the strength of electromagnetic repulsion, but when the temperature reached 20 million degrees, even the strong atomic force was overcome; two hydrogen nuclei fused into deuterium. Out of further such collisions came the qualitatively different atomic nucleus, that of helium, releasing enormous amounts of heat energy. By this same process of random encounter at the high temperature of stellar interiors and of even hotter supernova explosions, all 92 natural elements were formed, each a distinctively new emergent. Yet, there are linear aspects to this developmental sequence: Each successive atom in the developmental

---

[1]The notation for ego levels used in this chapter corresponds to the notation of the first edition of the scoring manual for the WUSCT (Loevinger & Wessler, 1970; Redmore, Loevinger, & Tamashiro, 1978). The current edition of the scoring manual (Hy & Loevinger, 1996) introduced several changes. See the Appendix to the introductory chapter of this volume for a comparison between the previous and the current system.

series contains more hadrons (electrons, protons, and neutrons), has a greater atomic weight, and a few other such quantitative properties.

Astronomy. In ancient times, curious observers of the heavens began to discriminate qualitative differences among the "thousand points of light" making up the night sky: the fixed stars and the wandering planets. With Galileo's telescope, it rapidly became possible to distinguish qualitative types among the stars. Modern astronomers' dominant theory of stellar evolution is again primarily phasic. Stars consume their hydrogen by fusion, creating enough heat to maintain a steady state. When this "fuel" is nearly gone, stars of the predominant *(main-sequence)* type in a short time expand enormously and form red giants. With the exhaustion of hydrogen, small stars (no bigger than our sun) collapse into white dwarfs. Larger stars go through a more complex series of changes in their methods of generating energy. Periods of expansion alternate with collapse, then a phase of extraordinary efflorescence as a nova or supernova, eventually a neutron star, and at last a black hole. Throughout it is a story of long, relatively steady states followed by rapid change to a new type of organization and internal process, marking milestones of novel self-organization. Stars are organized into larger systems of clusters and galaxies, among which (again) qualitatively different developmental types are distinguished.

In *biology*, most of us are familiar with the development of species, or the evolution of types of life. There is not yet any consensus on how, after the formation of carbon-based molecules of increasing size and complexity, aggregations of them suddenly acquired the property of self-replication and life emerged for the first time in an already ancient but inorganic universe—truly an extraordinary milestone! It marked the beginning of a slowly accelerating rush of organic development, from simple unicellular organisms to more complex ones. Again, part of the story can be told with polar variables: increasing numbers of cells and other dimensions of physical size and increasing differentiation and complexity of organization. Much more striking, however, is the true emergence of the myriad, qualitatively distinct forms of living beings: the species.

In another way, both incremental and phasic aspects of evolution can be seen. Darwin assumed that speciation would take place by slow, gradual, accretion of tiny changes, and indeed much of it seems to do so. In recent years, however, Gould and Eldredge proposed the theory of punctuated equilibrium to account for the striking fact that many species (e.g., the horseshoe crab) remain virtually unchanged for millions of years but then may undergo rapid transformation into new species.

If we look at the development of individual organisms rather than populations, both *botany* and *zoology* provide further material. All multicellular plants and animals start as unicellular ova or spores and grow larger in every way. Although after the egg hatches individuals of some species closely resemble their parents, merely growing bigger, even those go through some stages of (phasic) embryological development. Others traverse successive stages of strikingly diverse form, notably the larva, pupa, chrysalis, and imago of many insects.

The best known early discovery of striking developmental similarity across different types of living systems was Haeckel's "biogenetic law" that ontogeny recapitulates phylogeny. A few decades later, it became fashionable to criticize this notion, because the resemblances between embryological and fetal stages of mammals and the sequential evolution of other types of creatures were gross and somewhat superficial. Thanks to the serious, extended, scholarly reexamination given the topic by Steven J. Gould (1977), these similarities in developmental sequences can no longer be shrugged off.

Haeckel was, of course, wrong in interpreting them as guided and structured by a vaguely invoked, animistic reification of Progress. If both in phylogeny and in ontogeny, living systems go through similar stages, it is because both follow, not some external command, but the intrinsic dynamics of self-organization. Simon (1965) described one way it might happen: "A genetic program could be altered in the course of evolution by adding new processes that would modify a simpler form into a more complex one—to construct a gastrula, take a blastula and modify it!" (p. 75). This procedure, repeated, produces a sequence of stages, "each new stage in development representing the effect of an operator upon the previous one" (p. 75). Because the inherited genetic code for constructing any organism proceeds by first building subassemblies, and must start with a single cell, the inheritance of the basic sequence is inevitable.

In a great variety of sciences, dealing with both living and nonliving systems of great diversity, the first principle of ego development holds quite generally: that development proceeds both linearly and nonlinearly, in terms of polar variables of continuous growth and milestones of phase change.

2. Development is not Uniform: Some Individuals Change More Rapidly Than Others. Hence, at any one Time, Qualitatively Different Individuals Coexist, Giving Rise to a Typology

Again, the predominant temper of U.S. psychology was opposed to typological theories at the time Loevinger's appeared. The great majority of personality theorists rejected the notion of personality types, relying mainly on such polar variables as traits, needs, abilities, values, and so on. Even in psychopathology, long dominated by the medical model of separate diseases, a strong school of thought emphasized the lack of pure cases and the predominance of intermediate and mixed types. Yet in other sciences, the existence of types was so commonplace as to go virtually unremarked upon.

The earlier brief survey of astronomy, physics, chemistry, and biology found precisely the state of affairs Loevinger described: Galaxies and stars of many developmental stages can be observed today, giving rise to *observed types*. A virtual zoo of subatomic organizations of matter/energy is now described by physics, from quarks to protons—all qualitatively distinctive *types* coexisting, differing from one another in structure and distinguished by large jumps in mass. The evolution of matter produced 92 observable, qualitatively distinct types of atoms. Just so in the course of biological evolution. Alhough many types of organisms have disappeared, representatives from virtually every phase from the simplest to the most complex, from single cells (e.g., amoeba) to the blue whale, are alive today.

We might here take note of some of the stages of *social evolution*, from mating couples (forming stable dyads in many species) to larger and more complex groups in a number of social species besides *H. sapiens*. Human groupings began with the family, expanded to clans banded together by the necessities of survival and living by hunting and gathering. That is the first type of what can be called societies, one that exists today (e.g., in forest pygmies). Miller (1978) tabulated eight leading taxonomies of society in sociology and anthropology, noting that, "They classify the societies by the stages through which they appear to have passed in going from primitive to fully developed systems" (p. 754). Miller reported that other authors stress polar indices of degree or complexity of civilization; both approaches are valid, yielding different information.

3. The Qualitatively Distinct Features, or Milestones, That Make up a Developmental Stage are Aspects of the Whole Person's Behavior and of Relationships to Other Persons, but Also of Internal Organization or Structure

Again, Loevinger struck out in a direction opposed to the general analytic trend of contemporary U.S. psychology, but one in harmony with systems theory. Various authors (e.g., Miller, 1978; Rapoport, 1978; von Bertalanffy, 1968) agreed that a defining characteristic of GST is its opposition to reductionism, its insistence on observing whole systems at their own level. At the same time, it differs from earlier holisms in not opposing analysis as long as it is accompanied by a study of the ways the parts and functions of a system are organized.

It hardly seems necessary to exemplify this point in the various sciences. Indeed, one might say that it was the existence of different systemic levels at which observations of totalities were possible that gave rise to the array of separate scientific disciplines. And a notable aspect in the development of many sciences during the past 200 years has been an increasing emphasis on structure (in the sense of pattern). In the physicochemical sciences, for example, crystallography and structural chemistry have shown the major importance of the ways atoms are organized in molecules.

4. There is an Invariable Sequence of Stages, None of Which can be Skipped, for Each Builds on, Incorporates, and Transmutes the Previous one

Loevinger (1976) attributes these points to Piaget and Inhelder (e.g., 1969), who promulgated them in another field, cognitive development. Even there, other researchers by no means uniformly accept the proposition, and apparent exceptions can be found in ED, also. The existence of pathological and phenotypic variants does not invalidate the basic point, however: we do not reject the proposition that mammals have four limbs because an occasional calf is born with one too many or too few, and because cetaceans have only vestigial remains of missing limbs.

By and large, the developmental sequences described for other types of systems show a similar degree of invariance to that in ED. The evolution of matter presents the purest example, rigidly adhering to this rule: The subatomic particles are subassemblies of hadrons, which are the invariably necessary constituents of atoms, and molecules cannot exist without the prior development of atoms.

Because organic evolution has taken place (so far as we know) only once, here on earth, we cannot say how far the phylogenetic sequence of types of life is invariant. It is difficult, however, to imagine a possible world in which life would not be originally unicellular, then going through increasingly complex types of multicellular creatures. There have been relatively few opportunities for societies to develop without outside interference (at least for their initial stages), but the sequences of early stages in the eastern and western hemispheres are, so far as social scientists can determine, the same.The developmental sequences of embryology occur reliably in fixed sequence, as do the strikingly different ontogenetic stages of butterflies, frogs, and other species with manifestly phasic development. Notice, however, that the numbers of stages and many of their qualitative features differ markedly from one species to another.

5. Development Proceeds Jerkily, the Time Occupied
by Each Stage Varying, so That Periods of Rapid Change
Alternate With Plateaus of Indefinite Length During
Which Slow or Negligible Change Takes Place

The invariant sequence of ego developmental stages thus does not imply that they can be given specific age slots. One person may pass rapidly through the sequence, attaining the main features of the Autonomous stage in adolescence, while others progress much more slowly to the same endpoint late in life. In either case, however, swift advances and plateaus alternate. Piaget made such observations in his studies of cognitive development.

Loevinger (1976) cited Kuhn (1970) as having noticed the same sequence in the growth of science: Long periods of "normal science" are followed by briefer "scientific revolutions," in which the previously prevailing paradigm is altered. She added, ". . . the idea of tradition-bound periods broken by periods of radical change has always been current in fields such as art, politics, and literature . . . " (p. 306).

The phase changes of many nonliving systems sometimes occur so quickly as to be almost instantaneous, notably the fusion-induced transmutation of elements. The transformation of an ordinary star into a nova contrasts a steady state lasting millions of years with a transitional stage of a few of our days, although most of the other phase changes take much longer.

In biological evolution, there are striking differences in the length of what corresponds to developmental phases: the existence of species. As noted above, the theory of punctuated equilibrium proposes as a general rule the alternation of more or less long periods of equilibrium or steady state, and spurts of rapid speciation punctuating them. Miller (1978) cited the following as one of 15 points of similarity in organic and societal evolution: "Periods of stability of form and process may be succeeded by brief periods in which profound changes result in new system organization and capacities" (p. 856).

In the development of various other sorts of living systems, the same alternating pattern occurs. Though in human embryology and in the phasic ontogeny of insects and amphibians the time spent in each stage is predictable within narrow limits, one society differs greatly from another in the length of time each remains in any one stage before making a rapid transition to the next.

6. Later Developmental Stages are Generally More
Complex Than Earlier Stages: They Have More Distinctive
Qualities and More Intricate Internal Organization

This is a familiar property of the stages of ED. Indeed, the increase in complexity plays such a large role as to call into question whether the changes from I–4 (Conscientious) to I–6 (Integrated) are as truly phasic as are the earlier ones. If complexity is viewed as a combination of both increased differentiation and more thorough integration, it summarizes Werner's (1940/1964) conceptualization of the main trend in mental development in various species and in societies.

Miller (1978) noted that several students of societal development primarily arrange societies on a scale of increasing complexity. He concluded: "Increase in complexity appears to be fundamental in societal evolution" (p. 756). It is surely arguable that atoms are more complex than hadrons, uranium more so than hydrogen, and organic molecules far more complex than any of their constituents. We are so familiar with the tendency of the later stages of biological evolution to produce more complex organisms that some authors have thought it intrinsic to the process. Nevertheless, some species (e.g., parasites) evolved to lower degrees of complexity, and devolving, senescent stages may be distinguished at such different systemic levels as those of human personality and stars.[2]

Let us see where we have come so far. For all six of the major propositions making up Loevinger's conception of ED, there appear to be impressive similarities (or isomorphies) in the development of other systems. The analogies to other types of living systems are most striking, but in a way it seems to me even more remarkable that many nonliving systems develop in similar ways. The time may be ripe for the beginnings of a general theory of the development of systems.

GENERAL SYSTEMS THEORY

That is squarely in the province of GST. It has emerged since the 1960s, as people grounded in various disciplines have been struck by just such isomorphies, homomorphies, or analogies across disciplinary boundaries. GST became an attempt to formulate hypotheses about the nature, behavior, structure, and dynamics of systems of whatever kind and to test them in a number of different sciences.

A critical property of GST is that it postulates emergent order: At one systemic level, processes that look random and unpredictable work together to produce observable and lawful regularities and pattern at higher levels. If the phenomena that interest you seem unlawful, intractable to scientific study, the general systems approach implies that you should

---

[2]In some contexts, Loevinger (e.g., 1976) advanced the proposition that the highest levels of development are characterized by creativity/generativity. I am neglecting the idea here, because it does not seem to have the level of generality of her other propositions about ED, and it is clearly difficult to extend to other systemic levels.

try looking at the next higher systemic level. This principle suggests a reason that two equally good scientists may study the same phenomena, one finding unfolding patterns of phase changes whereas the other sees only a maze of individual differences in the operation of many polar variables. In this way, both Heath (e.g., 1965, 1991) and Loevinger may be right, although some of their statements seem mutually contradictory.

In a retrospective survey (Boulding, 1986), a founder and first president of the Society, remarked that there was as yet no "definitive textbook in the field" (p. 4). The somewhat smaller area of living systems is, however, dominated by Miller's (1978) *Living Systems*. I use it here as a principal source, supplemented by briefer works on the growth or evolution of systems, and by the recent work of Thelen and Smith (1994; see also Smith & Thelen, 1993). This last pair of books explicitly grew out of GST, but emphasized nonlinear dynamic systems in development.

First, some definitions. Miller (1978) defined *system* as "a set of interacting units with relationships among them" (p. 16). This definition is similar to that of Bertalanffy (1968): systems are "sets of elements standing in interaction" (p. 38). Rapoport (1978) emphasized a different aspect: "a system is a portion of the world that maintains some sort of organization in the face of disturbing influences . . . [it] maintains its identity in spite of changes [going] on within it" (p. 153).

There are two views of systems here, which emerged near the beginning of systems science. On the one hand, some (including those who work with mathematical models of systems) tend to define them in a relatively weak, or *loosely coupled*, sense, whereas those who work with empirical (largely living) systems put forward a strong sense, of systems as *tightly coupled*—interdependently organized.[3] We can go beyond this dichotomous situation and resolve the conflict by taking the position that systems exist in all degrees of coupling, a property that can in principle be quantified and thus entered into a mathematical theory.

Another important, often unrecognized, property of natural systems is that they are *self-organizing*. In stark contrast to the ancient tradition of the "argument from design" for the existence of God, natural systems do not require the services of a designer or creator to assemble themselves, though man-made or artificial systems (e.g., a computer) do make that requirement.

---

[3]Mathematical relationships, being precise, seem to imply "tightness" of a kind that is not meant. Any group of elements can be considered a mathematical set; the fact that we chose them out of some kind of interest does not give them any inherent tendency to hang together, which is what coupling refers to.

Let us see, next, what general systems theorists have had to say about systemic development. It happens that the very first yearbook of the Society for General Systems Research contained a paper by Boulding (1956), on a general theory of growth. There, he introduced the concept of structural growth, in which the aggregate which "grows" consists of a complex structure of interrelated parts and in which the growth process involves change in the relation of the parts. Yet Boulding did not mention phasic development as such, not even in his 1978 book, *Ecodynamics*.

My search of the volumes of *General Systems* did not turn up any other paper devoted entirely to developmental theory, except that a number of papers were concerned with biological evolution and parallels to it in other realms. Virtually all of these studies focused on the *mechanism* of evolution: blind or random variation, a selective device, and a means of retaining the variants that passed screening; and several authors noted homologies between evolution and learning. Beginning while Darwin was still alive, many writers were struck by resemblances between biological and sociocultural evolution (e.g., Spencer, 1896; Spengler, 1926; Toynbee, 1946). Less speculative works on the same topic have come from general systems theorists: Gerard, Kluckhohn, and Rapoport (1956) tabulated nine points of correspondence between these two kinds of evolution, and Miller (1978) listed 15 (plus 6 differences).

A strong new theory of development has arisen from a seemingly unrelated novelty in systems theory since the 1970s. That has been variously called the *dynamics of nonlinear systems, chaos theory*, and the *new sciences of complexity* (see Gleick, 1987, for an accessible introduction). Before then, there was not a satisfactory treatment of emergence, the relationship between levels of systems. The strong tendency of 19th century science was reductionist: to believe that the proper course of science was analytic, looking for more microscopic order rather than that of macroscopic observation. Thus, the hope of Freud's mentors was that biology could be eventually reduced to and replaced by the ever more sophisticated study of chemistry and physics (Holt, 1989). For awhile, exciting findings in molecular biology seemed to be realizing such hopes, and many of the best minds in psychology grew pessimistic about the possibility of making much progress in the study of molar behavior. The alternative insistence on the reality of emergence could too readily become mystical, as it had with Bergson (1911).

The new sciences of complexity find, however, that there is often a beautiful mathematical order hidden in what looks like a random mess, a state of affairs called chaos. This discovery that predictable pattern and regularity can appear at a higher systemic level out of chaos is, I believe, the first genuine theory of emergence. It has inspired an innovative, fresh look at developmental theory by psychologists who have been deeply immersed in what might look like quite atomistic studies of early childhood. Esther Thelen, who studied the details of how babies learn to walk, and Linda Smith, who worked on the early stages in the learning of language, became increasingly dissatisfied with available developmental theories, and then noticed the concern of the new sciences of complexity with precisely the problem of how complex systems arise.

Chaos theorists (e.g., Kauffman, 1993) distinguish several mathematically describable "regimes": random, chaotic, stably ordered, and one intermediate between the last two, which Kauffman called "poised" (p. 19). A random regime is totally devoid of order, thus contains no coupled systems; chaotic regimes are phenotypically the same, yet contain the hidden seeds of patterned organization, which emerges in the other two regimes. In the ordered regime, pattern is frozen into structure.[4] In the poised regime, however, patterns emerge from system dynamics, hence are free to change—thus to develop. Living systems occur only in this intermediate, "narrow third complex regime poised on the boundary of chaos" (p. 19).

This new approach to the emergence of complexity, which has had a major impact on many fields of science, calls into question the prevailing fundamental assumption about the nature of order and pattern in nature—structuralism—and proposes to replace or at least greatly supplement it by elegant mathematical theories of self-organization. It would take up too much space to summarize the argument at all convincingly, but I urge any interested reader to consult Thelen and Smith (1994), Smith and Thelen (1993), and Kauffman (1993).

Complex patterned organization does not have to be built, piece by piece, according to a fixed blueprint; computer simulations and simple chemical systems demonstrate that it can and does arise spontaneously from the intrinsic dynamics of systems of simple elements, granted enough mutual interaction. That is the process of self-organization.

---

[4]Note that I am using "structure" in a particular way, based on Thelen and Smith's (1994) trenchant critique of structural theories of development. As often used, structure may refer merely to pattern or organization, but its connotation of stability and permanence subtly encourages us to believe that wherever we see persistent patterning there must be structure in the sense of the ordered regime. But consider a vortex. It has a distinctive, persistent, instantly recognizable form, although a whirlpool and a tornado's funnel are made of quite different substances, neither contains any static parts, and both are constantly changing. Both, moreover, are regular patterns that emerge from prior chaotic states. Hence, it is clearer to refrain from referring to such emergent forms as "structures."

From the background of their detailed empirical studies of how children learn to speak and to walk, Thelen and Smith (1994) first assert basic propositions with which we are familiar:

> Development is linear and quantitative as growth is always incremental. At the same time, development is also nonlinear and qualitative, since complexity involves new forms and abilities. . . . The sweep of development . . . is progressive or directional. The changes, both qualitative and quantitative, are not reversible. (p. xiv)

Noting that research in infant development some time ago transcended simple nativism or environmentalism, they reported that the prevailing interactionist consensus has become inadequate to account for the detail of many kinds of findings: "Our visions of linearity, uniformity, inevitable sequencing, and even irreversibility break down" (p. xvi) as we get closer to the detail of actual data. For example,

> At a global level, the intellectual differences between children of different ages are much as Piaget described them. Nevertheless, the scientific consensus is that the part of Piaget's theory that postulated monolithic changes in the logicomathematical structures that underlie cognition is wrong. [His theory] dramatically failed to capture the complexity and messiness of cognitive development in detail. . . . All of cognition does not move forward in lock-step. (pp. 21-22)

They begin their alternative theory by noting

> that all biological systems belong to a class of systems that are both *complex* and . . . exist *far from thermal equilibrium* [Kauffman's poised regime]. (p. 51)

> When sufficient energy is pumped into [open systems with many components free to interact nonlinearly], new ordered structures may spontaneously appear . . . (p. 54)

> In self-organization, the system *selects* or is *attracted* to one preferred configuration out of many possible states, but behavioral variability is an essential precursor ("order out of chaos"). (p. 56)

Bronowski (1972) referred to this selective phenomenon as *stratified stability*, the fact that a given class of systems can exist at a (finite) number of stable configurations at increasing levels of complexity. His phrase has the advantage of not implying any of the animism or personification one tends to read into a term like "attractor," a configuration that is "preferred" only because it is one of a few that are inherently *stable*.

The process of change just described requires one more specification: It requires an *order parameter,* something (often a source of energy) that brings about a phase change. Consider, for example, the gait of horses:

> As the horse continually increases its speed [the order parameter], its gait shifts discontinuously from a walk to a trot to a gallop with no stable intermediate pattern. . . . The preferred gait at any speed level is also the energetically most efficient. (p. 62)

> Phase shifts result from the amplification of normally occurring fluctuations of noise. As the control parameter is scaled up, there are critical values where the internal fluctuations overwhelm the system stability and the system . . . [moves into] new stable modes. (p. 64)

A possible danger of these (now modish) ideas and concepts is that they may lead us to believe that, to explain personality change, we need only invoke systems dynamics, as if the mathematics of nonlinear systems had causal efficacy. It is a remarkable fact of nature that systems behave in such similar ways regardless of what they are made of and of what the forces are that couple their components together. But in any particular science, the theory only prompts us to look for and identify those components and forces in our own data.

IMPLICATIONS FOR RESEARCH
IN EGO DEVELOPMENT

These are the basic ideas, nonmathematically expressed. Let us see how they might be applied to ED. One of the important differences between physical and biological or social systems is that the components of physical systems respond to a narrower range of perturbing factors, and they fall into much more stable modes or phases under the influence of simpler and more predictable control parameters. Nevertheless, Thelen and Smith proceeded to show how applicable they are to the behavioral realms of walking and talking, and there is every reason to expect they will be fruitful in the study of adult development, too.

A first implication for ED is a shift of focus from the sequence of stages to the processes of change. Phase changes in behavior will be heralded, the theory tells us, by a time of increased instability or variability (which Scott, 1979, called *critical periods*), under the influence of some control parameter. What might that be? One obviously possible cause of the disruption of long-term behavioral stability is bodily changes, anatomical and hormonal, like those of puberty and senescence. Other possibilities are exposure to modeling of adult (and immature) patterns by role models within the family and outside, notably in the mass media; changes in family dynamics, like growing tensions between parents; or changes induced by larger external systems, like economic stress, or pressures of cultural expectations and values.

A further implication of this approach is the need to shift ED research from a focus on sentence completions to more direct and differentiated measures of behavior, the stability of which can be quantified. Then we can start looking for control parameters and test hypotheses of the kinds advanced in the preceding paragraph.

From the dynamic systems perspective, the extensive *décalage* or variance of item scores in any given WUSCTED protocol takes on a new meaning. The set of levels sampled by item scores may correspond to sets of attractors with relatively shallow basins of attraction: that is, several strata of stability between which a person can move relatively easily, depending on the demands of the situation. Thus, a Nixon could be a cursing Delta when scheming action against his enemies, and a Conscientious father and husband in his family. In his studies of Nazi doctors, Lifton (1986) described his subjects' similar but more extreme behavioral shifts between developmental levels within a day, comparable to the fluctuations of multiple personalities.

Detailed studies of such short-time shifts should teach us a good deal about ED. They might lead to the discovery of more precisely what parts of a pattern like Delta are tightly coupled and reliably occur together, what brings about transition to other patterns, and in which components variability begins to increase in a critical, transitional phase.

At least in the realm of physical systems, the tightness of coupling is easily identified with the strength of the forces that hold the system together. Thus, atomic nuclei, bound by the strong force, resist deformation from external or internal influences more tenaciously than any other systems; whereas those like the solar system or galaxies, held together only by the relatively weak force of gravity, do not put up much resistance against disruption.

Living systems, at least those beyond the level of individual organisms, are held together only negligibly by the four physical forces. What, then, is responsible for the coupling of groups (families, institutions, nations, supranational systems) and their resistance to deformation? Freud (1921) had an answer: "A group is clearly held together by a power of some kind: and to what power could this feat be better ascribed than to Eros, which holds together everything in the world?" (p. 92). No doubt sexual attraction plays a large part in the coupling of dyads, the nuclei of families. And Freud made a pretty good case that "emotional bonds" between members and the leader, or among members themselves, hold many kinds of groups together, although his conviction that the forces involved were ultimately those of a mythical psychic energy vitiate his contribution.

There is a good deal of evidence (see Holt, 1971) for the existence of innate readiness to recognize other members of one's own species and act less aggressively toward them than to others, which may be related to the human capacity for identification-based empathy. The concept of imprinting refers to a largely unexplicated process of pair-bonding, which can function across species. Various kinds of learning, including emotional, play a part in group cohesion.

Turning to ED, we must concede that its stages are rather loosely coupled, although the issue needs much more intensive study. Once we have observational methods that will permit more precise definition and measurement of the constituent elements of each stage, it will be possible to study the question of what holds the components together. Cognitive dissonance may play a role here.

CONCLUSION

With only minor modifications, Loevinger's conception seems so compatible with GST that it can only help the development of ED theory to ground it explicitly on GST and exploit that and the theories of living systems and complexity more systematically. Moreover, her approach to development emphasizes aspects that for years were neglected by most systems theorists, although it has been possible to find the properties of development she highlights at a variety of systemic levels, including many nonliving as well as living systems. A general theory of the development of systems therefore begins to seem possible, one that promises to guide research into fruitful new realms.

Ultimately, it will be desirable to make explicit the grounding of developmental psychology in systems philosophy, as I urged elsewhere (Holt, 1989) for psychoanalysis. Scientific theories are abstracted ideational systems, and their relation to metatheories like metaphysics has some homologies to the nesting or hierarchy of concrete systems. Another task for the future is to investigate the developmental stages through which theories go and their similarity to the sequence of ED. In the latter, let us recall, the highest developmental level is characterized by a high degree of internal consistency (integrity) and a concern for larger implications.

II

CONSTRUCT VALIDITY

6

Ego Development in Children and Adolescents: Another Side of the Impulsive, Self-Protective, and Conformist Ego Levels

P. Michiel Westenberg
Judith Jonckheer
Philip D. A. Treffers
Martine J. Drewes
Academic Centre for Child and Adolescent Psychiatry
Curium, Leiden University

When making a Dutch scoring manual for the Washington University Sentence Completion Test (WUSCT) we inadvertently addressed a fundamental question: To what extent is Loevinger's developmental model and scoring manual applicable to children and adolescents? Scoring categories in the United States were derived mainly from older respondents (large majority was older than 18), whereas scoring categories for the Dutch manual were derived mainly from young respondents. Despite this methodological difference in manual construction, there are numerous similarities between Dutch and U.S. scoring categories, supporting the cross-age and cross-national validity of ego development theory. However, several consistent differences emerged between the two scoring manuals, mainly with respect to the Impulsive, Self-Protective, and Conformist levels. Impulsive protocols ($N = 491$) were characterized by vulnerability and a dependent coping style, by receptivity to concrete rules and guidance generally, and by empathic impulses and positive interactions. Self-Protective protocols ($N = 650$) were characterized by self-focused forms of control, by instrumental but appreciative relations, and by a self-sufficient attitude and a live-and-let-live philosophy of life. Conformist protocols ($N = 798$) were characterized by equality and reciprocity in relations, by the emphasis on (interpersonal) feelings, and by a helpful attitude and a communal philosophy of life. The current findings suggest a more balanced picture of the earliest developmental levels than originally proposed, at least when referring to the development of children and adolescents.

BACKGROUND: CLINICAL RESEARCH ON CHILDREN AND ADOLESCENTS

Inspired by the results of research on the developmental underpinnings of psychopathology in children and adolescents (e.g., Block, Block, & Keyes, 1988; Borst & Noam, 1993; Browning & Quinlan, 1985; Gjerde, 1995; Hauser, Powers, & Noam, 1991; Kegan, 1986; Noam et al., 1984; Rierdan & Koff, 1993; Selman & Schultz, 1990; Westen, 1989), we embarked on a large-scale research project to study the relation of Loevinger's (1976) model of ego development to specific forms of psychopathology. One of several ideas was to compare a psychiatric, outpatient population (age 8–18) with a representative sample from the nonpsychiatric population. This research design (psychiatric vs. nonpsychiatric subjects) sought to meet two goals: (a) to study the extent to which psychopathology (in particular the behavior disorders) is related to developmental delay, and (b) to produce a Dutch scoring manual for the WUSCT. Indeed, a Dutch scoring manual for children and adolescents became our first priority, because the clinical research could only be conducted with a reliable and valid manual.

Ego Development in Children and Adolescents

Loevinger's scoring manual and the corresponding descriptions of the ego levels were based mostly on SCT data obtained from (young) adults. The original manual (Loevinger & Wessler, 1970) is based mainly on subjects who were older than 16 years of age: more than 85% were older than 16, and only 0.8% were below age 10. For the revised scoring manual, the collected samples almost exclusively consisted of (young) adults: "The largest single source of subjects for most of the subsamples in our present manual construction sample has been students, mostly of college age or older, or college graduates" (Loevinger, in press).

Due to the age composition of the samples, the U.S. manuals are based on a relatively small number of low level subjects (see Table 6.1). With respect to manual construction, Loevinger (in press) acknowledged the limitations imposed by the skewed distribution of ego levels in their sample: ". . . one cannot extrapolate very far to ego levels that are underrepresented. There are fewer [Impulsive and Self-Protective] subjects than would be optimal to give a fair representation of the possible answers and modes of thought at those levels."

TABLE 6.1
Distribution of Ego Levels: Comparison of American and Dutch Samples

	E2[a]	E3	E4	E5	E6	E7	E8–9	Total
Original U.S. manual[b] (Loevinger & Wessler, 1970)	62	82	589	403	374	88	42	1,640
Revised U.S. manual (Loevinger, in press)	20	47	180	428	367	101	17	1,160
Dutch manual (Westenberg et al., in press)	491	650	798	618	199	16	1	2,773

[a]This is the new notation proposed by Hy and Loevinger (1996): E2—Impulsive level, E3—Self-Protective, E4—Conformist, E5—Self-Aware, E6—Conscientious, E7—Individualistic, E8—Autonomous, E9—Integrated. (See Appendix of introduction to this volume.)
[b]Subjects classified in the then-used but currently omitted transitional levels were proportionally distributed among the two adjacent levels.

The age and ego level characteristics of the samples upon which Loevinger's scoring manuals are based cast doubt on the applicability of the manuals to children and adolescents. Yet, many studies were conducted with children and adolescents (see Cohn, 1991), and the WUSCT appears to be reliable and valid also in age groups requiring discriminations in the low-level range; the WUSCT has been used in studies of children as young as 9 years of age (e.g., Avery & Ryan, 1988) and in many studies of adolescents (e.g., Westenberg & Block, 1993). Moreover, the WUSCT was used in research in several other countries (see Carlson & Westenberg, in press), and, as noted, was used in clinical research on children and adolescents. None of these studies reported shortcomings of Loevinger's ego development model or scoring manual when used with young, clinical, or foreign populations.

Expectations

The broad applicability of the WUSCT and scoring manual led us to expect that our data from 8–18-year-old subjects could be scored readily with the U.S. scoring manual, and that it would not be an extraordinary effort to produce a Dutch scoring manual. We were mistaken, however, and it would take several years before we were able to return to clinical research. The present study was the first systematic attempt to develop a scoring manual for 8–18-year-olds. The fact that our young subjects represented a large proportion of low-level subjects had a significant impact on the scoring manual and consequently on the description of the earliest ego levels.

MAKING A DUTCH SCORING MANUAL
FOR CHILDREN AND ADOLESCENTS

The evolution and precise details of this mammoth project cannot be fully described here. A brief overview is presented to provide the most basic information on the methods and procedures followed to develop the scoring manual. The research details were described elsewhere (Westenberg, Jonckheer, & Treffers, in press).

Two Subsequent Studies

In two rounds of research we used SCT protocols from 2,773 subjects (age 8–25) to construct and cross-validate a Dutch scoring manual for ego development. Although we planned to develop a scoring manual for 8–18 year-olds, the age limit was extended to 25 years of age, to be sure that a sufficient number of Self-Aware and Conscientious subjects were included to represent these levels in the scoring manual.

Microvalidation. To construct and evaluate the Dutch scoring manual, we closely followed the microvalidation procedure used by Hy and Loevinger (1996) to revise the U.S. manual (Loevinger, in press). The only difference is that Hy and Loevinger started with the original manuals (Loevinger, Wessler, & Redmore, 1970; Redmore, Loevinger, & Tamashiro, 1978) to produce the revised manual, whereas we basically started with their revised manual (Hy & Loevinger, 1996) to produce a Dutch manual.[1]

Subjects. The total sample comprised two subsamples. An outpatient sample was obtained through the regular intake procedure at Curium, the Academic Centre for Child and Adolescent Psychiatry of Leiden University ($N = 544$). A representative comparison sample was recruited through elementary and high schools, universities, and other educational institutes (ranging from scouting clubs for youth to training programs for nurses; $N = 2,229$). The total sample consisted of an almost equal proportion of males and females, and about the same number of subjects at each age (between 120 and 200 subjects per age cohort).

The distribution of the subjects across three age cohorts is presented in Table 6.2, as is the distribution of ego levels within and across these age cohorts. Table 6.1 shows that the Impulsive and Self-Protective ego levels

---

[1]Comparisons were, in fact, based on the prepublication version provided by Loevinger, but were checked against the published version of the revised manual (Hy & Loevinger, 1996).

TABLE 6.2
Distribution of Ego Levels Across Three Age Cohorts

	E2[a]	E3	E4	E5	E6	Total
Age 8–12	414	270	84	2	-	770
row %	53.8	35.1	10.9	.3	-	
column %	84.3	41.6	10.5	.4	-	27.9
Age 13–18	76	354	486	190	38	1144
row %	6.6	30.9	42.5	16.6	3.3	
column %	15.4	54.4	60.9	30.7	19.1	41.5
Age 19–25	1	26	228	426	161	842
row %	.1	3.1	27.1	50.6	19.1	
column %	.3	4.0	28.6	68.9	80.9	30.6
Total	491	650	798	618	199	2756
row %	17.8	23.6	29.0	22.4	7.2	

[a]See Table 6.1 for meaning of labels.

were underrepresented in the U.S. samples, whereas the highest ego levels were underrepresented or absent in the Dutch sample.

Dutch SCT. In the first round of research we used Form 81 of the WUSCT (Loevinger, 1985) and scored the corresponding completions with the revised scoring manual (Hy & Loevinger, 1996). Eight items were added from previous versions of the WUSCT, for which original scoring manuals were available (Loevinger et al., 1970; Redmore et al., 1978), and seven new items were used (e.g., concerning fears and friends). Items were added because of the possibility that certain items of Form 81 would not perform according to expectations, due to the cultural difference or to the age difference with Loevinger's samples. On the basis of the results of both studies, the number of items was reduced to 32 items, a sufficient number to obtain reliable total protocol scores. A detailed discussion of the criteria for item selection may be found in Westenberg, Treffers, and Drews (in press).

The following analyses are restricted to the 29 items for which American scoring manuals were available. Of these 29 American item manuals, 26 item manuals have been revised (Hy & Loevinger, 1996), and three manuals have not been revised.

Dutch Scoring Manual. On average, about 80% of Dutch sentence completions could be categorized with the scoring categories of the U.S.

item manuals. Additional categories were constructed for the unratable responses. The classification of the scoring categories at a particular ego level was determined by means of the microvalidation procedure. A few examples are presented to illustrate the use and consequence of this procedure. The response category "My conscience bothers me if—*I lie, cheat*" is classified at the Conformist level in the U.S. manual. This classification is repeated in the Dutch manual, because this response was also most prevalent on Conformist protocols of the present study.[2] In contrast, the response category "When I am criticized—*it doesn't bother me*," placed at the Conformist level in theU.S. manual, was most prevalent on Self-Protective protocols of this study. Hence this response category was relocated to the Self-Protective level in the Dutch scoring manual.[3]

Moreover, on the basis of the U.S. manual, we had several very large and heterogeneous response categories. If these categories were split into multiple, more homogeneous categories, the different subcategories emerged at different ego levels. For example, the response category "When people are helpless—*I (try to) help them*" (classified at the Conformist level in the U.S. manual) was split into three subcategories: "*—I help them*" (most prevalent at the Impulsive level in our data), "*—I sometimes help them, if I know them*" (at Self-Protective level), and "*—I try to help them*" (at Conformist level).

The microvalidation procedure was applied in Study 1 and 2 for each of the 2,254 scoring categories of the Dutch manual, and resulted in a consistent and stable classification of scoring categories. The internal consistency of item scores and the test–retest stability of total protocol scores is satisfactory (Westenberg et al., in press).

SIMILARITIES AND DIFFERENCES BETWEEN THE U.S. AND DUTCH SCORING MANUALS

Statistical Analyses

Of all Dutch response categories with content equivalents in the U.S. manual, 51% emerged at the same ego level, 41% emerged at an adjacent level (one level up or down), and 8% emerged at two or more levels from

---

[2]The microvalidation procedure takes baserates into account. For details, see Loevinger (in press).

[3]A word of caution: One should not confuse a response category with an item stem. A response category represents a cluster of similar responses to the same item stem. Averaged across the 32 items, an item manual contains about 80 response categories. If one category is moved to another level, that does not affect the other categories. Hence the term microvalidation

the classification in the U.S. manual.[4] About 18% of the Dutch response categories did not have content equivalents in the U.S. manual.

If categories did not emerge at the same level in the Dutch manual, they mostly "dropped" to a lower level (79%), whereas fewer categories "climbed" to a higher level (21%). Moreover, this downshift of categories did not equally occur at all levels, but selectively occurred at the low end of the ego level scale. Downshifts occurred mainly from the Conformist level to the Self-Protective or Impulsive levels and from the Self-Protective to the Impulsive level, whereas relatively few categories dropped from the Conscientious level. For example, 65% of Dutch Impulsive response categories—with content-equivalents in the U.S. manual—were classified at the Self-Protective or Conformist ego levels in the U.S. manual, whereas only 7% of Dutch Conscientious categories were classified at higher levels in the American manual. Similarly, new response categories in the Dutch manual emerged mainly at the Impulsive and Self-Protective levels, and hardly at the Conformist through Conscientious level.

This particular pattern of the differences between the two manuals is not consistent with normally occurring error variance, cannot be explained in terms of drifting ratings, and the downward shift is neither an artifact of relative group size, nor a consequence of ceiling or floor effects.

Conceptual Analyses[5]

In case of a difference (downshift or new category) between the U.S. and Dutch manuals, it had to be decided whether the difference was consistent or inconsistent with Loevinger's description of the corresponding ego level. Some of the differences appeared assimilable by the current description, whereas other differences appeared to require accommodations in the description. As an example of the former, responses indicating unrestrained emotions dropped from the Conformist level (e.g., "If I can't get what I want—*I fight for it, I get angry*") and the Self-Protective level (e.g., "When I am criticized—*I get angry, mad, have a fit*") in the U.S. manual to the Impulsive level in the Dutch manual. This change appears to be consistent with Loevinger's description of the Impulsive person, whereas the classification in the U.S. manual appeared inconsistent with the controlling and conforming nature of the Self-Protective and Conformist person, respectively. Such downshifts validate Loevinger's descriptions of the ego

---

[4]Developmental milestones are no longer distinguished on the basis of full stages versus transitional levels, but are all referred to as ego levels (Hy & Loevinger, 1996).

[5]A full report on the conceptual comparison between the two manuals, category-by-category, may be obtained from the authors.

levels, and strengthen the connection between the theory and the measure.

Some differences, however, were more surprising in light of Loevinger's description of the ego levels, and appeared to require accommodation. For example, the response category "When people are helpless—*I help (them)*" dropped from the Conformist level in the U.S. manual to the Impulsive level in the Dutch manual. This is not a trivial category, because this response was given by 34% of the Impulsive subjects and was one of the most reliable indicators of that level. In contrast, the U.S. manual does not include any prosocial responses at the Impulsive level, and prosocial responses appear inconsistent with the egocentric and receiving interpersonal style of the Impulsive person as described by Loevinger.

With respect to the downshift of a response category, one issue remains to be addressed: Does it affect the level from which it descended? This is particularly relevant at the Conformist level. Of the response categories classified at the Conformist level in the U.S. manual, 38% dropped down to lower levels in the Dutch manual. This cannot be without any consequence to the description of the Conformist level. For example, what is the consequence if the response "When people are helpless—*I help (them)*" is moved to the Impulsive level? Is the Conformist level less prosocial or less behavior-oriented than assumed? Or was this response misclassified in the U.S. manual?

ADJUSTMENTS IN THE DESCRIPTIONS
OF THE FIRST THREE EGO LEVELS

Whether differences between the U.S. and Dutch manuals should lead to adjustments in the descriptions of the corresponding ego levels is not an easy matter. Statistical and conceptual analyses of individual response categories are necessary but not sufficient conditions to distinguish between trivial and important differences. Nothing less but the total pattern of responses conveys what a stage is "all about." Like Loevinger and colleagues, we had to extract from varied sentence completions some common dimension or meaning. The interpretive component of "reading" clusters of responses is most difficult to grasp and convey, because it is based on years of experience with a massive data set. In any case, an avalanche of response categories cannot be without consequence to the descriptions of the corresponding ego levels. That fact emboldened us to present our interpretations of the differences and our proposals for adjustments. The following presentation will be limited to the Impulsive through Conformist levels, because the differences were much less significant for the higher levels.

Impulsive Level

Of the 271 response categories in the Dutch manual for the Impulsive level, about 20% were classified at that level in the U.S. manual, whereas an additional 20% were classified at the Self-Protective level, 20% at the Conformist level, and 40% were not present in the U.S. manual.

Not all these differences resulted in changes of our understanding of the Impulsive person,[6] because many of the differences were consistent with Loevinger's current description. The Impulsive response categories in the Dutch manual agree with Loevinger's description in the following aspects: preoccupation with (aggressive) impulses, dependency on others for impulse control and need satisfaction, description of inner life in terms of simple wants and basic emotions (including physical malaise), reduction of abstract ideas to concrete-specific examples, and dichotomization of the world into good and bad, nice or mean (to me).

Some differences, though, led to adjustments of our view of the Impulsive person, because they appeared to be inconsistent with Loevinger's current description. Adjustments were due mainly to new response categories and to those categories coming from the Conformist level. Three features of Loevinger's description of the Impulsive level—the blatant aggression, the oppositional–defiant attitude, and the egocentric perspective—were not characteristic of the great majority of Impulsive protocols in our study.

Vulnerability and Dependency. The U.S. manual (Hy & Loevinger, 1996) reports that "one of the most reliable indicators of an [Impulsive] protocol is blatant and unsocialized expression of impulses, mainly hostile and sexual ones" (p. 9), and the provided examples indicate that hostile impulses are manifested in response to items not specifically pulling for aggression (e.g., "Men are lucky because—*they beat on women*"; "When I am with a man—*want to shoot him*" [p. 10]). In the present findings, too, Impulsive protocols contain aggressive impulsivity, but less blatantly and less unexpectedly. Aggressive impulses are not spontaneously displayed in response to innocuous items, but are expressed mostly in response to items implicating the frustration of dependency needs (e.g., "If I can't get what I want—*I hit them*"). And even in response to the frustration of needs, aggression is not the predominant response. Negative emotions (e.g., "If I

---

[6]Throughout this chapter we are referring to the Impulsive person, the Self-Protective person, and so forth. Our sample, however, is limited to young persons. But for the sake of brevity and convenience we decided to use the unqualified person. In the Discussion we return to this issue.

can't get what I want—*I get angry*"), simple evaluations (e.g.,"—*it is no fun*"), and dependency (e.g., "—*I ask my father*") are the most reliable and characteristic indicators of an Impulsive protocol.

Congruent with Loevinger's findings, the Impulsive person in our data is concerned with aggressive impulses. In addition to the preoccupation with one's own aggressive impulses, however, the Impulsive person in our data appears to be concerned more with being the victim of aggression. A reliable indicator of Impulsive protocols is the concern with meanness and aggression by others (e.g., "My main problem is—*to be hit, caught, teased, called names*"). The concern over being victimized is broadly represented in the Dutch manual for various items, but is present for only one item in the U.S. manual ("I just can't stand people who—*fight, scold, are angry, mean*"). Connected with the concern about being the victim of aggression, is the desire to be strong physically (e.g., "I am—*strong*"; "Sometimes I wished that—*I was strong, stronger, strongest*"). The importance of physical strength is absent in the U.S. manual, but is broadly present in the Dutch manual for the Impulsive level.

The sense of vulnerability captured by these categories adds to the dependent interpersonal style of the Impulsive person. As reported by Loevinger, the Impulsive person expects to be cared for and given to. In our data, the Impulsive subject also wants to be protected from physical threats (e.g., "A good father—*is strong*").

Vulnerability and dependency are striking and reliable indicators of an Impulsive protocol. The Impulsive person appears to lack the ability to independently cope with difficult situations, and reacts with unrestrained emotions (e.g., "When I am criticized—*I get mad, angry, I cry*"), with avoidance ("—*I walk away, through*"), or with assistance-seeking ("—*I tell someone, my mother, teacher*"). These responses are also present in the U.S. manual, but variously at the Impulsive, Self-Protective, or the Conformist level. In the Dutch manual, all such responses emerged at the Impulsive level. Consistent with Loevinger's hypothesis, the display of primary emotions may be viewed as manifestations of impulsivity. Our data suggest that impulsive emotions may simultaneously be viewed as primitive ways to cope with difficult situations (e.g., "When they avoided me—*I cry for help*").

This interpretation is supported by the inclination of the Impulsive person to run away from difficult situations, a tendency also represented in the U.S. manual. In Loevinger's (Hy & Loevinger, 1996) description of the Impulsive person, running away from difficult situations is seen as a manifestation of limited causal thinking. "Running away, running home, or going to one's own room are common responses, as if whatever is wrong is located in the place rather than the situation" (p. 10). Our findings suggest that limited causal thinking adds to the lack of effective coping strategies, and prompts the Impulsive person to run away. Alternatively, running away may be seen as a primitive coping strategy based on the belief that trouble is located in the place. At any rate, running away is a simple way to deal with difficult situations. The possibility that this coping strategy is fueled by the dependent orientation is reinforced by the frequent response that they seek help or protection. Indeed, running away and running to someone are sometimes combined in the same response (e.g., "When they avoided me—*I go home, run to mother*"). Running away from situations and running to others appear to be in line with each other; the Impulsive person runs away, often to seek help.

Receptiveness to Rules and Guidance Generally.   Another prominent feature of Loevinger's Impulsive person is oppositional–defiance. Impulsive people are dependent on others for control, but they resent being controlled. Rules are seen as arbitrary, punishments as retaliatory. This oppositional–defiant stance is to affirm and protect a yet fragile sense of identity: "The growing sense of self is affirmed by the word 'No'" (Hy & Loevinger, 1996, p. 5). In our data, however, we find relatively few direct manifestations of an oppositional attitude. In contrast, the great majority of Impulsive protocols convey the impression that the Impulsive person is receptive to rules and guidance generally.

As Loevinger argued, and both manuals demonstrate, the Impulsive person does not focus on the reasons for rules, but just describes what the rules are ("Rules are—*rules*"; "—*things you should (not) do*"; "—*do not fight, kick, curse*"). Loevinger points to the "tautological" and concrete aspects of such responses, but these responses may simultaneously be expressive of a receptive attitude toward rules. The latter interpretation is supported by a varied set of categories. The Impulsive person: (a) argues that misbehavior could be stopped with immediate and personally administered interventions (e.g., "Crime and delinquency could be halted if—*you say so, you have to*"; "—*they are told to stop*"; "When a child will not join in group activities—*s/he has to do it anyways*"); (b) thinks that people should just not misbehave or stop misbehaving (e.g., "Crime and delinquency could be halted if—*they didn't do it, they were sweet, nice*"); and (c) is not only concerned about other people's misbehavior, but is also geared toward one's own proper behavior (e.g., "My conscience bothers me if—*I have done something wrong*"). These responses were not present in the U.S. manual for the Impulsive level, but some were classified at higher levels.

Receptiveness to rules and guidance may be fueled by the sense of vulnerability, because rules and controls provide security against meanness (e.g., "Rules are—*do not fight, kick, curse*"; "—*that you should be nice*"). Specific rules and immediate consequences, personally enforced, are accepted ways to regulate behavior. In this sense, the Impulsive person is impulsive, because behavior is not regulated by means of long-term consequences. On the other hand, clear and specific rules applied in a predictable environment are desired ways to control (aggressive) impulses.

Empathic Impulses and Positive Interactions. According to Loevinger's (Hy & Loevinger, 1996) description, the Impulsive person is self-centered and receiving: "Good guys give to me, mean ones don't" (p. 5). Indeed, both the U.S. manual and the Dutch manual indicate that the Impulsive person likes to be cared for (e.g., "A good father/ mother—*takes care of me, cooks well, gives me money, presents*"). At the same time, however, a crucial difference emerged in our data. The Dutch manual contains several prosocial categories at the Impulsive level (e.g., "I feel sorry—*for someone, him, Frank*"; "When people are helpless—*I don't like it*"; "—*I help (them)*"). These responses are reliable and frequent indicators of Impulsive protocols (40% and 34%, respectively), whereas the U.S. manual does not include any such categories at the Impulsive level. Indeed, prosocial responses appear inconsistent with Loevinger's description of the Impulsive person.

There are two ways to assimilate prosocial responses to Loevinger's description of the Impulsive level: by broadening the impulsivity concept to include empathic impulses (next to aggressive and sexual ones), or by seeing prosocial responses as motivated by personal distress. First, prosocial response categories at the Impulsive level may be interpreted in terms of impulsive empathy based on the dependent orientation: others need help, just as I need others to help me. Help is offered impulsively, without a moment's thought about the possibilities, consequences, and preferences of the needy. Unwittingly, the Impulsive person simply assumes that others need help and protection as much as they do. Second, seeing helplessness in others is aversive, because it represents a feared situation. The aversive state in oneself is relieved by helping. But regardless of the impulsive mode of and egocentric reasons for helping, the impulsiveness and egocentrism of the Impulsive person do not always imply the negative connotation of these concepts. The Impulsive person may jump to the rescue of others.

In addition to prosocial categories, the Dutch manual includes many categories indicating that the Impulsive person enjoys interactions with other people. Literally, they like to do fun things with parents and friends, with whom they generally have positive relations (e.g., "Being with other people—*is doing fun things*"; "My father—*is fun, takes me places*"). In contrast, the U.S. manual stresses the negative aspects of parent–child relations.

For example, "My father—*is mean, bad* [unqualified rejection]" is the leading category in the U.S. manual for the Impulsive level (p. 238), whereas "My father—*is nice, fun*" is the leading category in the Dutch manual (given by 38% of Impulsive subjects).

Conclusion. In addition to impulsiveness, dependency appears to be the unifying concept behind a diverse set of phenomena. A dependent interpersonal style is also part of Loevinger's description of the Impulsive level, but was limited to receiving care and things. Dependency appears to be the connecting thread between empathic impulses, a receptive attitude toward rules and controls, and dependent coping with frustrations. Dependency is accentuated by a sense of vulnerability, especially with regard to aggressive impulses. Dependency is also related to aspects shared by both manuals, such as the dependency on others for impulse control and need satisfaction, and the tendency to dichotomize the world into good or bad, nice or mean to me.

Self-Protective Level

Of the 430 response categories in the Dutch manual for the Self-Protective level, about 35% were classified at the same level in the U.S. manual, whereas about 35% were classified at the Conformist level, and 30% were not present in the U.S. manual.

Not all these differences resulted in changes of our understanding of the Self-Protective person, because many of the differences were consistent with Loevinger's current description. The Self-Protective response categories in the Dutch manual agree with Loevinger's description in the following aspects: the preoccupation with control (resents being controlled by others, prefers to be in charge), the pursuit of hedonistic aims (without work or school, life is a party), an opportunistic morality (with staying out of trouble as a main concern), and a punitive attitude (strict surveillance and harsh consequences).

Some differences led to adjustments of our view of the Self-Protective person, because they appeared to be inconsistent with Loevinger's current description. Adjustments were due mainly to new response categories and to those categories coming from the Conformist level, and indicated that an outright manipulative and exploitative attitude toward other people is not characteristic of the great majority of Self-Protective protocols in the present sample.

Self-Focused Forms of Control. According to the U.S. manual, "[c]ontrol is the leading issue as the child develops beyond the

Impulsive level, that is, controlling and being controlled by his or her own impulses and by other people" (p. 10). In the U.S. manual, the predominant manifestation of the need for control is to control others, and this concern is expressed in an authoritarian ("Raising a family—*I want my family to obey me*"), punitive ("When a child will not join in group activities—*he should be punished*"), retaliatory ("When I am criticized—*I mean talk about him*"), exploitative ("Women are lucky because—*they can get married and live off the men*"), and manipulative ("The thing I like about myself is—*the way to handle boys*") attitude toward other people (pp. 10–11).

In the present study, too, control appears to be a central concern, but interpersonally malignant forms of control are supplemented by self-focused forms of control. For example, frequent strategies to deal with criticism are to disavow hurt feelings (e.g., "When I am criticized—*it doesn't bother me*"), to ignore the insult ("—*I ignore them, don't listen to it*"), or to keep quiet ("—*I don't react*"). These responses were classified at the Conformist level in the U.S. manual. The emergence of these categories at the Self-Protective level suggests that control is not always achieved by means of domination or manipulation. Self-Protective people also use self-focused forms of control and other psychological strategies to stay in charge. In fact, some of these self-focused strategies appear to indicate manipulation of one's own feelings (e.g., "When they avoided me—*I really don't care*"). Pretended indifference to social difficulties is paralleled by the denial of problems generally (e.g., "My main problem is—*I don't have any problems*"). Incidentally, the downshift of these categories from the Conformist to the Self-Protective level is consistent with the expectation that Conformists are not indifferent to social difficulties.

The emphasis on self-control is verified by the disappearance of categories indicating a lack of control. This set of categories was classified at the Self-Protective level in the U.S. manual, but moved to the Impulsive level in the Dutch manual (e.g. "When I am criticized—*I get mad, I become angry*") where they fit the general impulsiveness of the Impulsive person. Self-control is further verified by the addition of a set of categories indicating the realization that a lack or loss of self-control may cause troubles (e.g., "My main problem is—*I quickly get angry*"). The latter categories were placed at the Conformist level in the U.S. manual.

In contrast with the dependent attitude of the Impulsive person, who expects others to provide care and protection, Self-Protective persons are able to hold their own. Often, the emphasis is on the protection of one's own feelings, and not just on self-protection through controlling others.

Positive and Instrumental Relations. Loevinger described the interpersonal style as manipulative, exploitative, and wary: "They want immediate gratification and, if they can, will exploit others for their ends. Seeing interpersonal relations as exploitative, they are themselves wary and self-protective" (Hy & Loevinger, 1996, p. 5). Correspondingly, the U.S. manual includes very few positive statements about (relations with) other people. Our findings, however, indicate that the social attitude of the Self-Protective person is not as negative as is suggested by Loevinger's characterization. The great majority of our Self-Protective subjects respond with positive statements regarding parents and friends. One of the most reliable and frequent indicators of Self-Protective protocols is the appreciation of parents (e.g., "A good father–mother—*is mine*"), and the need for friends (e.g., A girl–boy feels good when—*s/he has friends, a friend*"). Both responses were classified at the Conformist level in the U.S. manual, but emerged at the Self-Protective level in the Dutch manual.

Our data suggest a difference between Self-Protective and Conformist responses concerning social relations; to *have* good friends is what counts for the Self-Protective person, to *be* a good friend is what counts for the Conformist person. At the Self-Protective level, parents and friends are good to have, because they may be helpful in reaching one's own objectives (e.g., "A good father–mother—*is useful, is a job half done*"). Relationships are instrumental; you scratch my back, I scratch yours. For example, some categories indicate the willingness to assist people who are likely to help them (e.g., "When people are helpless—*I help them if they are friends, family*"). But despite the instrumental tone of Self-Protective protocols, we find few indicators of the manipulative, exploitative, and wary attitude.

Detached Empathy and Live-and-let-Live Philosophy of Life. The U.S. manual, both in terms of the global description and individual response categories, suggests that the Self-Protective person is indifferent to the welfare of others (e.g., "When people are helpless—*I don't care*"), unless they are friends or relatives ("I feel sorry for—*for my sister*"). In our data, however, we found two indicators of the opposite:

1. A reliable indicator of a Self-Protective protocol is to feel sorry for certain groups of people (e.g., "I feel sorry—*for poor people, for people in* [name of a country at war]"). These categories were classified at the Conformist level in the U.S. manual. Emergence of such categories at the Self-Protective level suggests a concern with people who are in dire straits beyond their own control. Control is a central preoccupation of Self-Protective people, who like to be in charge of their own life. Because of this need for self-determination, the Self-Protective person feels sorry

for people whose circumstances prevent them from controlling their own lives.

Congruent with the U.S. manual, however, Self-Protective persons appear to lack the motivation to act on their pity, perhaps because compassion is overshadowed by the value put on self-reliance ("everyone should stand on their own feet"), perhaps because they respond negatively to the perceived demands of people in need, and perhaps because empathy is experienced as a sign of weakness and is covered up under a facade of toughness, or a combination thereof.

2. Characteristic of Self-Protective protocols is a live-and-let-live philosophy of life. Others are expected to have the same need for self-assertion and freedom they crave for themselves; everyone wants and should be allowed to be independent and take care of themselves. The live-and-let-live attitude does not emerge as a salient issue in the U.S. manual for the Self-Protective level. For example, the U.S. manual for the item "When a child will not join in group activities—" lists predominantly punitive ("—force–punish him) and derogatory ("—he is a loser, she has a problem") responses (p. 89). In contrast, our data indicate that the Self-Protective person responds with a mixture of indifference and permissiveness ("—I don't mind, it's up to him, leave her alone"). These categories were classified at the Conformist level in the U.S. manual, where they did not fit with the value put on social activities. The live-and-let-live attitude may come through as uncaring, but may also be seen as responsive to the need to "do one's own thing."

Yet, a derogatory attitude is also present in the Dutch manual for the Self-Protective level (e.g., "When a child will not join in group activities— it's 'cause she is stupid"). The combination of a derogatory attitude with the live-and-let-live philosophy, suggests that the Self-Protective person looks down upon and rejects people with different views, but is not driven to change their views—as if they think, "others are stupid to think or behave differently, but it is their mistake and none of my business." In other words, live-and-let-live should not be confused with genuine tolerance or cultural relativity.

Conclusion. Aside from control, self-sufficiency appears to be a leading motive. Self-sufficiency is expressed through self-focused as opposed to other-focused forms of control, through detached perspective-taking (emphasizing self-reliance), and a live-and-let-live philosophy of life. Self-sufficiency also appears to be related to the aspects both manuals have in common: The need for self-sufficiency is expressed in resentment of control by others, in the dislike of obligations (work, school), self-assertion through the pursuit of hedonistic wishes, in the independency afforded by having lots of money, and in the attempt to ignore rules in pursuit of one's own desires.

Conformist Level

Of the 434 response categories in the Dutch manual for the Conformist level, about 60% were classified at the same level in the U.S. manual, whereas 20% were classified at the Self-Aware level, and 20% were not present in the U.S. manual.

The large overlap between the two manuals suggests many correspondences between the Conformist response categories in the Dutch manual and Loevinger's description of the Conformist person. The Conformist response categories in the Dutch manual agree with Loevinger's description of the Conformist person in the following aspects: the Conformist appears to be other-centered (identifies self with others), accepts the rules of one's reference group (whether according to conventional or unconventional norms), is preoccupied with social acceptability and fearful of social disapproval, perceives inner life in terms of global emotions (e.g., happy and love), and views work as a duty.

Next to the many similarities, there are some differences between Loevinger's description of the Conformist level and our findings. The differences for the Impulsive and Self-Protective level were due mainly to additional categories (also from the Conformist level), whereas the differences for the Conformist level were due also to the departure of many categories to lower levels. The present findings indicate that the emphasis on conformity is supplemented by an altruistic and communal orientation.

Helpful. In the U.S. manual, a helpful interpersonal style is attributed to the Self-Aware level (p. 4, Table 1.1). In contrast, our findings suggest that the helpful attitude is characteristic of the Conformist person, because related response categories dropped down from the Self-Aware level in the U.S. manual to the Conformist level in the Dutch manual (e.g., "When people are helpless—*I like to help them*"). In the U.S. manual, such responses were deemed to be characteristic of Self-Aware protocols, because the emphasis is on feelings and not on behavior ("I *like* to help them"). In contrast, the Conformist person was deemed to be focused on prosocial behavior and not on feelings (e.g., "When people are helpless—*I try to help them*"). In the present findings, however, both sets of responses emerged at the Conformist level. The "feeling" aspect of the helpful attitude is consistent with the Conformist's general focus on global feelings.

A helpful attitude spurred by emotional involvement is generally characteristic of Conformist protocols. Several response categories indicate that the Conformist person is affected by the distress of others, that someone's fate is taken to heart (e.g., "When people are helpless—*I feel sorry, sad, bad*"). The affective response may be one of the reasons why the Conformist is impelled to reach out, whereas the more detached attitude of the Self-Protective person does not motivate helping behavior. For the Conformist person, helping people in need is an emotional and moral imperative. Indeed, the helpful attitude is a cherished trait (e.g., "The thing I like about myself—*I want (like) to help others*"; "—*I am caring, loving toward others*"). The latter response categories were classified at the Self-Aware level in the U.S. manual, but dropped down to the Conformist level in the Dutch manual.

This type of concern with other people cannot be explained entirely in terms of Conformity, unless it is viewed as a "good feeling to have" and as a way to meet the wishes and expectations of others. It appears, however, as if the Conformist person is intrinsically motivated to alleviate the distress of others, not out of Conformity but out of sympathy.

Aside from the downshift of the helpful attitude, the Self-Aware level is almost identical in the Dutch and U.S. manuals. The present data confirmed the most typical features of the Self-Aware level, such as allowing for exceptions, the concern with adjustment, and the inner orientation on personal feelings and ideas.

Equality and Reciprocity.   Loevinger's description in the manual suggests that the Conformist person blindly follows rules and social standards to obtain social acceptance, and that the content of the rules is arbitrary: "Rules are accepted *just* [italics added] because they are the rules," and "[w]hat is conventional and socially approved is right," but "a person who rigidly conforms to some unconventional sex norms is still a Conformist" (p. 5). Moreover, the U.S. manual stresses conformity to concrete rules in specific situations, with particular emphasis on proper behavior and appearance. In our findings, however, concrete-specific responses are less typical and mostly appeared on Impulsive protocols. More importantly, rules are not entirely arbitrary but are tied to particular ground rules, such as equality and reciprocity.

Conformist protocols are characterized by the concern about reciprocal relations between like-minded partners. Others are not just there for you, but you are there for them as well. You are there for each other. Good relations are defined by reciprocal enjoyment (e.g.," My father—*and I get along with each other*"), and bad relations are defined by its absence ("—*don't get on with each other*"). Reciprocal relations imply the participation of equal partners, important to one another on an equal footing. Despite age and role differences between parent and child, parents are viewed as equal partners in reciprocal relations (e.g., "A good father–mother—*is (like) a good friend*"). Conversely, she disapproves of parents who advocate hierarchical relations (e.g., "A good father—*should be a friend instead of an authority figure*" [Hy & Loevinger, 1996, p. 141]).

In addition to equality in personal relationships, equality is a general concern expressed in several ways, as in a communal instead of competitive attitude, and in the belief in uniformity of capacities, needs, thoughts, and behavior. Inequality is viewed as the source of many problems and superior behavior is a source of irritation ("I just can't stand people who—*are conceited, arrogant*"). The restoration or implementation of equality is the panacea (e.g., "Crime and delinquency could be halted if—*everything was equal in the world*"). The emphasis on equality gives rise to a special brand of idealism: All were better if all were equal (e.g., "If I were in charge—*everyone should be equal*"). (These reponses should be contrasted with the post-Conformist notion of equal opportunities.) If one's reference group (parents, peers, or society) favors hierarchical and competitive relations, one may reject these conventions and seek alliance with unconventional but egalitarian groups. Thus, the decision to adhere to conventional or unconventional rules is not solely based on accidental group membership, but depends partly on the presence or absence of egalitarian values.

Egalitarian responses are present in the U.S. manual for the Conformist level, and equality is part of Loevinger's description of the Conformist level ("the same size fits all"). But the presence of contradictory response categories may have pushed the egalitarian view to the background. For example, competitiveness (e.g., "A man feels good when—*he wins something*" [p. 165]) and egocentrism (e.g., "A woman feels good when—*she gets her way*" [p. 199]) are inconsistent with the emphasis on equality and altruism, but were placed at the Conformist level in the U.S. manual. In the Dutch manual, however, contradictory categories dropped to lower levels, allowing the egalitarian view to come to the fore.

In addition to the sharper focus on egalitarianism, the downshift of categories also caused a sharper contrast with the lower levels. For example, the U.S. manual for the Conformist level presents a punitive solution to crime and delinquency as the leading response category ("Crime and delinquency could be halted if—*the death penalty was reinstated*" [p. 174]). Even though the punitive attitude displayed in this response did not explicitly enter into Loevinger's description of the Conformist person, the presence of such categories in the manual may have overshadowed other Conformist response categories. With a punitive attitude as the leading response category at the Conformist level, the emphasis is on rigid conformity to rules. In the Dutch manual, however, punitive response categories appeared at the Self-Protective level. In the absence of such categories, the emphasis shifts to other response categories, such as the concern with social equality and social controls. The Conformist proposes a firm but prosocial approach to misbehavior, very different from the punitive and indifferent attitude of the Self-Protective person.

Interpersonal Feelings. Loevinger argued that "[i]nterpersonal interactions are described primarily in terms of actions rather than feelings" (Loevinger, 1987b, pp. 227–228; see also Hy & Loevinger, 1996). In contrast, the present findings indicate that the emphasis on actions is typical of Impulsive and Self-Protective protocols, whereas the emphasis on feelings is more characteristic of Conformist protocols.

Consistent with Loevinger's observations, however, "[i]nner states are perceived in the simplest language (sad, happy, glad, angry, love, and understanding)" (Hy & Loevinger, 1996, p. 5). But even though feelings are expressed in cliché-like terms, the present findings suggest that feelings are key in several respects. First, as discussed before, prosocial behavior is fueled by sympathy (e.g., "When people are helpless—*I feel sorry*"). Feelings are important in doing what is deemed to be right, and not doing the right thing makes one feel bad. Second, social interactions are valued in their own right. It is enjoyable to be with others. It "feels right" (e.g., "When I am with a girl–boy—*I feel happy, good*"). Conversely, problems with or the lack of social contacts is very distressing, because pleasant social interactions are crucial to one's sense of well-being (e.g., "When they avoided me—*I feel sad, unhappy, lonely*"). Third, the Conformist reports emotional support as one of the most important facets of interpersonal interactions ("A good father–mother—*loves, cares about his or her children*"), and their lack is distressing. Fourth, well-being is defined in terms of feeling good or being happy ("A woman–man feels good when—*he or she is happy*"), and lack of well-being as feeling bad or unhappy. Indeed, if people felt well, they would behave well ("Crime and delinquency could be halted if—*everyone were happy*").

The impression that the Conformist person is geared toward global emotions, and not to concrete behaviors in specific situations, is reinforced by the downshift of a number of Conformist categories of the U.S. manual to lower levels in the Dutch manual. Three examples of such downshifts: (a) concrete-specific responses dropped to the Impulsive level (e.g., "My mother and I—*live together*"), (b) the focus on demographics dropped to the Self-Protective level (e.g., "I am—[Demographics: age, sex, occupation]"), and (c) indifference to social difficulties and the general denial of difficulties dropped to the Self-Protective level (e.g., "When I am criticized—*it doesn't bother me*"; "Sometimes I worry about—*nothing*"). The downshift of such categories to lower levels allowed the feeling-tone of Conformist protocols to come to the fore, and caused a sharper contrast with the indifferent and detached attitude of the Self-Protective person.

The detached and indifferent attitude of the Self-protective person disconnects "knowing" from "doing"; he or she perceives distress in others but does not care, knows the rules but feels no remorse for violations. In contrast, the Conformist person feels the distress of others and is impelled to reach out, feels remorse when rules are violated.

Conclusion. The inclusion of a large number of Impulsive and Self-Protective subjects results, paradoxically, in a more distinctive portrait of the Conformist person. The presence of many pre-Conformist subjects caused a downshift of Conformist categories allowing already present aspects to come to the fore. In addition to being rule-bound and focused on social desirability, the Conformist is also motivated by the need for communality: equal and reciprocal relations, helpful attitude and egalitarian values, and positive feelings in self and others. The need for communality is also related to the aspects both manuals have in common, such as being other-centered, submission to the rules and norms of one's reference group, and the importance of social approval.

DISCUSSION

The present findings indicate that ego development in Dutch youth resembles ego development in older subjects as described by Loevinger and her colleagues. The overall congruence between the two sets of results attests to the abstract power and cross-national value of Loevinger's ego development theory. Yet, differences between the Dutch and U.S. manuals emerged and had to be accounted for: Were these differences between the manuals with or without relevance to Loevinger's overall description of each ego level? Some differences between the two manuals did not contradict but validated Loevinger's description of the corresponding ego level, and strengthened the connection between the theory and the measure. Other differences between the two manuals appeared inconsistent with Loevinger's description and required adjustments of these levels. Some of the adjustments represented elaborations of already existing concepts, such as the elaboration of the dependency concept at the Impulsive level. Some of the adjustments represented a more balanced view of a level, such as the combination of self-protection with self-sufficiency. Some of the adjustments represent a contradiction with the present description, such as the receptivity to rules and guidance at the

Impulsive level. And some of the adjustments represented novel elements, such as the emphasis on reciprocal relations at the Conformist level.

The present findings suggest a more balanced picture of the lowest developmental levels. Both positive and negative elements are present at the Impulsive thru Conformist levels, at least among children and adolescents. Loevinger's description of the earliest levels appear to emphasize the malignant side, whereas the present findings put greater emphasis on the good-natured side of these levels. Four possible explanations of these differences are discussed: First, our subjects were relatively young as compared to Loevinger's subjects. In addition, ego level and age were closely related. For example, 84% of Impulsive subjects were 8- to 12-year-olds. Therefore we should have spoken of the Impulsive 8–12-year-old, instead of speaking of the Impulsive person. The same applies more-or-less to the other ego levels. Should we then speak of the 8-12-year-old subtype of the Impulsive person, as opposed to the adult subtype presented by Loevinger? In fact, this is the premise of ego development theory: Adult personality types are related but not identical to development occurring during childhood and adolescence (John, Pals, & Westenberg, in press; Loevinger, 1976). And this premise of Loevinger's model appears to be supported by our findings. There are clear conceptual links between Loevinger's descriptions of ego development in (young) adults and our descriptions of the same levels of development in a much younger cohort. Herein lies the importance of integrating child with adult data, to arrive at an abstract description applicable to both. The present data may have contributed to that discussion.

The second explanation of the differences between the present and Loevinger's findings lies in the number of Impulsive and Self-Protective subjects. Compared to the U.S. scoring manual, the Dutch manual was based on a much larger pool of Impulsive and Self-Protective subjects. This allowed for a more detailed and distinctive picture of the Impulsive and Self-Protective levels. The importance of the number of low level subjects was anticipated by Loevinger (1993b): "If there are almost no cases at the extremes, one will never be able to verify what responses belong there. Responses typical for extreme cases will occur occasionally at median levels and, if there are few or no extreme cases, be wrongly assigned there" (p. 9). For example, the U.S. manual classified virtually all prosocial responses into one heterogeneous basket at the Conformist level, even though a substantial proportion of Impulsive and Self-Protective subjects may have replied with prosocial responses. The many Impulsive and Self-protective subjects in our sample, in contrast, allowed for the subtle distinctions between Impulsive, Self-Protective, and Conformist protocols with regard to the different kinds of prosocial responses. The paradoxical result of the large number of Impulsive and Self-Protective subjects is a more distinctive portrait of the Conformist person. Hy and Loevinger (1996) argued that the "Conformist person is, almost by definition, the least distinctive type" (p. 12). However, our findings suggest that a lack of distinctiveness is not inevitable, but may have been due to the small number of Impulsive and Self-Protective subjects in the samples used to construct the U.S. manual.

The third explanation of the differences between the two sets of findings lies in the fact that low-level adults are delayed in their development, as compared with the majority of their age peers. Research indicated that developmental delay is associated with the severity of psychopathology (e.g., Kapfhammer, Neumeier, & Scherer, 1993; Noam & Houlihan, 1990), and the pathology may have seeped into the descriptions of those levels most likely associated with developmental delay in adults: the Impulsive and Self-Protective levels. This explanation is supported by information on the samples used to develop the original U.S. manual. A substantial portion of the youngest (hence low level?) subjects were from clinical samples: "child guidance," "house of detention," and "institutionalized delinquent" subjects (Loevinger & Wessler, 1970, p. 30). It is not unlikely that the low level subjects came from these groups, and that the scoring clues for low ego level may thus be contaminated by behavior problems or low verbal intelligence. In fact, the jumping-off point for Loevinger's work was the four-stage sequence developed by Sullivan, Grant, and Grant (1957), whose sequence was based on research with delinquent adolescents.

Fourth, the cultural or national difference is the most obvious but least likely explanation of the differences between the U.S. and Dutch manuals. Considering the age difference between the two samples, the overlap in the content of the responses was impressive. Dutch and U.S. respondents basically display the same associations to incompleted sentences. Moreover, the selective downshift of response categories cannot be explained in terms of culture. There is no reason to suppose that Dutch culture would cause a downshift from medium to low levels but prevent a downshift from high to medium levels. And finally, the differences found in the present study are consistent with the findings of U.S. studies. For example, the vulnerability of the Dutch Impulsive subject (mainly age 8–12) corresponds to the finding by Silverman, LaGreca, and Wasserstein (1995), that 7–12-year-old "children worried most intensely about events that pertain to security or personal safety" (p. 677).

As yet, we cannot present data on the validity of the Dutch scoring manual, whereas Loevinger's manual has accummulated an impressive body of evidence (see Cohn, 1991; Hauser, 1976; Loevinger, 1979). All we can do at this point is to identify parallels in the literature. For example, our finding of empathic impulses at the Impulsive level is anticipated by the finding that young children display prosocial impulses (Blasi, 1984). Some of the present findings appear closer to alternative accounts of development (e.g., Blasi, 1984; Selman, 1980).

Further comparisons and future studies will have to determine the validity of our interpretations of the differences between the Dutch and U.S. manuals. Are Impulsive thru Conformist youngsters the way we claim them to be? Are Impulsive thru Conformist youngsters indeed different from their adult counterparts in ways that correspond to the differences between the Dutch and U.S. manuals (good-natured vs. malignant)? Is it also possible to identify adults who are more like their youthful and good-natured counterparts, and to identify children and adolescents who are more like the malignant adults? And if two subtypes can be distinguished for each level, what is the relation between them: Is the malignant adult type always foreshadowed by the malignant child type?

The current findings suggest that in terms of the most abstract meaning of ego development, people basically follow the same developmental path, although at a different pace and to a different extent. In terms of the more concrete manifestations of ego development, however, people may follow different developmental trajectories according to the different subtypes identifiable within ego levels.

ACKNOWLEDGMENTS

This research was supported by grants from the Nationaal Fonds Geestelijke Volksgezondheid (National Fund for Mental Health, Utrecht) and the Frijling–Prins Fund (Amsterdam). We thank Jane Loevinger, who continuously informed us about the revision of the scoring manual for ego development, enabling us to develop a Dutch manual for the SCT and to make the comparisons presented in this chapter. We are indebted to our coworkers in Curium, particularly Arnold W. Goedhart, Els C. Koudijs, and Berend M. Siebelink, responsible for the systematic collection of patient data, as well as to the large number of schools, subjects, and ego development raters involved in this project. This chapter greatly benefitted from comments by Augusto Blasi, Lawrence D. Cohn, and Sophie R. Borst.

Correspondence concerning the present chapter may be directed to p.m.westenberg@thuisnet.leidenuniv.nl.

7

How Are Dimensions of Adult Personality Related to Ego Development? An Application of the Typological Approach

Jennifer L. Pals
Oliver P. John
Department of Psychology
University of California at Berkeley

When asked to complete the sentence, "Sometimes she wished that . . . ," one person writes, "she were dead," another writes, "she could go on a trip," and a third writes, "she had six other lives to lead, concurrently, and could skip among them at will." What kinds of people might generate these rather different responses? Jane Loevinger would say these three individuals differ in their ego development, with the first at the Self-Protective stage, the second at the Self-Aware stage, and the third at the Individualistic stage. Alternatively, York and John's (1992) personality typology would suggest that the three individuals differ in their basic modes of adaptation, with each of them exemplifying a different personality prototype: the first appears Conflicted; the second, Traditional; and the third, Individuated. How are these two accounts related? More generally, how is ego development related to personality in adulthood? This is the topic of the present chapter.

Loevinger's (1976) theory of ego development offers a comprehensive and in-depth account of personality development. According to this theory, ego development proceeds through a set of nine stages, which represent successive degrees of complexity and sophistication in the organization of experience: Symbiotic (1), Impulsive (2), Self-Protective (3), Conformist (4), Self-Aware (5), Conscientious (6), Individualistic (7), Autonomous (8), and Integrated (9). A considerable body of research has examined how Loevinger's conception of ego development is related to specific dimensions of personality in adulthood. In the first part of this chapter, we review these studies and consider how they might be organized and integrated. We propose that the personality attributes that characterize adults who are low, middle, and high in ego development form organized patterns similar to three basic personality types. In the second part of the chapter, we review recent empirical research on these three types and their links to ego development in a study of adult women. In the third part, we turn to measurement issues; specifically, we compare Block's (1978) California Adult Q–Set (CAQ), an all-purpose personality assessment instrument used by York and John (1992) to measure their adult personality types, to the Sentence Completion Test (SCT; Loevinger & Wessler, 1970), a projective test serving as the standard for measuring ego development.

RELATIONS BETWEEN EGO DEVELOPMENT AND PERSONALITY DIMENSIONS IN ADULT SAMPLES

The relative level of complexity and sophistication characterizing the organization of experience at different levels of ego development is manifested in the way the individual thinks, feels, and behaves. Many studies, some of which are reviewed here, linked ego level as measured by the SCT with other individual difference measures in order to highlight these differences. We divide our review into seven sections. The first four primarily address cognitive aspects of the individual's experience, including beliefs and values, artistic interests, complexity of thought and creativity, and self-awareness. Individual differences in these four domains have all been linked to openness to experience, a broad personality trait related to wide interests, an active imagination, and an appreciation for the new and unfamiliar (see Costa & McCrae, 1992). The next two sections consider interpersonal functioning in relationships and adherence to and transcendence of traditional gender roles. Finally, we discuss psychological adjustment, well-being, and impulsivity.

Beliefs and Values

According to ego development theory, individuals at high levels of ego development should have an open-minded, unconventional approach to beliefs and values. Using their Openness to Values scale, McCrae and Costa (1980) found support for this hypothesis; ego development was also related to a scale measuring liberal thinking. College students high in ego development were more likely to question fundamental religious beliefs and to be open to different religions, whereas those at lower ego levels reported little or no questioning (McAdams, Booth, & Selvik, 1981).

Tolerance, defined as being nonjudgmental toward the beliefs and values held by others, was also associated with high ego development (Helson & Roberts, 1994; White, 1985). In contrast, having authoritarian attitudes (not being open about beliefs and values) was associated with the Self-Protective and Conformist stages (Browning, 1983; McCrae & Costa, 1980). A related idea is the concept of *compliance,* which Westenberg and Block (1993) defined as adherence to convention. Compliance suggests that the individual uncritically adopts beliefs and values dictated by a group or external standard. As with authoritarian attitudes, compliance was most pronounced at the Conformist stage (Westenberg & Block, 1993). Although being open and unconventional about beliefs and values is linearly and positively related to ego development, being closed and conventional appears to be curvilinearly related, being most pronounced at the Conformist stage.

Artistic and Cultural Interests

Appreciation of artistic and cultural products and activities is another domain of individual differences associated with ego development in adulthood. Several studies show that appreciating, understanding, and ultimately being influenced by the creative products of the cultural world involves a level of psychological complexity and openness typically found only in individuals of high ego level. For example, ego level was correlated with openness to aesthetic and artistic experiences (McCrae & Costa, 1980). Cultural sophistication, defined as a component of intellectualism, also increased with successive ego levels (Westenberg & Block, 1993). Finally, men who were described as culturally sophisticated when they were sophomores in college tended to also be high in ego development 30 years later (Vaillant & McCullough, 1987).

Cognitive Complexity and Creativity

Individuals at the highest ego levels tend to be open to unfamiliar ways of thinking, have the capacity to process information in new and complex ways, and generate original ideas. For example, the Ideas subscale of McCrae and Costa's (1980) openness construct was correlated with ego level. Helson and Roberts (1994) showed that women high in ego level were open to thinking about difficult life experiences in new ways; apparently, high ego level leads the individual to construct new schemas, thus accommodating rather than assimilating life experience. As college students, men who were viewed as creative

and ideational (Vaillant & McCullough, 1987) and women who were
nominated for their creativity (Helson & Roberts, 1994) tended to achieve
high ego levels in middle adulthood.

Self-Awareness

Several studies suggest that individuals at the post-Conformist levels of
ego development are characterized by a high degree of self-awareness,
which allows for a heightened understanding of and appreciation for the
richness of one's own inner life and self-development. For example,
Westenberg and Block (1993) showed that psychological mindedness
(introspectiveness, self-knowledge, and a general awareness and
examination of motives in self and others) increased with ego level, and
Helson and Roberts (1994) showed that achieving the Individualistic level
or higher by midlife was associated with an increase in psychological
mindedness from early to middle adulthood. Those high in ego level also
tended to have a more internal locus of control according to Rotter's
internal-external scale (White, 1985), suggesting a tendency to recognize
internal psychological causation. Helson and Wink (1987) showed that
the amount of change recognized in oneself during college predicted ego
level in middle adulthood, suggesting that being aware of self-development
is associated with ego development.

Interpersonal Functioning

Loevinger's (1976) theory suggests that individuals at higher ego levels have
a greater capacity to form and maintain intimate relationships with others.
Consistent with this hypothesis, subjects at and above the Self-Aware stage
scored significantly higher on empathy than did subjects at lower levels
(Carlozzi, Gaa, & Liberman, 1983). Moreover, ego level was consistently related
to nurturance, affiliation, and satisfaction with watching one's children develop
(White, 1985). Women high in ego level were genuinely concerned about
others but also appreciated them as separate and autonomous individuals
(Helson & Wink, 1987). Ego level was also related to the capacity for
interpersonal closeness in young men and women (Westenberg & Block, 1993).
Although the capacity for intimacy is linearly related to ego level, friendly,
interpersonally pleasant behavior should be curvilinearly related. According
to Loevinger, trying to please others is characteristic of the Conformist stage's
interpersonal style; and, indeed, friendliness was most pronounced at the
Conformist stage in young adults (Westenberg & Block, 1993). Individuals at
the Conformist stage are more concerned with fitting in and being accepted
than with forming and maintaining intimate connections with others.

Traditional Gender Roles:
Adherence and Transcendence

Adherence to traditional gender roles is an aspect of conformity characteristic of the middle range of ego development that is transcended at the highest levels. Indeed, adults at the highest ego levels, especially women, were shown to behave in ways that do not conform to traditional sex roles. In her study of women in a nurse practitioner training program, White (1985) found a positive association between ego level and leadership potential—a traditionally masculine characteristic. Helson and Roberts (1994) showed that women who had reached the Individualistic stage by age 43 had increased in achievement via independence since their early 20s. That sample of women graduated from college in 1958 and 1960 and entered adulthood just as the roles available to women were expanding. Status level in work, recognition for work, and time in the labor force were all positively associated with ego level at age 43 (Helson & Wink, 1987), showing that those who took the more progressive path in life also tended to achieve high levels of ego development. As discussed later in this chapter, the women in this sample who scored in the middle of the ego development continuum tended to adhere to the traditional gender role for women (John, Pals, & Westenberg, in press).

It seems that a hallmark of high ego development is an integration of both masculine and feminine strengths: "Self-development at higher levels apparently goes hand in hand with an awareness of emotional interdependence and granting of appropriate autonomy to others as well as to self. If this seems a complex blend of caring and autonomy, . . . it is precisely this complexity that the individual at higher ego levels is successfully mastering" (White, 1985, p. 572). Prager and Bailey (1985) found that the men and women who scored in the androgynous range on the Bem Sex Role Inventory reached the higher stages of ego development, whereas the masculine and feminine sex-typed individuals were more likely to score at the Conformist stage. More evidence for this integration of masculine and feminine characteristics comes from McAdams, Ruetzel, and Foley (1986), who showed that ego level was related to having both instrumental and interpersonal goals.

Psychological Adjustment,
Well-Being, and Impulsivity

Loevinger (1976) argued that ego development is independent of mental health and that maladjustment, in one form or another, can occur at any ego level. The research findings, however, are complex and not easily summarized. In some studies, ego level was not related to neuroticism (McCrae & Costa, 1980), subjective well-being (McCrae & Costa, 1983), and various indices of mental health (Vaillant & McCullough, 1987). In other studies, however, ego level was related positively to resiliency (Westenberg & Block, 1993), personal adjustment, well-being, and health, and negatively to aggression (White, 1985) and impulsivity (Starrett, 1983).

How can we make sense of these seemingly contradictory sets of findings? Some important relations might be obscured by the breadth, and thus heterogeneity, of the personality traits studied in relation to ego development. For example, although the broad trait of neuroticism was unrelated to ego level, Westenberg and Block (1993) argued that neuroticism is developmentally heterogeneous; some facets should be related negatively to ego development and others should be unrelated. Indeed, in McCrae and Costa's (1983) research, two of their neuroticism facets—fear and anger temperament—yielded modest but significant negative correlations with ego level. These correlations make theoretical sense, as fear of retaliation and fear of being caught are characteristic of the Impulsive and Self-Protective stages, respectively, and the Self-Protective stage is also characterized by externalized, hostile feelings such as intense anger.

Similarly, some facets of the broad trait of impulsivity (vs. inhibition of impulse) are related to ego development. Starrett (1983) studied various facets of impulsiveness and found that the unsocialized expression of hostile and antisocial impulses was the facet most strongly associated with low ego level. The relation between ego level and impulsiveness might be curvilinear rather than linear. For example, Westenberg and Block (1993) showed that impulse control and need regulation were weakest at the pre-Conformist stages (especially at the Impulsive stage) and strongest at the Conscientious stage, followed by a loosening of impulse control at the Individualistic stage. As a point of speculation, perhaps the more moderate level of impulse control found in persons at the Individualistic level is due to their greater understanding of their needs and impulses and their more relaxed spontaneity in the way they experience and express these inner states.

A second factor that might influence the relations between ego development and adjustment in different studies is the range of ego levels represented in the sample (Westenberg & Block, 1993). After all, ego development is a set of qualitatively distinct stages and not simply a quantitative continuum, particularly with regard to the domain of psychological adjustment. Labouvie-Vief (1993) concluded that, "The protocols of lower-ego-level adults . . . are typically characterized by what strikes one as a high level of hostility, rigidity, and foreclosed thinking: all indices, it would appear, of a degree of pathology" (p. 35). More specifically, in adult samples, mental health and ego level might be truly independent of each other at the Conformist stage and above but highly associated at the pre-Conformist stages. Therefore, if an adult sample has no subjects who score in the pre-Conformist range, positive correlations between ego level and indices of psychological adjustment are not likely to be obtained. For example, Vaillant and McCullough (1987), who found no relations with indices of mental health, had a sample of middle-aged men who ranged from the Self-Aware to the Integrated stage—a sample restricted to the high end of ego development. When the whole range of ego development is represented equally, the presence of pathology at the low ego levels might lead to positive correlations with adjustment.

As ego development theory suggests, mature ego levels do not protect against the experience of psychological distress; indeed, the psychological-mindedness, cognitive complexity, and self-awareness characteristic of individuals at the highest stages might lead to a heightened responsiveness to internal conflict. Mature ego level should influence the way such conflict and distress are managed by the individual. Westenberg and Block (1993) showed that high ego levels are associated with *resiliency* (defined broadly as the capacity for flexible and resourceful adaptation to internal and external stressors) and suggested resiliency promotes more mature management of conflict. Helson and Wink (1987) showed that the sophisticated coping mechanisms of intellectualization and tolerance for ambiguity were positively correlated with ego level. Ego level was also positively correlated with number of psychiatric visits over the course of adulthood (Vaillant & McCullough, 1987), suggesting that high ego level individuals deal with psychological problems in constructive, problem-focused ways. This proactive stance contrasts with the defensive and hostile response to problems typical of the lowest ego levels.

There is also some evidence to suggest that the subjective experience of well-being may have a curvilinear relation with ego development, with a peak somewhere in the Conformist to Conscientious range. Helson and Wink (1987) compared two conceptions of maturity, *competence* (defined as effective functioning in society) and ego development. They concluded that adjustment "is likely to be maximal near the middle range of ego level" (p. 540). They found that women who were both high on competence and moderate on ego level (Self-Aware or Conscientious) had the happiest marriages and were the most emotionally secure. Women at the highest ego levels had marital and emotional problems regardless of their level of competence: Those low in competence showed substantial emotional problems (e.g., breakdowns, extended psychotherapy), whereas the problems of those high in competence were less severe, and "may be attributed to the strong urge to self-actualize that does not fit easily into the social system" (p. 540).

Conclusions

In this section, we considered the empirical relations between ego development and several personality trait constructs. Some of these relations were linear, increasing monotonically with increases in ego development. In particular, the higher individuals are in ego development, the more they are open to experience, appreciate alternative values and new ideas, and have aesthetic interests. They are more creative and psychologically minded, and think in more complex ways. Finally, they have more mature, mutually respectful relationships, adopt more androgynous gender role identities, and they are more responsive to psychological conflict.

Other relations were not linear but peaked at middle or moderate levels of ego development. Thus, individuals at middle levels are the most compliant, interpersonally pleasant, and authoritarian. They are more likely to tightly control their needs and feelings and closely follow gender norms. At the same time, they feel the most emotionally secure. Finally, some traits seem characteristic of only the small subset of adults at the very low end of ego development: they show signs of maladjustment, especially hostile impulsivity, fear, and anger. When we consider these patterns of linear and nonlinear relations, they suggest that particular personality characteristics are associated with three regions of the ego development continuum. We suggest they form three patterns or configurations that work together in systematic ways. In fact, a similar set of trait configurations were noted independently in the literature on adult personality types. These types, and how they relate to ego development, are the focus of the following discussion.

EGO DEVELOPMENT AND PERSONALITY
TYPES: INSTRUCTIVE CONVERGENCES

The typological approach takes a person-centered view emphasizing the patterns of attributes shared by particular groups of individuals; it attempts to represent the infinite variety of personality structures with a small and parsimonious set of distinct person categories, defined as independently as possible. This approach, we believe, provides a useful framework for understanding the relations between ego development and the adult personality literature. In fact, although Loevinger (1993b) focuses on stages, she likened her stages to types:

Stages are qualitatively different points along a more or less hypothetical continuum. Ego development is the term for the common element in the stage sequence and the corresponding dimension of individual differences, a *quasi-typology*. There is an underlying assumption that the *types* found in adult life represent the trace of developmental stages. (pp. 6-7, emphases added)

Thus, Loevinger's notion of types is unique in that she postulates an underlying developmental sequence connecting the types to each other. How are Loevinger's developmental types connected with those found in the recent literature on empirically derived adult personality types?

Three Basic Personality Types:
The Inductive Approach

Psychologists have proposed a variety of general personality typologies. Most of them are based on the theories of Freud, Jung, Rank, Horney, and other psychotherapists. However, these theoretically derived typologies seldom hold up to the rigorous empirical standards of replicability, construct validity, and generalizability across diverse populations. Until recently, empirically derived, or *inductive*, personality typologies were rare, primarily because well-accepted procedures for identifying types were lacking. One way to derive types involves identifying groups of individuals who have similar personality profiles across multiple dimensions. This approach has the advantage of identifying general types—that is, types based on a person's overall configuration of attributes. This multidimensional approach requires a method for determining the similarity between two individuals' personality profiles and for identifying distinct groups of individuals. Several recent studies used inverse factor analysis as the method of choice (see Robins, John, Caspi, Moffitt, & Stouthamer-Loeber, 1996; York & John, 1992). This method uses the intercorrelations among people, rather than among variables, and thus focuses on the similarity between two individuals' personality profiles. The factors generated by an inverse factor analysis can be interpreted as personality types because they represent sets of people whose personality profiles are similar to each other within each set, but distinct (i.e., uncorrelated) from the profiles of the other sets. Finally, inverse factor analysis is consistent with a prototype conception of types: It does not force the classification of individuals into just one type but determines how similar each individual is to each type. Factor loadings serve to indicate the degree to which an individual's personality configuration resembles, or is prototypical of, the personality configuration defining the type factor (see York & John, 1992).

Robins, John, and Caspi (in press) reviewed the findings from eight studies of personality types using the inductive approach, representing a wide range of samples of males and females from several different cultures, including Europe, the U.S., Iceland, and New Zealand. Similar sets of three personality types emerged in each of these studies. Future research may identify additional types, and the definition of the types may differ slightly as a function of age and gender. Nonetheless, the generalizability of these three types was so substantial that Robins et al. (in press) concluded that these three form a minimally necessary set that any comprehensive typology will have to include.

York and John (1992): An Example of the Three Types in Adult Women

In adult women, these three personality types have been labeled *Individuated, Traditional,* and *Conflicted* (York & John, 1992). The women in this study were participants in the Mills Longitudinal Study (Helson, 1967) and were first assessed in the late 1950s when they were seniors in college. The types were derived via inverse factor analysis of CAQ (Block, 1978) personality descriptions obtained from raters who read extensive data files about the subjects from a follow-up assessment at age 43. The CAQ consists of 100 widely ranging statements about behavioral, affective, and cognitive attributes, which provide a comprehensive, generally applicable, and standardized language for describing a broad range of individual differences in personality functioning. Each type is defined by a unique CAQ profile across the 100 items. York and John (1992) used subjects' loadings on these type factors (i.e., the similarity between the individual subject's CAQ profile and each of the type's CAQ profile) to classify the subjects into nonoverlapping groups and provided extensive construct validity for their interpretation of the types (see also Ostrove & John, 1994).

John et al. (in press) examined the relations between these empirically derived types and ego development in the same sample of women. In addition to CAQ personality descriptions at age 43, the SCT was also administered to the women at that age ($N = 83$) and scored by two raters according to Loevinger's procedures (Picano, 1984). Thus, each woman received both a type classification and an ego level. How were these two systems related?

Types and Stages: Hypotheses and Relations

Would one expect each personality type to correspond to a single stage in Loevinger's model? Instead, John et al. (in press) proposed a set of *regional hypotheses,* mapping several adjacent ego stages, or regions of the ego development continuum, onto each personality type. The eight measurable ego stages form a sequence of gradual and continuous transitions capturing the reorganization of various features of psychological functioning. Sets of adjacent stages will share many, although certainly not all, of these features. The three personality types, in contrast, represent a smaller number of prototype categories chosen to be maximally independent and nonoverlapping. Thus, if this typology and ego development have hit on the same "true" features of personality functioning, each of the three personality types should map onto a region of the ego development continuum, with each region defined by several adjacent ego levels.

John et al. (in press) tested three specific hypotheses regarding York and John's (1992) Individuated, Traditional, and Conflicted types. Consider the Individuated type first. York and John (1992) found that the Individuated type shows a strong drive toward individualistic achievement and reaches exceptionally high levels of self-actualization and creativity. Self and others are viewed as autonomous individuals, yet able to connect with each other. Some CAQ items highly characteristic of the Individuated type include: "Values independence," "Has high aspirations for self," "Is introspective," and "Has warmth; affectionate." Therefore, the Individuated type should predominate in the highest stages of ego development, Individualistic, Autonomous, and Integrated. This prediction is consistent with findings already discussed in that the Individuated type captures a configuration of characteristics—openness, autonomy, creativity, interpersonal maturity—shown to be related positively to ego development. Table 7.1 provides some example sentence completions by Individuated subjects illustrating these characteristics.

The Traditional type adopts the prevailing cultural norms, emphasizes the fulfillment of duties and responsibilities, and is concerned with belonging and gaining acceptance at the cost of self-expression. The self adapts to the needs of others. Some highly characteristic CAQ items include: "Has a sex-typed, feminine style," "Is conforming," "Overcontrols needs, impulses," "Is giving," and "Is prone to guilt feelings." Thus, individuals of the Traditional personality type should be found primarily in the middle region of the ego development continuum, namely the Conformist, Self-Aware and Conscientious stages. Characteristics shown to predominate in the middle range of ego development—adherence to traditional gender roles, conformity, and heightened impulse control, for example—corroborate this prediction. Again, the sentence completions by Traditional type members in Table 7.1 illustrate these points.

TABLE 7.1

Example SCT Responses from Individuals Classified Into Each of the York and John (1992) Types

Type	Raising a family . . .	What gets me into trouble is . . .	Sometimes she wished that . . .	When she though of her mother, she . . .
Individuated	is not easy, but is one of life's greatest satisfactions and opportunities for intimacy.	my openness.	she had six other lives to lead, concurrently, and could skip among them at will.	had to deal with a deep and complex tangle of emotions and feelings—certainly not a superficial relationship.
Traditional	has been a wonderful experience.	arguing with my husband.	she could go on a trip.	missed her, and wished she were still around.
Conflicted	is a drag.	headaches.	she were dead.	screamed.

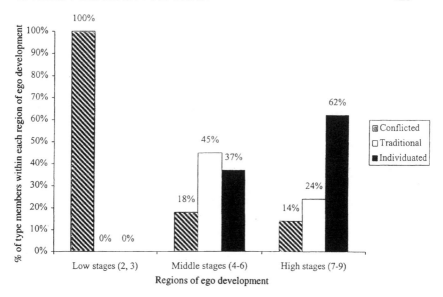

FIG. 7.1. Distribution of personality types (in %) within each region of ego development (adapted from John et al., in press).

The Conflicted type is defined by indications of psychological problems involving both intrapersonal and interpersonal difficulties. The self is marked by ambivalent feelings regarding both autonomy and intimacy. Some CAQ items highly characteristic of this type include: "Has hostility towards others," "Is basically anxious," "Is generally fearful," "Is dissatisfied with self," and "Lacks personal meaning in life." As was noted, the connection between ego development and psychological adjustment is quite complex. Thus, although the Conflicted type may appear at any level of ego development, those few adults who score in the pre-Conformist region (Impulsive and Self-Protective) of ego development should be members of the Conflicted type. Table 7.1, again, provides some relevant example sentence completions.

John et al.'s (in press) findings indeed showed that the three types were differentially distributed across the stages of ego development as predicted. Figure 7.1 summarizes the frequency of each type within each hypothesis-relevant region along the ego development continuum. All of the women (100%) who scored in the low region of ego development on the SCT were members of the Conflicted type, compared with only 18% and 14% in the middle and high regions, respectively. The largest percentage of the women in the middle region were members of the Traditional type. Finally, as predicted, the vast majority of the women in the high region were members of the Individuated type. There were a number of additional findings not apparent in Fig. 7.1. First, the Traditional type was the only type found at the Conformist stage. Second, the proportion of Individuated type members within each post-Conformist ego level increased with each successive level. A final note about Fig. 7.1 is that, although all the individuals at the lowest stages were Conflicted type members, consistent with predictions, there were also Conflicted type members in the other two regions of ego development, a finding that reflects the complexity of the previously discussed relation between ego level and psychological adjustment.

These findings suggest that observer based, broadly defined personality types in adulthood emphasize the similarities of adjacent ego levels within specific regions of the ego development continuum. This analysis highlights the ways in which, for example, Conformist, Self-Aware, and Conscientious individuals are similar in their personality functioning. Conversely, these findings also help us to elaborate the personality types by considering how, for example, a Traditional type member at the Conformist stage may be different from a Traditional type member at the Conscientious stage. These within-type distinctions elucidate important differences in assessment between the two systems. After all, "The SCT, being a free-response test, requires the respondent to display his or her own frame of reference. That gives a glimpse of personality structure that objective tests cannot match" (Loevinger, 1993b, p. 12). This "glimpse of personality" highlights motivational and experiential processes, and therefore captures finer distinctions than do the CAQ-based types.

Focusing on this example of the Traditional type, let us consider how ego level offers a way of assessing differentiation within a broad personality type. The Traditional type was the most prevalent in the middle range of ego development; it was also the most prevalent at the Conformist, Self-Aware, and Conscientious levels examined separately. Note, however, that according to Loevinger's theory, major developmental changes take place between the Conformist and Conscientious stages; the individual increases in self-awareness and in the capacity to appreciate multiple perspectives, and achieves a richer understanding and experience of inner life. How is it that the same personality type can bridge this developmental transition? The answer lies in the different levels of personality functioning that the types and stages capture. One example will illustrate this point. As was noted, a CAQ item highly characteristic of the Traditional type is "Is prone to guilt feelings." Loevinger (1993b) pointed out that guilt feelings are common at both the Conformist and Conscientious levels; what differs is *why* the individual feels guilt. Conformist individuals feel guilty for breaking rules, whereas Conscientious individuals feel guilty for the consequences of their behavior. The experience of guilt feelings is characteristic of the Traditional type in general, but the psychological reasons for experiencing guilt differ importantly for Traditional type members at the Conformist and Conscientious stages.

To summarize, John et al. (in press) found support for their three regional hypotheses relating ego development to personality types in a sample of adult women. The Individuated type was most prevalent in the highest stages, the Traditional type in the middle range of stages, and all the women found at the lowest stages were members of the Conflicted type. The types provide a frame of reference for recognizing similarities among certain sets of stages in the ego development continuum, and ego development provides a frame of reference for understanding important differences that exist within each of the three types. An important point emerging from the interpretation of John et al.'s (in press) results is that the choice of measurement instruments is crucial for understanding how these two systems of personality structure and functioning are related. The projective SCT and the observer-based CAQ profiles seem to capture related but unique perspectives on personality. A pragmatic question one might ask is whether these perspectives on personality can be obtained with other assessment instruments. For example, might there be other ways of measuring ego development? This is the issue to which we now turn.

MEASUREMENT ISSUES: WHAT THE CAQ CAN AND CANNOT TELL US ABOUT EGO DEVELOPMENT

Our discussion of the relation between York and John's (1992) typology and stages of ego development shows that the "glimpse of personality" offered by the SCT is both trenchant and subtle. As a projective test, the SCT requires subjects to reveal their own frame of reference in the way they organize experience, resulting in eight meaningful, sequentially organized stage categories. How essential is the projective nature of the SCT in measuring ego development? Or, can more structured personality assessment instruments capture ego level as well? For example, the CAQ is a well-validated measure of personality functioning. How well can it discriminate among ego levels? If one views the stages of ego development as an eight-category typology, we can ask whether the eight "types" can be recaptured with the inverse factor analytical techniques used by York and John (1992). The answer is no; as we noted, CAQ analyses typically result in no more than three replicable type factors (see Robins et al., in press).

However, the CAQ can be used in another way to index ego development. Rather than inferring constructs via factor analysis, the CAQ can be used to conceptually define existing personality constructs (see Block, 1978, 1991). An expert can generate a CAQ profile of a construct by sorting the 100 CAQ items in a manner that reflects the theoretical definition of that construct. In this way, two experts on ego development theory, Jane Loevinger and Lawrence D. Cohn, generated CAQ profiles of seven of the ego levels from Impulsive (2) to Autonomous (8).[1]

Given the general validity of the CAQ and the level of expertise behind the CAQ ego level profiles, it seems likely that the profiles would reflect at least some important aspects of the stages. However, any expert-sorted CAQ profile is only as good as the 100 items allow it to be. A stringent test of the validity of the ego level profiles is whether they can actually discriminate among the ego levels and indicate an individual's level of ego functioning as defined by the SCT criterion measure. We examined this question in the Mills Longitudinal Study. For each subject, we computed an index of similarity between her individual CAQ profile and each of the seven CAQ ego level profiles by correlating them across the 100 items. This created an individual difference variable for each ego level defined by the subjects' similarity scores for that ego level. We refer to these individual difference variables as *CAQ ego level profile scores*.

Figure 7.2 graphs the means of these seven profile scores for the women at each SCT-measured stage of ego development. The stages along the bottom represent SCT-measured ego level, and each line in the figure represents a CAQ ego level profile. Therefore, each point on the graph reflects the similarity between the individuals' CAQ profiles and a particular CAQ ego level profile averaged for the individuals at each SCT-measured stage. For example, the women who scored at the Conformist stage (4) according to the SCT had the highest average similarity to the Conformist stage CAQ profile.

What does this figure tell us about the validity of the CAQ profiles as measures of ego level? If the CAQ ego level profiles had discriminant validity, each of the lines in Fig. 7.2 would have a distinct pattern with a clear peak at the corresponding SCT-measured stage. In other words, the individual CAQ profiles of women at a given SCT-measured stage would be very similar to the corresponding CAQ ego level profile and relatively dissimilar to the other CAQ ego level profiles. The Impulsive and Conformist profiles showed the pattern expected by the validity predictions, but the patterns for the other CAQ ego level profiles were less clear. In fact, the overall pattern in Fig. 7.2 suggests that the CAQ ego

---

[1]The preverbal first stage is typically not measured and the Integrated Stage (9) was not attempted because the experts felt that the CAQ did not contain unique indicators of this stage (cf. Westenberg & Block, 1993).

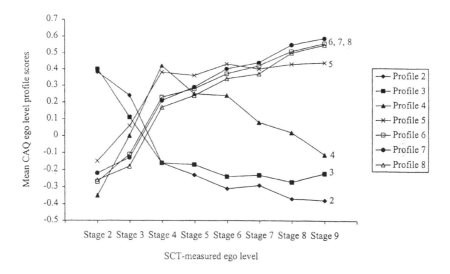

FIG. 7.2. Mean CAQ ego level profile scores as a function of SCT-measured ego level.

level profiles tap into the three-way distinction of pre-Conformist (Stages 2 and 3), Conformist (4), and post-Conformist (6, 7, and 8), with the Self-Aware stage (5) occupying a transitional position between Conformity and post-Conformity. Specifically, the patterns of the two pre-Conformist CAQ profiles were very similar; their highest mean scores were at SCT-measured Stages 2 and 3, and were consistently lower at the Conformist and post-Conformist SCT-measured stages. The Conformist CAQ profile, in contrast, had low mean scores for the women at the pre-Conformist stages on the SCT, peaked at the Conformist stage, and fell off in the post-Conformist range. Finally, the women's scores on the post-Conformist CAQ profiles showed very similar patterns, increasing more or less linearly from low means for the pre-Conformist stages to high means for the post-Conformist range on the SCT.

These findings suggest that the CAQ is sensitive to the theoretically meaningful distinction between pre-Conformist, Conformist, and post-Conformist regions of the ego development continuum but does not seem to discriminate among the individual stages within the pre- and post-Conformist regions. This conclusion is supported by the intercorrelations among the seven CAQ ego level profile scores which can be represented by two factors. The first factor was bipolar, contrasting the pre-Conformist and post-Conformist stages, and the second factor was defined primarily by the Conformist profile. Thus, the conceptually derived CAQ ego profiles capture three regions of ego development, and these regions are similar to those delineated by York and John's (1992) personality types.

This excursion into the issue of measuring ego development with the CAQ convinced us that the SCT is an integral and invaluable part of Loevinger's theory. As Loevinger said, the SCT captures a "glimpse of personality" other assessment measures do not. In our view, the CAQ is an all-purpose personality assessment instrument that captures broad themes of ego development but lacks the subtlety of the more finely graded distinctions among the individual stages captured by the SCT.

CONCLUSIONS

In this chapter, we examined how ego development is related to individual personality trait dimensions and found evidence that three regions of the ego development continuum can be characterized by particular configurations of traits. These configurations, we argued, are similar to three empirically derived personality types that emerged repeatedly in a series of independent studies (see Robins et al., 1996). We then reviewed a recent study showing these three types to be related to the stages of ego development in meaningful and instructive ways. The types and the stages offer different but related perspectives on personality. They are distinct in that the three observer based types are objectively measured and focus on behavior and life outcomes, whereas the eight projectively measured stages focus on the processes and motivations underlying subjective experience. Yet, the evidence for John et al.'s (in press) regional hypothesis suggests that these two distinct perspectives hit upon something important about the nature of personality functioning. The configurations of characteristics captured by the three personality types (Conflicted, Traditional, Individuated) point not to specific stages but to developmentally meaningful regions (pre-Conformist, Conformist to Conscientious, and Individualistic and above) along the continuum of ego development.

Many interesting questions remain. For example, do each of the personality types follow different courses of ego development over time? Perhaps personality is stable at the level of the type and develops at the level of ego functioning. As a point of speculation, the personality structure of the Individuated type at the start of one's adult life might predispose the individual to the kinds of experiences that would facilitate further ego development over the course of adulthood. Another interesting approach would be to use ego development as a starting point to examine the differentiation of experience within the Conflicted type. Indeed, although all of the women at the lowest stages were of the Conflicted type, John et al. (in press) also found many Conflicted type members in the post-Conformist range. What distinguishes the experience and psychological make-up of Conflicted individuals at the highest ego levels with Conflicted individuals at the lowest ego levels? Finally, how is a single ego level manifested differently by individuals of different personality types? For example, how might the experience of the Conscientious stage differ for individuals of the Individuated and Traditional types? These questions show how the work on adult personality types and on ego development can stimulate one another and that much research remains to be done in order to achieve a full integration of these two approaches.

ACKNOWLEDGMENTS

The writing of this chapter was supported by Grants MH–49255 and MH–43948 from the National Institute of Mental Health. Additional support for the first author came from a National Science Foundation Graduate Fellowship. We are indebted to Ravenna Helson, who supported this project in numerous ways. James Picano's dissertation work on the SCT data is also gratefully acknowledged. This chapter benefitted from thoughtful comments by Ravenna Helson, Richard W. Robins, and the three editors of this volume.

8

Age Trends in Personality Development: A Quantitative Review

Lawrence D. Cohn
Department of Psychology
The University of Texas at El Paso

When I was a boy of 14, my father was so ignorant I could hardly stand to have the old man around. But when I got to be twenty-one I was astonished at how much he had learned in seven years.

—Mark Twain (cited in Loeb, 1996, p. 5)

When do individuals cease to mature? Both common wisdom and empirical evidence provide equivocal answers to this question. Some findings suggest that maturity increases throughout adulthood, whereas other findings suggest that people reach their upper limit of development by the end of adolescence and then resist further growth. The present review contributes to this debate by examining a large body of new evidence: longitudinal, cross-sectional and related findings obtained from more than 90 studies using Loevinger's Washington University Sentence Completion Test of Ego Development (WUSCT; Loevinger & Wessler, 1970). The WUSCT is a comprehensive measure of maturity assessesing development within many domains, including impulse control, conscious preoccupations, and interpersonal style. Because of its broad focus, the WUSCT provides an opportunity to move beyond studies of age trends in maturity focusing on single aspects of development (e.g., moral maturity). Although many studies of personality change restrict their analysis to age trends in polar variables (e.g., neuroticism, openness to experience), the WUSCT assesses change in milestone variables, providing an opportunity to examine age trends in aspects of development often overlooked in studies of personality change.

Knowing when most people cease to mature should provide some insight into the more fundamental question of what makes people mature. What experiences act as pacers for development? This question touches on the basic nature of Loevinger's model of personality growth: what changes, and why? Understanding how change occurs has emerged as the fundamental puzzle facing theories of cognitive growth (Siegler, 1995) and it may well be the central puzzle facing stage theories of personality growth. Loevinger (1976) addressed issues of change and stability in her discussion of *pacers*, proposing that people mature when exposed to slightly more complex interpersonal environments than their own level of development. Only a limited number of studies have addressed this issue (e.g., Sprinthall, 1994), leaving several basic questions unanswered: Is growth gradual or abrupt? Does it simultaneously occur across all dimensions of ego development, or does growth first appear in one dimension (e.g., psychological insight) and then extend to others (e.g., perspective taking)? What pacers are appropriate for each developmental stage and, perhaps more importantly, are there individual differences in responsivity to different pacers? Identifying the trajectory of ego development across adulthood should provide some insight into these questions.

Several recent findings suggest that personality traits stabilize by early adulthood. Some of these traits are related to maturity, providing indirect evidence that ego development also stabilizes by early adulthood. For example, a cross-sectional study of approximately 10,000 adults, ages 35–85, revealed virtually no age changes in neuroticism, extraversion, and openness to experience, a trait that is associated with advances in ego development (McCrae & Costa, 1980, 1990). Longitudinal data supported the age trends observed in cross-sectional testings. Studies of moral development also suggest that maturity stabilizes by early adulthood. Rest (1979) reviewed findings from longitudinal and cross-sectional studies of moral maturity as measured by the Defining Issues Test and concluded that "adults in general seem to slow down in moral development in their 20s and to plateau after leaving school" (p. 143).

In contrast to the above findings, several studies suggest that development continues throughout adulthood. A 20-year longitudinal study of adult women, for example, revealed significant increases in toleration and psychological mindedness, two traits associated with increasing maturity (Helson & Roberts, 1994). Using a different index of development, Vaillant (1977) observed increasing use of mature defense mechanisms among a sample of Harvard men studied longitudinally for 40 years.

What growth patterns are expected in the domain of ego development? Loevinger hypothesized that ego level increases during adolescence and then stabilizes for most individuals by early adulthood. She noted that ". . . whatever the SCT measures it is relatively stable in adult life, approximately after high school graduation" (Loevinger et al., 1985, p. 960). The evidence supporting this hypothesis was limited to a small number of studies (e.g., Loevinger et al., 1985; Redmore & Loevinger, 1979). This chapter expands the data set used to test Loevinger's hypothesis. First, I examine age trends in ego development using data from 30 cross-sectional studies; next, I examine age trends in development using data from 16 longitudinal studies. Finally, I use regression analysis to examine age trends in ego development among 144 sample means obtained from studies not included in the previous two analyses. *In toto,* this review summarizes evidence obtained from studies of 12,370 subjects.

METHOD

Literature Search and Effect Size Indices

Studies using the WUSCT served as the primary source data.[1] Studies conducted prior to 1986 were identified through bibliographies cited in earlier reviews (Cohn, 1991; Hauser, 1976; Loevinger, 1979a); studies published between 1986-1995 were identified using a computer search of PSYCINFO with the key words *Loevinger, Washington University Sentence Completion Test (WUSCT),* and *ego development.* Studies of clinical populations were excluded from the analysis.

When possible, the correlation between age and ego level was recovered from each study. Some studies only reported descriptive statistics (e.g., mean WUSCT scores among different age groups) or only reported the results of F-tests or t-tests comparing the WUSCT scores of two age groups. In these cases, t-values were converted into Pearson rs using formulas provided in Glass, McGaw, and Smith (1981). The correlation between age and ego level was set to 0 when authors did not provide the results of statistical tests but did report that age changes in WUSCT scores were nonsignificant. When authors only reported that age differences in WUSCT scores were "significant," then t was assigned the value associated with a significant mean difference at $p = .05$.

---

[1]A complete list of studies used in the meta-analysis is available from the author.

RESULTS

Cross Sectional Studies

Correlations between age and WUSCT scores were recovered from 30 studies involving 4,330 participants (Table 8.1). These correlations were used to test the hypothesis that advances in ego development are large during adolescence and small during adulthood. Subject samples were first assigned to one of three categories: (a) adolescents (ages 11–20), (b) adults (ages 20–65+), and (c) cross-Generational (i.e., samples comprised of adolescents and adults). For each age group, a weighted estimate of the population correlation was calculated (Hedges & Olkin, 1985). Sample correlations were initially transformed using Fisher's r to z' transformation and the z' values were then weighted as a function of the study's sample size. The weighted z' values were subsequently converted back into estimates of r.

Among adolescent samples, the weighted estimate of the population correlation between age and ego level was $r = .40$ (95% confidence interval: .35 to .44); among adults, the weighted estimate of the population correlation between age and ego level was $r = .04$ (95% confidence interval: -.025 to.10). There was significant variability among sample correlations within each age group indicating the presence of at least one moderating variable per group. Despite this heterogeneity, both findings support Loevinger's hypothesis that maturity increases during the adolescent years and stabilizes during adulthood.

Among cross-generational samples the weighted estimate of the population correlation between age and ego level was .27. The latter value is close to the mean correlation of adolescent and adult samples combined, suggesting that the association between age and ego level observed in samples comprised of both adolescents and adults is most likely due to advances made during the adolescent years rather than the adult years.

TABLE 8.1
Age Trends in Ego Development: Cross-Sectional Findings

Study	Age[a] Range	N	Sex[b]	r Ego/Age
Child and Adolescent Samples				
Avery & Ryan	9–12	92	1, 2	.06
Hirsch	10.5–12.8	93	1, 2	.27
McCammon	11–16	80	1, 2	.18
Lerner	11–20	59	1, 2	.53

(continued)

TABLE 8.1
(CONTINUED)

Coor	12–15	23	1	.53
	12–15	24	2	.48
	13–16	10	1	.11
	13–16	17	2	.36
Novy et al.	12–17	61	1, 2	.33[c]
Cohn	12–17	112	1, 2	.50
Sullivan et al.	12–17	120	1, 2	.65
Gfellner	12–18	420	1, 2	.48
Starrett	13.7–17	43	1	.71
	13.5–16.9[b]	55	1	.74
Hoppe & Loevinger	13.7–17.9	107	1	.42
Head & Shayer	14–17	117	1	.38
	14–17	111	2	.18
Hansel	14–18	99	1	.19
	14–18	116	2	.02
Levit	14.6–19	66	1, 2	.33
Adams & Jones	15–18	137	2	ns trend

Adult Samples

Lockett	18/21–35/47	60	2	.27
Nettles & Loevinger	18–58	107	1	-.06
	20–68	107	1	-.11
Busche & Gibbs	20–58	64	1, 2	.29
Bursik	22–62	104	2	.ns
White	23–59	97	1	.20
Suzman	25–45	272	1, 2	(.26)[d]
McAdams et al.	35–49	50	1, 2	ns
McCrae & Costa	35–80	239	1	.01
Acklin	30–49	40	1, 2	.21
	50–60+	40	1, 2	.11
Streich & Swensen	40–73	64	1	.11
	42–74	64	2	-.31

Cross-Generational Samples

Labouvie-Vief et al.	10–77	100	1, 2	.49
Blanchard-Fields	14–46	60	1, 2	.49
Snarey & Blasi	14–27[b]	20	1	.19
	14–27[b]	20	2	.12
Browning	16–25	930	1, 2	.27
Snarey & Blasi	17–72	42	1, 2	.44
Hansel	13–91	221	1, 2	-.13

[a]Among adolescent samples, the correlation between grade and ego level was often used in lieu of the correlation between age and ego level.
[b]1 = males, 2 = females.
[c]Kendall's correlation coefficient.
[d]Correlation of WUSCT and education.

Longitudinal Studies

Longitudinal data were recovered from 16 studies involving 39 samples and 1,862 respondents (Table 8.2). Test–retest periods ranged from 1 to 9 years. To test the hypothesis that advances in ego development are greatest

TABLE 8.2
Age Trends in Ego Development: Longitudinal Findings

Study	Age/Grade at First Testing	Years to Retest	N	Sex[a]	% Gain/ %Regress	Repeated Measures Test
Petersen & Crockett	6th	2	78	2	NA	ns
Jacobson et al.	12-15	2	42	1, 2	NA	ns
Gfellner	7th/8th	4	123	1,2	58/0	$t = 11.4$
Martin & Redmore	6th	6	32	1, 2	94/NA	$t = 10.4$
Nichols	7th	2	28	1, 2	NA	$t = 1.1$
	7th	2	29	1, 2	NA	$t = 2.6$
Redmore	8th	4	50	1	NA	$Z = 5.7$
	8th	4	9	1	NA	$T = 0$
	8th	4	25	1	NA	$T = 12$
	9th	3	33	1	NA	$T = 27$
	9th	3	27	1, 2	NA	$T = 0$
	10th	2	16	2	NA	$T = 3$
	11th	2.5	23	1	NA	ns
Westenberg & Block	14th	9	51	1	NA	$t = 4.7$
	14th	9	53	2	NA	$t = 5.1$
Kitchner et al.	11th	2	16		-	ns
Redmore	13th	4	57	1, 2	40/10	$t = 3.9$
			40	1, 2		$t = 2.7$
Ruprecht	13th	4	17	1	70/12	$t = 2.1$
	13th	4	36	2	39/17	$t = 2.2$
Whitely	13th	.9	119	1, 2	NA	$t = 3.3$
Adams & Fitch	13th	1	148	1, 2	23/21	ns
Kitchner et al.	15th	2	27		NA	ns
	17th	2	13		NA	ns
Loevinger et al.	13th	4	76	1	NA	$t = 0.83$
	13th	3	46	1	NA	$t = -0.45$
	13th	4	63	1	NA	$t = 1.6$
	13th	4	62	2	NA	$t = 1.87$
	13th	3	17	2	NA	$t = -0.53$
	13th	4	34	2	NA	$t = -1.89$
	13th	4	56	1	NA	$t = 2.07$
	13th	4	36	1	NA	$t = 1.94$
	13th	4	67	1	NA	$t = 1.63$
	13th	4	47	1	NA	$t = -0.78$
	13th	4	8	2	NA	$t = 0.58$
	13th	4	23	2	NA	$t = 1.42$
	13th	4	35	2	NA	$t = -1.16$
White	27	2	97	2	22/32	ns, but time by ego signif.
Bursik	22-62	1	96	2		group by time signif.

Note. NA = not available; ns = nonsignificant.
[a]1 = males, 2 = females.

during adolescence and least during adulthood I grouped the samples into two homogeneous age groups: adolescents (first testing occurred between 6th and 11th grades) and (b) college age. Only two studies reported longitudinal data for noncollege adults, hence no statistical analyses were conducted for this age group.

Significant increases in WUSCT scores occurred in 11 of the 16 adolescent samples; in contrast, only 6 of the 21 college samples displayed significant growth across testings (marginally significant growth was displayed in three additional samples). Among adolescents, the estimated population correlation between age and ego level was .41 (confidence interval: .32 to .51). This finding is comparable to the population correlation estimated from cross-sectional data, but the comparison should be interpreted with caution due to significant heterogeneity among sample correlations within both data sets.

Among college-age adults, the estimated population correlation was .13 (confidence interval: .06 to .19). There was not significant heterogeneity among the sample correlations. These findings suggests that development is present during the college years, but is less dramatic than the growth associated with adolescence.

Scatterplot of Sample Means

One final strategy was used to assess age trends in ego development. I identified 56 additional studies reporting the mean age and WUSCT scores of participants. These data were not used in the two preceding analyses and thus provided an opportunity for a third independent test of Loevinger's hypothesis. Data from 144 samples were entered into a regression analysis in which the mean ego level of each sample was regressed onto the mean age of the samples. Curvilinear regression revealed significant linear and quadratic trends. The Pearson correlation between age and ego level was .52; the multiple R (combining linear and quadratic components) was .68. The presence of a quadratic trend in WUSCT scores supports the hypothesis that ego development increases during adolescence and stabilizes during adulthood.

The age trend suggested by the above finding is clearly depicted in Fig. 8.1, which presents a distribution of 252 sample means (WUSCT scores) by age. These data were recovered from 79 of the studies reviewed in this chapter. As expected, curvilinear regression revealed significant linear and quadratic trends. The Pearson correlation between age and ego level was .48; the multiple R (combining linear and quadratic components) was .67. Inspection of Fig. 8.1 indicates that mean WUSCT scores rise during adolescence and then stabilize during early adulthood.

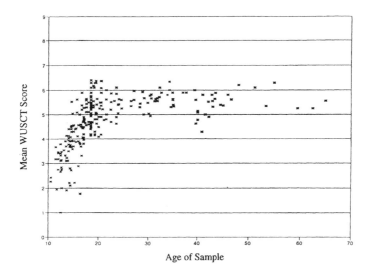

FIG. 8.1. Scatterplot of 252 sample means by age of sample (data recovered from 79 studies involving 11,032 participants). Key: 0 = Impulsive stage, 2 = Self-protective stage, 4 = Conformist stage, 6 = Conscientious stage.

DISCUSSION

When do people cease to mature? This question is inextricably tied to a related query: What makes people mature? What experiences act as pacers for development? The current review provides a tentative answer to the first question and, in so doing, brings the second query to the forefront for future study.

These findings support Loevinger's hypothesis that ego development stabilizes for most individuals by early adulthood. The consistency of findings across three independent data sets involving more than 12,000 subjects suggests that unknown sampling biases do not account for the age trends revealed here, despite limitations and confounds associated with each analysis (e.g., restricted age ranges and possible SES differences between samples). For some reason development slows down long before most individuals reach the upper stages of maturity. The mean WUSCT scores for adult samples in this review lay mainly between the Self-Aware and Conscientious stages of development (see Fig. 8.1). This finding is consistent with data obtained from a national probability sample of young adults, which also identified the Self-Aware stage as the modal level of development (Holt, 1980).

What accounts for the apparent lack of growth during adulthood? Are adults more resistant to change or are they simply exposed to fewer pacers for development? Few studies addressed this issue, although Loevinger leaned towards the latter explanation. She noted (1976) that "the ego is a structure of expectations not about natural phenomena but primarily about interpersonal ones" (p. 311). Development, she suggested, occurs when interpersonal environments disconfirm expectations that are characteristic of a specific stage. From this vantage point, we expect to see marked personality growth during childhood and adolescence because family and school experiences typically expose teenagers to interpersonal environments that challenge pre-Conformist expectations and preoccupations. During adulthood, development may be less likely because adults have more freedom to pick and choose their interpersonal worlds and, hence, are more likely to seek out environments that reinforce their own orientation and beliefs. Adults do not have fewer novel experiences than do adolescents; rather, adults may have fewer experiences that effectively challenge their expectations.

Several studies sought to facilitate development by exposing participants to peer mentoring and counseling experiences. Such experiences are thought to increase a person's capacity for perspective taking and, hence, their ego level. At least eight studies (mainly comprised of high school students) have reported significant advances in WUSCT scores following such interventions, although participants do not, on average, advance beyond the Self-Aware stage (e.g., Bernier & Rustad, 1977; Hurt, 1977; Locke & Zimmerman, 1987; Nichols, 1981; Slaughter, 1983). In two additional studies, adults did not mature in response to role taking experiences or training experiences designed to increase one's capacity for perspective taking and coping with inner conflict (Bernier, 1980; Bushe & Gibbs, 1990). However, adults in the latter studies scored at the Self-Aware stage or higher at pretesting, suggesting that role-taking experiences may facilitate development mainly among individuals at pre-Conscientious levels of development.

Education has also been proposed as a developmental pacer to the extent that schooling exposes students to different views and thereby encourages perspective taking. Here, too, such experiences may facilitate development through the Self-Aware stage but not much beyond, as suggested earlier. Correlations between ego level and education are typically high among high school samples and low to moderate in magnitude among adult samples. This pattern of findings is consistent with the suggestion that perspective taking experiences facilitate growth mainly through the pre-Conscientious stages of development.

Let me summarize the discussion thus far. During adolescence, the movement away from an egocentric orientation toward an interpersonal one may be due, in part, to the conformist expectations of junior and senior high school. Secondary schools encourage the growth of cooperation, obedience to rules, and the regulation of impulses. Teenagers who are unable to adapt to these constraints are not likely to succeed in school. Gfellner's (1986) longitudinal data support this proposition: Students at the lowest ego levels were the most likely to become school dropouts and unavailable for retesting. Notably her findings raise the possibility that the current review overestimates maturation during adolescence due to attrition in 11th- and 12th-grade samples of teens at the lowest ego levels.

High school and college environments that encourage perspective taking and reflectiveness are likely to facilitate movement away from the Conformist stage to the Self-Aware and, possibly, Conscientious stages. Many studies support this general proposition and the current findings also provide partial support for this claim. Among college samples, the average correlation between age and WUSCT scores was significant, although small. Because the present analyses utilize group data, however, the current review probably underestimates the degree of growth occurring among the subset of students who mature during college. One avenue for future research will be to identify the types of students who are likely to mature in response to college experiences.

Are there any social experiences, shared by large segments of the adult population, that facilitate development beyond the Self-Aware or Conscientious stages? Thus far, no such pacers have been identified or even proposed. Growth beyond the Self-Aware stage is characterized by a unique set of changes that entail the emergence of self-evaluated standards, psychological insight, role conception, tolerance, and a recognition of inner conflict (Loevinger & Wessler, 1970). Some types of graduate education may contribute to development in these domains but thus far the impact of such training has been limited. For example, clinical training and expertise should facilitate the growth of psychological insight and a respect for individual differences. Yet several studies suggest that counseling and clinical psychology students (beginning and advanced) have WUSCT scores at the level of most adults, between the Self-Aware and Conscientious stages of development (e.g., Bernier, 1980; Borders & Fong, 1989; Slomowitz, 1981). At least two studies noted a small relationship between ego level and personal experience in psychotherapy (e.g., Helson & Wink, 1987; Vaillant & McCullough, 1987) but it is not yet known if the pursuit of psychotherapy is a cause or consequence of ego development.

Stability did not characterize all of the adult samples examined in this review. Bursik (1991), for example, reported significant gains in ego development over a 1-year period among a subset of divorced women. White (1985) reported gains among a subset of female nurses studied longitudinally over a 2-year period, and Helson and Roberts (1994) reported gains in two traits related to ego development (toleration and psychological mindedness) over a 20-year period. These findings highlight a key point that might otherwise be lost in the current analyses of group data: Individual development occurs during adulthood, although it does not seem to characterize most people. One direction for future research will be to identify the characteristics of people who are likely to mature during adulthood. For example, Helson and Roberts (1994) found different developmental trajectories, over a 20-year period, among women initially classified at the Conformist and Self-Aware stages versus women classified at the Conscientious and Individualistic stages. Women who were initially classified at or below the Self-Aware stage were less likely to show evidence of ego development than were women at higher stages. Are women in the former group more resistant to change, or are they simply exposed to fewer developmentally appropriate pacers, or both? Additional longitudinal studies are needed to investigate these questions.

Attempts to identify stage-appropriate pacers may obscure the importance of another issue, one that is rarely addressed: individual differences among adults at the same developmental level. Adults at a specific ego stage (e.g., Conformist stage) share a common level of development but differ in many other aspects of their personality. How do these differences influence a person's response to developmental pacers? For example, college experiences facilitate personality growth among some Conformist students, but not all of them. Why? The efficacy of some pacers may depend upon the presence of other personality traits, for example, sociability, shyness, or neuroticism. Here, too, is an avenue for future research.

The present review provides a preliminary assessment of age trends in ego development. Longitudinal studies are now needed to address many of the questions and hypotheses suggested by these data.

ACKNOWLEDGMENTS

I gratefully acknowledge the helpful comments of Augusto Blasi and Michiel Westenberg on an earlier draft of this manuscript. Statistical advice provided by Michael Strube is also gratefully acknowledged.

Understanding Changes in Girls' Relationships and in Ego Development: Three Studies of Adolescent Girls

Annie G. Rogers
Human Development and Psychology
Harvard University

CONCEPTS AND METHODS

This chapter is an empirical and theoretical exploration of changes in girls' relationships and in ego development during adolescence using two different approaches: Loevinger's ego development theory, and a voice-centered understanding of women's psychological development grounded in the work of Carol Gilligan and members of the Harvard Project on Women's Psychology and Girls' Development. Drawing on the strengths of the distinct methods from each of these two approaches, I articulate and illustrate an integrative methodology for understanding changes in the relational development of adolescent girls that, in turn, affect ego development, using data from a longitudinal project presented in three studies.

Each of the two approaches I describe is rooted in particular methodological and developmental traditions. I elucidate the evolution of each approach before proceeding, beginning with Loevinger's ego development conception.

Loevinger's Ego Development Theory

The ego, as conceived by Loevinger, is the self: *das Ich* as Freud called it, the unity of personality, a framework for actively constructing a meaningful world, the self-consciously known "I." The construction of meaning is not only something the ego does, but what the ego is. According to

Loevinger, the ego is a structure of personality, by definition relatively stable, changing very gradually. Ego development theory attempts to explain changes in the development of self over time through a sequence of qualitatively different structures or stages. Nine different levels of development were distinguished by Loevinger and her colleagues. Structural changes in impulse control, character, interpersonal relations, conscious preoccupations, and cognitive style define the stages of ego development (see Loevinger, 1979d). Nothing less than a complete pattern of structural changes defines a shift in ego level. Although Loevinger does not claim her theory is universal, this view of the ego does not specifically take into account cultural constraints, including the constraints of race, class or gender, in the ways individuals make sense of their worlds.

Loevinger's theory of ego development has evolved in response to data from the Washington University Sentence Completion Test (SCT). The test consists of 36 sentence stems. The individual taking the test simply completes these stems. The responses to the stems are scored for signs of ego level one item at a time by two independent raters. Construct validity for the SCT as a measure of ego development is substantial (Loevinger, 1979a). There are many parallels among stages and stage sequences described by various developmental theorists working in a common tradition. In fact, many developmental theories formed in the tradition of Piaget's work, including Loevinger's, embrace a philosophical assumption that qualitative differences in meaning-making are not random or coincidental, but are expressions of underlying structural developments. Loevinger's theory is perhaps among the most integrative of such theories. It also stands out as a model of theory grounded in a consciously chosen measurement strategy.

Loevinger argued that a developmental view was antagonistic to classical psychometrics. She saw that the logical polarities on which trait measurement relies did not easily correspond to a developmental sequence. Loevinger described her concept as a milestone variable, in contrast to a polar variable, which can be measured simply by gradations of increase in the trait to be studied. The scoring algorithm for ego development, she decided, would include an entire distribution of test responses. The scoring structure for various ego levels was based on ogive rules, that is, cumulative distributions of ego level scores, with cutting points for each ego level. She carefully matched her scoring algorithm to her quantification strategy and her concept of ego development. Using an *ogive* distribution for relatively broad ranges of responses allowed Loevinger and her colleagues to identify the most probable signs for each ego level they delineated. Thus, she constructed a developmental concept, quantification strategy, and scoring algorithm that were logically consistent.

A Voice-Centered Theory of Women's Psychological Development

The voice-centered, relational approach to studying women's development explored in this chapter is historically indebted to the work of Carol Gilligan (1982/1993). A voice-centered conception of psychological development is grounded in her observation that by listening carefully to women one could discern a different voice, that is, a voice that spoke about relationships and responsivity. Gilligan called this voice an *ethic of care* and linked it with women's voices conceptually and empirically. She contrasted this voice with a voice of justice, autonomy, and individual rights that was represented with far greater regularity in theories of human development and was clearly discernible in women's and men's narratives of moral choices (Gilligan, 1982/1993; Gilligan & Attanucci, 1988). More recently, she described voice as the core of the self. Gilligan (1982/1993) argued that having a voice makes us human, but also that "speaking depends upon listening and being heard; it is an intensely relational act" (p. xiv). Thus, voice is both the core of self and a key to understanding relationships.

A voice-centered approach to studying relational development and Loevinger's theory of ego development rely on different methods and developmental assumptions. I have worked within both frameworks over the past 10 years. These experiences led me to a particular understanding of developmental processes in young women, and to the exploration of voice as a psychological conception and a method of studying development.

Defining voice as *polyphonic* and *relational,* members of the Harvard Project designed an interpretive method that entails reading interviews multiple times for various voices (Brown et al., 1988; Brown & Gilligan, 1992; Gilligan, Brown, & Rogers, 1990; Rogers, Brown, & Tappan, 1993). By polyphonic, we mean that voices are nuanced by different layers of meanings, as well as by shifting tones, emphases and pauses, contradictions, gaps, and silences. By relational, we mean that what is voiced depends on a relational context; the hearer, as much as the speaker, determines what will be said and how it will be spoken. Thus, uncovering different layers of voice and meaning involves multiple readings or listenings. The method involves first reading an interview for the story or plot. We attend to the dramatic rendering of a story or several storylines constructed by the interviewee. This reading includes attending to recurrent words and images, central metaphors, contradictions in the story, as well as revisions and silences. The second reading, a reading for self, traces the voice of "I" speaking in the text who is also an actor or protagonist in the stories she or he tells. We note how the story is conveyed, including shifts in narrative position—the use of first-, second-, or third-person voice. This reading for self is underlined in a colored pencil. Subsequent readings of an interview for additional voices (each in a different colored pencil) depend on the researcher's empirical questions. Each additional voice reading is defined inferentially from the data. Worksheets accompany each voice reading, so that independent readers can check and argue with one another's interpretations. This method is systematic and very flexible. In different studies, voice-centered readings were used to create case studies or profiles, as well as to discern how groups differ or change over time.

Our theoretical understanding of women's psychological development is grounded in empirical studies with girls that rely in turn on voice-centered methods. As is the case with Loevinger's theory of ego development, the theory and method are recursive. The most fundamental finding of the Harvard Project, that girls struggle against or resist losing the capacity to voice their thoughts and feelings in early adolescence, is grounded in extensive readings of girls' voices in longitudinal interviews (Brown & Gilligan, 1992; Gilligan et al., 1990; Rogers et al., 1993). We would not have heard this struggle without listening to girls' multiple, sometimes contradictory, voices. Using voice-centered methods, we documented a process of girls silencing themselves, or speaking as if speaking itself were dangerous, but speaking nevertheless. At adolescence, we heard girls begin to doubt themselves about the veracity or sanity of their own thoughts and feelings. At the same time, we heard these girls resist making a series of disconnections between their own experiences and what was said to be "reality." What we heard and how we interpreted what we heard depended on the individual girl speaking, on the responses of her interviewer, and on our interpretive strategy. Without the voice-centered method, we might have missed the process of self-silencing and the struggle for voice altogether. Using other methods, we might have seen and heard only those aspects of voice fitting fixed categories that, in turn, corresponded with particular preconceived conceptions of psychological maturity.

A voice-centered method of reading interview texts and the derivation of a theory of women's psychological development based on longitudinal empirical studies of girls offers another way to consider some dynamic processes of development—particularly regarding women's relational and internalized representations of various voices. Using this method, it is possible to document changes in voice over time along with changes in ego development.

The specific ways each approach understands and investigates development makes it possible to combine and modify the two approaches so that, taken together, they enlarge our understanding of both relational development and ego development in adolescent girls.

ILLUSTRATION OF METHODS

I begin by describing the longitudinal study from which the following illustrations are drawn. The girls were participants in a 5-year longitudinal study involving four age-cohort groups of girls, ranging in age from 7 to 18, attending a private girls' school in the Midwest.[1] Approximately 25% of the girls received partial or full scholarships, and 86% were White, whereas 14% represented diverse racial and ethnic groups. In this study, socioeconomic status (SES) was not associated with race or ethnicity. This chapter focuses on two of the longitudinal cohort groups—girls in early and midadolescence—specifically 38 girls who were followed from 7th to 9th grade and 64 girls who were followed from 10th to 12th grade.

This study was designed to explore the ways girls understand themselves and their relationships. As a number of studies document, adolescence appears to be a time of psychological risk and vulnerability for girls, comparable to early childhood for boys (see Elder, Nguyen, & Caspi, 1985; Petersen, 1988). The move into adolescence affects girls' self-conceptions, and for example, marks a sharp drop in self-confidence, primarily among White and Latina girls (Block, 1990; Greenburg-Lake Analysis Group, 1991). Girls begin to develop disparaging body images at this time and to experience problems around eating (Garner, 1981). In addition, girls tend to lose ground in their assessments of their academic achievement and in their aspirations at adolescence. There is clearly a need to understand why adolescence is a time of psychological vulnerability and risk for girls.

We were particularly interested in changes in girls' ego development and their relational development in early adolescence. We explored these changes in two ways: through the SCT, and through annual in-depth clinical interviews designed specifically to interpret girls' concepts of self and relationships.

A cohort of 38 early adolescent girls completed the SCT in the seventh grade, and repeated the test again in the ninth grade. A cohort of 64 girls at midadolescence filled out the SCT in the 10th grade and again in the 12th grade. All testing was done in a group administration. The responses to the SCT were scored for ego development by two trained independent raters. Ego levels were derived for each girl using Loevinger's ogive rules. Reliability of ego development rating was assessed in terms of the raters' agreements on ego levels (Kappa = .79), as well as a correlation of the raters' assessments of the item responses as a whole ($r = .84$).

---

[1]Lyn Mikel Brown was the Project Director and Carol Gilligan was the Principal Investigator of this study.

Each girl also participated in a semistructured in-depth clinical interview with a trained female interviewer. The interview consisted of four major sections: The girls were asked to describe themselves in the first section, to tell a story of their own moral conflict and choice in the second, to think about a set of scenarios about learning and comment on their own learning in the third, and to consider how society constructs the ideal woman and speak about their own views and plans for the future in the final section. Participants were interviewed once a year for 3 years, and girls whose cases were particularly interesting were interviewed for 5 years. Whenever possible, the girls were interviewed by the same woman throughout the study.

In order to explain the types of analyses that follow and my efforts to integrate different methods, it is important for readers to understand the empirical work that was the basis for new questions about girls' psychological development. My dissertation research (Rogers, 1987a) investigated gender differences in ego development along the same lines as Gilligan's description of gender differences in moral thinking (Gilligan, 1982/1993). Three hundred ninety-five adolescents ranging in age from 12 to 19 (199 girls and 196 boys) filled out the SCT. I coded these data for ego development using standard procedures. I also created a reliable and valid way of measuring care and justice concerns using manuals constructed for content coding of SCT data (Rogers, 1987b; 1987c). This study revealed that girls were significantly more likely than boys to write sentence responses reflecting issues of care and connection; and boys were significantly more likely to respond in terms of individual rights and issues of justice ($p < .001$). This finding was very robust and held up across all ego levels, and is graphically represented in Fig. 9.1.

For both boys and girls, an increasing articulation of moral concerns in both the justice and care domains was associated with increasing ego development levels. However, the correlation of care thinking with ego development was significantly higher for the girls ($r = .55$) than for the boys ($r = .35$). In other words, concerns about how to care for both self and others in relationships was highlighted in girls' development.

From this work, I became interested in using the SCT as a way to explore other aspects of the psychological development of girls in adolescence. I was particularly interested in answering the following questions:

1. How do girls' voices change during adolescence in different domains of development?

2. What are changing self-conceptions for girls in adolescence as revealed by ego development trajectories?

Mean Justice Score

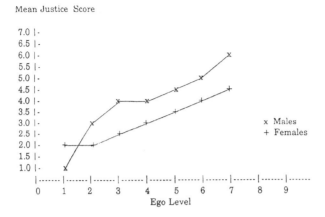

Mean Care Score

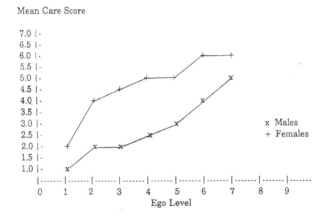

FIG. 9.1. Mean justice scores and mean care scores on sex and ego level.
Note: Males *n* = 122. Females *n* = 125. Ego level numbers refer to nine scorable
stages: Impulsive, Self-protective, Self protective–Conformist, Conformist,
Conscientious–Conformist, Conscientious, Individualistic, Autonomous, and
Integrated.

3. How do girls consider relationships during adolescence, and how
does this construction of relationships affect their psychological well being,
as revealed by semistructured clinical interviews?

These questions became an impetus for undertaking different kinds of
data analysis in three progressive studies.

Study One

How do girls' voices change during adolescence in different domains of development? The first analysis involved a developmental comparison of the 7th and 10th-grade groups of girls using only the SCT data. Their sentence completions were scored for ego development level and were also analyzed for themes of voice in different domains of development using a method designed for use with the SCT data. Although it is not the way Loevinger describes her measure, the SCT can also be used as measure of the ways in which adolescents develop in different domains as revealed by the use of distinctive voices. The phrases comprising the sentence stems of the test, written in the colloquial or everyday vernacular of U.S. speech, require individuals to consider where they stand in relation to themselves, their relationships, and the rules, norms, and values of their culture. The content of the test responses constitutes an elegant and rich view of development in these areas, if the stems are scored for the content of responses as well as for structural signs of stage development. In order to code the test responses for content in these areas, I used a manual created for this purpose: *Developmental Voices: A Method for Identifying a Fugue of Themes in Sentence Completions* (Rogers, 1988). This method required two independent raters to identify specific sets of themes as a voice in sentence completions, allowing that several voices might, at times, overlap in the same sentence completion. The idea that various voices may overlap in a text was derived from a method of reading interview texts (see Brown et al., 1988). Although SCT responses are much shorter than are passages from interviews, the concept of reading with different conceptual lenses made it possible to discern distinct voices in sentence completions. The new method defined voices in three domains: cultural, relational, and moral development.

Conceptualizing these clusters of themes as voices, two raters reliably identified six voices in girls' sentence completions in two samples—38 7th graders and 64 10th graders. The first two voices, *resistance* and *capitulation*, elaborate themes of self in relation to cultural conventions of feminine identity and behavior (primarily for White, upper-middle class girls). The second two voices, *connection* and *independence*, represent themes of self in relation to others. The final set of voices, *care* and *justice*, reveal the moral concerns identified by Gilligan (1982/1993). A few examples of themes of each voice from the 7th and 10th-grade girls' sentence completions are presented here to give readers a realistic understanding of how the sentence completions were coded (see Table 9.1.).

TABLE 9.1
Illustrated Coding of Thematic Voices on the SCT

---

1. Voice of resistance (themes: resistance, self-assertion, self-confidence, self-respect)
- What gets me into trouble is . . . chewing gum and not having my shirt tucked in (but usually it's worth it)
- Rules are . . . supposed to be the guidelines for life, but I can't say I'm convinced of that.

2. Voice of capitulation (themes: capitulation to norms of "good girl" or "good women" behavior, self-doubt, self-abnegation)
- Sometimes she wished that . . . I was a blonde, and I wish I weren't so ugly too.
- When they avoided me . . . I feel unimportant, unwanted, as though I am a fly on the wall.

3. Voice of connection (themes: connection, attachment, relationship, distressful disconnection)
- The thing I like about myself is . . . I have a best friend and we do lots of neat things togther.
- My mother and I . . . don't have enough time together, which I resent sometimes.

4. Voice of independence (themes: separation, independence, autonomy, individuality)
- When a child won't join in group activities . . . don't consider her an outsider, but someone who is an individual.
- When people are helpless . . . they should be helped to become independent.

5. Voice of care (themes: love, care, attention to needs, hurt, isolation)
- I am . . . someone who cares about people, and wishes for life to be better.
- I feel sorry . . . for my grandfather, who just lost his wife after being married for 45 years.

6. Voice of justice (themes: fairness, justice, equality, freedom from oppression)
- A good mother . . . will listen to her child's opinion, and consider it too.
- Women are lucky because . . . we have some equal rights, but not entirely equal.

The initial analysis involved a comparison of the two cohort groups of adolescent girls, but did not involve any longitudinal data. The following table (see Table 9.2) lists the means and standard deviations in the SCT data for the 7th grade and 10th-grade girls.

Because samples were relatively small and we had no directional hypotheses, the differences in the groups were tested with a series of two-tailed t-tests. The 10th-grade girls responded with significantly more themes about care and connection ($t[100] = 2.28, p = .05$) than were present in the seventh graders' sentence completions ($t(100) = 2.54, p = .01$). Additionally, ego development was moderately to highly correlated with these two voices (.72 with care and .58 with connection) for the two samples

TABLE 9.2
Menas and Standard Deviations of Voices in Girls' SCT Responses

| | 7th Graders | | 10th Graders | |
	M	SD	M	SD
Resistance	6.23	1.52	4.77	1.08
Capitulation	3.94	1.63	5.89	1.15
Connection	5.47	2.02	7.12	1.14
Independence	4.39	1.76	4.94	1.44
Care	5.89	1.47	7.28	2.08
Justice	6.37	2.16	6.66	2.39

Note. 7th graders: $n = 38$. 10th graders: $n = 64$.

as a single group. However, there were negligible and nonsignificant differences in the justice and independence themes for the two groups, and (correlations with ego development were respectively only .09 and .12). The themes of resistance and capitulation showed striking reversals with increasing age. The seventh graders' sentence completions showed significantly more themes of resistance, self-assertion, self-confidence, and self-respect than did the tenth graders' responses ($t[100] = 3.32$, $p = .01$). Conversely, themes of capitulation to norms of conventional feminine behavior, including self-doubt and self-abnegation, were significantly higher for the tenth grade group ($t[100] = 3.95$, $p = .01$).

A qualitative, thematic analysis revealed two patterns in girls' psychological development: on the one hand, a clear progression in development along the lines of Loevinger's ego development theory; and on the other hand, a struggle for voice and self knowledge, and a loss of psychological resilience.[2] The quantitative and qualitative comparative analysis of girls' sentence completions pointed to a pattern of losses in the older group that did not fit a hierarchical stage description of development. An alternative model of development would consider both gains and losses in development over time. What was striking in the analysis of these data was that some voices appeared to drop dramatically as the girls matured, whereas others grew stronger or more elaborate. Evidence that a voice of resistance was on the wane while themes of capitulation were increasing by midadolescence, suggested that there were changes in voice that could be identified reliably—and related to progression or regression in ego development.

---

[2]The qualitative analysis was conducted in collaboration with Carol Gilligan and was funded by the American Association of University Women and the Spencer foundation.

Study Two

What are changing self-conceptions for girls in adolescence as revealed by ego development trajectories? In order to answer this second research question, I was interested in following the trajectories of development for these girls, using their longitudinal ego development scores. The girls had been followed for 3 years (respectively in 7th, 8th, and 9th grades, and in 10th, 11th, and 12th grades). We chose to focus on the broadest range of possible changes, looking at the 7th graders again in 9th grade, and the 10th graders again in 12th grade. Using three trajectories of ego development (progression, stability, and regression), it became clear that the girls' ego development trajectories varied widely throughout adolescence. Using a sign test to see if decreases in ego development at two points in time were significant, I found that a significant number of girls in each of the two groups had regressed in ego development ($p < .05$). Nineteen of 38 girls regressed at least one level between the 7th and 9th grades, and 35 of 64 girls regressed between the 10th and 12th grades.

Loevinger also found that a significant number of college women (but not men) regressed in ego development in her longitudinal sample (Loevinger et al., 1985). What might explain this repeated pattern in girls' and young women's ego development? If the SCT picked up changes in girls' responses marking a struggle with cultural conventions, as a purely thematic analysis of the sentence stem responses had shown, then might the movement through the conventional and postconventional stages of ego development be particularly fraught for girls? Were some educationally privileged girls (a characteristic of both the Loevinger sample and our sample) facing such strong cultural pressures to conform in adolescence that, in effect, they were moving from a relatively simple but critical perspective on conventions at early adolescence into a capitulation to conventions at mid- and late adolescence? To answer these questions we turned to the longitudinal interview data.

Study Three

In a third study, we explored particular changes in girls' conceptions of relationships in the annual interviews of the two cohort groups of adolescents previously discussed in order to illuminate the finding of regression in ego development on the SCT (Rogers et al., 1993). How do girls who regressed in ego development consider relationships during adolescence? We wondered if and how their construction of relationships affected their psychological well being. In other words, might some changes in the kinds of distress they experienced in relationships help to explain their regression in ego development? Initially, we faced a methodological problem: how to reliably identify signs of psychological distress and psychological resilience in girls' narratives about themselves and their relationships. We also sought to understand in what ways the themes of voice revealed in girls' private written responses to the SCT in study one might be similar to and different from their interview responses, which reflected a social and dialogic process.

Drawing on experience interpreting girls' interviews and on developmental findings (Brown, 1989; Rogers, 1987a), we outlined signs of psychological distress and resilience in a pilot sample. We then chose to focus on the interviews of the girls who had regressed in ego development, to see if we might better understand their developmental struggles. Using the voice-centered method (Brown et al., 1988; Brown & Gilligan, 1992; Gilligan et al., 1990), we read each girl's first- and third-year interview three different times.

The first time through the text, we read or listened for *self*: the voice of the I speaking in the text, attending to recurrent words or images, inconsistencies, revisions and absences in the stories told, as well as shifts in first-, second-, and third-person voice.

The second time through, we read for a *voice of psychological distress*, garnering evidence of the ways the girl spoke painfully about (a) capitulation to debilitating conventions of conventional female behavior, and (b) evidence of denial or psychological resistance to knowing her own thoughts and feelings.

The third time through, we read the interviews for a *voice of psychological resilience*, searching for evidence of an active and sometimes politically informed resistance to restrictive gender-role stereotypes, and for evidence of speaking about genuine relationships in which girls felt free to voice their real thoughts and feelings. Comparisons of each of two readers' independent interpretations of the presence of these voices in 20 examples of narration yielded an agreement of 92% (Kappa = .88).

These voices were not conceptualized as mutually exclusive. In other words, the same text could be interpreted in more than one way. We did not select parts of the text to exemplify a voice in the actual data analysis, but followed a single voice throughout the entire interview. However, examples of the voices of psychological distress and psychological resilience drawn from the interviews are presented here to give some indication of how we actually interpreted interview passages (Table 9.3).

Following the three interpretive readings of each set of longitudinal interviews, we wrote case summaries which included examples from the various categories of voices and notes on how prevalent they were in a girl's interviews over time. We also culled examples of the voice readings

TABLE 9.3
Illustrated Examples of the Voices of Psychological Distress and Resilience

---

Voice of psychological distress:

When my brother is around and he is talking to my parents, you kind of get the feeling that they're listening to him and neither of them are listening to me . . . it kind of bothers me . . . but, I don't know, my brother either he had a greater problem, it was because he had a problem or something, they were probably trying to concentrate on what he was trying to say and then I was telling them something, it wasn't as important. (Janet, age 13)

Voice of psychological resilience:

If I have something to say that's in my heart, you know, and I think it's right, I speak up . . . I got that from my mother. My mother, I've always heard my mother speak up to what's wrong and what's right, and even it it's hard to say, you know, she's been like that and it sort of grew on me. (Andrea, age 15)

---

by grade level and followed the girls in their cohort groups over time. From this analysis, we noted certain commonalities among girls who had regressed in ego development between the 7th and 9th grades, and two distinct patterns among the girls who regressed between the 10th and 12th grades. It is not possible to summarize the details of our analysis in this paper (see Rogers et al., 1993), so I point out only the most striking changes we found.

As seventh graders, many of the girls impressed us as unusually lively, intelligent, and vital. Many of the girls shifted back and forth between a clear resistance to conventions of "good girl" behavior and an undoing of their own struggles to know and name their own experiences in their relationships, often introduced by the phrases "I mean" or "I don't know." As seventh graders, the girls spoke of the necessity to protect themselves sometimes by not speaking, particularly as they imagined shocked or avoidant responses from others. By the ninth grade, much of their vitality and open resistance seemed watered down. The girls had entered highly privatized relationships, relationships where confidentiality became the most frequently mentioned basis for trust. At the same time, they spoke about frequent betrayals of trust and the impossibility of speaking genuinely, not so much to protect themselves, but in order to protect others from being hurt. A process of self-silencing had become automatic for many of the girls, and this self-silencing was justified as selfless caring for others and often accompanied by signs of psychological distress—complaints of inexplicable moods, feelings of depression and exhaustion, and an expressed wish to escape or go away from the situations with which they found themselves confronted. Although this was a common pattern, the girls appeared to be doing well in school and maintaining relationships, and only two girls (5% of the sample) revealed distress to such a degree that we wondered if they were clinically depressed or experiencing severe dissociation.

Among the girls we followed from 10th to 12th grade, we saw two distinct developmental patterns. As 10th graders, these girls clearly subscribed to many of the conventions of maturity and success espoused by their parents and private girls' school—they wanted to be young superwomen, to do everything superbly well, and not to inconvenience anyone or hurt or disturb anyone, even if this meant suppressing their own needs. They were acutely aware of others' expectations and were willing to engage in relationships the girls themselves described as shallow or false. Some girls also deliberately hid their strengths from boys—in order to keep boys interested, they explained. Most of these girls continued the pattern of pleasing others and more deeply internalized conventions between the 10th through 12th grade, although there were bursts of protest about the demands and expectations of others, or suddenly expressed wishes that someone could break through the facades they had created and really care for them. Another smaller group of girls (8 of the 35 who had regressed) revealed a different pattern of development, however. These girls spoke with candor and complexity about their relationships throughout adolescence in the 12th grade. They were self-reflective and startlingly honest about what they saw and felt from day to day. At times they were openly irreverent about the values and norms of their school. This small group of resistors of the status quo was comprised of girls of color, working-class girls, and girls who hinted at family violence and abuse. Other girls in the group shared those characteristics. What was unique in this group was the fact that each girl described a vital confiding relationship in her life, most often with a woman, whether a mother or teacher or adult friend.

The way we understood the phenomenon of a regression in ego development among adolescent girls depended on discerning these patterns from our interpretive analyses of their longitudinal interviews. We randomly chose five girls from each cohort group who did not regress in ego development to comprise a small comparison group. We did not hear the strong struggle to know one's own thoughts and feelings and to actively resist social expectations, nor did we see the same degree of capitulation and the undoing of self-knowledge among those girls, nor the clear signs of psychological distress.

Thus, the regression in ego development we found may be interpreted in light of girls' active struggles in their relationships with mixed messages about conventions of growing into young women—conventions that would have them claim a sense of personal authority and compete scholastically on the one hand, while also modulating their strong feelings, foregoing their own wishes, dismissing their perceptions, and silencing themselves in the name of caring for and not hurting or disturbing others. This struggle was so fraught for some girls, we surmised, that the movement through the stages of ego development was diverted or turned back for a period of time during their adolescence. Of course, this is only one plausible explanation, and the changes in voice that we identified could be seen themselves as evidence of progression toward an ultimately more complex understanding of relationships. Further research on the relationship between ego development and changes in young women's voices, particularly beyond adolescence, would clarify some of these issues.

CONCLUSION

I explored some of the methodological and theoretical possibilities of combining two approaches to studying development here, and argued for the utility of drawing on the strengths of each approach to enlarge our understanding of ego development and relational development in adolescent girls. This integrative approach extends a well-developed body of literature on ego development theory, and offers a way to understand groups that are not well-represented in psychological theory and research.

Since the 1980s, we have seen an increasing call to pay attention to the different developmental vulnerabilities and strengths of both girls and boys, children and adolescents of color, and young people growing up in different cultures and historical times (Feldman & Elliot, 1990)—yet our methods of research and basic assumptions about human development do not commonly accommodate these concerns. Many stage theories of human development rely on assumptions that development is hierarchical, growth proceeds in an invariant sequence, and changing structures represent universal forms of thought. Recently these assumptions were challenged and alternatives explored. For example, developmentalists have begun to use ecological methods specifying the particularities of different contexts of development (Bronfenbrenner, 1992) as vital alternatives to studying development. These alternatives raise key questions about epistemology, methodology, and definitions of development for research psychologists. What is the philosophical basis for a particular theory? In what ways do our methods inform and limit our theories? How do we define human development? The methods used in the three studies presented in this chapter are intended to extend these questions into the area of personality development, and specifically ego development theory.

III

RELATED DEVELOPMENTAL MODELS

10

Ego Development and the Ethical Voices of Justice and Care: An Eriksonian Interpretation

John Snarey
Emory University

"One of the most troublesome things about current stage theories is their proliferation," Jane Loevinger (1987b) remarked. Going on to discuss stage theories of moral development and ego development, among others, she concluded that "if the stages really reflect a common 'deep structure,' the stages of those variables should all proceed in tandem." She then asked, "If they are not all evidence of the same structure, how many structures are there, and what should be the relations among them? Those are among the questions remaining to be answered in this field of research" (p. 242). In this chapter, I apply Loevinger's questions to the relationship of ego and moral development.

Developmental researchers often study the relationship of ego and ethical maturity, usually using the models and measures advanced by Jane Loevinger (1966a, 1994) and Lawrence Kohlberg (1958; Kohlberg, Boyd, & Levine, 1990). Most studies have focused on the relationship between ego development and moral development, although some studies have also attempted to examine moral maturity as a strand of development within ego development (for reviews, see Loevinger, 1979a; Lee & Snarey, 1988). Yet the complex relationship between ego and moral growth has remained stubbornly difficult to unravel. To clarify the problem, it will be helpful to begin by reviewing how Loevinger and Kohlberg conceptualized the relationship of ego and ethical development.

BACKGROUND

"Ego," according to Erik Erikson (1964), is "an age-old term which in the scholastics stood for the unity of body and soul, and in philosophy in general for the *permanency* of conscious experience" (p. 147). Jane Loevinger's model of ego development is similar in some respects to such a pre-Freudian conception of the ego as well as with Erikson's own post-Freudian model. Loevinger (1976), that is, used the concept of ego development in a holistic sense to refer to the process and course of an individual's "striving to master, to integrate, to make sense of experience" (p. 59). "That human beings, developing, go through an ordered sequence" of stages in ego development "is the premise" of Loevinger's theory (Blasi, 1976, p. 45). Loevinger (1994) postulates that ego development proceeds by stages through an invariant hierarchical sequence characterized by qualitative changes in complexity as the developing ego integrates various "strands" of personality: "motives, moral judgment, . . . cognitive complexity, interpersonal integration, and above all, ways of perceiving oneself and others" (p. 5). Ego development is thus differentiated, with each strand performing its role, but ego development as a whole is a structural unity, inseparable for analysis by individual domain or function.

No "grand" theory is always consistent, of course, as Loevinger's reviewers consistently pointed out (cf. Blanck, 1976; Broughton & Zahaykevich, 1977, 1988; Noam, 1993). For instance, Loevinger described "ego development" in the following ways: synonymous with the development of the self, sharply differentiated from the development of the self, encompassing the strand of self development, and close to the Eriksonian concept of ego identity development (cf. Loevinger, 1976, pp. 375, 393, 445; 1984, pp. 49–51, 57–58; 1986, pp. 187–188; Loevinger & Blasi, 1991, pp. 150–151; Loevinger & Knoll, 1983, pp. 202–203). Much of this confusion may be more apparent than real, however, if we judge by the clarity of Loevinger's overall life work and accept her right to engage in what she studies—developmental change. What Loevinger clearly has had in mind is the integrity and wholeness of ego development.

Loevinger (1976) viewed "moral development" as a facet of the single coherent process of ego development. Moral development, that is, is understood (1979b) as a "more restricted realm than ego development" and, thus, ego development "encompasses the complexity of moral judgment" as one of the primary strands of development within ego development (p. 3). Loevinger noted two expectations regarding the empirical relationship between ego and moral development: When comparing strands within the unity of the developing ego, one should not be able to establish statistically differentiated factors or to otherwise find different strands showing significantly different or inconsistent courses of development (Loevinger, 1979a, 1987b). When analyzing the relationship between ego and moral development stage scores, the minimal empirical expectation is that they should show a significant, positive, and moderately strong correlation (Loevinger, 1979a, 1984, 1987b, 1993a). Loevinger has not been explicit beyond these expectations, perhaps because she believes that ego development is neither separate nor separable from moral development (Loevinger, 1983). Nevertheless, one can note additional implicit expectations. The logic underlying the bulk of Loevinger's writings appears to lead to *ego primacy*—a decalage relationship in which ego development would be expected to be higher than, or equal to, moral development because, in effect, ego development functions to lead or place a ceiling on moral development. Some fragments of Loevinger's writings, such as her comments on William Perry's model of intellectual and ethical development (Loevinger, 1983), however, imply that the leading edge of growth is variable—new growth will occur first in ego development for some individuals, in moral development for other individuals, and in still some other developmental domain for still other persons. In this approach, however, no mechanism of development across ego and moral stages is provided.

Lawrence Kohlberg's (1979, 1983, 1984) perspective on the relationship between ego and moral development also evolved as new theoretical and empirical studies appeared. Kohlberg (1986) concluded that the two sets of stages are "partially isomorphic"—that is, rough but significant parallels exist between virtually all of the stages in the ego and moral schemas (p. 503). The correspondence can be seen, for instance, when Loevinger's stage I–3[1] (conformity to external rules and preoccupation with appearance and social acceptability) is compared to Kohlberg's Stage M–3 (typically motivated by a need to live up to what is expected by people close to you and to be seen by others as a good person). Despite similarities at this level of comparison, however, Kohlberg (1979, 1986) viewed the two schemas as far from identical. He noted that the two theories make different claims regarding the nature of the constructs, the relationship between the constructs, and development across stages. Kohlberg's model, for instance, applies most directly to issues of moral decision making and action; Loevinger's model specifies content that is broadly related to, among other things, interpersonal and cognitive styles. For Kohlberg, the strand of ego development Loevinger calls cognitive style points to the

---

[1]The notation for ego levels used in this chapter corresponds to the notation of the first edition of the scoring manual for the WUSCT (Loevinger & Wessler, 1970; Redmore, Loevinger, & Tamashiro, 1978). The current edition of the scoring manual (Hy & Loevinger, 1996) introduced several changes. See the Appendix to the introductory chapter of this volume for a comparison between the previous and the current system.

domain of cognitive development as defined by Piaget and others. Loevinger's strand of interpersonal style and self-concerns indicates, for Kohlberg, the domain of social cognition studied by Robert Selman and others. And Loevinger's strand of impulse control and character suggests, in part, the course of moral judgment development. Thus, in Kohlberg's (1986) words, "Moral development is one aspect or component" of ego development (p. 502). Kohlberg concluded that the cognitive development strand was more general than, and served as the foundation for, moral structures, and that cognitive and moral structures, in turn, were more general than, and served as a foundation for, ego structures.

Kohlberg's interpretation leads to an empirical expectation of *moral primacy* in the relationship between moral and ego development because development in a more generally fundamental and prior domain is necessary, but insufficient, for the corresponding level of development in a broader and more inclusive secondary domain. This decalage allows the various strands of development to be separated out and empirically isolated. Kohlberg, thus, hypothesized a sequence of necessary-but-not-sufficient relationships between developmental domains: He noted that attaining particular stages of cognitive development was empirically shown to be a necessary but not sufficient condition for attaining corresponding social perspective-taking stages, and that cognitive and social perspective-taking development,were shown to precede the equivalent level of moral stage development. Kohlberg speculated that moral development may function as a necessary but not sufficient foundation for the developmental construction of corresponding ego stage structures (for reviews, see Kohlberg, 1983, 1986; Loevinger, 1986).

The form of sequencing between ego and moral development stages is important because it implies an empirically observable mechanism of development across stages of the two systems. Ego primacy and moral primacy each assume that stages of one construct are asymmetrically related to stages of the second construct. The most conclusive evidence for ego primacy, short of regular and frequent monitoring of moral and ego stage change, is demonstrating that, at any single point in time, all or most research participants have an ego stage equal to or exceeding the corresponding moral stage (or vice versa, for moral primacy).

It may now be possible to bring a measure of resolution to this controversy. In this chapter, I summarize the major study to date of the relationship between moral and ego development, report results of a new study of the relationship of justice and care reasoning within ego development, and present an Eriksonian interpretation of the general findings.

STUDY 1: ETHICAL DEVELOPMENT
AND EGO DEVELOPMENT

Previous studies addressing the empirical relationship between ego and moral development stages produced conflicting portraits (for review, see Lee & Snarey, 1988). Difficulties in defining the connection were due primarily to three factors: disparate methods of assessing ego and moral growth, small sample sizes, and difficulty taking into consideration moderating variables (e.g., age, gender, education). Loren Lee and I (1988), attempted to address these three factors by conducting a comprehensive secondary analysis of the combined data from previous studies.

Research Method

Sample

We obtained the individual case records from nine prior investigations that had administered both Loevinger's Sentence Completion Test (SCT) and Kohlberg's Moral Judgment Interview (MJI). Our composite sample included 567 persons. Of these, 130 people had two or more longitudinally gathered sets of scores, giving a total of 787 concurrent measurements of ego and moral development; 668 of the 787 case records included complete demographic background information. The study participants ranged in age from 11 to 82 years; 47% were adolescents aged 11 to 18 years, 33% were young adults between aged 19 to 29 years, 9% were middle-adulthood participants aged 30 to 49 years, and 11% were older adults aged 50 to 82 years. Overall, females made up 65% of the study participants. The adolescent, young adult, and middle-adult age groups each included a similar majority of female participants, whereas the older adult group was equally divided between males and females. A majority of 53% of the study participants had attended or graduated from college, compared with 41% who had a high school education or less, and 6% who held a postgraduate degree.

Measures

SCT ego development stage scores and MJI moral development stage scores, as reported here, were calculated according to Loevinger's and Kohlberg's standard scoring algorithms. In addition, two sets of indices were calculated to examine the relationship between ego (I) and moral (M) stage development (Rogosa, 1983).

I–M Continuous Index. This index provides a quantitative measure of the separation in ego and moral scores. It is the result of subtracting a person's moral stage score from his or her ego stage score (I minus M). Based on the logical similarities between specific ego and moral stages (Kohlberg, 1983; Kohlberg & Kramer, 1969; cf. Krebs & Hesteren, 1994; Lee & Snarey, 1988), we used the following 9-point scales for both models: 1 = M–1 and I–2; 2 = M–1/2 and I–2/Delta; 3 = M–2 and I–Delta; 4 = M–2/ 3 and I–Delta/3; 5 = M–3 and I–3; 6 = M–3/4 and I–3/4; 7 = M–4 and I–4; 8 = M–4/5 and I–4/5; 9 = M–5 and I–5. Thus, a single unit in the I–M continuum indicates a half-stage difference (e.g., a score of 2.0 means that the ego score exceeds the moral score by one full stage).

I:M Categorical Ranking. This index categorizes the relationship more succinctly by showing, for a specific person at a particular testing time, whether the ego stage is higher than the moral stage (I > M category), is equivalent to the moral stage (I = M category), or is lower than the moral stage (M > I category).

Results and Discussion

The data provide clear evidence that ego development and moral development are empirically related to one another across the life span. We found that when ego and moral stage scores were plotted, they extended in a relatively broad diagonal from lower ego and moral stage scores to higher ego and moral stage scores, yielding a strikingly high correlation ($r = .65, p < .0001$). Stage 3/4 was the modal stage for both ego development ($n = 263$) and moral development ($n = 260$), and 101 people scored at stage 3/4 on both measures. What did not emerge from the data was evidence for a consistent one-to-one correspondence between stages in the two systems. When both whole and half-stage positions in both models were juxtaposed, for instance, approximately 13% of the cases were scored at directly corresponding ego and moral stages. When only whole-stage parallels were juxtaposed, approximately 28% of the cases were scored at corresponding stages. When other possible models of correspondence between specific stages in the two models were used, they did not improve the percentage of persons who scored at corresponding stages. Measurement error, of course, cannot account for the lack of correspondence between scores for 72% or more of the cases. Lee and I concluded that the conceptual parallels between certain ego and moral stages falls short of an empirical stage-per-stage identity. The association of ego and moral stage scores simply does not support a rigid overall stage-by-stage isomorphism.

Gender (coded as femaleness) showed a low but significant correlation with ego stages ($r = .22, p < .0001$), indicating that women were somewhat

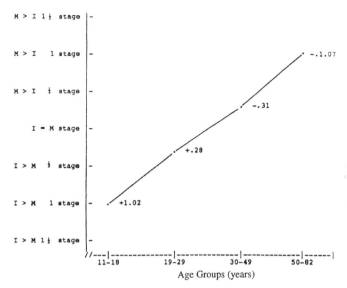

Ego-Moral Index (I minus M)

```
 M > I  1½ stage  |-

 M > I   1 stage  |-                                         • -.1.07

 M > I    ½ stage |-

 I = M stage      |-

 I > M    ½ stage |-                    • +.28

 I > M   1 stage  |-      ./ +1.02

 I > M  1½ stage  |-
                  //---|--------------|--------------|--------------|------|
                      11-18          19-29          30-49          50-82
                                  Age Groups (years)
```

FIG. 10.1. Changes in the relationship between moral (M) and ego (I) stage scores as a linear function of age across the life span.

more likely to have higher ego scores than men. There was no significant correlation between gender and moral stage scores. There was, however, a significant gender difference in the ego–moral relationship. Men in the sample were more likely to display a mean index that was negative (indicating a higher moral stage), whereas women were more likely to display a mean index that was positive (indicating a higher ego stage). These results are consistent with the idea that there are gender differences in ego development and in the ego–moral relationship, and with the weight of the literature indicating that women and men do not differ significantly in moral judgment development (cf. Brabeck, 1983).

Age was moderately correlated with ego stage ($r = .31$, $p < .0001$) and highly correlated with moral stage ($r = .54$, $p < .0001$). Age had a strong and significant effect on the ego–moral relationship. When case records were partitioned by age periods, adolescents ($n = 311$), young adults ($n = 221$), middle-aged adults ($n = 61$), and older adults ($n = 75$) emerged as significantly different in terms of their I:M categorical ranking. Most adolescents and young adults demonstrated an I > M relationship; those in middle adulthood most frequently showed an I = M relationship; in later adulthood, cases were concentrated primarily in the M > I bracket.

Figure 10.1 shows that the age effect continued when these groups were compared on the I–M Continuous Index: The group means are significantly different during adolescence and early adulthood versus middle adulthood and versus later adulthood. For both categorical and quantitative contrasts, a linear trend analysis was significant. This suggests that, with other factors held constant, changes in the relationship between ego and moral stage scores may be predicted, in part, as a linear function of age. Figure 10.1 also vividly demonstrates that there is not a universal sequence in ego and moral correspondence across the entire life span. The data, that is, do not support either an ego primacy or moral primacy hypothesis. Rather, it appears that for earlier periods in the life cycle, ego development is the first order of business, and that for later periods, moral development becomes predominant. These patterns remained stable even after taking into consideration known variations between the combined studies in measurement-related factors such as test administration and scoring reliability.

Multiple regression analysis was used to separate the contribution of individual subject variables to explaining the variance in ego development, moral development, and the ego–moral relationship. When ego stage is entered as a dependent variable in a stepwise regression procedure, age, then sex, and then education enter the equation and together account for 15.8% of the stage variance. When moral stage is the dependent variable in a similar stepwise regression procedure, age and then education enter the equation and together account for 37.5% of the stage variance; the contribution of gender was not significant. When the I–M Continuous Index was entered as a dependent variable in a stepwise regression procedure, age, then sex, then years of education accounted for 6.2%, 4.6%, and 1.6% of the variance successively, for a total of 12.4%.

Combining these cross-sectional analyses with parallel analyses of the smaller longitudinal subsample (cf. Lee & Snarey, 1988), it is it possible to present a tentative developmental pathway that a typical (modal) person will take with regard to the ego–moral relationship:

During adolescence, the typical youth is likely to score at an ego stage higher than her or his moral stage (hence, a high positive I–M Index). This is true for both genders, but more pronounced for females. Furthermore, although adolescents may progress to new stages in ego and moral development, typical adolescents, male and female, are unlikely to change their initial I:M status (i.e., they will not experience a categorical switch during this period).

In the early adulthood years (ages 19 to 29), the modal individual is likely to change I:M categories at least once; a complete "reversal" would not be uncommon (e.g., a switch from I > M to M > I). This is true for both sexes, although males are twice as likely to change I:M status. Collectively, the net direction of all those changing I:M categories will be towards the M > I pole. The modal individual, however, will still remain at I > M or

I = M; this is especially true for women. A young adult who has an advanced postgraduate education, however, also has a clear tendency, regardless of gender, to move towards the M > I side of the continuum.

In middle adulthood (ages 30 to 49), the modal man or woman will likely be matched very well on ego and moral stage (i.e., the I–M Index will be close to zero). Similarly, the modal man or woman is also unlikely to change his or her I:M status. The middle adult years, according to our data, are characterized by balance and stability.

In the more mature years of adulthood (age 50+ in our sample), the ego and moral development scores for both the modal man and woman will most likely come to rest at the M > I pole of the ego-moral continuum. For modal individuals of both sexes, the chances of having an M > I status, and a larger negative I–M Continuous Index, also increase with higher levels of educational attainment. The mature years are characterized by new growth in the moral domain.

STUDY 2: ETHICAL DEVELOPMENT
WITHIN EGO DEVELOPMENT

What is the relationship of moral and ego development in terms of the moral voices of justice and care within ego development? Loevinger's model, of course, is based on an assumed unity of various strands of development. The empirical evidence for structural unity is usually understood to mean that people's responses to test items will be internally consistent or homogeneous. Several studies found a single general factor or underlying unity across sentence stem responses scored for ego development stage. Loevinger's (1979a) review of these studies clearly acknowledges, however, that such statistical analyses actually provide no evidence to contradict the thesis that there are separable lines of development because "the source of that unity . . . is methodological," that is, it is a product of the method used to construct the scoring manual (p. 286). States Loevinger (1993b), "there is no proof of the indivisibility of ego development" (p. 61).

Annie Rogers (1987) has developed a method for separately assessing the moral development voices of justice and care in SCT and, therefore, of potentially clarifying the relationship of moral development within ego development. "At the heart of the ethic of care," Rogers (1987) stated, is "the ability to perceive and respond to the needs of others in order to prevent hurt or harm." In contrast, Rogers continued, "the necessity to treat others equally and to judge them fairly lies at the heart of the ethic of justice" (pp. 1–2; cf. Gilligan, 1982). Rogers selected 14 items from each form of the SCT and then constructed a content rating system for scoring responses to these stems for the voice of justice and for the voice of care. She demonstrated that it is possible to use the SCT to measure in a reliable manner the frequency with which a person uses each voice. The scoring system also had acceptable construct validity for research purposes. Rogers (1987a), for instance, showed that justice orientation scores and care orientation scores were significantly correlated with independent Gilligan-based ratings of interviews for the same voice but not with interview ratings for the opposite voice.

Research Method

Sample

A sample of kibbutz members was used to study the moral voices of justice and care within ego development. The participants included 56 adults (26 women and 30 men) who ranged in age from 51 to 57 years, with a mean age of 53. All were original founders of a kibbutz or collective community in northern Israel. Their community is a member of the National Kibbutz Federation, the federation most consistent with the traditional socialist values upon which kibbutz systems of production and consumption are based. (For a more detailed description of the sample, see Snarey & Lydens, 1990.)

Measures

The research instruments included Loevinger's SCT and Kohlberg's MJI. The participants were tested or interviewed individually in their homes.

Ego Development. Each person completed Loevinger's SCT (Form 11–68), which includes 36 incomplete sentence stems. Loevinger's standard scoring manual (Loevinger, Wessler, & Redmore, 1970) and standard ogive scoring algorithm (Loevinger & Wessler, 1970) were used to assign each protocol a total protocol rating on an ordinal scale ranging from 1 (Stage 2) to 9 (Stage 6). All interviews were scored by an expert rater, and 15 randomly selected protocols were rescored by a second expert rater. Both raters were blind to all information about the study participants other than the fact that they were kibbutz residents; the interrater reliability coefficient was .85.

Care and Justice. The SCT was also scored for justice and care using Rogers' (1987a, 1988) manual. To ensure raters do not assume that the two moral orientations are mutually exclusive categories, Rogers' system includes two submanuals—the *Care Orientation Manual* and the *Justice Orientation Manual*, which are used independently. Rogers' scoring system thus yields two scores: frequency of stems completed with care reasoning, and frequency of stems completed with justice reasoning. One of the test items, for instance, is the incomplete sentence stem: "A good father...." Completing this stem with ". . . is loving, kind, and available for his children" would be rated as an example of care reasoning. Stating that "A good father . . . has a duty to bring up his children to be responsible" would be rated as reflecting a justice orientation, and " . . . is one like mine" would be rated as unscorable. Because Rogers designated 14 stems as potentially scorable for either, both, or neither justice and care, both scores may range from 0 to 14. These frequency counts are "content rating systems of justice and care thinking" that do not attempt to distinguish specific stages of moral development (Rogers, 1987a, p. 26).

For this study, two raters were trained in the use of Rogers' manual and scoring procedures. Each then independently scored 28 sets of sentence stems from Rogers' scoring practice cases, 2 each for the 14 stems used in this study. The interrater reliability coefficients, for both justice and care scores, were always greater than or equal to .82 when comparing the scores assigned by the two raters and when comparing either rater and Rogers' scores for the same practice stems. Each rater, blinded to all information about the study participants, then independently scored one half of the sentence completion tests included in this study, plus an overlapping set of 15 SCTs for reliability assessment. The interrater reliability coefficients were .73 for justice scores and .75 for care scores.

Moral Judgment Development. Each person was administered Kohlberg's MJI (Form A), which includes three moral dilemmas. To ascertain the participants' level of moral reasoning, we scored the interviews with the standardized scoring manual (Colby & Kohlberg, 1987). The interviews were randomly divided between two blinded expert raters who assigned each interview a global moral stage score from Kohlberg's ordinal scale ranging from 1 (Stage 1) to 9 (Stage 5). Fifteen of the interviews were randomly selected and independently scored by both expert raters; the interrater reliability coefficient was .92.

Results and Discussion

The kibbutz founders' justice scores ranged from 2 to 11, with a mean frequency of 6.2, and their care scores ranged from 0 to 12, with a mean frequency of 6.0. The care and justice scores were significantly correlated ($r = .49$, $p < .001$). Nearly all adults (98%) made some use of both moral voices, and a majority (77%) had frequency scores of 4 or higher for both orientations. Only 16% had identical justice and care scores, but this figure rose to 50% when results from those whose frequency scores were within 1 point of each other were included. Among all those with nonidentical justice and care scores, a relatively similar number had higher justice than care scores (45%) compared with those who had higher care than justice scores (55%). Overall, these findings show that for adult kibbutz founders, the ethic of justice and the ethic of care are highly interrelated, but there is no decalage or divergent relationship between justice and care within ego development.

There were no significant gender differences regarding preference for using an ethic of justice or care. A series of ANOVA procedures also indicated that there were no significant interaction effects between gender and either ego or moral development in the use of either an ethic of justice or an ethic of care. In contrast to Rogers' (1987a) finding that adolescents (aged 12 to 20) showed a notable degree of gender-related discord between the voices of justice and care, the older adult women and men in this study orchestrated the two voices with a notable degree of harmony. These findings are consistent with gender-by-age trends previously reported for ego development (Cohn, 1991).

The participants' scores on Loevinger's SCT showed a positive and statistically significant linear relationship with both care orientation scores ($r = .39, p < .01$) and justice orientation scores ($r = .31, p < .05$). This finding lends some support to the idea that Loevinger's measure taps both justice and care and that the frequency of use of justice and care orientations may be understood as an approximate index of developmental maturity. It is helpful to place the present findings in the context of Rogers' (1987a) prior finding—that adolescent boys tend to use justice reasoning more than adolescent girls do, whereas adolescent girls tend to use care reasoning more than adolescent boys do.

The solid plot lines in Fig. 10.2 display the findings for justice reasoning in relation to ego development. It is notable that adult men and women, at all stages of ego development, used justice reasoning markedly more than did male or female adolescents in Rogers' study. As the solid plot lines in Fig. 10. 3 show, except for Stage 3, adult men and women also use care reasoning more frequently than do female or male adolescents at the same stage of ego development. There is apparently a maturational–experiential gain in moral development across the life span, even when ego stage is held constant. As adults age, that is, they may continue to mature in moral development without necessarily showing an equivalent increase in ego development, which provides further validation of the results of the previously summarized Lee and Snarey study.

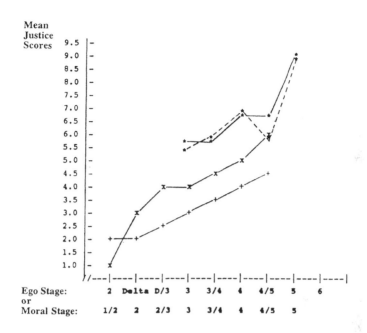

FIG. 10.2. Plot of mean justice scores on ego stage scores or moral stage scores for gender–age groups.

   ___ Adults; justice scores plotted with ego stages.

   *----*Adults; justice scores plotted with moral stages.

   x___x Male adolescents; justice scores plotted with ego stages (Rogers, 1987a).

   +___+ Female adolescents; justice scores plotted with ego stages (Rogers, 1987a).

The dashed plot lines in Figs. 10.2 and 10.3 show the complex relationship between Kohlberg's stages of moral development and Rogers' voices of justice and care reasoning. Because the relationship is not consistently linear, the correlation coefficients were weak and nonsignificant between moral development scores and both justice scores ($r = .16$) and care scores ($r = .17$). The dashed plot lines display clearly, however, that moral judgment stages are not statistically independent of either justice or care scores: There is a positive linear trend, followed by a sharp fall, which is again followed by a positive linear trend. This pattern can be quantitatively seen by comparing the correlation coefficients before the fall, with those during and after the fall. Moral development scores at the conventional stages (Stages 3, 3/4, and 4) are positively correlated with both justice scores ($r = .23$, $p = ns$) and care scores ($r = .36$, $p < .05$). During the transition from Stage 4 to Stage 4/5, however, moral development

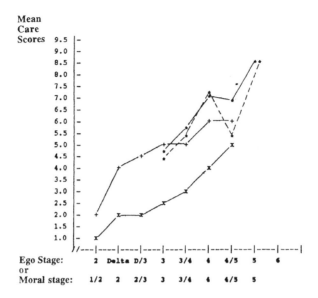

Mean
Care
Scores

FIG. 10.3. Plot of mean care scores on ego stage scores or moral stage scores
for gender–age groups.
   ___ Adults; care scores plotted with ego stages.
   *----*Adults; care scores plotted with moral stages.
   +___+ Female adolescents; care scores plotted with ego stages (Rogers, 1987a).
   x___x Male adolescents; care scores plotted with ego stages (Rogers, 1987a).

scores are negatively correlated with both justice scores ($r = -.22$) and care
scores ($r = -.32$). Then, at the postconventional segment of the plot line
(Stages 4/5 and 5), moral development scores are again positively but
more strongly correlated with both justice scores ($r = .50$) and care scores
($r = .45$). Moral development shows a somewhat stronger relationship
with care than with justice scores before and during the fall, but a somewhat
stronger relationship with justice than care scores after the fall. This pattern
modestly supports the idea that the voice of care can be heard within the
conventional stages of Kohlberg's model, whereas the voice of justice is
given primacy at the postconventional stages.
     The complex relationship of justice and care orientations with moral
development, in contrast to the linear relationship of justice and care with
ego development, supports the idea that moral and ego development can
be differentiated. In particular, the tendency of persons who scored at
Stage 4/5 of moral development to regress in the use of both care and
justice orientations, but for persons at Stage 4/5 of ego development not
to exhibit such declines, differentiates the models. It is noteworthy that

this apparent regression in relation to moral stage development is consistent with Kohlberg's unique conceptualization of one type of transition from Stage 4 to Stage 5 in moral development. Kohlberg (1973) originally noted that a few college students in his original sample appeared to regress to a form of moral relativism as they moved out of Stage 4 conventional moral reasoning but not yet into Stage 5 postconventional moral reasoning. He called this relativistic stage Stage 4 -1/2, to distinguish it from the typical transition Stage 4/5. Kohlberg (1984) subsequently moderated his understanding of Stage 4-1/2 as a unique transitional stage but he retained the idea that "some form of subjectivism or relativism is a necessary but not sufficient condition for movement to Stage 5 " (p. 440). The results of this study suggest that relativism (whether it be regarded as a temporary regression, a type of transition, or as a genuine stage in moral development) can characterize the movement from Stage 4 to Stage 5 during adulthood as well as during adolescence and it can characterize the moral voice of care as well as the voice of justice.

Those persons who had attained Stage 5 in ego development or moral development consistently demonstrated the highest levels and fullest synchronization of the ethical voices of justice and care (Figs. 10.2 and 10.3). This finding supports Rogers' (1987a) Gilligan-based claim that maturity involves, at least in part, "the ability to represent both moral orientations and sustain perspectives within each" (p. 54). It also would seem to illustrate Blasi's (1995) thesis that "morality and identity or the self-concept are separate psychological systems which only slowly, and sometimes imperfectly, come together and become integrated" (p. 229). Finally, the finding that a group of women and men who had founded an Israeli kibbutz showed a frequent and integrated use of both communitarian care and social justice orientations is consistent with prior research suggesting that kibbutz founders aimed to create a "caring and just community" (Snarey & Blasi, 1980).

AN ERIKSONIAN INTERPRETATION

The full developmental ripening of a human life requires the synchronization and integration of a stable identity and mature morality. Thus, it is not surprising that developmental researchers often study the relationship of ego and ethical maturity. I applied Loevinger's questions to the relationship of ego and moral stage development by using a composite sample spanning early adolescence to later adulthood (Study 1) and by placing the findings for adults within the context of prior findings for adolescents (Study 2). The data from both studies support Loevinger's and Kohlberg's common contention that ego development and moral development are significantly related to one another across the life span. In contrast, the data do not support a thesis of moral primacy (that is, ego development is not completely reducible to a dependent position in a moral–ego decalage relationship). The data also show the fallacy of an ego-primacy thesis and of the contention that ego development is all inclusive (that is, moral development does not behave as if it was simply a strand or facet of ego development).

Neither Kohlberg's nor Loevinger's prior theorizing about the ego–moral relationship predicts the intricate patterns documented by these two studies. How does one best interpret the complex relationship of moral development with and within ego development? The perspective of Erik H. Erikson (1950, 1964) provides a useful interpretative framework.

Loevinger, who was briefly a student of Erikson's at Berkeley (Loevinger, 1993b), also pointed to his chronicle of psychosocial development as the only psychoanalytic model of ego development compatible with her own (Loevinger, 1966b, 1986). As Loevinger (1986) stated, Erikson's use of the term *ego development*, "applying the term to development taking place throughout adolescence, is closer to our usage and incompatible with most other psychoanalytic usages" (p. 187; cf. 1976). Others also noted similarities between the process and course of ego identity formation in Erikson's model and ego development in Loevinger's model (cf. Blasi, 1988; Blasi & Milton, 1991; Vaillant, 1987). I would further venture to theorize that Erikson's more pluralistic and multifarious unifying ego is capable of making sense of the developmental patterns reported in this chapter.

First, the adolescent's preoccupation with identity achievement is consistent with achieving higher levels of ego development than with moral development. Ego identity formation, although a constant strand of development throughout life, is an overwhelming preoccupation during adolescence, and it is during this decade that SCT ego levels increase most steadily. It appears that, as adolescents search for a durable set of values on which they can base an inner sense of ego identity, boys tend to establish a favorable ratio of justice in relation to care and girls tend to establish a favorable ratio of care compared to justice. The origin of this difference is a matter of debate, of course, but it probably reflects the fact that these adolescents live in a gender-differentiated, male-dominated society. The voice of justice may have an initial elective affinity among privileged or dominant groups and the voice of care may have an initial elective affinity among nonadvantaged or subordinate groups (Snarey, 1995; Snarey, Friedman, & Blasi, 1986).

Second, during early adulthood, making greater strides in moral than in ego development is consistent with the characteristics Erikson assigns to this period—the fruit harvested from the achievement of identity is the virtue of fidelity, and the task of young adulthood is the realization of intimacy, which gives rise to the virtue of mature love. Fidelity and love, that is, both represent successive capacities for social–moral commitments that are freely made but ethically binding.

Third, the subsequent stability in ego and moral development, and in the ego–moral relationship, during middle adulthood corresponds to the seventh level in Erikson's model—generativity. Here the individual's focus shifts more strikingly from personal development to the development, care, and continuity of the next generation. It is an inherently conservative phase of life in the sense that the task is to pass on to other younger adults those values, ideas, and things one has come to value. Thus, consistent with the stability and balance of one's own development, the person's psychosocial virtue or ego strength is an ability to care for the development of others.

The moral dynamics of psychosocial transitions during mature adulthood are also evident. Although care and justice orientation scores among older adults followed a clear linear trend in relation to ego stages, care and justice orientation scores also showed a striking, although apparently temporary, decline in relation to Stage 4/5 of moral development. The MJIs of persons at Stage 4/5 suggested that their lower frequencies for both care and justice orientations generally reflected a conscious tension between their need to become more caring of and fair to themselves as individuals versus their need to continue caring for and protecting the rights of others. The apparent tension between individualistic, seemingly selfish behavior and communitarian, seemingly self-sacrificing behavior was also expressed in some moral dilemma discussions as a conscious philosophical tension about how and why one should live morally when the very "caring and just community" one has devoted one's life creating is still all too often unjust and uncaring. Here we see an expression of the Eriksonian struggle between integrity—acceptance of limits, finitude, and one's one and only life cycle—versus despair, a melancholic inability to accept life's finitude and the fact that one is now too old to try alternative life paths. Erikson defined this struggle as the primary polar tension of the eighth stage of the life cycle.

Finally, the older adult years are again characterized by new growth in moral development, whereas ego levels continue to remain relatively stable. As a decline in the use of care or justice orientations, for instance, despair was no longer evident among those persons who scored at Stage 5 of ego development or Stage 5 of moral development. This suggests that these persons successfully established a favorable ratio of ego integrity over ego despair. The sentence completions of these persons showed a level of complexity and discernment suggesting their lives also evidence the virtue Erikson assigns to maturity: wisdom. Arlin (1990) and Sprinthall and colleagues (Sprinthall, Reiman, & Thies-Sprinthall, 1993), for instance, conceptualized Eriksonian wisdom as a critical indicator of adult development in a way that is consistent with our findings on moral stage development. Erikson's model functions well as an integrative framework for the empirical relationship of moral and ego development.

The Eriksonian perspective raises the fundamental question of construct validity: What does the SCT really measure? Does it measure one strand of development or that which unifies the strands? The data presented in this chapter show that Loevinger's and Kohlberg's measures tap separable structures that, together, weave complexly intertwined developmental patterns. These patterns suggest that the SCT as deciphered by Loevinger's scoring system actually operationalizes a strand of ego development—ego identity, just as the Moral Judgment Interview as interpreted by Kohlberg's scoring system operationalizes a strand of ego development—ethical development. From an Eriksonian perspective, this is not a cause for despair. Ego identity and generative ethics, for instance, both have a place of integrity in personality development across the life span.

Any study must balance the knowledge accrued against the questions remaining to be explored. The present research indicates that without understanding the contribution of factors such as age and gender it is difficult to objectively portray the ego–moral relationship as it changes across a person's life span. Yet, chronological age provides only the barest outline for explaining development because it stands for a life of significant influences and experiences, such as family history (Hauser, Powers, & Noam, 1991), workplace experiences (Snarey & Lydens, 1990), and socially defined seasons of life (Neugarten, 1979). Similarly, there are a multitude of major life influences and experiences behind gender, such as variations in biological maturation (Cohn, 1991), family relations (Lasser & Snarey, 1989), and social opportunities (Snarey et al., 1986). Which of these influences and experiences may moderate changes in the ego and moral status across the life span are topics for further investigation.

ACKNOWLEDGMENTS

Special thanks to Augusto Blasi, John Gibbs, Russell Hanford, Scott Lilienfeld, Annie Rogers, and Norman Sprinthall for their helpful suggestions.

CHAPTER
11

Ego Development and Interpersonal Development in Young Adulthood: A Between-Model Comparison

Lynn Hickey Schultz
Robert L. Selman
Harvard University
Judge Baker Children's Center

Loevinger's (1976) conceptualization of ego development as an evolving system of meaning-making encompasses a broad range of an individual's functioning and perception of inner and outer experience. In Loevinger's theory, ego development represents a "master trait" (Loevinger & Wessler, 1970; Tellegen, 1988), a framework of meaning governing how individuals master and interpret experience. At each level along the continuum of ego development, ego functioning is aligned with synchronous development in various ego domains (self, cognition, character, morality, and interpersonal relating) in a characteristic frame of reference. These frameworks represent a sequence of stages of socioemotional development.

In Loevinger's conceptualization, interpersonal development is a component of sequential changes in the structure of character, meaning, and world view. Within the ego development construct, individuals at lower levels of development have limited abilities to relate to others, with a progression at higher levels toward individuals having strengths that facilitate intimate, collaborative relationships. Interpersonal development in this model is emphasized equally with character development and other ego domains.

In contrast, Selman and colleagues developed a model of personality focusing specifically on interpersonal development by differentiating and contextualizing several psychosocial components (e.g., Selman, 1980; Selman & Schultz, 1990). In this model, interpersonal functioning is characterized not by a decontextualized master trait, but rather by the contextual use of a core social–cognitive process, the coordination of social perspectives. According to this model, the capacity to coordinate the perspectives of self and others underlies social reasoning and social behavior, and is the fundamental element of what Loevinger terms *ego development* (Selman, 1980). In the interpersonal model, character development involves treating other people well, interacting in all situations with respect for others, which requires consistently incorporating the perspectives of others in one's social dealings.

This chapter describes an assessment of young adult social development based on this model of interpersonal development and compares it to ego development as assessed by Loevinger's method. The interpersonal development measure, which focuses on a specific aspect of ego development—the maturity of close peer relationships—will be used to address the question of how the construct of ego development is related to developmental aspects of intimacy and autonomy in close peer relationships, that is, to a relationship-specific measure of personality development. In other words, we examine how the "master trait" of ego development is related to a subdomain of relationship maturity described as a profile across components of psychosocial functioning.

The chapter includes a general description of the theoretical model of interpersonal development and how the model is operationalized in the young adult assessment, the Close Peer Relationship Interview and Developmental Relationship Scales (Schultz, 1993; Schultz, Hauser, Selman, & Allen, in preparation). The description of the Close Peer Relationship interview methodology is followed by a between-model comparison to clarify how the interpersonal model is similar to and different from the ego development model and to contrast the research methods these two developmental models generate. Finally, we use case material from a study that used both the Loevinger Sentence Completion Test and the Close Peer Relationship assessment in a longitudinal study of ego and social development. The case is used to illuminate the convergence and divergence in theory and empirical findings between the ego and interpersonal frameworks.

THE BETWEEN-MODEL COMPARISON: THEORY

The Tripartite Interpersonal Model

The premise of the developmental theory and interpersonal model underlying the close peer relationship assessment is that the developing ability to differentiate and coordinate the social perspectives of self and others, both cognitively and emotionally, is a core human process underlying social thought and action. *Social perspective coordination* is the individual's capacity to differentiate and integrate the self's and others' points of view through an understanding of the relation between the thoughts, feelings, and wishes of each person. This capacity to coordinate social perspectives seems a uniquely powerful descriptive tool for assessing social development: when it is operationalized in a particular domain of social thought or action, we view social perspective coordination as a key social–cognitive skill or ability in persons and as both an analytic tool for researchers (Selman, 1980) and a diagnostic tool for clinicians (Selman & Schultz, 1990).

The tripartite interpersonal model was developed by the Group for the Study of Interpersonal Development during 25 years of basic and applied research on children aged 4 to 16 (Selman et al., 1992). In this developmental interpersonal model, psychosocial functioning is represented by three interacting processes, namely interpersonal understanding, action (social behavior), and meaning. As described in Table 11.1, each of the three psychosocial processes in the model undergoes developmental transformation based on the underlying social–cognitive process of social perspective coordination.

TABLE 11.1
Developmental Relationship Scale Levels

UNDERSTANDING

Interpersonal Understanding Levels

0 Egocentric	The physical and psychological characteristics of persons are undifferentiated, and subjective perspectives of self and other are not recognized.
1 Differentiated	The physical and psychological characteristics of persons and the subjective perspectives of self and other are differentiated, but relating of perspectives is one-way.
2 Reflexive	Persons have the ability to take a self-reflective or second-person perspective on own thoughts and actions and realize that others can also; two-way reciprocity in the concept of the relations between self and others.
3 Mutual	Persons have the ability to take a third-person perspective, to step outside the self as a system; coordination of perspectives of self and other(s) in a generalized other perspective.
4 Intersubjective	New notions emerge of the unconscious and of the personality as a product of traits, beliefs, and values—a system with its own developmental history. Abstraction of multiple mutual perspectives to a societal, conventional, legal, or moral perspective that all individuals can share.

(continued)

TABLE 11.1
(CONTINUED)

MEANING

Interpersonal Meaning Levels

0 Polarized	Intimacy and autonomy issues are polarized: either enmeshment or lack of any dependence.
1 Simplistic	Closeness seen as doing things together and independence as doing things separately; intimacy based on similarity, autonomy on difference.
2 Trusting	"Being there" emotionally when others need support but having own opinions, thoughts, and feelings; self-disclosure without fear of betrayal.
3 Integrated	Intimacy and autonomy issues are integrated although not balanced (equally valued).
4 Interdependent	Committed and balanced interdependence, with limitations in intimacy and autonomy capacities contextualized in terms of both partners' personal histories.

ACTION

Interpersonal Negotiation Levels

0 Impulsive	Physically aggressive (hit, fight) or withdrawing (flee, hide).
1 Unilateral	One-way control (bully, order) or appeasing (give in, obey).
2 Reciprocal	Persuasive or deferential trades, exchanges, deals.
3 Collaborative	Use of self- and shared reflection in dialogue leading to compromise and the construction of mutually satisfactory resolutions.
4 Interpretive	The negotiation of intimacy in an integration of support and challenge, holding and interpretation.

Shared Interpersonal Experience Levels

0 Situation-Based	Interactions are coincidental, due to an external situation (e.g., work) and remain at a surface level.
1 Action-Based	Shared activities and routine talk.
2 Feeling-Based	Shared feelings and opinions with joint reflection on experiences, with more meaning and emotional connection ascribed because of other's involvement.
3 Identity-Based	Shared communication in discussion of own relationship and of inner vulnerabilities, internal struggles, insecurities, and identity.
4 Boundary-Based	Boundaries are negotiated in self-reflective discussions about issues unique to relationship, leading to growth of each person and of the relationship.

Interpersonal Understanding. Interpersonal understanding is what the developing individual understands to be the core psychological and social qualities of persons and relationships (Selman, 1980). Conceptually, this construct represents a social–cognitive competency that is necessary but not sufficient for mature developmental levels of interpersonal action (i.e., for mature relationships).

The interpersonal understanding component is the most decontextualized and thus the closest of the three components to ego development. Historically, it was been assessed with reflective interviews to elicit subjects' reasoning about transactions, exchanges, and relations between individuals with differing roles and perspectives, and about the nature of the experience of conflicting or alternative perspectives within the same individual. Because these interviews focus on the understanding of human psychology and relationships in general rather than specific hypothetical or real relationships, they minimize the inherent affective pull of the social content in the perspective taking operation by decontextualizing the content. Thus, the interpersonal understanding stages represent relatively abstract knowledge about persons and relationships rather than understanding of specific personal relationships (except in the case of the early childhood phase of development when children do not differentiate the two). Even so, because the social content is inextricable from the social–cognitive operation, interpersonal understanding is still influenced by social context, although less so than are the other components of the interpersonal model.

Interpersonal Action. The developmental levels of interpersonal action in the model are also based on the core operation of social perspective coordination as we observe how a person interacts with others in certain ways as if he or she had a certain level of (social–cognitive) understanding of the self in relation to other (Selman & Schultz, 1990). The construct of interpersonal action includes both autonomy and intimacy processes. Autonomy interactions are operationalized in the construct of *interpersonal negotiation* strategies, defined as the ways in which individuals in situations of social conflict deal with the self and another person to gain control over inner and interpersonal disequilibrium. Relatedness interactions in the interpersonal model are operationalized in the construct of *shared experience*, defined as the relatively harmonious experiencing of emotional and physical connections with another person through self-disclosure, doing things together, and spending time together.

A key underlying assumption of the interpersonal relationship model is that persons do not consistently reason or act at the same developmental level in different interpersonal contexts; even within a single context the developmental level of action often is not consistent with the level of thought. This can occur in calm interviews but is more common in actual social interaction. The use of social perspective coordination in interpersonal action is limited by the highest level of interpersonal understanding achieved, but is not directly determined by it. Although the core underlying capacity for social perspective coordination is thought to be structural–developmental, the use of this capacity in actual social interaction is dependent on the social, emotional, and even political context of the interpersonal relationships involved, thus lending a contextual dimension to our developmental theory of interpersonal action, distinct from its intellectual origins in the work of Piaget (1954) and Kohlberg (1969).

Personal Meaning. The third component of the interpersonal model, *personal meaning*, is conceptualized to be the process by which individuals connect their behavior to their own life histories, which involves a developing capacity to appreciate consciously and express explicitly the implicit embeddedness of behavior in the complex fabric of past and present relationships (Levitt & Selman, 1996). The construct of developmental levels of personal meaning was developed in studies of adolescents' risk-taking behavior in the context of their relationships, particularly fighting in relation to friendship (e.g., Selman et al., 1992).

The personal meaning of relationships—that is, interpersonal meaning—includes the values, attitudes, and beliefs held by the individual about a particular relationship, like a specific friendship (why this friendship is important to me). In the interpersonal model, interpersonal meaning functions as the affective component integrating or reconciling persons' social–cognitive understanding of relationships in general with their actual social interaction in particular, real-life relationships. With the construct of interpersonal understanding, we developmentally analyze the use of the perspective coordination operation in abstract conceptions of what makes a good friend, whereas with the construct of interpersonal meaning, the developmental analysis focuses on perspective coordination in reflection about particular relationships to real-life close friends or intimate partners. The interpersonal meaning of the relationship is close to the psychoanalytic constructs of object relations or working models of attachment, that is, how a person's past history of social interaction with significant others affects current interaction, of how characteristic patterns or tendencies in interpersonal relations are related to intrapsychic structures deriving from the internalization of aspects of relationships with significant others.

To adapt this relationship model to the young adults' interview responses we had to expand the interpersonal model into adulthood, when relationships take on new levels of complexity. Extending the developmental model into adulthood entailed the identification and description of new higher levels of interpersonal action and meaning as well as descriptions of how the lower levels are manifest in young adult relationships. Recently, using the Piagetian and Neo-Piagetian notion that development within a particular skill domain follows a course that is repeated on successive intellectual planes (Fischer, 1980; Piaget, 1954), Kane (1994; Kane, Raya, & Ayoub, 1997) described a developmental model of social perspective coordination and peer relationships on the plane of prereflective awareness in preschool children that parallels our model of perspective coordination and relationships on the plane of reflective understanding in older children and adolescents. We are currently exploring the possibility that adult social cognition and relationships form a third tier of interpersonal development based on more fully developed self-reflective capacities.

The Continuum From Ego Development to Interpersonal Development in Thought, Action, and Meaning

Both the interpersonal and ego development models have origins in the same hierarchical developmental paradigm and share an intellectual heritage in the thinking and writing of Baldwin (1906), Mead (1934), Piaget (1954), and Sullivan (1953). Developmental levels in both the interpersonal (perspective-taking) and ego development constructs chart increasing differentiation and integration in psychosocial development. However, there are conceptual differences between the interpersonal and ego development models somewhat linked to their differing methods. Interpersonal issues are central to the definition and assessment of ego development stages, yet the projective sentence completion technique plays down social context so that the ego development stages are more abstract constructs than are the interpersonal developmental levels. The interpersonal model provides a contextualized assessment of actual, particular relationships and still maintains a developmental system. The interpersonal model is a measure of the self in a particular relationship, in which developmental levels of differentiated psychosocial processes are assessed within specific interpersonal relationships (e.g., close friend or romantic partner). The ego development measure, in contrast, assesses integrative processes of the self across a range of domains (cognitive, social, moral) globally rather than contextually.

Figure 11.1 shows the three psychosocial components of the interpersonal relationship model in relation to ego development on a continuum from assessments of personality to assessments of action, from a greater level of theoretical abstraction to more concrete observation. Because ego development is more removed from context and behavior than interpersonal understanding, it is placed at the left end of the continuum. Within the construct of interpersonal understanding, the closest of the psychosocial components to ego development in terms of

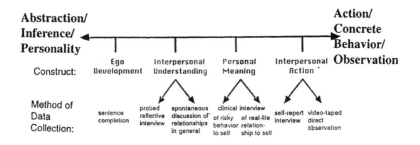

FIG. 11.1.Three psychosocial components of the interpersonal relationship model in relation to Loevinger's model of ego development.

degree of theoretical abstraction, we can distinguish between its assessment in probed reflective interviews versus its assessment as more spontaneous reflection, which is one step away from developmental assessment of social–cognitive competence and closer to developmental assessment of performance or action. The latter is how interpersonal understanding is assessed in the Close Peer Relationship Interview, as subjects discuss their own particular relationships.

Interpersonal action—operationalized in the constructs of interpersonal negotiation and shared interpersonal experience—is placed closest to observed action at the right end of the continuum. We can assess the constructs of interpersonal negotiation and shared experience closer to action by observing actual social interaction, or somewhat further away by obtaining self-reports of social interaction (as in the Close Peer Relationship Interview). Falling in between interpersonal understanding and interpersonal action on the continuum is personal meaning, which links action and understanding as subjects relate past personal and relationship history to current relationship patterns and actions.

Moving from left to right along the continuum, each of the psychosocial processes are increasingly influenced by immediate context and affect. Emotion plays a larger role relative to cognition in the psychosocial processes that are closer to action, as the target of inquiry moves from social reasoning to social behavior, from partially decontextualized abstraction to contextual particularity. To understand the relation between level of interpersonal action and level of interpersonal understanding requires an assessment of level of interpersonal meaning, which is reflective yet inherently interactive: meaning-making is distinguished by the relation of a particular behavior or particular relationship to the self. Reflection is a necessary component of meaning making but is incomplete in and of itself because a crucial component of meaning-making is the consideration of action in a particular context, the point at which the self engages with the world.

The Close Peer Relationship Interview and the Developmental Relationship Scales

The Close Peer Relationship assessment is based on a construct of relationship development defined as the growth of both intimacy and autonomy processes that move toward interdependence, or integration of intimacy and autonomy. The processes of autonomy and relatedness in interpersonal development have been recognized in disciplines as diverse as developmental psychology and psychoanalysis. Converging lines of research and theory suggest that (a) there is an interplay between autonomy and relatedness, connection and individuation, in human development (e.g., Cooper, Grotevant, & Condon, 1983; Gilligan, 1982; Stern, 1985), and (b) interpersonal maturity involves an "interdependence," or balance between autonomy and relatedness (e.g., Sullivan, 1953; White, Speisman, Costos, & Smith, 1987). Ego development is also considered to be related to the attainment of autonomy and relatedness in relationships (Allen, Hauser, Bell, & O'Connor, 1994; Hauser & Levine, 1993; White et al., 1987).

The concepts of interpersonal development as interplay between intimacy and autonomy and of interpersonal maturity as interdependence have a long history in the development of the three psychosocial components in the interpersonal model. Selman's (1980) research on the growth of interpersonal understanding suggests that as the capacity to coordinate social perspectives from a fourth-person perspective develops in late adolescence, a new understanding of *interdependent* friendship emerges, of how friends can be mutually close and intimate yet still grant each other a certain degree of autonomy and independence. Moreover, each of the three psychosocial components are comprised of dual intimacy and autonomy aspects. Interpersonal understanding is based on both *concepts of persons*, describing notions of how an individual functions psychologically (the understanding of internal complexity), and *concepts of relations*, describing the closely related notions of how these individual perspectives are related, how viewpoints are mutually understood and coordinated. Interpersonal action, as we described, is comprised of both intimacy and autonomy functions (i.e., shared experience and interpersonal negotiation). The personal meaning of risky behavior reflects the differentiation and integration of the influence of the self and others on action, and the interpersonal meaning of particular relationships reflects the differentiation and integration of the conceptualization of, and attitudes toward, intimacy and autonomy in that relationship.

The Close Peer Relationship Interview is a semistructured instrument lasting between 1 and 2 hours that probes aspects of autonomy and relatedness in two close peer relationships (best friend and romantic partner, if possible). Within each of these two close peer relationships, experiences of closeness, shared activities, and self-disclosure, on the one hand, and experiences of autonomy and conflict resolution, on the other, are probed with questions about recent experiences, observations, thoughts, and actions that have taken place between these peers. For example, subjects are asked to what extent they share their personal problems and worries with the other person (relatedness–intimacy), and to describe the last time they got upset or frustrated with the other person (autonomy).

The Developmental Relationship Scales (Schultz, 1993) were constructed from the Close Peer Relationship Interview by adapting previous developmental scales (Levitt & Selman, 1996; Selman, 1980, Selman & Schultz, 1990). The scales assess self-reported autonomy and relatedness interactions and reflections about the young adults' two closest peer relationships. There are four scales:

1. Autonomy interactions, or *interpersonal negotiation.*
2. Intimacy–Relatedness interactions, or *shared experience.*
3. Reflections on intimacy and autonomy and the degree to which intimacy and autonomy issues are integrated in an interdependent relationship, or the *interpersonal meaning* of the relationship.
4. Conceptions of personality and relations within the relationship, or *interpersonal understanding.*

Table 11.1 presents the five developmental levels of each of the four Developmental Relationship Scales. The two interpersonal action scales are given multiple scores to reflect the inherent contextual influence on the expression of developmental levels of social action: *interpersonal negotiation* is scored for highest, lowest, and predominant levels, and *shared experience* is scored for highest and predominant levels.

The Between-Model Comparison: Data

The Close Peer Relationship Interview and Loevinger's Sentence Completion Test (SCT) were both included as measures in a study of adolescent paths to young adult social development (Hauser & Allen, 1991). The 146 subjects, originally sampled from a high school and a psychiatric hospital to create a range of ego functioning scores, were studied intensively throughout middle adolescence (ages 14–17) with measures including repeated assessments of adolescent and parental levels of ego development with the SCT (Hauser et al., 1984). The Close Peer Relationship assessment was included in the follow-up study when the subjects were 24 to 26 years old, along with the SCT, measures of security of attachment representations, and other measures of social development.

Analyses of most of the sample from this study (n = 133) indicate that ego development is moderately positively correlated with three[1] of the Developmental Relationship Scales: r = .48 with interpersonal negotiation and r = .57 with both shared experience and interpersonal meaning. The moderate size of this association between the ego and interpersonal scores supports the construct validity of these peer relationship scales, suggesting that they share some variation in common with ego level but also tap some different aspects of personality. The Close Peer Relationship Interview was also used in a parallel longitudinal study of 111 subjects (Jacobson, Hauser, Powers, & Noam, 1981) when the subjects were an average of 23 years old. In this slightly younger sample, the correlations between ego development and the four Developmental Relationship Scales were more varied in an order that is somewhat congruent with the concrete to abstract continuum: r = .31 with interpersonal negotiation, r = .43 with shared experience, r = .32 with interpersonal meaning, and r = .47 with interpersonal understanding. This empirical evidence that interpersonal understanding has a stronger relationship with ego development and interpersonal negotiation has a weaker one supports the theoretically predicted ordering of the relationship between ego development and the four interpersonal relationship scales shown in Fig. 11.1. However, the results suggest that whereas conflictual action (i.e., interpersonal negotiation) is less congruent with the levels of ego development and interpersonal understanding, action fostering relatedness and connection—coded as sharing experience in this interpersonal model—seems to be more closely associated with ego development level. Young adults appear to be able to put their interpersonal understanding into action in nonconflictual interactions with their close peers, but can less consistently do so in negotiating autonomy issues.

Our hypothesis is that higher levels of ego development are theoretically necessary but not sufficient for higher levels of maturity in

---

[1]Interpersonal understanding was scored later than the other scales for this sample and the scores were not available for these analyses.

close peer interactions, and that other factors—degree of security of attachment is one example (cf. Weiss, 1982)—also operate to influence these close interpersonal relationships. Regression analyses using an overall relationship maturity score computed as an average of the four interpersonal development scores provide some support for this notion. The quality of attachment was assessed in the young adult study with the Adult Attachment Interview (Main & Goldwyn, 1984). Security of attachment scores significantly predict the overall relationship maturity scores after controlling for ego development level.[2] This suggests that security of attachment is an important factor in how maturely young adults relate to close peers, over and above complexity of ego development. At any given stage of ego development, young adults with insecure parental attachments seem to score lower on the developmental assessment of close relationships and hence appear to be less mature in relating to their best friends and romantic partners.

These statistical results suggest how the ego development and relationship assessments empirically converge and differ. It is clear that persons with higher levels of ego development tend to have more developmentally mature peer relationships, yet the details of how the close peer relationship measure differs from the ego development measure get lost in the group comparisons. We now turn to a case study to illuminate the empirical between-model comparison and to address the question of how the interpersonal relationship measure is related to the ego development measure. The case example of a woman named Sarah illustrates how a Close Peer Relationship Interview is coded with the four Developmental Relationship Scales.

Sarah

Sarah was recruited for the longitudinal study from the public high school of a middle class suburb where she was a good student and very socially involved. During adolescence her ego development showed an *accelerated pattern* (Hauser, Powers, & Noam, & 1991). She was an unusually mature adolescent who comprehended complexities in personal relationships and could articulate subtle aspects of her highly differentiated affective and inner life. As a young adult, Sarah had earned a Master's degree and taught 10th-grade English in a public school. Her father had died 6 months

---

[2]This regression analysis had an $F(2,128) = 41.1$, $p < .0001$, with an R^2 of .39. The t-values for the predictors of the relationship maturity scores were as follows: intercept, $t = 2.0$, $p = .0506$; ego development item sum score, $t = 7.4$, $p = .0001$; security of attachment, $t = 2.9$, $p = .0044$.

prior to her participation in the young adult study at age 25. In the Close Peer Relationship Interview, Sarah's discussion of her relationships with her best friend, Anne, and her boyfriend, James, featured a complex interweaving of reflection throughout the reports of her social interactions and patterns.

Shared Experience. Sarah's experiences of sharing and connection with Anne and James include dancing, listening to music, going for walks on the beach, travelling together, and going to art shows. However, their most intense shared experiences focus on conversations about self development and relationships:

> DO YOU SHARE YOUR PERSONAL PROBLEMS AND WORRIES WITH ANNE?
> Yeah, she's been through just about everything with me. I mean, my personal difficulties with my parents and my own internal struggle. Always been very supportive of that. You know, to what's happening and to what, how I feel about work, and what's happening there, to a lot of my personal relationships, both with my friends and with my lovers.
>
> HOW DOES SHE RESPOND?
> Anne—it varies. I mean, she's very there in some arenas and very uncomfortable in others, because there are things that she's still working out in her own self. Like when I went through a really hard time right after college, she really didn't understand that. And then when she started going through it after she finally finished college, she'd—we could finally connect and understand that we were questioning a lot about ourselves, about our strengths, about our weaknesses, about what's important to us. But it was only until she was able to experience it herself that she was able to sort of understand why I was upset, why I was confused, why it was hard.

In these examples, Sarah shares not only deep feelings but also very personal insecurities, vulnerabilities, and internal struggles with Anne, making their shared experience at least Level 3. But Sarah seems to go beyond the Level 3 sharing of communication to the Level 4 sharing of boundaries in her reported interactions. In connecting with Anne about their respective personal struggles to grow up and in urging Anne "not to sell herself short" in her relationship with her boyfriend, Sarah creates a context of supportive challenge with a conscious goal to promote growth in their own relationship at the same time both are trying to grow as individuals and in other relationships. This level of "negotiation of intimacy" propels an ongoing expansion of the relationship toward greater closeness and interdependence.

Sarah's shared experience with her boyfriend, James, is also quite varied, with a similar focus on intense interchanges about personal struggles and relationships—their own relationship and those each has with other significant persons:

> And in terms of emotions, he's also trying to work through the past and sort of grow and mature and come into his adulthood. And so I see things in him, as he's doing and expressing it better, just so much like me. He cries, which I mean—he will be honest about his confusion. He will be honest about not necessarily feeling like he knows where he's going, and how that makes him feel. And, you know, he was really honest about his past relationships. About what he's afraid of in the relationship that we have. What he can give and what he can't give. And he also has been clear about the internal struggle that he goes through.
>
> WHAT DO YOU TEND TO TALK ABOUT WHEN YOU'RE TOGETHER?
> We talk about—I made it real clear to him where I was at, because he came into my life right after my Dad died. And so we talk about our sort of dreams and our fears, and what's happening. Sort of around every day. And our goals. And our frustrations, with each other, with ourselves, with our relationship, and our joys as well.
>
> DO YOU SHARE YOUR PERSONAL PROBLEMS AND WORRIES WITH JAMES?
> Anywhere from, you know, how I feel about my Dad's death. You know, I'm very confused because I hate him. And I just remember him giving me permission to hate my Dad right now. So that, I mean, that's sort of like a very intimate and very hard and difficult thing, but that's how close we are. I mean, it's to tell him exactly how I feel. You know, telling him that Sundays were really, really hard. And wondering if I'm going to slit my wrist. That I can trust him enough to say something like that, knowing that he's not going to like freak out. That it's sort of a passing frustration, and that's the way that I will verbalize it to him and him not freaking out or anything. And he's really available and there. And honest about when he feels like I'm not being as there for him as he's been there for me.

Sarah and James discuss their relationship and its boundaries (e.g., what they can and cannot give to each other) and their intimacy is deepening as they get to know one another. There is evidence in these excerpts that James, in giving Sarah "permission to hate" her father and challenging her about not "being there" for him, is pushing on the boundaries to broaden the relationship, which is characteristic of Level 4. However, other elements of Level 4 shared experience are missing. For example, it is not clear whether they openly discuss and negotiate boundaries in self-reflective discussions about issues unique to their particular relationship. Therefore, Sarah's highest level shared experience with James is scored at Level 3/4.

Interpersonal Negotiation. Many of the conflicts Sarah describes with Anne occur when Anne acts less than maturely—being a "brat," having a tantrum, being "manipulative":

> WHEN WAS THE LAST TIME YOU GOT UPSET WITH HER?
> It was Sunday. And I was trying to be very—she was being, what seemed to be very irrational. She did this in front of all our guests, and it's not like her. And she's sort of taking a tantrum. You know, "Why aren't you helping?" You know, "I'm doing everything." And screaming this across the room. You know, in the kitchen screaming. And all these people sort of looking at her. And I'm saying, "Anne," you know, "what needs to be done?" You know, "Things seem to be okay here." And her just sort of screaming back. And I moved her into the pantry and I said, "Anne, why are you doing this?" I said, "You've got to calm down." And still not calming down. "I'm sorry." So I said that everyone could still hear. And I was just like, "Oh you've got to be insane." And I was, you know, when, afterwards we were in the living room, then I said, "Okay, we've got to hug now." Gave a hug. And then thought, "Okay, something's been cleared." And just as I was about to leave the house with my boyfriend, she said, "You're not going to leave this mess." I'd cleaned up the kitchen. And she—"Not going to leave this mess for me." And I looked at her and I was like, "Anne, there's not a mess here. But obviously there are still bits left over." And I stayed with that. I've not always been good with staying with things. Always sort of want to solve them right away and talk to the person right away. But I really let myself be with it. And waited 'til the next day to talk to her, which was kind of—because it was, then it was not so emotional. That we were removed from what had occurred. And to think about it. And both of us had thought about it. And she didn't go to work that next day. I didn't realize that she took a mental health day for herself, and I was coming back from work, just going to James's from there. And we-I saw her. I'd been thinking about her, and then I just saw her walking down the road, and thought, you know, "This happened for a reason." Picked her up and took her home. And then we talked about it.

This example shows a number of qualities of higher level interpersonal negotiation. First, it is a series of interactions in which some of Sarah's actions seem at a much lower developmental level when considered out of context (e.g., unilaterally ordering her to calm down). Second, in being able to "stay with it," with simply saying only what Anne could hear at the time and not trying to "reason" with her when she had come to realize that it would not have worked, Sarah was able to come back to the negotiation when both of them were removed from an overly emotional immediate context and had a chance to think about what had happened. Sarah achieves at least a third-person perspective in a collaborative negotiation; although without knowledge of exactly how they talked about it, it is not clear if the negotiation is merely collaborative or whether it reaches the higher interpretive level.

Sarah returns to this incident in another part of the peer interview. She describes talking through the conflict with Anne, with a focus more on what is happening in the relationship and what needs to be changed in the relationship (what Anne's jealousy is about) rather than the immediate source of the conflict (the events at the brunch). There is a sense that this disagreement brought them closer through the work of trying to resolve it. This questioning of self and other and resulting compromise leading to growth in each individual and in the relationship itself is a hallmark of interpretive (Level 4) negotiation.

Sarah's negotiations with Anne are predominantly collaborative, although she occasionally reaches the interpretive level, as in the example. However, as in most relationships, some of Sarah's strategies with Anne are reciprocal or unilateral, depending on the interpersonal context of the moment, particularly on Anne's actions. In the following example, Sarah's strategies stay at the unilateral level, although her interpersonal understanding of these less mature episodes in their relationship is at a higher level:

WHEN YOU GET INTO DISAGREEMENTS WITH HER AND HAVE TO DEAL WITH HER BEING SORT OF MANIPULATIVE, DO YOU LIKE THE WAY YOU HANDLE IT?
Usually, yeah, usually. I mean, I'll get frustrated and I'll get mad and I'll let her know. You know, like, "Anne, I—you know, stop it. I'm not really happy with what you're doing. I think the way that I'm doing the dishes is fine, and if you can't handle that, that's your problem."

Sarah's interpersonal negotiations with James do not reach the same interpretive level as with Anne, but she does describe a rather abstract pattern ("acting" rather than "reacting") that seems to imply collaboration in her conflict resolution strategies with him. Sarah's negotiations with James are predominantly at a reciprocal level, incorporating a second-person perspective, but she also reported a number of examples of unilateral negotiations, such as the following:

This is probably the first time I've ever been as assertive that I am. In this relationship versus other relationships that I've been in. Sort of asserting what's good for me, what's not good for me. You know, what— I've always been pretty good about this is what I want to do, and this is what I don't want to do. But just—I remember one of the conversations, it was not a great way to react. But I just remember saying, "Listen, you know, I just—I went through a relationship with somebody for 10 months, and they just could never become committed to it. And I'm not going to waste my time doing that." And I said that, you know, like over dinner. "I'm not going to waste my time. And you better think about what I'm saying, about what I need and what I don't need, and decide." You know, one of those sort of like, sort of cool, calm, collected, assertive. So, and that was the first time I'd ever done anything like that, ever. So I'm, I think that I'm pretty assertive in it.

Even when Sarah is acting in a unilateral mode with James, she tends to have some perspective on it (e.g., "it was not a great way to react").

Interpersonal Meaning. Sarah emphasized how the trust she felt in her relationships with Anne and James allowed her the freedom to be both close and autonomous and allowed the relationships to grow and be transformed through each person's ability to synthesize feelings of independence and dependence. About her relationship with Anne, Sarah articulates a high level perspective on independence (e.g., independence in terms of assertion of self and independence of abstract traits like imagination). Although she fails to integrate this notion with a sense of concomitant dependence in her abstract reflection, she does describe concrete patterns of interdependence with Anne that balance intimacy and autonomy issues, so Sarah's interpersonal meaning is coded at the transitional 3/4 level.

Sarah's high level of meaning with regard to intimacy and autonomy in her close relationships is more explicit in the following reflections on her relationship with James.

WHAT DOES INDEPENDENCE MEAN TO YOU IN THE RELATIONSHIP? It definitely means remaining a singular person. Someone once wrote about these two people dancing very closely to one another, but always sort of having their two feet to step on. And I think that's what independence means to me. Is always carrying out the things that I've wanted to carry out that are important to me in my life. But sharing those things with another person, and growing with that person, within that. So it's always—it's like creating a rainbow, but having—you're part of the colors and they're part of the colors. And there are part of the colors that are mixed. But you always hold on to your colors.

ARE THERE ANY WISHES OR FEELINGS THAT INTERFERE WITH
THIS FEELING OF INDEPENDENCE?
It does come back to that, still wanting for that stability, and that does
get you. So that is a wish. Not that I know that I'm necessarily ready
to go out and try to make come true. That sometimes gets in the way.
I mean, I have to be real careful about asserting who I am and not
feeding into that as a need. Waiting until it's a want and a ready,
instead of a need. And, you know, fulfilling it by losing, getting a
part of my color, or forgetting to be more assertive and independent.

In describing her relationship with her boyfriend, Sarah uses two
metaphors—two people dancing closely together and the colors in a
rainbow—that embody the integration of a strong sense of self-identity
with a strong sense of needing the other person emotionally—and a
balance between this intimacy and autonomy, that is the hallmark of
the Level 4 articulation of interdependence in close peer relationships.
However, whether she actually values each equally in the relationship
is questionable. She comments on both the insecurity she feels in the
relationship because of her recent loss of her father and her wish for
stability (i.e., marriage), suggesting a significant imbalance between
her sense of connection and her sense of self in the relationship, which
is Level 3 interpersonal meaning of the relationship.

Interpersonal Understanding. Sarah's complex understanding of
persons and relations pervades her reports of her interactions with her
close peers. Her interpersonal understanding is at the highest level of
in-depth, societal–symbolic social perspective coordination, that is,
fourth-person perspective taking. Her conceptions of personality
portray individuals as complex self-systems in which actions, thoughts,
and feelings are understood to be psychologically determined, but not
necessarily available to conscious awareness and self-reflective
understanding. This notion of the unconscious is implicit in Sarah's
differentiation of "acting" versus "reacting" in conflicts with her
boyfriend. In discussing her interaction with Anne, we see that Sarah's
conceptions of persons and of interpersonal relations merge in a
complex process in which her relationship with Anne is seen as part of
her personality structure, and Sarah's subjective sense of herself is seen
as tied in part to the relationship. In acknowledging her difficulty in
debating Jewish issues with non-Jewish men without becoming overly
emotionally involved and losing a broader perspective, Sarah implies
that persons can abstract multiple mutual perspectives to a societal or

moral perspective, and that if such a generalized other point of view (of a social system, or, in this case, of a particular cultural group) is shared, accurate communication and understanding will be facilitated, whereas if it is not shared, misunderstanding and conflict are likely.

Summary. Figure 11.2 graphs Sarah's ego development levels from age 14 to age 25 and the interpersonal development levels of her closest peer relationships at age 25. The left vertical axis plots the ego development stages and the right vertical axis plots the corresponding levels of social perspective coordination, according to Selman's (1980) conceptual mapping of the two developmental systems. The four interpersonal development scores are graphed across both relationships, with the two interpersonal action scores (shared experience and interpersonal negotiation) graphed at both the highest and predominant developmental levels.

As complicated as the right side of Fig. 11.2 may seem, it demonstrates that the one point representing level of ego development at age 25 on the left side represents a more dynamic process in actual social relationships. The graphs in Fig. 11.2 begin to suggest an answer to the research question posed earlier: how the "master trait" of ego development is related to a subdomain of relationship maturity described as a profile across components of psychosocial functioning. Sarah's relatively high ego development score is congruent with the interpersonal development scores for her close peer relationships. However, Fig. 11.2 suggests that the relationship measure has the ability to differentiate a range of interpersonal performance relative to interpersonal capacity. Sarah's interpersonal understanding and highest levels of interpersonal action (shared experience and interpersonal negotiation), were at an in-depth, fourth-person perspective level and her interpersonal meaning is at a transitional 3/ 4 level in her best friend relationship. However, in her relationship with her boyfriend, the highest levels of action and interpersonal meaning were at lower levels, with the discrepancy between developmental levels being most pronounced for the interpersonal negotiation component. Thus, Sarah's highest negotiation strategies with her boyfriend (Level 3) do not match her level of interpersonal understanding or the highest level of strategies she has attained with her best friend. Why that is is unknown, although we could speculate about various possible explanations—that she has not known her boyfriend long enough or that unresolved conflicts with her father affect her romantic relationships.

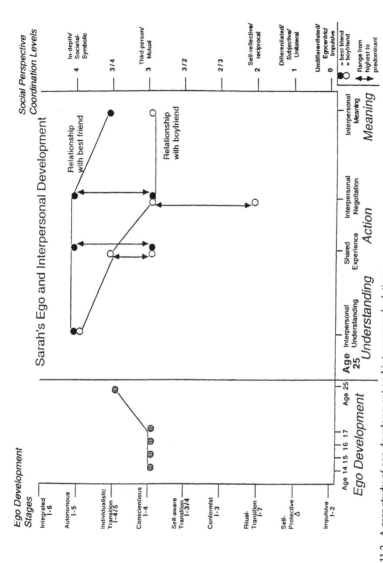

FIG. 11.2. A case study of ego development and interpersonal relations.
Note. The notation for ego levels used in this chapter corresponds to the notation of the first edition of the scoring manual for the WUSCT (Loevinger & Wessler, 1970; Redmore, Loevinger, & Tamashiro, 1978). The current edition of the scoring manual (Hy & Loevinger, 1996) introduced several changes. See the Appendix to the introductory chapter of this volume for a comparison between the previous and the current system.

DISCUSSION

The ego development and interpersonal development measures share some strengths and weaknesses deriving from their partial common heritage in the structural–developmental tradition. Both measures are able to assess developmental complexity in personality that is increasingly advantageous for living in the modern world. In both systems, conceptualization and method are in line with one another, and the developmental stages or levels are constantly being refined on the basis of empirical data.

The differences in the two measures derive from differences in their methods and underlying theoretical constructs. The sentence completion methodology of the ego development assessment has some advantages over the qualitative interview methodology of the interpersonal development assessment in large scale research because it is easier and quicker to administer. The single score of the master trait construct of ego development may be easier to interpret and manipulate statistically than the multiple scores of the interpersonal model, although an overall relationship maturity score can be generated from the latter measure.

Both measures are good research tools, but the tripartite model of interpersonal relationships gives the interpersonal measure a clinical utility the ego development measure and model lack. The usefulness of the interpersonal relationship assessment for clinical practice derives from its specification of the relation between interpersonal thought and action and its sensitivity to context. It provides a map to chart the repertoire of strategies a person uses in different interpersonal contexts and relationships, and the relation of this to what the person could do and what it means to him or her. The juxtaposition of understanding, action, and meaning in the interpersonal development model illuminates how the affective complexity of specific contexts shapes social behavior.

The case of Sarah illustrates how the profile across the understanding, action, and meaning components generated by the interpersonal assessment contextualizes development within and across relationships. Sarah's interpersonal relationship pattern is, relatively speaking, high thought–high action, one of three common patterns we have identified. However, the interpersonal model assessment of particular relationships reveals gaps between Sarah's best friend and romantic relationships in certain areas, particularly in her ability to negotiate conflict.

A second group of young adults show a low thought–low action (and low ego development) pattern. Individuals with high–high and low–low patterns show some overlap in interpersonal functioning (e.g., the use of unilateral and reciprocal negotiation strategies), yet high–high individuals like Sarah have the capacity to use collaborative and even interpretive strategies in relationships when appropriate, and so have more flexibility in responding to the relationship complexities of the modern world. The third group—those with high thought and low action within a particular relationship—are the most challenging to assess. In these cases of gap between thought and action, interpersonal meaning, which we believe mediates between thought and action, also tends to be low. The high ego development and interpersonal understanding scores for these individuals with thought–action gaps paint part of the picture of their interpersonal development but leave out other important aspects. The ego development measure is related to clinical diagnosis to the extent that psychopathology tends to be associated with lower ego development stages (Hauser, 1976); yet, because subjects get credit for occasional insights, it tends to produce false positives of maturity—subjects who are not able to put their higher-stage ego development into practice in their close peer relationships.

A major task of early adulthood is to initiate and sustain close and intimate long term relationships with other adults, outside the family of origin, in both personal and work contexts. As adolescents move into young adulthood, peer relationships become increasingly influential in psychological and social development. The developmental perspective on young adult close peer relationships offered by the interpersonal relationship model offers a way to explore early adults' closest peer relationships, which form the cutting edge of their social development, and to track how their relationship capacity and actual relationships change or remain stable in new phases of adulthood.

ACKNOWLEDGMENTS

This research was supported by an NIMH-funded postdoctoral fellowship in the Clinical Research Training Program and a Livingston Fellowship, both from the Department of Psychiatry, Harvard Medical School, to Lynn Schultz. We would like to thank Stuart Hauser and Joseph Allen for their support and the use of data from their Young Adult Development Project.

12

Ego Development and Attachment: Converging Platforms for Understanding Close Relationships

Stuart T. Hauser
Emily B. Gerber
Joseph P. Allen
Department of Psychiatry
Harvard Medical School
Judge Baker Children's Center
University of Virginia at Charlottesville

Models linking early regulatory experiences, or attachment, and later psychopathology suggest directions for continued investigation. A principal focus of study remains tracing the origins and causes of individual variations within personality functioning. . . . it is important to build on current research—investigating mechanisms that link developmental processes (e.g., cognition and affect) and provide continuity in development—How do affective regulatory styles and representational processes mediate behavior? How do defensive processes develop?

—Carlson & Sroufe (1995, p. 609)

Concluding their masterful review of attachment theory and developmental psychology, Carlson and Sroufe (1995) highlight key questions about mechanisms linking cognitive and affective processes, and about how we can understand the ways that individual processes (e.g., cognition) can shape behaviors (e.g., peer relationships). Their call for these new integrative research directions in developmental psychopathology converges with: (a) study of close relationships, an emerging domain within social sciences characterized by proliferating contributions from ethology, psychology, and sociology (Bowlby, 1980, 1988, 1989; Hazan & Shaver, 1994; Loevinger, 1994; Weiss, 1994); and (b) research focusing on continuity of attachment across the life span (e.g., Rothbard & Shaver, 1994; Sperling & Berman, 1994).

Curiously, a paradigm given scant attention in otherwise broad reaching reviews of attachment theory is ego development (e.g., Carlson & Sroufe, 1995; Hazan & Shaver, 1994; Rothbard & Shaver, 1994). This omission is problematic, in light of several important parallels between attachment theory and ego development. Central in both frameworks are inner representations—constructions, working models, cognitive styles. In addition, the complex interplay between cognitive and affective processes is addressed by studies of ego development and attachment. When we turn to an emergent direction within attachment theory, adult attachment, we find the most specific convergences: coherence of discourse, syntheses of perceptions and cognitions, personal frameworks of meaning (Hauser, 1993).

Most broadly, attachment and ego development research converge with respect to their insistence upon continuously sustaining bidirectional paths between theory construction and empirical assessment; ". . . a well articulated feedback loop between [ego development] theory and data" (Loevinger, 1976, p. 433); "I emphasize that theory and measurement [of attachment] are inextricably linked . . . questions of measurement can in fact have significant theoretical implications" (Bartholemew, 1994, p. 26).

Recognizing these intersections between ego development and attachment, this chapter is in the spirit of more deeply exploring their meaning and implications. Given the range of attachment research (e.g., Carlson & Sroufe, 1994) we deliberately restrict our scope to adult attachment representations, and extend previous work along these lines, based on conceptual (Hauser, 1993; Hauser & Smith, 1991) and empirical (Hauser & Allen, 1991) observations. Through a theoretically guided longitudinal study of adolescents becoming young adults, we have had the unique opportunity to trace ego development antecedents of young adult attachment representations and close relationships. Proceeding from conceptual to empirical analyses, we first review pertinent conceptual domains and then examine results of new analyses from our study, focusing on longitudinal links between adolescent ego development and adult attachment representations.

EGO DEVELOPMENT

A perspective within psychoanalysis, ego psychology builds on earlier conceptualizations based on hypothesized biological drives. Echoing goals of attachment theory, ego psychology represents an appreciation of biological and psychological views of individuals, together with an awareness of social and cultural forces, thereby broadening the scope of psychoanalysis from the study of unconscious processes and psychopathology to the exploration of adaptive processes within a matrix of interpersonal, familial, societal and cultural influences (Hauser & Safyer, 1995). Ego development is a central construct for ego psychology theory (Hartmann, 1939; Loevinger, 1976) and for many practitioners (Hauser & Smith, 1991). Although ego processes and ego development are certainly connected, the nature of their linkages is still not fully clarified (e.g., Haan, 1977; Hauser, 1993; Hauser & Daffner, 1980; Hauser & Safyer, 1995). Two prevailing models of ego development illustrate ego processes–ego development questions (Hauser, 1976). One model is based on multiple ego processes, defining ego development in terms of how these processes unfold, and are used by the individual to manage internal and external conflicts, as well as to develop new competencies. Characterizing the second model, conceptualized by Loevinger, is the special place of one ego process, the *synthetic function*, in defining ego development (Hauser, 1976, 1993; Loevinger, 1976). This model has clear theoretical connections with adult attachment representations, and has been incorporated in numerous relevant empirical investigations (Cohn, 1991; Hauser, 1976, 1993; Loevinger, 1976, 1993a).

Dramatically advancing our understanding of ego development has been the availability of an assessment approach that includes a psychometrically robust sentence completion test (SCT)and theoretically driven scoring system (Loevinger & Wessler, 1970; Loevinger, Wessler & Redmore, 1970). Over the past 20 years, over 280 studies used this approach to study ego development from psychological and sociocultural perspectives (Cohn, 1991; Hauser, 1976, 1993; Loevinger, 1976, 1979a). Embedded in much of this research is close attention to intersections between an individual's level of ego development and other aspects of his or her psychological functioning—inner representations, empathy, emotional security, impulsiveness, psychological-mindedness, openness to experience (Hauser, 1976, 1993).

Loevinger's model of ego development assumes each person has a customary orientation to the self and to the world and that there is a continuum (ego development) along which these frames of reference can be arrayed. "In general, development is marked by a more differentiated perception of one's self, of the social world, and the relations of one's feelings and thoughts and feelings to others" (Candee, 1974, p. 621). From this perspective, the ego is conceived of as a relatively stable structure, maintaining its coherence by initially screening out information that would disrupt its homeostasis. Yet, this definition does not postulate that the developing individual is completely shielded from disequilibrium.

Qualitative changes occur, usually gradually, in developing children *and* adults as they encounger experiences with their current frameworks of meaning. Such inconsistencies may trigger periods of disequilibrium, and in favorable circumstances may lead to shifts to higher ego development levels (Loevinger, 1976; Loevinger et al., 1970).

Stages of ego development vary along several dimensions—impulse control, conscious concerns, interpersonal and cognitive style (Loevinger, 1976; Loevinger et al., 1970). Individuals at the earliest (preconformist) stages are impulsive and fearful, favoring stereotypes and dependent or exploitative interpersonal styles. Their most prominent conscious concerns are immediate gratification and avoidance of punishment (Loevinger, 1976). At the conformist stages, an individual's conscious concerns shift to social acceptance and approval. Inner states are verbally expressed for the most part as clichés, stereotypes, and generalizations. Nonetheless, there is a gradual increase in self-awareness and an appreciation of the multiple possibilities and outcomes expected from a given situation or experience.

As individuals reach the most advanced (postconformist) stages, their self awareness and capacity for introspection are most noteworthy. Social norms are no longer seen as immutable; they are followed because they are understood as just, not because their violation leads to punishment and disapproval. Interpersonal relationships are guided by principles of mutuality and empathy, alongside a growing appreciation of interest in individual differences. In most groups, it is more unusual to find individuals functioning in ways reflecting these more advanced stages, which usually emerge during late adolescence and adulthood. Moving beyond specific stages, most germane to our interest in ego development and adult attachment representations are those components of ego development contributing to how an individual integrates outer and inner experiences with perceptions of interpersonal relationships.

EGO DEVELOPMENT AND ITS NEIGHBORING
DISCIPLINES: FOUR THEMES

A major benefit of the accumulating predictive validity studies is our greater awareness of neighboring theoretical perspectives (e.g., Blasi, 1993; Costa & McCrae, 1993; Hauser, 1993; Loevinger, 1976, 1979b, 1983; McCrae & Costa, 1983; Selman, 1993; Thorne, 1993; Vaillant & McCullough, 1987). This chapter's explorations of ego development and attachment representations clearly extends these outreach efforts. In a festschrift dedicated to Henry Murray (Zucker, Aronoff, & Rabin, 1984), Loevinger (1984) argued that ego development can most appropriately be viewed as a form of "self-theory," referring to ". . . a kind of filter, template, or frame of reference for one's perceptions and conceptions of the interpersonal world" (p.49). This template is not simply a static theoretical entity:

> I am convinced that the self, ego, I, or me is in some real sense, not created by our definition. My purpose is to comprehend the way the person navigates through life, not to create artificially demarcated entities [self, ego, I, me]. . . . What I have called ego development is, I believe, the closest we can come at present to tracing the developmental sequences of the self, or major aspects of it. (p. 50)

In other words, assessing ego development is a way of tapping this template, discovering the "filter" through which the child, adolescent, or adult is experiencing his or her interpersonal world.   We know that individuals vary greatly with respect to the framework of meaning that they impose upon their experience (Hauser, 1976). Broad outlines of such variation are apparent in our descriptions of the ego development stages. To be sure, Loevinger is investigating individuals' constructions, their meaning-making. Yet pressing questions arise: What is being constructed? What is the developmental nature of these constructions? What are the relations of the constructions to other representations, such as those so relevant to adult attachment?

Perceptions and conceptions of the interpersonal world are among the most striking aspects of ego development. But more is included in this model. Cognitive style, cognitive complexity, impulse control, and conscious preoccupations are repeatedly cited as components of ego development (Hauser, 1976, 1993; Loevinger, 1976, 1984; Loevinger & Wessler, 1970). These components are not merely discrete properties; they are dynamically interconnected along a continuum of increasing self-integration, differentiation, and complexity of thought.

In addition, there are at least four specific motifs embedded within the ego development perspective (Hauser, 1993): (a) psychological-mindedness, (b) integration and coherence of perceptions and cognitions, (c) agency, active mastery; and (d) interpersonal relationships. These motifs are strongly implied as one reads up the sequence of advancing levels of development. The four themes suggest connections between ego development and adult attachment representations.

PSYCHOLOGICAL-MINDEDNESS

Included among "conscious concerns" in Loevinger's model of ego development, this multifaceted strength encompasses several aspects of awareness: recognition that one's internal states are separate from those of others; self-reflection; knowledge that inner feelings and standards can stand apart, and yet are not totally isolated from those of others; and awareness of the psychological impact of one's actions, emotional expressions, and verbal expressions on another person (e.g., Loewald, 1980; Vaillant & McCullough, 1987). This monitoring of self and others is comparable to *metacognition*, discussed by Main and Hesse (1990) with respect to adult attachment representations.

INTEGRATION AND COHERENCE OF PERCEPTIONS AND COGNITIONS

One cannot synthesize inner representations through bypassing complexity, by reducing diverse ideas and perspectives to one overriding scaffolding (e.g., psychological or sociological), or truncating ideas and perceptions so that they artificially fit together. Rather, the experience of coherence comes about through recognizing, constructing, a network of connections of thoughts and perceptions relevant to the topic at hand. For example, the coherent completion to a given sentence stem on the SCT may be highly relevant to the sentence stem and it may reflect the individual's integrated perceptions and thoughts related to an issue touched on by the stem.

To become conscious of experience as repetitive of one's past is to assume an active role. In doing so, one lifts the experience to a new plane and puts it within the scope of the ego as an integrating agent. In active repetition, the old is mastered, not eliminated or abolished but dissolved and reconstructed (Loevinger, 1976). Coherence is a salient dimension in the study of adult attachment representations; and is one of the major criteria used for assessing and classifying adult attachment representations (Main, Kaplan, & Cassidy, 1985).

AGENCY, ACTIVE MASTERY

This theme could be included under the rubric of psychological-mindedness. Yet its distinctiveness merits separate discussion. The basic idea is that a person thinks he or she can influence their surroundings— immediate environment and even larger institutional contexts. For instance, one may believe: that he or she is able, within limits, to shape ongoing relationships; has affected previous ones; and will meaningfully influence future relationships. These beliefs contrast starkly with perceiving oneself to be a victim, at the mercy of the environment. Active or passive orientation to the world is reflected in each of the ego development stages and in how individuals complete specific sentence stems. Activity and passivity are also important considerations in distinguishing among attachment representations.

INTERPERSONAL RELATIONSHIPS

Earlier reviews of ego development studies covered many investigations of social functioning (Hauser, 1976; Loevinger, 1979a). Since then, a series of papers amplified support of the view that there are theoretically meaningful connections between ego development and aspects of interpersonal relationships (e.g., Browning, 1986, 1987; Hauser, 1978, 1993; Helson & Wink, 1987; McCrae & Costa, 1980; Rosznafsky, 1981; Vaillant & McCullough, 1987; White, 1985). The most persuasive data supporting this claim are based on actual behavioral ratings or naturalistic data, thereby circumventing the bias inherent in data drawn from multiple self reports. Several studies used this important design (Frank & Quinlan, 1976; Hauser, 1978; Helson & Wink, 1987; Rosznafsky, 1981; Vaillant & McCullough, 1987). The thrust of the findings is that higher levels of ego development are associated with increased nurturance, trust, interpersonal sensitivity, valuing of individuality, psychological mindedness, responsibility, and inner control. These studies lead us, in turn, to the personal relationship field, where attachment theory has been an influential new paradigm (Hazan & Shaver, 1994; Rothbard & Shaver, 1994).

ADULT ATTACHMENT REPRESENTATIONS

Attachment theory was conceptualized by John Bowlby (e.g., 1973, 1980, 1988) " . . . to explain the nature of a child's ties to his or her parent in terms of its biological function and to account for the disturbing behavioral responses observed in infants subjected to prolonged separations from significant attachment figures" (Van IJzendoorn, 1995a, p. 387). Over a decade ago, Mary Main and her colleagues (Main, Kaplan, & Cassidy, 1985) offered a new hypothesis signaling a move from the level of behaviors (of infants and children) to mental representations (of parents). In brief, they argued that "an adult's evaluation of childhood experiences and their influence on current functioning becomes organized into a relatively stable 'state of mind' with respect to attachment" (Main et al., 1985, p. 68; Van IJzendoorn, 1995, p. 387). Referred to as a *mental representation*, this state of mind is then defined as a system of rules "for the organization of information relevant to attachment and for obtaining or limiting access to that information" (Main et al., 1985, p. 67).

This shift to mental representations stimulated several lines of research focusing on predicting infant–parent attachment relationships, parents' responsiveness to infant attachment signals, and adult close relationships (e.g., Bartholemew, 1994; Crowell & Waters, 1994; Hazan & Shaver, 1994). In his comprehensive meta-analysis of the Adult Attachment Interview (AAI), a major approach for assessing adult attachment, Van IJzendoorn (1995a) considered the reliability and validity of this interview assessment, concluding that ". . . the AAI shows the predicted associations with infant attachment and parental responsiveness, and its predictive validity is also supported in clinical studies" (p. 400). Another direction in adult attachment research addresses individual differences in adult attachment representations, raising important questions about developmental, cognitive, and affective determinants of variations among individuals (Bartholemew, 1994; Belsky & Cassidy, 1994). For example, do adults holding insecure attachment representations function at earlier stages of ego development? Are specific components of ego development systematically related to aspects of adult attachment representations? Such questions about individual variation organize our new explorations of links between ego development and adult attachment.[1]

ASSESSING ADULT ATTACHMENT REPRESENTATIONS AND ADULT ATTACHMENT STATUS

Van IJzendoorn (1995a), concurring with many other observers, considered "The Introduction of the Adult Attachment Interview (AAI; George, Kaplan & Main, 1985) . . . [to reflect] a simple but revolutionary shift in attention from the objective description of childhood experiences to the current mental representation of these experiences and from the contents of autobiographical memories to the form in which the autobiography is presented" (p. 388). Originally developed with parents of young children, the AAI is a semistructured interview probing the degree to which adults can access, and openly reflect on, their relationships with early significant caregivers, tapping several dimensions—coherence, metacognition (reflecting on one's mental processes), derogation of attachments—that are key features of attachment representations. The interview consists of

---

[1]To be sure, many other issues could also be taken up: To what extent are attachment representations consciously held? How general or specific are these representations? (Bartholemew, 1994). Under what conditions are these representations likely to be activated and influence close relationships? Does their influence, for instance, vary with the dynamics and phase of the relationship—courtship, early marriage, termination? These related questions, for now, reach beyond the scope of this chapter—which addresses the possible interface between ego development and adult attachment representations.

15 questions asked in a set order, with standardized probes. Questions inquire about specific descriptions of attachment figures, supportive or contradicting memories, and current relationships with attachment figures. Other questions ask the participant to recall memories and descriptions of events from early childhood in which the subject was upset, physically hurt, ill, felt rejected, threatened, and/or experienced loss (i.e., events that would typically activate his or her attachment system). Of much importance is the fact that the interview includes probes designed to evoke memories exemplifying words the individual has used to describe experiences with attachment figures (for instance, subjects choose five words they believe characterize their early relationship with their mother, and are then asked to provide associated memories). Subjects are also asked about alternative attachment figures, and to reflect on how childhood experiences and parental behaviors affected the course of their development. A significant portion of the AAI addresses abuse experiences and loss of key figures through death, as a child and as an adult. Hence, with minimal involvement on the part of the interviewer, the AAI is designed to elicit a subject's *representations* of significant attachment figures and attachment experiences.

Coding of the AAI transcripts is based on the ways in which these experiences and their attributed effects on current functioning are reflected on and evaluated (Van IJzendoorn, 1995a). Although several dimensions are assessed (e.g., derogation of attachment, idealization, passivity of thought) one aspect of attachment representations, *coherence,* is central: "The nature of an adult's attachment representation is considered to become manifest in the coherence of his or her discourse during the AAI" (van IJzendoorn, 1995a, p. 388). Drawing from Grice (1975), the AAI coding manual presents several scoring systems to assess subjects' coherence in their use of language (Main & Goldwyn, 1994).

Three major *adult attachment classifications* can be derived from application of the Main and Goldwyn (1994) coding system to AAI transcripts. A subject is classified as *secure* or autonomous when his or her descriptions of attachment-related experiences are coherent and consistent; "their responses are clear, relevant, and reasonably succinct" (Van IJzendoorn, 1995a, p. 388). In contrast, subjects are classified as *dismissing* when they present attachment figures in a very positive way, using terms that are contradicted or unsupported elsewhere in the interview. The dismissing subject appears to be unaware of inconsistencies and contradictions. In addition, these subjects frequently insist that they are unable to remember childhood attachment experiences. Recent studies note that they do not lack memory for other childhood events (Bakermans-Kranenburg & Van IJzendoorn, 1993; Sagi et al., 1994). These observations are consistent with the view that dismissing subjects minimize their attention to attachment-related experiences (Main, 1990).

Preoccupied subjects describe a confused, angry, or passive involvement with attachment figures, using jargon and long entangled sentences. Intense emotional memories are apparent, together with few indications that the speaker has integrated these strongly expressed, often lucid, constructions with one another or with descriptions of the present. In these subjects, ". . . the interview questions seem to stimulate excessive attention to attachment-related memories at the cost of loss of focus on the discourse context (i.e., once started on a given [attachment-related] topic the participant becomes lost or confused or cannot stop talking; Main, 1990)" (Van IJzendoorn, 1995a, p. 388). Dismissing and preoccupied subjects are classified as insecure (Main & Goldwyn, in press).

A final category is *unresolved–disorganized* with respect to likely traumatic experiences involving loss or abuse. Indices of this classification, assessed through the AAI, include momentary lapses in the monitoring of discourse (e.g., confusions of time and subject) during or immediately following discussion of such experiences. Subjects classified as unresolved–disorganized are always given a second major category assignment (preoccupied, dismissing, secure) (Main & Hesse, 1990).

ADULT ATTACHMENT REPRESENTATIONS AND EGO DEVELOPMENT: EMPIRICAL STUDIES

Theoretical analyses of ego development and adult attachment representations, then, highlight meaningful connections between these frameworks. Until now, other than occasional suggestions of possible links (e.g. Carlson & Sroufe, 1995; Hauser & Smith, 1991; Van IJzendoorn, 1995b)—and preliminary findings pointing to expected links (Hauser & Allen, 1991)—empirical studies of associations between Main's personality–interpersonal framework (Kobak, 1994) and Loevinger's personality–developmental perspective have not been reported. Through new analyses, drawn from our longitudinal research, we are now in an excellent position to consider one highly relevant question: Does adolescent ego development predict young adult attachment representations?

In the most recent phase of our program (Hauser et al., 1984; Hauser, 1993; Hauser & Allen, 1991), we follow a sample of 143 middle adolescents who were former psychiatric patients and a demographically comparable group of nonpatients into their young adulthood. Guiding these studies are explorations of how adolescent socioemotional development and family experience may shape attachment, close relationships, and other aspects of adaptation in adult years. Consistent with theoretical expectations, we find that adolescents with higher ego development levels are classified as expressing secure attachment status in young adulthood, in contrast to significantly lower adolescent ego development levels for unresolved, preoccupied, and dismissive young adults. In addition, adolescent ego development predicts young adult attachment coherence ($r = .41; p < .0001$). Moreover, arrested paths of adolescent ego development (Hauser, 1993) are associated with dismissing and preoccupied attachment in young adult years (Hauser & Allen, 1991). Finally, even after adolescent psychopathology is accounted for (through multiple regression analyses), adolescent ego development continues to be a significant predictor of coherence of young adult attachment representations.

One way to understand these findings is through recognizing the key role—for ego development and attachment—of processes leading to coherence or synthesis of representations and constructions. Moreover, there are likely other psychological processes shaping both ego development stages and adult attachment status, including the capacity to tolerate and reconcile inner conflicts, balanced needs for autonomy and relatedness, ability to reflect on internal and external events (psychological mindedness), and curiosity. These dimensions, discussed as embedded within the ego development framework, are also conjectured to be closely associated with the ability to construct coherent, cohesive, and plausible internal representations of attachment (Main, 1990). Also of interest are questions about causal direction. On the one hand, early attachment experiences can facilitate or obstruct advances in ego development, as they influence the emergence of key ego strengths like self-reflection, delay of gratification, tolerance of ambiguity, and intense affect. Alternatively, early and emergent ego processes of self reflection, affect tolerance, and synthetic abilities may provide the requisite conditions for constructing those coherent attachment representations classified as secure. Because attachment representations were not assessed in adolescence, we cannot firmly argue for one or the other of these alternative directions of influence. Nor can we discover whether both attachment and ego development assessments are ultimately indexing a third underlying dimension, yet unmeasured. About one matter we can be sure. Attachment and ego development are not simply different names for the same phenomena (a problem of discriminant validity). Our findings indicate that, at most, 16% of the variance in adult attachment coherence is explained by adolescent ego development. Observing a significant but modest relationship between ego development and attachment suggests the hypothesis that ego development is likely a necessary but not sufficient condition for security of attachment in young adulthood.

Ego development refers to syntheses, complexity of thought, self-reflection. Yet it does not cover all aspects of emotion regulation, interpersonal distance, intimacy, trust, and commitment in close relationships. Such dimensions are within the domain of attachment theory, particularly that newest branch focusing on adult attachment representations. Carlson and Sroufe (1995) expressed a similar point of view:

> Attachment . . . organization regulates the processing of emotional information and provides direction in interpersonal relationships. Developing cognitive and linguistic capabilities increase the complexity of processing of emotional information and the meaning assigned to experience. More complex representations and beliefs concerning relationships with caregivers, the self, and the world develop. (p. 598)

Through these excellent measures and a relevant database we can now investigate—in some detail—the interplay between ego development and attachment in childhood years, and from these years into different phases of adulthood. As we follow our subjects from young adulthood to parenthood, we can identify ways parental differences in ego development and attachment representations may shape parental behaviors and cognitions about parenting. Major new questions can be explored empirically: For instance, do advances in ego development lead to overarching transformations in attachment representations or in specific dimensions of these representations? Or do dramatic changes in attachment status (e.g., changing from securely attached to dismissive) become reflected in unexpected ego development regressions? By engaging adult attachment and ego development theory in conceptual and empirical dialogue, we begin to cover broader theoretical terrain, probing new frontiers about psychosocial development.

CONCLUDING COMMENTS

Loevinger's notion of the ego as a self's "guiding fiction," adapted from Adler (Loevinger, 1976, p. 9), resonates with adult attachment representations conceived of as memories of childhood experiences of their relationship with primary caregivers. Both attachment theory and ego development rely on the accumulation of past layers of emotional, interpersonal and cognitive experiences. For ego development, Loevinger (1976) argued that this amounts to taking an active role in perceiving "conscious experience as repetitive of one's past . . . in doing so, one lifts the experience to a new plane and puts it within the scope of the ego as an integrating agent. . . ." (p. 334). In a similar way, Bowlby (1989) conceived of working attachment models as the key to how adults organize their orientation to the world, involving expectations of self and other relationships to partners, children and parents, based on current perceptions of their previous child–parent attachment relationships. These representations represent "principal features of the world about the person, about him and himself as an agent in it. Such working models determine his expectations and forecasts, and provide him with tools for constructing plans of action" (p. 117).

Although there is evidence for some stability of attachment classifications (Van IJzendoorn, 1995a) and ego development stages (Hauser, 1993) over time, both attachment and ego development perspectives share an optimism about human potential for change and flexible adaption in the face of normative stressors, like the transition to parenthood or traumatic events, like the sudden loss of a child or spouse. As a response to environmental changes, revised attachment representations may become more coherent, and transitions from lower to higher stages of ego development may occur, revealing varied developmental paths that may be traced over time (Hauser, 1993).

Despite their shared optimism about human potential for growth, both the ego development and attachment perspectives identify childhood as a particularly important phase of development when children are more vulnerable than adolescents and adults to stressors ranging from marital discord to abuse. As a consequence of early serious psychosocial stressors, young adults may become arrested at earlier stages of ego development and construct insecure representations. When an adult has endured such adverse conditions, the significance of his or her arrested ego development or insecure attachment patterns is not always readily apparent. Are these levels and patterns necessarily indicative of significant psychopathology? Or can one understand these patterns and levels as indexing special forms of adaptation to a particular set of life events, a repertoire of responses enabling the child and then adult to creatively cope with severe adversity?

We have argued that higher levels of ego development are likely a necessary, but not sufficient condition to sustain secure attachment representations. However, although we can specify processes contributing to coherence of attachment representations and to higher levels of ego development, we have not yet precisely conceptualized how these constructs differ. The ability to restructure and flexibly adapt in domains outside the interpersonal, for example, can indicate higher levels of ego development. But such abilities, alone, do not lead to a secure attachment.

We may find connections between attachment representations and ego development in terms of information processing constructs, relevant to the central motifs of coherence, psychological-mindedness and agency.

Crittenden (1992) observed that children achieve secure attachment via the coherent processing of information by procedural, semantic, and episodic memory systems. This tripartite information-processing system is linked with cognitive development: procedural memory involves encoding of sensory stimuli and behavioral responses; semantic memory allows the child to create verbal representations of their experience; and episodic memory involves episodes of specific, sequential narrative experiences that may be recollected like a story accompanied by the sounds, smells, and feelings associated with the event. Synthesis is achieved when children develop coherent integrations of their representations of external events, their own behaviors and inner experiences (feelings and beliefs). In other words, securely attached children are able to retrieve and coherently interpret their various stored memories of events. Attachment figures who selectively attend to their infant's signals facilitate an attachment relationship in which the infant learns that he or she cannot reliably depend on consistent strategies to obtain care when aroused. Attachment figures' inconsistent or dismissive responses provide discordant or negative feedback about the self in relation to the environment; in turn, these infants become anxiously attached children employing strategies like distortion, defensiveness, and repression to manage discrepancies between their internal states and environmental responses.

Can the differing strategies employed by children with insecure and secure attachments be viewed as an attempt to master a known environment? At a distance, these strategies could be considered adaptive or maladaptive. But within the context of their lives, children's engagement in certain behaviors might be an attempt at immediate mastery, regardless of subsequent outcome. For example, a child classified as dismissing might engage in disruptive behaviors to attract the attention of a neglectful parent. However, when this strategy is generalized to other settings, like school, it becomes maladaptive. And consider a child with a secure attachment classification. At home, this child experiences caring, sensitive and supportive responses. How might this child handle conflict with the "class bully"? Would this encounter prove more difficult for the secure child to master than the dismissing child? Would the dismissing child be more adept at countering unprovoked aggression from a peer? These questions illustrate how both attachment representations and ego development conceptualize the convergence of outer realities with inner experiences. A child's mastery of the home environment may or may not generalize easily to other environments. This lack of success is usually interpreted as maladaptive. How a child (and adult) approaches challenging experiences likely depends on context, ego development, and attachment representations.

Whether classified as secure or insecure, adolescents with higher ego development levels share an ability to master their environment; strategies employed in early attachment relationships become generalizable to other environments and feedback received from the environment continues to be positive, leaving the adolescent psychologically intact or providing room for psychological growth. This behavior may appear to be maladaptive. For example, consider an adolescent who sells drugs to establish financial independence from a controlling or neglectful parent. Appearing dysfunctional from an external perspective, within the framework of the adolescent's plan to achieve greater fiscal autonomy, his or her actions may be adaptive. Higher levels of ego development cannot be equated with mental health. Rather, levels of ego development and attachment representations combine to determine psychological response to the environment. In other psychiatric samples, Noam (1993) found that higher levels of ego development are related to internalizing disorders, whereas lower ego levels are related to externalizing disorders.

These final comments, stimulated by the interplay between two historically different perspectives, raise many intriguing questions. With the exception of recent contributions by Kobak, Allen, and Hauser (1993) and Hauser and colleagues (Hauser & Safyer, 1995; Hauser & Smith, 1991), there are no focused discussions about the surface and deep paths between what now appear to be obvious theoretical 'neighbors.' New work reexamining emotion processes and development (e.g., Campos, Campos, & Barrett, 1989; Hauser & Huffman, 1994; Hauser & Safyer, 1994, 1995) should enhance our understanding of the intersection of ego development, internal representations, and interpersonal relationships, thereby deepening our knowledge of the evolution of developmental pathways through adolescent and adult years. At the most practical level, such advances in our knowledge promise to yield new insights about why some individuals, seemingly at great risk for later psychopathology, lead optimal lives, whereas others show surprising signs of disorder following low-risk, "normal" childhood and adolescent years.

ACKNOWLEDGMENTS

Preparation of this chapter was supported in part by: an NIMH Research Scientist Development Award # KO5MH70178; NIMH R01 MH44934, "Across generations: Family life and mental health," and by a grant from the Catherine T. and John D. MacArthur Foundation for partial support to Stuart Hauser while a Fellow at the Center for Advanced Study in the Behavioral Sciences, Stanford, California, 1993–1994.

The Role of Ego Development in the Adult Self

Gisela Labouvie-Vief
Manfred Diehl
Department of Psychology
Wayne State University
University of Colorado — Colorado Springs

Since the 1970s, Jane Loevinger's theory of ego development (Loevinger, 1976, 1993b; Loevinger & Wessler, 1970) provided an influential approach to the study of personality development. Her theory and method have been attractive because they have provided a strategy differing in significant ways from more trait-oriented personality measurement. That strategy is informed by a theory of transitions and transformations in cognitive–emotional complexity, assumed to form part of a normal course of impulse control and ego processes. The theory thus provides a bridge between cognitive and psychodynamic conceptions of personality development. Because the model carries levels of ego development through all of the life span, it has been crucial in recent efforts to extend the notion of development beyond adolescence and youth into mature and later adulthood (see e.g. Kegan, 1982; Labouvie-Vief, 1994; Noam, 1988b).

However, since the operationalization of the model, psychology has seen some significant reconceptualizations of the notion of the ego (see Greenberg & Mitchell, 1983; Kohut, 1977) on which Loevinger's method is based. As a result, several critics (see Labouvie-Vief, 1993; Noam, 1988b) began to surmise that Loevinger's approach remains aligned with the cognitive biases of past ego theories but does not fully address broader issues of affective integration of the *self*—a structure that is more encompassing than the ego and includes it. In this chapter, we provide an initial examination of this issue. We suggest that ego development, as defined by Loevinger, may be tied to cognitive correlates and reflect the effects of a particular set of developmental precursors—those related to education and enculturated knowledge systems. In contrast, we hypothesize that an emphasis on self-integration implies a broader emphasis on self and emotional processes rooted in family and relationship experiences.

TWO PATHWAYS OF DEVELOPMENT

Criticisms of the concept of the ego, and the notions of adult maturity to which it leads, arose early in the history of psychodynamic theories. They are perhaps signified most cogently by the disagreement between Freud and the individual he had hoped would continue his heritage, Carl Gustav Jung (see Jung, 1963). Jung felt that Freud's concept of the ego placed too much importance on rationality and its relation to secondary process and outer reality, and that as a result the nonrational parts were treated in a reductionistic way, as a depository of primitive, undeveloped tendencies only (see Whitmont, 1969). Jung proposed that, ideally, adaptation should consist of a genuine balance in which the rational and the nonrational mutually modify, support, and enrich each other. This structure, which encompassed the ego but transcended it, Jung called the *self*.

A somewhat related view of self processes was also proposed by Erikson (1984), for whom positive development required the joining of two developmental lines—one based on independence, initiative, and autonomy, the other rooted in the vicissitudes of human relatedness. In Erikson's theory, the second pathway places constraints on the first. These constraints are not so much a matter of limiting the level of ego development attained; rather, they are evident in the completeness of the integration permitted at a particular developmental level. Thus, for example, an adult with a developmental history predisposing him or her to vulnerability in the domain of basic trust still may display many signs of generativity; however, he or she will also give evidence that the radius of individuals to which generative concerns are extended is limited, and that a split is created between those worth caring for and those not.

The more radical Jungian and Eriksonian conceptions of self remained, however, at the periphery of academic study. Instead, the field of psychology began to study self-processes by reducing them—as Freud had done—to the cognitive system. Thus the rise of cognitive theories of behavior offered one avenue by which self-development could be studied.

Although Loevinger's theory was influenced by psychodynamic considerations, her methodological and empirical formulation of ego processes (see Loevinger, 1976, 1987b, 1993b; Loevinger & Wessler, 1970) also drew on then prevalent cognitive approaches, particularly the cognitive–developmentalism of Piaget (1965, 1981) and Kohlberg (1969, 1984). Piaget, too, had embarked on describing development as a tandem progression between two forms of thinking. One, *figurative thought*, was —like Freudian primary process—tied to the individual's inner states and desires. The other, *operative thought*, was able to abstract from figurative constraints. But even though Piaget asserted in some contexts that development was based on a dialectical interchange between figurative and operative thought, his theory of development asserted the priority of operative thought over the figurative. Piaget's writings show that he tended to equate development with a loss of organismic and imaginative relatedness, emphasizing instead the rise of objective, abstract structures of relating to the world (for extensive discussions of these issues see Labouvie-Vief, 1994; Riegel, 1973).

Loevinger did not specifically embrace these notions, yet her model —in line with the then prevalent zeitgeist—nevertheless incorporated elements of them. On the whole, this approach had an impressive impact on the field, and influenced a great volume of work on cognitive approaches to the self both in childhood (e.g. Damon & Hart 1988; Kegan, 1982; Selman, 1980) and adulthood (see Armon, 1984; Kegan, 1982; Labouvie-Vief, 1994; Labouvie-Vief, Chiodo, Goguen, Diehl, & Orwoll, 1995; Noam, Powers, Kilkenny, & Beedy, 1990). However, several critics pointed out that this approach, although useful in some ways, is limited in others.

On the theoretical side, several authors (e.g., Fischer & Ayoub, 1994; Labouvie-Vief, 1982; Noam, 1988b) suggested that it is useful to look at core affective systems like the attachment system on the one hand, and the cognitive system on the other, as somewhat independent though partially interacting systems. To do so may permit more powerful descriptions of developmental pathways, as well as how such pathways become derailed in the process of ontogeny. Traditionally, within hierarchical models of development the two are mapped into a single structure; thus more maladaptive ego or self-processes are thought to occupy lower levels on a dimension of cognitive–emotional complexity. Vaillant's (1977, 1993) hierarchy of defenses is a good example of that view. Loevinger's measure of ego development to some extent also embodies that assumption.

An alternative view that emerged since the 1980s proposes that processes of self-fragmentation often cannot easily be mapped into a simple hierarchy of complexity. Very powerful processes of distortion and fragmentation are only possible as cognitive–developmental structures mature (see Fischer & Ayoub, 1994; Labouvie-Vief, 1982; Noam, 1988b). Thus, as Fischer and Ayoub (1994) pointed out, even very fragmented developmental lines can show great cognitive complexity. These authors proposed that forms of self-fragmentation should not be viewed as lower levels of maturity, but as separate lines of development modulated by a fragmented self-system that can yet achieve high levels of complexity. Or, as Noam (1988b) suggested, it appears to be useful to differentiate issues of self-complexity from issues of self-integration.

On the empirical side, several studies also suggested that ego level as measured by Loevinger's SCT may place special emphasis on a dimension rooted in reflective and relatively conscious cognitive processes. Working with an adult sample, for example, Vaillant and McCullough (1987) found that ego level appeared to be part of a cluster quite distinct from a cluster composed of such variables as global adjustment, maturity of defense, lack of alcoholism, no visits to psychiatrists, and warm childhood environment. The ego level cluster, in contrast, was defined by aspects of maturity quite independent of general mental health parameters such as articulateness, intuition, citation in *Who's Who in America*, and frequent use of sublimation. Thus, this cluster suggested a component related to conceptual and creative complexity.

Helson and Wink (1987) compared the correlates of two aspects of maturity: ego level and competence as assessed by Gough's (1987) California Psychological Inventory (CPI). Helson and Wink argued that these two measures reflect quite different conceptual approaches to psychosocial maturity. One concept, exemplified by ego development, assumes that maturity comes with growth in cognitive complexity, tolerance of ambiguity, and objectivity. A second concept of maturity and competence, instead, emphasizes alignment with social norms and the regulation of behavior by reducing friction and obtaining rewards in social life. In our own research, too, we are finding evidence that different lines related to self-development appear to form rather different patterns. A first line is exemplified by cognitively based self and value, such as ego development or related levels of representation of self and others (e.g., Labouvie-Vief et al., 1995). A second line, in contrast, appears to tap aspects of self-vulnerability as indicated by measures related to defense mechanisms and family climate. These two components appear to be quite independent.

The notion that ego level and self–affective integration constitute somewhat separate components of development dovetails with the suggestions of several other developmentalists. Labouvie-Vief (1994), for example, proposed that rationality and feeling–imagination, or logos and mythos, are two independent processing systems. Epstein (1994) also suggested two processing systems, one based on abstract–rational processes, the other on personalized, felt experience. Both conceptualizations are echoed by Bruner's (1986) distinction between paradigmatic and narrative processes, or Pascual-Leone's (1984) distinction between logical and organismic processes. Such differentiations, which follow Freud's and Piaget's conceptualizations discussed earlier, suggest that as students of personality development, we may have relied too heavily on self-descriptions and self-reflections as indicators of ego processes. Such reflective processes may be primarily dependent on collective representations as they are mediated by institutions such as the educational system. In turn, a different aspect of development may be rooted much more strongly in certain figurative and organismic constraints on development. Those constraints may be related to a line of development running parallel to the reflective line rather than being integrated within it, and that is primarily mediated by the human attachment system first postulated by Freud and since elaborated in attachment formulations (see Bowlby, 1988; Bretherton, 1985).

To propose that we think of ego–self development in terms of not a single system, but of the coordination and interplay of two somewhat separate systems does not mean, of course, that any one theory aligns itself with one or the other set of processes. Rather, most theories—as discussed earlier in the case of Freud and Piaget—involve some sort of mediation of the two. Thus, as Blasi (1980) noted, Loevinger's model of ego development probably would occupy a less extreme position on the cognitive complexity pole than would Piagetian formal thought, because it is oriented not on objects but on subjects' inner states. Hauser's (1993) research showed that ego level and attachment processes appear to share common variance. Nevertheless, we suggest that even Loevinger's model is relatively closely aligned with the cognitive complexity pole, although being somewhat more independent of the self-integration versus self-fragmentation pole. In the remainder of this chapter, we provide a preliminary empirical test of this hypothesis.

EMPIRICAL SUPPORT

In this section, we offer an empirical analysis suggesting that Loevinger's model of ego development appears to be more aligned with a developmental line relating to cognitive complexity, although being more independent of a line relating to integration of the self and originating out of the vicissitudes of human attachments. For purposes of our analyses, we rely on a model of ego processes offered by Haan (1977) to operationalize aspects of cognitive complexity and self-integration–fragmentation. This model is quite in line with a conception of relatively independent systems related to cognitive complexity and self-integration.

Haan provided a taxonomy describing ego processes as having a *mature* mode (coping) and an *immature* mode (defense). In the mature mode (coping), the individual responds to the requirements of the situation in a flexible and adaptive manner, using cognitive mechanisms in differentiated ways to think about and integrate conscious and preconscious elements. Thus, coping involves behaviors such as logical analysis, striving for objectivity, and understanding of others, but also some affect–impulse regulating endeavors such as sublimation or suppression. In the immature mode (defense), the person responds to the requirements of the situation in a rigid and undifferentiated manner involving ways of thinking that distort the situation and may include elements that are not part of the situation. Thus, defense involves behaviors such as intellectualization, rationalization, projection, or regression (see Haan, 1977).

Although Haan developed her taxonomy so that each coping strategy is lined up with a corresponding defense mechanism, these processes should not necessarily be seen as opposite ends on a single dimension. Rather, mechanisms of coping and defense are different in nature and psychological impact, and separate scales are used to measure coping processes on one hand, and defense mechanisms on the other (see Joffe & Naditch, 1977).

Because processes of coping and defense refer to the typical ways in which the ego deals with conflict and ambiguity, they are inseparably related to the concept of ego development as outlined by Loevinger (1976). However, we believe that strategies of coping and defense are differentially related to ego level. We suggest that ego level is more strongly aligned with cognitive aspects of personality and is, therefore, also positively related to the coping mode as defined by Haan (1977). In contrast, we also suggest that processes of defense show stronger relations to affective processes as they are indicated by an individual's attachment status and family history.

In our analyses, ego level is considered a mediator rather than an outcome variable in itself because two of the four dimensions along which Loevinger organizes the stages of ego level are related to how individuals control their affective and cognitive impulses and how they negotiate ambiguity and conflict (Loevinger, 1976). Individuals' specific ways of controlling impulses and tolerating ambiguity and conflict, however, have their behavioral manifestation in strategies of coping and defense and, therefore, styles of coping seem to be the more appropriate outcome variables. We believe that this conceptualization has two major advantages. First, it underscores the central role ego development plays in the larger context of social and personality development. Second, from a conceptual and statistical point of view, this notion is consistent with Baron and

Kenny's (1986) moderator–mediator distinction and directs the focus to models examining the role of ego level within a larger network of developmental and socialization variables.

METHOD

Participants and Procedure

Participants in this study were 333 individuals (159 men, 174 women) who had been recruited for a project focusing on cognitive–emotional maturity and self-development across the life span. Participants had been recruited from three suburban communities of a large midwestern metropolitan area representing low, medium, and high socioeconomic (SES)levels. The sample was stratified by age representing the following age groups: adolescents (age 15 to 19; n = 25), young adults (age 20 to 29; n = 54), adults (age 30-45; n = 86), middle-aged adults (age 46 to 59; n = 72), older adults (age 60 to 69; n = 51), and elderly adults (age 70 and older; n = 45).

Participants' mean age was 46.6 (SD = 18.7), ranging from 15 to 87 years of age. Participants' annual family income ranged from less than $10,000 to over $150,000, with an average of about $55,000. The majority of respondents were White and most of the adult participants were married. Compared to the general population, the study sample was well-educated. Most of the adolescents (65.4%) were still in high school. Of the adults, 1.9% had not received a high school diploma. About 30% of the adults had attended some college and 19.8% had received a degree. Fifteen percent of the adults had pursued some education beyond bachelor level without receiving a final degree, and 20.5% of the adults had earned a graduate degree.

Participants completed two 3-hour testing sessions scheduled approximately 2 weeks apart. The measures were administered in small groups of two to ten participants by specially trained student assistants. Testing was conducted at locations in the participants' communities. The test battery consisted of a comprehensive personal background questionnaire and a total of 22 measures focusing on emotional and cognitive development. In concert, the instruments assessed participants' cognitive and personality development, attachment styles and family climate, styles of coping and defense, and representations of self and other.

Measures

The measures described here focus on emotional and cognitive aspects of personality development such as ego level, attachment style, and intellectual abilities. In addition, we are interested in participants' ways of self–environment organization as assessed by their styles of coping and defense.

Ego Development. Loevinger's Sentence Completion Test (SCT; Loevinger & Wessler, 1970) was used to assess participants' level of ego development. Participants were asked to complete the short form (Form 81), which consists of 18 sentence stems (Hy & Loevinger, 1989). Responses for each stem were classified according to the nine level system, ranging from impulsive to integrated.

Protocols were scored by a rater trained in the scoring procedure developed by Loevinger and Wessler (1970). As total ego level score, the item sum score was computed using the procedure suggested by Loevinger and Wessler (1970). Rater reliability was assessed by having a second rater score a random subsample of 40 protocols. Interrater reliability (Pearson product–moment correlation) was .94 for the set of double-coded protocols.

Attachment Style. Participants' attachment style was assessed using Bartholomew and Horowitz's (1991) adaptation of Hazan and Shaver's (1987) attachment measure. This measure consists of four short paragraphs describing four attachment styles: secure, dismissing, preoccupied, and fearful. Participants are asked to make ratings on a 5-point scale ranging from 1 *(very unlike me)* to 5 *(very like me)* of the degree to which they believe they resemble each of the four styles.

The *secure* attachment style refers to persons' ways of relating to others which are characterized by ease in emotional closeness, comfort in depending on others and having others depend on them, and by a confidence that they are accepted by others. Participants with a *dismissing* attachment style feel comfortable without close emotional relationships and prefer not to depend on others or to have others depend on them. It is important to them to feel independent and self-sufficient. Individuals with a *preoccupied* attachment style want to be completely emotionally intimate with others, they are uncomfortable without close relationships, but at the same time worry that others do not value them as much as they value others. Finally, individuals with a *fearful* attachment style are uncomfortable getting close to others; they want emotional closeness, but find it difficult to trust others completely or to depend on them. Fearfully attached individuals worry that they will be hurt if they allow themselves to become too close to others. For the purposes of this study, participants' ratings on the dismissing, preoccupied, and fearful items were combined into a global rating of *insecure* attachment style.

Family Climate. Participants' family climate was assessed using the Colorado Self-Report Measure of Family Functioning (CSRMFF; Bloom, 1985). The CSRMFF is a 60-item questionnaire which asks participants to indicate on a 4-point scaleranging from 1 *(very untrue in my family)* to 4 *(very true in my family)* to what extent their current family can be described by the respective item. Items of the CSRMFF form 15 factor analytically derived scales such as cohesion, expressiveness, conflict, democratic family style, permissive family style, or conflict (see Bloom, 1985).

To obtain a more parsimonious number of variables for describing the perceived family climate, the intercorrelations among the 15 scales were factor analyzed. Results showed that the 15 scales formed 4 factors: Positive Family Climate, Control–Organization, Enmeshment, and Negative Family Climate. For this study, we were only interested in positive and negative family climate as correlates of ego development. Thus, linear composites were formed including the scales Cohesion, Expressiveness, Democratic Family Style, Family Sociability, and Family Idealization for Positive Family Climate. The scales Conflict and Authoritarian Family Style formed the negative family climate factor.

The *Positive Family Climate* factor is indicative of the extent to which family members help and support each other (cohesion), allow and encourage the expression of feelings and opinions (expressiveness), make decisions based upon the full participation of all family members (democratic family style), seek and get pleasure from social interactions with others (sociability), and prize and value their family (family idealization). The *Negative Family Climate* factor is indicative of the extent to which family members get angry, criticize, and fight with each other (conflict) and the extent to which parents are the locus of rule-making and punishment in the event of rule-breaking (authoritarian family style). The correlation between the positive and negative family climate factor was -.60.

Cognitive Abilities and Education. Study participants' cognitive abilities were assessed within the framework of crystallized and fluid intelligence (Cattell, 1971). In particular, the Vocabulary test (V–3) and the Subtraction and Multiplication test (N–3) from the Educational Testing Service Kit of Factor-Referenced Cognitive Tests (Ekstrom, French, Harman, & Dermen, 1976) were used as markers of crystallized intelligence. The Vocabulary test assessed participants' verbal comprehension and required the selection of a synonym for a given stimulus word from five alternatives. The Subtraction and

Multiplication test assessed participants' ability to perform simple numerical operations and required the subtraction of two-digit numbers and the multiplication of a two-digit number with a single-digit number.

The Letter Set test (I–1) and the Figure Classification test (I–3) from the Kit of Factor-Referenced Cognitive Tests (Ekstrom et al., 1976) were used as markers of fluid intelligence. The Letter Set test assessed participants' inductive reasoning and required the elimination of one letter set because of its dissimilarity with four other letter sets. The Figure Classification test assessed participants' figural reasoning and required participants to match individual figures with groups of stimulus figures based on certain rules.

All intelligence tests were administered under standard timed conditions and a total score was calculated for each test by adding the number of correct responses. Linear composites were generated by adding participants' vocabulary and subtraction–multiplication scores for crystallized intelligence and their letter set and figure classification scores for fluid intelligence. In addition to indices of crystallized and fluid intelligence, the number of years of formal education was used as another global indicator of participants' cognitive development and a proxy of their out-of-family socialization.

Coping and Defense. Participants' coping and defense styles were assessed using the coping and defense scales developed by Joffe and Naditch (1977). These scales are based on items from the CPI (Gough, 1987) and represent the taxonomy of processes of coping and defending established by Haan (1977).

For the purposes of this study, the correlations among the 20 coping and defense scales were factor analyzed and scores for two factors were calculated. The first factor was labeled *Cognitive Coping* and included the coping scales intellectuality, logical analysis, objectivity, concentration, substitution, and sublimation. The second factor was labeled *Defensive Coping* and included the defense scales regression, displacement, projection, regression in the service of the ego, isolation, and rationalization. In addition, this factor also incorporated participants' score on the Immature Defense Style Scale by Bond, Gardner, Christian, and Sigal (1983).

RESULTS

In the following, we first present bivariate correlations, showing that in a life-span sample, ego level shows a different pattern of correlations with attachment styles, family climate, and cognitive variables than do two distinct modes of coping. These correlations are followed by findings from path analyses, which examined the role of ego level in the context of individuals' self-environment organization.

Bivariate Relations

In a first step, the bivariate relations between attachment-related, family-related, and cognition-related variables and ego level, cognitive coping, and defensive coping were assessed. The resulting bivariate correlations are shown in Table 13.1.

TABLE 13.1
Bivariate Correlations Between Attachment Style, Family Climate, Cognition and Ego
Level, Cognitive Coping and Defensive Coping (N = 333)

Domain–Variable	Ego Level	Cognitive Coping	Defensive Coping
Attachment			
Secure Relationship	.01	.21***	-.30***
Dismissing Relationship	-.09	-.02	.03
Preoccupied Relationship	-.07	-.13*	.17**
Fearful Relationship	-.15*	-.22***	.43***
Family Climate			
Cohesion	-.01	.04	-.27***
Family Idealization	-.08	-.04	-.30***
Expressiveness	-.10	.02	-.24***
Organization	.03	-.06	-.20***
Family Sociability	-.04	.07	-.22***
Democratic Family Style	-.09	.03	-.22***
Conflict	-.03	-.03	.29***
Disengagement	-.17**	-.07	.23***
External Locus of Control	-.04	-.21***	.35***
Enmeshment	.05	-.10	.21***
Permissive Family Style	-.09	-.10	.29***
Authoritarian Family Style	.06	.03	.09
Cognition–Education			
Crystallized Intelligence	.30***	.24***	-.15**
Fluid Intelligence	-.06	.21***	.22***
Education	.36***	.37***	-.23***

Note. The Correlations between ego level and cognitive coping and between ego level and defensive coping were .32 and -.29, p's < .001; respectively; the correlation between cognitive and defensive coping was -.41, p < .001. *p < .05; **p < .01; ***p < .001.

As Table 13.1 shows, ego level was scarcely related to attachment variables or variables describing the family climate. Ego level was negatively related to fearful attachment and disengagement but to none of the other attachment and family climate variables. Higher scores on fearful attachment and higher scores on disengagement were associated with lower ego level scores and vice versa. Ego level, however, showed significant positive correlations with crystallized intelligence and education. Thus, ego level clearly shared more variance with cognitive variables than with attachment or family climate variables.

A somewhat similar pattern of correlations was found for cognitive coping, which was positively related to crystallized and fluid intelligence, education and ego level ($r = .32$, $p < .001$). This pattern was expected because cognitive coping represents efforts that rely strongly on individuals' use of rational problem solving skills. As further expected, there was a lack of statistically significant relations with family climate variables (except for external locus of control). However, contrary to our expectations, cognitive coping was also negatively correlated with preoccupied and fearful attachment and positively with secure attachment relationships.

For defensive coping, the pattern closely corresponded to our predictions. Defensive coping was negatively related to secure attachment and the family climate variables of cohesion, family idealization, expressiveness, organization, family sociability, and democratic family style (see Table 13.1). Specifically, higher scores on defensive coping were associated with lower scores on secure attachment and lower scores on scales describing individuals' families as providing mutual help and support, encouraging free expression of opinions and feelings, or the involvement of all family members in decision making. In addition, use of defensive coping was negatively related to crystallized intelligence, education, and ego level ($r = -.29$, $p < .001$). This pattern of relations was complemented by significant positive correlations between defense and preoccupied and fearful attachment and the family climate variables of conflict, disengagement, external locus of control, enmeshment, and permissive family style. Thus, higher scores on defense were associated with higher scores on insecure attachment styles and a family climate characterized by greater conflict, more disengagement, more permissiveness, more enmeshment and a greater sense of external locus of control.

In concert, these correlations showed that coping and defense, as two ways of self-environment organization, were differently related to attachment styles and family climate variables than was ego level. Although these correlations do not permit any statements in terms of causality, they seem to suggest that for the more fragmenting processes of defense, the relationship to attachment and family variables is more pervasive than for the more integrative processes of coping.

Path Analyses

The second part of the analyses focused on the examination of a model of relations between attachment style, family climate, cognitive variables, and coping and defense, which incorporated ego level as a mediating variable. The model proposed that ego level would mediate the effects of the cognitive variables on participants' ways of coping and defending but would not mediate the effects of attachment and family climate.

LISREL 8 (Jöreskog & Sörbom, 1993) was used to estimate the path analysis models. Initially, fully recursive models were estimated allowing all exogenous variables (i.e., attachment, family climate, education, cognitive variables) to predict ego level and the outcome variables, cognitive coping, and defense, simultaneously. These models contained several statistically nonsignificant paths; thus, the reduced models were estimated retaining only the significant paths. The resulting model for cognitive coping is shown in Fig. 13.1; the coefficients shown in Fig. 13.1 are the path coefficients (ßs) provided by LISREL 8.

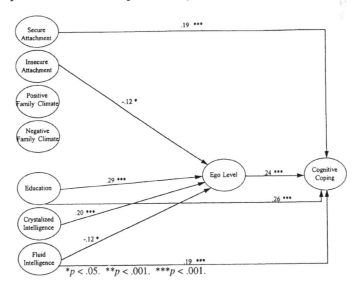

FIG. 13.1. Reduced path model for cognitive coping.

As expected, ego level mediated the effects of education, crystallized, and fluid intelligence on participants' cognitive coping. In addition, education and fluid intelligence had significant direct effects on participants' cognitive coping; that is, a higher level of education and higher scores on measures of fluid intelligence were associated with higher scores on cognitive coping. In contrast, ego level only mediated the effect of insecure attachment style on cognitive coping. Secure attachment had a significant direct effect on cognitive coping, suggesting that its effect was independent of ego level. Ego level itself was positively related to cognitive coping indicating that a higher level of ego development was associated with greater use of cognitive coping as a style of person–environment organization. Taken together, these relations indicated that ego level and coping were primarily a function of the influence of cognitive variables, but were only slightly related to family climate or attachment styles.

Somewhat in contrast with our hypotheses was that ego level mediated the effect of insecure attachment, which exerted an indirect negative effect on cognitive coping. This hints at the possibility that ego development may be susceptible to developmental injury under difficult attachment conditions, but may not be fostered by positive attachment patterns, if the conditions for proper cognitive development are sufficiently developed. Rather, secure attachment seems to directly affect individuals' coping efforts.

Figure 13.2 shows the reduced path model for defensive coping. As

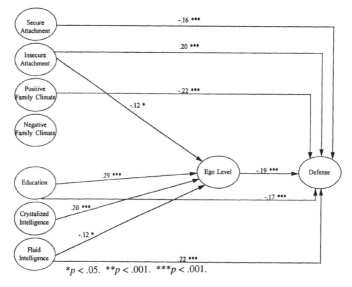

FIG. 13.2. Reduced path model for defensive coping.

can be seen in Fig.13.2, the pattern of significant relations for defensive coping was quite different from that found for cognitive coping. Secure attachment and positive family climate affected defensive coping in a direct, negative way; that is, lower scores on secure attachment and positive family climate were associated with higher scores on defensive coping. Furthermore, insecure attachment style affected use of defenses directly and indirectly via ego level. Higher scores on insecure attachment were associated with higher scores on defensive coping. In the same vein, higher scores on insecure attachment were associated with lower ego level scores and, in turn, lower ego level scores were associated with higher scores on defensive coping.

Again, ego level mediated the effects of education, crystallized, and fluid intelligence on participants' use of defensive strategies. In addition, education had a significant, direct, negative effect on participants' defensive coping. Fluid intelligence showed a significant, positive relation with defensive coping, suggesting that greater use of defenses may not necessarily indicate a lower level of intellectual functioning.

Findings from these path analyses allow three important conclusions. First, ego level was more a mediator of the effects of cognitive variables and education on styles of person–environment organization than it was a mediator of the effects of adult attachment styles and indices of family climate. Second, cognitive variables, attachment styles, and family climate variables showed different patterns of relations with cognitive coping than with defensive coping. In particular, attachment styles and positive family climate had significant direct effects on individuals' use of defensive behaviors. Third, although the absolute magnitude of the effect of ego level on cognitive coping and defensive coping was about the same, the direction of the influence was positive with regard to cognitive coping and negative with regard to defensive coping.

CONCLUSIONS

In this chapter, we suggested that ego level may be a construct more closely aligned with cognitive processes than with affectively mediated aspects of self-integration or self-fragmentation. Because cognitive organization and self-integration do not always function in tandem, we propose that certain aspects of lack of integration of self are not sensitively captured by the concept of ego development as operationalized by Loevinger's SCT. Our data provided some support of that notion. Somewhat in contradiction to our hypothesis, cognitive coping and defensive coping themselves were moderately negatively (-.41) correlated, and showed similar relationships to cognitive variables and ego level. However, in support of our hypothesis, ego development nevertheless appears to play a somewhat different role in each of those relationships. As far as cognitive coping is concerned, ego development mediated the effects of education and intelligence and, to some extent, of insecure attachment. Although these relationships also held for defensive coping, defensive coping was also significantly related to insecure attachment, secure attachment and positive family climate. These variables, then, exerted an effect on defensive coping processes independently of the role of ego level.

Our analyses indicate, then, that ego development shows a strong relationship with cognitive variables and education, suggesting that it may be a component closely aligned to crystallized intelligence or culturally acquired knowledge. Additional support for this proposition comes from analyses in which we examined a measurement model of cognitive complexity across the life span. In the context of this model, the goodness-of-fit of the model to the observed data was best when ego level was specified as representing a dimension of cognitive complexity which was distinct from crystallized intelligence and from reflective cognition as assessed via representation of self and others.

Thus, although ego development mediates the effects of cognition on cognitive coping and defensive coping, it only partially mediates the effects of attachment styles and family climate on less mature forms of self-environment organization, such as the use of mechanisms of fragmentation and distortion. Use of these processes appears to reflect the additional contribution of systems that are related to the development of trust and secure attachments and are regulated by the family's emotional climate. Our data also indicated that ego level played a role in mediating the relation between insecure attachment style and coping and defense. This hints at the possibility that ego development may be affected by negative attachment conditions but may not benefit from positive attachment conditions, if circumstances for proper cognitive development exist. However, more research is needed to examine whether this conclusion is warranted.

Why should defensive processes show a different relationship to ego level and attachment processes than do cognitive coping processes? One reason may be that defensive processes are more likely to deal with negative affect that is difficult to assimilate, whereas cognitive coping deals with affect that can be assimilated and transformed into conceptual systems. Such an interpretation is in line with much theorizing that suggests that individuals often isolate or "split off" negative experiences into separate structures (see Clark & Watson, 1991; Ogilvie, 1987; Ogilvie & Clark, 1992). Indeed, Ogilvie and Clark (1992) reported that such negative *part-structures of the self* are particularly likely to be described in terms of concrete, felt language, whereas features of the desired–ideal self are more likely to be referred to in terms of relatively abstract language.

Suggesting that the two systems of cognitive and emotional organization are not identical does not, however, imply that they are truly independent. One current challenge to developmental theory is to map out how aspects of cognitive complexity and self-integration interweave. One way to do that is to formulate superordinate systems or theories in which the integration or lack of integration is specifically analyzed (see Fischer & Ayoub, 1994; Noam, 1988b). At the current time, however, the notion of a high level of ego development does not necessarily imply that such an interweaving and integration within a single structure has occurred. Thus, it will be necessary in the future to examine more carefully those features of higher levels of ego development that truly indicate self-integration and to differentiate them from those that point to issues of self-fragmentation. Such a focus, we surmise, will contribute to transforming the current concept of ego development to one that is more closely aligned to theories of the self that, like Jung's, include the ego as merely one structure of self-regulation.

ACKNOWLEDGMENTS

We would like to thank the editors of this volume for their constructive and helpful comments on earlier versions of this chapter.

On Becoming the Same Age as One's Mother: Ego Development and the Growth of Subject–Subject Relationship

Ruthellen Josselson
Towson State University and
The Fielding Institute

We might think of psychoanalytic theory as having undergone a developmental sequence akin to the stages of ego development outlined by Jane Loevinger—from a preoccupation with drive and impulse to a concern with object relations to an interest in intersubjectivity. This evolution has afforded an ever-more complex view of the person in his or her world. My aim in this chapter will be to reconsider the psychoanalytic story of development as told from an intersubjective, relational perspective and to explore its implications for adult development in the light of Loevinger's model of ego development.

Object relations theory gave full recognition to the processes by which relations with others had profound meaning for the formation and maintenance of the self. From good-enough mothering to persecutory introjects, theorists postulated that representations of experience with others were the foundation of self-experience. All representations of the self were formed as part of a matrix of self-representation, object-representation, and an affective link between them, including, of course, drives and defenses. Much attention in this phase of theoretical development was devoted to explicating the formation of the self–other boundary (see Klein, 1987; Mitchell, 1988; Skolnick & Warshaw, 1992 for reviews.) Theorists pondered how the self precipitates out of an initial infantile self–other merger, and they constructed psychological development as an ongoing process of continual separation–individuation, which firmed the divide between self and other through internalizing the functions of the other that the self needs. In simplified form, these concerns formed the core of object relations theory—the processes through which "others" became internalized as objects and served the psychological equilibrium of the self. In this approach, the aim was to formulate and describe processes that occur within an increasingly autonomous individual. With these concepts, we could, perhaps, schematically explain phenomena up to the Conscientious level of ego development, working with the principle of increasing and increasingly complex differentiation and structuralization at each stage of growth.

More recently, however, many thinkers within the psychoanalytic paradigm began to extend the conception of the object beyond that which is internalized (Benjamin,1988, 1992; Sampson, 1993; Stolorow & Atwood, 1992). Perhaps the truly startling discovery of early life is not that there are others to be made use of and represented but that these others have their own subjectivity. The revolutionary observational work of Daniel Stern (1985) pointed to the importance of the mother-child system, regulated through processes of attunement. Stern demonstrated that the infant, rather than being psychologically merged with the mother from birth, is born psychically separate but primed to recognize and be recognized. The organization of experience, then, is not solely a property of an individual but a function of an interpersonal system.The developmental problem is to connect, to form relationships with preexisting others.

From this grew increasing recognition that a neglected aspect of psychological development concerned not object relations but subject–subject relations. The more problematic and challenging aspects of psychological and emotional development concern the articulation of self with others who are also selves. In this view, the experience of self is intertwined with an intersubjective context that forms, sustains, and allows expression of self.[1]

In the history of psychology, these problems of the relationship between self and other–subject and of the relationship between self as subject and self as object of an other (subject), although of great interest to William James, were primarily bequeathed to philosophy rather than to academic psychology. The development of intersubjectivity is a complex matter bringing to the forefront the murky borderland of human interconnection. Others are, in part, a product of our own construal, whereas we are in part an amalgam of what others have made of us. And yet we must form ongoing relationships with the others who retain a reality

---

[1]Benjamin (1988, 1992) regards intersubjective theory and intrapsychic theory as complementary (rather than mutually exclusive) ways of understanding the psyche.

independent of our mutual representations and misrepresentations. We can never fully know another in his or her wholeness, yet, as Buber suggested, true "I–thou" relations are possible through "making the other present," through our empathic capacity to "imagine the real." And these processes, Buber suggested (1965), are at the heart of human development. "For the inmost growth of the self is not accomplished, as people like to suppose today, in man's relation to himself, but in the relation between the one and the other . . . and in the knowledge that one is made present in his own self by the other" (p. 66).

Intersubjectivity is a framework for understanding the essential co-construction of reality occurring between self and others. It is also a developmental process in which increasing knowledge of others exists in tandem and in tension with knowledge of the self—interactively, recursively and, often, paradoxically. Intersubjectivity can be understood, then, both theoretically and experientially.

INTERSUBJECTIVITY AND EGO DEVELOPMENT

Loevinger's model of ego development belongs to an epoch of theory construction in psychology that was just beginning to discover postadolescent stages of personality development. Her work was prescient in its recognition that if we are to be able to describe any of the later aspects of human development, a theory of intersubjectivity is essential. Her concept of the ego went beyond the idea of an internal, monadic structure and included interactional patterns based on the growth of interpersonal understanding. Along this more transactional dimension are the developmental thrusts of late adolescent and adult growth - and the higher reaches of ego development.

In adulthood, there is no longer either biological or sociological press to grow. Indeed, the majority of adults function at no higher than the Conformist or Conscientious levels of ego development. The higher stages are distinguished by their more sophisticated and differentiated appreciation of the relation between self and other, in which both are increasingly appreciated as separate but exquisitely interacting.

I have always read Loevinger's ego development theory as a theory of increasing intersubjectivity, and I believe she anticipated much of what psychoanalysis is just beginning to explore. Loevinger and relational psychoanalysis both trace their lineage to the work of Harry Stack Sullivan. Loevinger (1976) regarded Sullivan as the true "ancestor" of the ego development model, taking what he called the *self system* as "a frame of reference for our perception and conception of the interpersonal world"

(p. 49). The essence of the ego, in her view, is making sense of experience —and this involves cognizance of the ways in which the intrapsychic is fundamentally intersubjective. At each level of ego development, the representation of the other shifts. Others move from being a part of oneself to a source of supply, to a necessary template for identification and molding of self at the Conformist stage to being more clearly differentiated in the Conscientious stage. But "to proceed beyond the Conscientious stage, a person must become more tolerant of himself and others" (p. 22). This greater "tolerance" at the highest stages of ego development is an increasingly complex experience of interpersonal life, in which one's separateness and connection are multilayered and shifting. (I think it unfortunate Loevinger named this stage the Autonomous stage when what defines it is a deepened understanding of one's relation to others as subjects in their own right.) Both Helson, Mitchell, and Hart (1985) and White (1985) found that higher levels of ego development are associated with responsible caring which cherishes the individuality of the other.

The hallmark of increasing intersubjectivity, according to Jessica Benjamin (1992), is the capacity for recognition. We most fully experience ourselves in the presence of someone who we most fully recognize as having his or her own subjectivity—for only another subject can recognize our subjectivity. Kohut's (1971) concept of the *selfobject* denotes the experience of the self in the presence of an other who is experienced as existing primarily to serve an internal function for the self. This defines a middle ground between others who are experienced as objects of need satisfaction and others who are fully subjects in their own right. Thus, interpersonal experience takes place at four levels—in alternating and interpenetrating ways. The other may be not be differentiated at all, as in merger; the other may be experienced as a need satisfier—an object who may or may not be internalized as part of the self; the other may be felt as a selfobject—separate but still part of the self; or the other may be represented as fully a subject—related to oneself but operating from their own center. Recognition of the other as subject is an unevenly realized task of development. At times, we may recognize someone as a separate subject only, in the next moment, to experience him as a selfobject. Or, we may acknowledge the subjectivity of some people but treat others as need gratifiers. As development progresses (optimally), there is an increase in intersubjective awareness, but this does not eliminate the other processes.

While the endpoint of the process of separation–individuation in object relations theory is internalization of the mother in the service of ego autonomy, the aim of intersubjective growth is the capacity to enjoy mutual recognition with another subject with the concomitant capacities for empathy, responsiveness and concern. This occurs through the growth of recognition of the mother's subjectivity—that is, her independent existence as a subject in her own right.

Ego development, then, goes beyond sufficient internalization of the other for the purpose of autonomous functioning. Its endpoint is not an "isolated mind." Rather, self-experience is shaped at every point in development by the intersubjective system in which it crystallizes (Stolorow & Atwood, 1992). "An intersubjective theory of the self is one that poses the question of how and whether the self can actually achieve a relationship to an outside other without, through identification, assimilating or being assimilated by it "(Benjamin, 1994, p. 231). The growth of the ego (in its essential function of meaning-making) entails the capacity to know another as a subject, different and separate from the self, but a subject available for interconnection with the self. Thus, the capacity for mutuality and mutual recognition emerges as a cardinal sign of progressive ego growth.

EGO DEVELOPMENT AS INCREASING
INTERSUBJECTIVE FUNCTIONING

Elsewhere (Josselson, 1992) I have detailed an effort to create a model of relationship that parses relationship into its components, each with a separate line of development. Issues of holding, attachment, and libidinal need for others are present in all stages of ego development (as outlined by Loevinger) as is the need for eye-to-eye validation, the "mirroring" explicated by Kohut. But it is in the more complex and developmentally mature capacities for mutuality, identification, embeddedness and concern (tending) that the stages of ego growth are most differentiated. As ego development becomes more mature and complex, the capacity to regard others as subjects opens the way for resonating with them, admiring them and becoming like them, affiliating with them and caring about them—as well as being in conflict with them or tolerating them. This is the developmental stream that we, as a discipline, are just beginning to explore.

The origins of intersubjectivity, according to Daniel Stern, occur at about 8 or 9 months when the infant makes the discovery that "there are other minds out there." What follows is a phase in which the infant explores sharing the inner world, a sharing that carries with it the experience of attunement. We might imagine a mother and child looking out the window at a squirrel eating a nut. The child points delightedly at the squirrel and makes cooing noises, glancing from time to time at the mother. Yet the child's wish is not that the mother look at him, but that she share his gaze and enjoy with him the antics of the squirrel. This is a prototype for the capacity for emotional resonance (mutuality). Unlike other aspects of relatedness, however, this need cannot be rooted in biological or ethological soil. There is no a priori reason why such sharing is pleasurable. It seems to serve no purpose other than some innate human propensity to relish this sort of experience. The consequence of such interconnection, however, makes possible the recognition of states of mind in the other, underlying all forms of concern and mutual understanding. But there are also failures of attunement. Later, the same child may come to have to learn, *I show mother the squirrel but she does not smile because she is depressed and so laden with worries that she cannot respond.)*

Striving for greater intersubjective connection does not replace the quest for increasing independence. Rather, connection and autonomy are two sides of a coin, always in tension. Throughout life, in qualitatively different ways at each stage, the developmental task is to preserve a self that is both distinct from but related to others.

An intersubjective reading of Loevinger's ego development stages would regard the self, in the earliest stages, as in the ascendant, seemingly obliterating recognition of the other as a meaningful other (subject). By the Conformist stage, the self and its own properties have been muted in favor of obeisance to the other. Only in the later stages of ego development is the conflict between autonomy and the need for relatedness fully realized and held in consciousness, forming the structure of more mature adult functioning.

Benjamin finds her philosophical ground in Hegel's analysis of the conflict between the self's wish for independence and the self's wish for the recognition of the other. Thus, the need for the other must always compromise the self's absoluteness. I draw also on the work of Mikhail Bakhtin (1981) who postulates a dialogical self, a self always responding to and anticipating a response of an other. The dialogical self is, therefore, fully intersubjective. Action is always an answer. Communication always involves a struggle with the realities of intersubjectivity, the barriers inherent in the very otherness of the other.

> The speaker strives to get a reading on his own word, and on his own conceptual system that determines this word, within the alien conceptual system of the understanding receiver; he enters into dialogical relationships with certain aspects of this system. The speaker breaks through the alien conceptual horizon of the listener, constructs his own utterance on alien territory, against his, the listener's apperceptive background. (p. 282)

As we grow, we become ever more aware of this process, of our distinctiveness in relation to our growing perception of the "alien-ness" of the other and of our efforts to bridge that divide as we get a reading on our own word on the horizon of the other.

Benjamin is critical of Mahler's account of the separation–individuation process because she believes that Mahler sets the goals of development too low. Although Benjamin grants the importance of independence as an outcome of this period, she notes that the child needs only to internalize the mother in order to achieve object constancy and to accept the disappointment of mother's leavings, which the child cannot control. But, Benjamin asserts, Mahler does not consider that the child may also shift to be able to recognize that mother may have her own center. Like in earlier infancy when the discovery of other minds led to the possibility of joyful mutuality in the sharing of inner states (which Stern stresses), an outcome of a successfully traversed rapprochement period is the capacity to contain the tension of different states of mind. This rapprochement—this containing of different states of mind—is, I think, a central thrust of ego development far beyond the end of childhood.

One can only wonder at the denial of maternal subjectivity in our infant-centered theory. Like young children, our theory embodies the fantasy that mother exists to meet the child's needs (or to fail at doing so). To regard the mother as a complex person with needs of her own has thus far eluded psychological theory. And it may be that increases in recognition of the (m)other are the bellwethers of progressive ego development.

THE HIGHER LEVELS OF EGO DEVELOPMENT

Progressive ego development—from childhood through adulthood—involves a continual restructuring of the experience of self and other, as Loevinger's ego development model suggests. At each stage, the capacity for intersubjective meaning-making grows more complex. Intersubjective recognitions provide another way of constructing experience, interconnecting with but not supplanting other forms such as the experience of others as objects or selfobjects. But it is unclear just what takes place. Is intersubjective awareness used more pervasively? More frequently? Only under certain circumstances, and if so, which? We may know that others operate from their own center, yet affectively demand that they be responsive to our own needs. And how do we come to terms with difference at the larger social levels—by finding ways of living together, or by asking that those who are other become first like us? Because we each experience from our own awareness, getting along with each other is difficult.

The experience of intersubjectivity is not an end state. Processes of projection, introjection, projective identification, and other forms of distortion occur throughout life, leaving us always with the task of sifting through and reworking our inner experience of others and self. We always continue to create our worlds, at least in part. Intersubjectivity does not imply the triumph of the external or a state of interpersonal harmony— that would be a sterile form of conformism. Rather, life becomes a process of breakdown and repair in relationships, discord followed by increases in understanding. This is what typifies the higher levels of ego function.

That progressive development involves the increasing definition of the boundary between self and other on the road to autonomy underlies all theories of ego development. Adolescence, for example, is seen as a second stage of separation and individuation, a period of increasing independence and personal responsibility (Blos, 1962; Josselson, 1980). But, as Kegan and others showed, such increasing self-determination coincides with new challenges in articulating the self with others, experiencing the self in an ever more complex and differentiated intersubjective world. As psychology more seriously tackles the problems of understanding adult development, issues of intersubjectivity, with all of its murkiness, rise to the fore.

AN EXAMPLE FROM IDENTITY RESEARCH

My own interest has been in tracking the growth of identity, an aspect of ego development, from adolescence to adulthood. In this work, I relied on Erikson's concept of identity which, in its stress on the mutual attunement and mutual regulation between the individual and society, is a fundamentally intersubjective phenomenon. In a 20-year longitudinal study of college-educated women's development, I found the most profound developmental changes to lie in this realm of intersubjectivity, in the way in which a woman positions her self experience in light of her experience of others as subjects (Josselson, 1996). But these revisions exist in a felt sense of the self, an orientation to one's place in one's world, and they are inordinately difficult to put into words. The most arduous task, as one women phrased it, was to maintain awareness of her needs and others' needs at the same time. Carol Gilligan (1982) described this inclusion of self in the ethic of care as the highest stage of female moral development, and it appears to be a central theme of ego development, as well.

Although I did not initially assess ego development according to Loevinger's model, the identity statuses (Marcia, 1966) into which I categorized my participants correlate with levels of ego development. Both late-adolescent Foreclosures and Diffusions generally score lower in ego development than Identity Achievements and Moratoriums (Adams & Shea, 1979 ; Ginsburg & Orlofsky, 1981), who are more likely to be located in postconformist levels. In my observation of these women as college seniors, Foreclosures and Diffusions also seemed to operate less from an intersubjective awareness than did those who were farther along in identity formation.[2]

Foreclosures were women who were assessed as college seniors to have an identity rooted in commitment without exploration. They had adopted their parents' goals and values without much internal debate. They regarded their parents as others whose approval was to be earned, and they held only stereotyped views of the others in their lives. They were oriented to goodness and followed prescribed forms of action. Their own inner lives or the inner lives of others seemed to have little interest for them. They felt secure in holding to firmly internalized, parentally derived, sources of self-esteem, a form of being which bought them freedom from anxiety. The Foreclosures lived with an inner conviction that if they are very good the world will treat them as an adored daughter, approve of them, protect them, and cherish them. To the world, they presented their conscientiousness, their moral purpose, their respect for rules and goodness in hopes of reward. They were both self-focused and selfless in their orientation. They were willing to put aside their own needs in order to be of service and to do right, thus selfless, but more deeply, they acted in their own interest, their wish to be seen as lovably angelic, and they were highly aware of their own goodness.

All of this was under pressure to change as these women moved through their 20s. They found that few, if any, people in the larger world were willing to treat them as adored daughters and many of them felt confused and frightened by this. Most of the Foreclosures found it difficult to make or maintain highly intimate relationships or friendships although they managed to get by with others on their dutifulness. It was usually not until their mid-30s that these women came to realize that relationships are not about "doing it right." Their Conformist or Conscientious orientation to relationship seemed no longer to serve them well. Instead, they were learning, relationships involve the flow of needs and responsiveness, of feelings and irrational fantasy, of blending of capability and tolerance of eccentricity. But this was hard-won learning, which necessitated leaving aside idealizations and coming to love people (as well as the self) for what they are, with all their limitations. Most profoundly, it also involved recognition that others, unlike the idealized parents of childhood, operate from their own centers. Rather than existing to approve or disapprove of their actions, other people act out of their own complex

---

[2]Marcia (1993), in summarizing empirical findings with regard to the identity statuses concluded that although a positive relationship between identity status and ego development is well-established, the exact nature of the relationship remains to be explicated.

motivations, of which concern for the other is only a part. These women, as they grew through adulthood, came to experience other people more and more in their otherness, and relationship took place more and more between clearly articulated and recognized selves.

Linda, at age 21, regarded her mother as "a perfect mother" and strove to be worthy of her mother's approval. Her greatest fear was of disappointing her—and indeed, Linda was doing well. A top student, engaged to a man her mother adored, she felt she was successfully doing all she was "supposed to" do in life. By age 32, struggling with her own perfectionism, she had come to think that perhaps her mother had been too demanding, had made her take too much responsibility after her father died when she was 11—and she recognized that her own demandingness was creating problems in her marriage. Her now more critical view of her mother was also more complex, as was her self-understanding. By age 43, however, now a mother of two children, Linda found herself thinking about how it must have been for her mother to have lost her husband at the same age. "I don't know how she did it," Linda said. "I couldn't do it alone. Now I see why she had to lean on me and my brother so much—it was all too much for her." At this age, Linda had become more forgiving of her own imperfections, including her perfectionism, and she felt herself to be in more empathic relationships with her family and her friends and more aware of her interest in understanding the contexts in which other people are who they are.

But these realizations were not limited to the Foreclosures. Women in the other groups also found their growth catalyzed by new understandings of their mothers. Gretchen, one of the Identity Achievements, at age 35, struggling to integrate a life of work and family, understood in a new way what it meant that her mother had given up the career she had been building to raise a family. "I always thought she didn't like me. Now I realize she just didn't like her life," Gretchen said. Just after her 40th birthday, Marlene, in the Moratorium group, whose Holocaust-survivor mother died when Marlene was 24, became interested in tracing her mother's history. "I'm now at an age where I can remember my mother at the same age and I really want to understand better how it must have been for her then." Marlene, who had always felt too different from her mother to identify with her, was now trying to relate her own experiences to her mother's in a new way.

For these women, as for others, becoming the same age as their mother was a marker event—even a metaphor—of a new way of organizing experience. The first object had now more fully become a subject, and the reverberations were felt, ripple-fashion, in all areas of their life. (But I do not exclude the possibility that gains in intersubjectivity in other realms of life may have made possible this understanding, or that the growth of intersubjective awareness takes place in a stepwise, checkered fashion.) To return to the example cited earlier, these women could now, in effect, look out the window at the squirrel from the perspective of their mother who was holding them and understand why she responded to them as she did, how this affected their own development, and at the same time experience themselves as in a new relationship to her, both internally and externally, as a woman just like themselves. Growth in intersubjective functioning invokes a process of reunderstanding of all of those people who seemed earlier to be only objects of self-experience, approvers or disapprovers of the self, withholders or givers of love, whose actions seemed to be responses to the self rather than actions obeying their own inner mechanisms which the self only influences in part. This greater understanding repositions self experience in a world of more-complex others who more fully operate from their own, often hidden and sometimes unfathomable, centers. And this, in turn, invokes a renarration of one's own history and understanding of self (Gergen & Gergen, 1988; McAdams, 1993; Vaillant,1977). Gretchen's adult recognition that her mother did not dislike her involved a complete reordering of her psychological world. And Marlene was in search of self-understanding through trying to find her mother in herself—as well as outside of herself. It was this greater awareness of the need to contain the tension of different minds that my participants, as they grew from adolescence into adulthood, groped to put into words. Identity itself seemed to become less rooted in social roles and more in their differentiating awareness of their embeddedness with others.

This revision in self–other understanding is ongoing, rather than a process that comes to an end. Such learning continues, often daily, throughout life. As I listened to my participants—at each age, in all the identity groups—I heard them struggling to refine this understanding, moving backwards and forwards, now churlishly demanding their own way, now resentfully doing what others want, but having moments of recognizing something in the other that helps them better understand their interaction, more and more articulating the self with others, struggling to maintain empathy, respect, and authenticity. In Benjamin's terms, their development is away from the experience of the self as passive or dominated (or dominating) and toward more equal connections with others where relatedness and mutuality are preserved despite recognition of difference.

Another one of the identity status groups, the Diffusions, at the other extreme from the Foreclosures, lacked a clear sense of themselves as they were about to graduate from college—a time when, for others, adolescence draws to a close. At the end of college, they still easily lost themselves in others and in impulses of the moment. They were caught by what was immediate in their lives and felt unable to plan a future for themselves or to regard themselves as other than infinitely malleable. Their developmental journey was marked by the challenge of trying to define a self by separating out from their ambivalent merger with others. For them, the needs and interests of others formed an overwhelming cacophony which they could escape only by fleeing the relationship itself. Growth into adulthood for the women in this group consisted of containing the self in relationship, erecting a boundary that would persist in the face of others' distinctiveness. Unclear about their own inner life, they persistently misjudged others, imagining them to be what they wished them to be. For the Diffusions, growth involved gaining greater clarity about both sides of this balance—who they are, who others are. They were grasping for intersubjective awareness, finding their own subjectivity by trying to more fully appreciate the otherness of others. Increasing differentiation coincides with increasing relationship to the world (Kegan, 1982). As they grew, both they and the people in their lives began to emerge from chiaroscuro and take on more definite shape. And this, too, was an arduous and longterm project—one that remains dynamic and continuing.

These processes of rebalancing self and other are easiest to observe in people like the Foreclosures and Diffusions where, in adolescence, there are visible imbalances in the experience of interpersonal boundaries. But even among women who were classified as Identity Achievements, those who had explored alternatives and made commitments, those whose ego development was farthest along at the end of college, adulthood involves progressive reworking of intersubjective experience. Ego development proceeds beyond the integration of identity and it seems to progress in terms of increasing intersubjective connection. In these groups, there is movement toward what Loevinger tried to capture in her description of the Autonomous and Integrated stages—not so much structural change as changes in position of the self vis-a-vis others. In my longitudinal study, what these women most stressed about their learning was learning about relationship—learning more about how to be with others, to tolerate and honor their differences rather than to engage in some process of mutual coercion where one or the other must "change," to accept others' awareness (and tolerance) of one's own imperfections, to be able to give and receive while containing the hatred that always accompanies dependency, to accept the inherent limitations of love, and so on. They move in the direction of what Benjamin termed an increased capacity for recognition—of self and of the indestructibility (and hence, independence) of the other. The growth of such interpersonal understanding was coincident with more complex awareness about the self, heralding a new way of making sense of experience, the core of Loevinger's concept of ego development.

INTERSUBJECTIVITY AND THE
CHALLENGES OF ADULTHOOD

Another theoretical polarization obscuring recognition of intersubjective growth is the bifurcation of adult development into the realms of love and work. Lest it be assumed that the realms in which adults learn about intersubjective experience are limited to family and friendship, I want to stress that adult development in career also implies maturation in an intersubjective awareness of the world. In the psychological understanding of adulthood, we have largely ignored the fact that much of "taking up adult work roles" involves interpersonal negotiation and learning to position the self intersubjectively in the maelstrom of the often contradictory needs of individuals and groups. (One of my participants, a highly successful trial lawyer, for example, attributes her success to having learned just how and when to "loosen up" the judge.) In the work world, articulating the self with others, appreciating the vagaries and dynamics of office politics, struggling with the inevitable problems of forming a task-oriented group—these are training exercises in higher forms of ego development (see Sinnott, 1993). It is in this more public realm that the enigmas of diversity and difference are unavoidable, and the challenges to the ego involve learning to accept difference without either assimilating the self to the other (through identification) or by reducing difference to sameness (see Benjamin, 1994; Sampson, 1993). In effect, the dilemmas of forming a society composed of others who are also subjects appear as the central challenges of adulthood. It may be that receptivity to the dialogic processes of intersubjective awareness is the mechanism driving development to higher levels of experience (Habermas, 1979; Leadbeater, 1989).

Ego development in adulthood, then, seems to turn on greater learning about the self in relation to a relational, intersubjective world that becomes, in circular fashion, ever more differentiated. The more we learn about ourselves in relation to others, the more there is yet to learn. There is no final stage. This is a region that, because of our limitations of language (and of current conceptualization) remains largely uncharted. To date, we have a growing literature speaking to the importance of understanding the self as growing "in-relation" (see Miller, 1976, 1987, 1988), intersubjectively, but future research is still necessary to better chart the terrain of the relational world and to understand how the reworking of adult self–other experience unfolds. The Autonomous person, wrote Loevinger, "recognizes the limitations to autonomy, that emotional interdependence is inevitable." In this way, her work anticipated the new frontier psychoanalytic theory is just beginning to explore.

IV

CLINICAL IMPLICATIONS

15

Ego Development, Pubertal Development, and Depressive Symptoms in Adolescent Girls

Jill Rierdan
Department of Psychology
University of Massachusetts at Boston

In this chapter, I have two goals. The narrow aim is to present empirical findings regarding ego development and depressive symptomatology among adolescent girls; the broader aim is to consider the relationship between ego development and the variety of psychopathologies over the life span. It is interest in this broader goal that informs the empirical inquiries presented, and that leads me to generalize beyond them. The organization of this chapter follows from these goals: The presentation of empirical studies on ego development, pubertal development, and depression in adolescent girls is preceded by (a) a general consideration of the field of developmental psychopathology, which is the broad context for the research, (b) a brief overview of Loevinger's views of ego development and psychopathology, and (c) the introduction of a model considering ego development in the context of predisposing, precipitating, perpetuating, and protective factors for the onset and avoidance of psychopathology. The empirical findings are followed by (d) a consideration of how the study of psychopathology might better be informed by attention to Loevinger's model of ego development.

CONTEXT: DEVELOPMENTAL PSYCHOPATHOLOGY

The field of developmental psychopathology was only recently christened (e.g., Cicchetti, 1984b), yet it is scarcely newborn. Its two fundamental assumptions—that an understanding of psychopathology requires an understanding of normal development, and that psychopathology is best understood as a maladaptive developmental variant, not defect or disease—were anticipated over 50 years ago by Heinz Werner (1948/1961) and Harry Stack Sullivan, whose lectures and writings in the 1920s and 1930s were published in 1962. Werner, cognitive–developmental psychologist and prolific empirical investigator, held the same lens to examination of the ontogenesis of mentation and to the comparison, at equivalent ages, of the psychological functioning of individuals differing in forms of psychopathology. The lens—his theoretical point of view—was the orthogenetic principle: Whenever development occurs, it proceeds from globality to increasing differentiation of parts and hierarchic integration. Werner looked for evidence of developmental patterns in the microgenesis of perceptions, in ontogenetic changes in motor behavior, perception, and language, and in comparison of the language, perception, and thought of psychotics, neurotics, and normals (as they were called at the time). Werner understood that observation is inherently dependent on theory. He looked for evidence to support his view of development; he did not believe that "development" would reveal itself to him in the data he collected.

Sullivan, a psychiatrist treating severely schizophrenic young adults, articulated a developmental theory of personality in terms of which he considered schizophrenic deviations. In so doing, he offered his one-genus postulate: "We are all more simply human than otherwise." It is this view, perhaps, that led to his ability to relate more successfully to schizophrenics than most at the time, and to facilitate not just symptom reduction or social adjustment, but personality development in those he treated.

My premise, consistent with the discipline of developmental psychopathology and influenced by the writings of Werner and Sullivan, is that the various psychopathologies are some of the many ways of being human, as comprehensible in principle—and comprehensible in terms of the *same* principles—as are the variety of adaptive developmental outcomes.

Within this perspective, considerations of development, personality, and psychopathology are inextricably linked. In terms of descriptive nosology, different psychopathologies are thought to be developmentally ordered, both in relation to each other and to more normative states of psychological functioning. This means that pathological conditions are seen as qualitatively, not simply quantitatively, different from various normative states, and also that there is continuity from normal to abnormal in relation to the same developmental principles. Further, in considering the same diagnosable states (e.g., depression, simple phobia) in individuals of different developmental levels, an assumption is made that symptom expression, configuration, and persistence, will vary.

In terms of the etiology of various psychopathologies, an assumption in developmental psychopathology is that different developmental stages or levels of organization render individuals more or less vulnerable; the persistence of ontogenetically more primitive states of personality organization, for example, is thought to render the individual more vulnerable to analogously primitive and pathological states in adulthood.

In terms of the sequelae of psychopathology, the experience of maladjustment is thought potentially to disrupt development, in terms of either inducing regression from more mature levels or by impeding expected advances. For children and adolescents, speculation has been that the experience of disorder and maladjustment may interrupt development, so that the child, recovering after some time, is less developmentally mature than would be expected from his or her chronological age.

Since the 1980s, when the field of developmental psychopathology sought to define itself and to articulate its central suppositions, other important changes were taking place in approaches to normal child and adolescent development and to the etiology of severe psychopathology. These changes pertain to a growing acceptance that multifactorial models are needed to understand normal and abnormal development. Replacing conceptions of one radical cause, theories in clinical psychology and psychiatry came to embrace, in the 1970s, diathesis-stress models, that is, explanations of psychopathology in terms of the interaction of biological vulnerability and psychosocial stressors. More recently, four classes of variables were identified—predisposing, precipitating, perpetuating, and protective—in attempting to understand acute and enduring psychopathologies and, as well, the avoidance of psychopathology by youngsters deemed "at risk."

Although terminology varies across time and disciplines, two points are generally accepted: (a) predisposing factors (or vulnerabilities) lead to maladjustment only with exposure to precipitating factors (i.e., risk experiences or stressors), and lead to enduring dysfunction only with the presence of perpetuating factors; vulnerabilities, in other words, do not inevitably conduce to maladjustment; (b) exposure to risk factors in the context of vulnerability may be mitigated by protective factors, so that maladjustment is avoided.

Rutter (e.g., 1986, 1990) addressed the importance of protective factors in accounting for the resilience of children who are both vulnerable and exposed to considerable risk. Protective factors facilitate a more adaptive reaction to a risk that under ordinary circumstances, for many vulnerable individuals, would lead to a maladaptive outcome. They do so by helping the individual more adaptively appraise and assign meaning to, or cope with risks to adjustment (Rutter, 1990). Protective factors are assumed to operate only in the presence of vulnerability and risk. Unlike positive factors, which are assumed to predict directly to well-being, protective factors have no direct relationship to (mal)adjustment. In the terminology of ANOVA, the protective factor will appear in a significant interaction term, where it changes the effect of another variable; it will not have a main or direct effect of its own.

It may be assumed that predisposing, precipitating, perpetuating, and protective factors may be primarily biological, psychological, or sociocultural (as if these distinctions might neatly be made); thus, multifactorial approaches to psychopathology are generally biopsychosocial models. This inelegant term is of value as it clarifies the obvious; we can no more expect to understand people in terms of one broad dimension of human life—biological, psychological, or sociocultural—than we can in terms of one variable. Our humanity, and that of our research participants and patients, is inextricably biopsychosocial, and so also must our theories be.

I suggest that biopsychosocial approaches to psychopathology be construed in broadly developmental terms. Some developmental stages may constitute vulnerabilities or predisposing conditions; others may be protective. Further, it may be that many of the life events which are cited as "precipitating events" gain this status because of their salience in relation to particular developmental levels, that is, they precipitate maladjustment because they are challenges for individuals with particular developmental vulnerabilities. Even with those events that are such egregious assaults on humanity that they are likely to precipitate dysfunction whatever the individual's developmental stage, the degree of ensuing dysfunction may vary with developmental level. Moreover, it seems likely that the developmental status of the individual might also relate to the likelihood of recovering following psychic disruption.

The suggestion that studies of the predisposing, precipitating, perpetuating, and protective variables in psychopathology be broadly developmental—that is, related to qualitative, not simply quantitative, change over time—may seem obvious and unnecessary to mention. Yet, most empirical studies in this field rely on chronological age as the meaning or index of development in "developmental" psychopathology. It is rare to see studies of the relationship between psychopathology and a developmentally ordered dimension, or to see a qualitative analysis of developmental differences in the phenomenology and organization of pathologies, although some exceptions appear in this volume.

Studies of age and psychopathology are valuable, but they are limited in what they can tell us. Wohlwill (1973) clarified that age is a marker, not a measure of development. As such, it is global and undifferentiated, a biopsychosocial net when used as an independent variable, a term scarcely more specific that "etc." when controlled for in studies of the relationship between other more discrete variables. It is important to study more defined, qualitative dimensions of development in empirical studies of developmental psychopathology, ones that are both age-related and also sensitive to individual differences within age. Just as an obvious example in the biological realm is pubertal development, an obvious example in the realm of personality is Loevinger's (1976) model and measure of ego development. How might ego development be construed in the biopsychosocial matrix of predisposing, precipitating, perpetuating, and protective factors for psychopathology? How might ego development and pubertal development interact?

EGO DEVELOPMENT AND
PSYCHOPATHOLOGY: AN OVERVIEW

At the same time Loevinger was publishing her early writings on ego development (e.g., Loevinger, 1966a), philosophers of science were writing of the "theory dependency of observation" (e.g., Hanson, 1958). They rejected the dichotomy between observation ("data") and theory, and contended that interpretation was inherent in the act of observation, whatever the object of scrutiny.

Loevinger's model of ego development seems consistent with this thesis, at the same time that the arena of concern is the more intensely personal, yet everyday realm, of individual experience. As Loevinger and Knoll (1983) wrote, meaning-making is synonymous with ego; ego development represents an outlook (Loevinger, 1994), a principle or organization, an active and integrating process (Loevinger, 1987a). Ego development is the personal theory mediating our personal and interpersonal experiences: a master trait.

As master trait, ego development can be described abstractly in terms of structural, or formal, properties, as well as content, or functional, properties, with the two inextricably related. In structural terms, ego development strives toward coherence (Loevinger, 1993), with increasing levels of differentiation and hierarchic integration (Loevinger & Knoll, 1983). In terms of content, ego development is manifest across four psychological–behavioral domains—impulse control and character, interpersonal relationships, conscious preoccupations, and cognitive style. Analogously, the 9 stages of ego development have formal and functional properties. Each stage corresponds in its prototypic state to a stable structure, with a coherent and unified organization; each stage can be typified thematically (e.g., Impulsive, Self-Protective, Conformist, . . . Autonomous, Integrated), with thematic differences reflecting different levels of complexity in structure. Ego development, as a whole, and each stage, in particular, is an abstraction (Loevinger, 1966a, 1979b, 1994)—inferred, not observed.

The structural–thematic focus of each stage constitutes its qualitative difference from all other stages and places it relative to other stages in an invariant sequence of increasingly more differentiated and integrated stages. The combined focus on structure and theme distinguishes Loevinger's developmental theory from that of Werner (1948/1961), who tended to focus on structure in his abstract characterization of development, and of Sullivan (1962), whose thematic analysis was more restricted.

It has been suggested that a theory of personality needs to be able to explain four phenomena: Change and consistency within the individual; differences and similarity between and among individuals. Ego development seems fully able to meet this requirement. Intraindividual change, of course, is what development describes, as the individual transforms and is transformed over the life cycle. Increases in ego development are significantly correlated with age, at least through adolescence (e.g., Redmore & Loevinger, 1979). Intraindividual consistency—or stability—can be explained in terms of the stabilizing of most adults at a particular developmental stage in early adulthood (e.g., Costa & McCrae, 1993). Individual differences reflect the manifestation of differences in stages of ego development (Loevinger, 1984). Evidence of such differences were found among adults in the absence of a significant relationship with age (Costa & McCrae, 1993) and within same-age cohorts of adolescents (e.g., Gold, 1980). Individual similarity can be accounted for, abstractly, in terms of a multitude of individuals being at the same developmental level, of which but 10 stages have been described conceptually. Holt (1980), for example, found that almost 40% of U.S. adults were at the Self-Aware stage.

Given this breadth of application—one which is explicitly developmental and also dealing with individual differences—ego development seems ideally suited as a dimension of study by those concerned with developmental psychopathology. Further, given the view of ego development as a master trait in terms of which individuals organize experience and act in the world, it seems that surely differences in ego development must be related to psychopathology. It seems, in other words, that Loevinger's concern with understanding *how* individuals organize their experience and act in the world must be related to the clinician's concern with understanding how *well* individuals organize and function in their worlds. Yet the relationship is far from clear.

From her provocative 1966 article in *American Psychologist* to her essays and commentary in the 1990s, Loevinger reiterates the *conceptual* independence of ego development and maladjustment or psychopathology. She contends, again and again, that ego development is *not* a continuum of adjustment or mental health. She noted (e.g., Loevinger, 1966a, 1968) that every stage has the potential for adjustment and growth, as well as maladjustment—certainly what one would expect, because these are stages in ordinary development and "normative" or modal at different ages, at least through the fifth or sixth stage of ego development.

To say that ego development and pathology are conceptually distinct and bear no necessary empirical relationship, is not to say, however, that no empirical relationship should be expected—an important distinction which has often been misstated. What are the results, then, of empirical research considering the relationship between ego development and psychopathology? Is there evidence that individuals at lower levels of ego development demonstrate psychopathology more often and with a greater degree of severity than do individuals at higher levels of ego development? Is there a symmetrical relationship between level of ego development and psychopathology such that low levels of ego development invariably relate to psychopathology and, in turn, psychopathology invariably relates to low levels of ego development?

With respect to the first issue, there are a number of studies (e.g., Gold, 1980; Helson & Wink, 1987) demonstrating a relationship between ego development and pathology. Studies include both genders, adolescents and adults, community and clinical samples, and those levels of ego development for age that are modal or above the mode. At the same time, there are a number of studies that did not find such a relationship (e.g., Vaillant & McCullough, 1987) or found that certain forms of pathology are more prevalent at higher developmental levels (e.g., Borst, Noam, & Bartok, 1991).

With respect to the issue of symmetry between lower levels of ego development and psychopathology, the data support what Loevinger would expect. Even in studies demonstrating significant linear relationships between ego and pathology, as well as those that did not, there are significant proportions of individuals at relatively low levels of ego development who do not evidence psychopathology, at least as assessed. Conversely, there are numerous reports of individuals warranting clinical diagnoses who score above the modal level of ego development for their age (e.g., Noam & Dill, 1991).

Is there a way of reconciling Loevinger's proposition that ego development and adjustment are conceptually distinct—supported by evidence that low or immature levels of ego development are not inherently

maladaptive nor high levels of ego development inherently adaptive—
with the intuition, and confirmation in some empirical studies, that there
is a meaningful relationship between ego development and
psychopathology? My view, of course, is that ego development be
considered within the biopsychosocial matrix of predisposing,
precipitating, perpetuating, and protective factors in the development of
psychopathologies.

EGO DEVELOPMENT AND DEVELOPMENTAL PSYCHOPATHOLOGY

At the simplest of levels, the relationship between ego development and
adjustment must take into account environmental demands and supports.
A child at a modal level of ego development, who is raised in Winnicott's
"average expectable environment," should be relatively well-adjusted.
Such a child should continue with an adequate level of adjustment, if
environmental demands increase in ways congruent with level of ego
development, and thus are sufficiently manageable and also sufficiently
challenging to support and facilitate continued development. It is assumed
that for most people, most of the time, such a congruence occurs, so that
most mature in ego development throughout childhood and adolescence
and maintain an adequate level of functioning. Such an assumption
accounts for the fact that only a minority of people are regarded as
maladjusted at any age or developmental level.

It is assumed that various psychopathologies emerge in adolescence
and early adulthood for one of three reasons. First, individuals at relatively
low levels of ego development—below the mode for their age—may be
unable to cope with normative age-graded stressors. This situation seems
analogous to what Hauser (1976) and Noam et al. (1984) described as age-
stage dysynchrony in their explanation of adolescent psychopathology,
and to what Loevinger (1968) postulated might be important in her early
writings on ego development and adjustment. Second, individuals at a
modal level of ego development may be confronted with stressors that are
normative (i.e., not deviant) but off-time relative to their age and maturity
level (e.g., adolescent pregnancy, death of a parent in childhood), so that
their ego functioning is inadequate for adaptive adjustment. Third,
individuals at a variety of levels of ego development may be confronted
by atypical, traumatic experiences (e.g., rape, hostage taking) which
surpass the capacities of most individuals whatever their level of ego
development, at least temporarily.

Considering ego development in the broad matrix of predisposing,
precipitating, perpetuating, and protective factors in the onset and

persistence of psychopathology, ego development is seen as constituting a context or lens affecting an individual's appraisal and subsequent coping with biological, psychological, and social risks. According to this model, relatively low levels of ego development would be seen as a possible predisposing factor for psychopathology with age-graded, off-time, or atypical conditions, but might be associated with well-being when the individual experiences a benign life course. Relatively high levels of ego development would be seen as a possible protective factor when the individual is confronted with off-time or atypical challenges, facilitating continued adjustment that would not likely be maintained by individuals at modal or low levels of ego development. At the same time, high levels of ego development would not be expected to be associated with unusual well-being, in general. The proposed model, then, does not assume a direct, linear relationship between ego development and psychopathology, but rather views levels of ego development as predisposing or protective factors that, in interaction with risk experiences (precipitating events), may conduce to or help avoid different degrees and forms of psychopathology.

This formulation seems consistent with Loevinger's admonition that ego development is not synonymous with adjustment and that there is no necessary relationship between ego development and adjustment. At the same time, it takes seriously the sense that a psychological dimension as fundamental and encompassing as ego development—a master trait—must be meaningfully related to psychopathology. In positing that ego development moderates response to life stressors, this model seems consistent with Loevinger's (1966b) contention that ego level might have a complex "triggering or facilitating" effect in relation to (mal)adjustment.

Evaluation of this model requires a research paradigm wherein level of ego development, presence of a life stressor, and a measure of psychopathology are obtained. The model was tested in studies of the impact of ego development for adolescent girls' depression, given presence–absence of a stressor related to pubertal timing.

EGO, PUBERTY, AND DEPRESSION
IN ADOLESCENT GIRLS

Loevinger (1979b) made clear the dynamic, reciprocal relationship between theory and observations about ego development. In this way, theory is a lens, not blinders, and when anomalous observations are made, the theory changes so as to render the anomalous, eventually, expected—postdicted, if not predicted.

My route to the view that ego development may be a moderator of response to stressors was guided by perplexing findings in my studies of adolescent girls' depression. The research, conducted with Elissa Koff, sought to clarify the complex relationships among the biological, psychological, and interpersonal changes taking place in early adolescence. The rapidity and breadth of change in early adolescence presents an opportunity for studying how individuals adapt to normative stressors and challenges; it is of interest to developmental psychopathologists because it is a watershed period for psychopathology, with gender-linked disorders such as depression increasing dramatically.

We undertook two major studies. In the first, we gave a large battery of measures, including Loevinger's SCT, to over 600 girls in sixth, seventh, eighth, and ninth grades, and tested each girl twice, in the fall and spring of a school year. In the second study, we followed a sample of 146 girls from the fall of the sixth grade through spring of the ninth, testing them every 6 months; measures of ego development were available for girls from the first test occasion.

Age-related increases in level of ego development among girls in the first study were consistent with the view of ego functioning as a developmental variable. There was a significant increase in ego functioning from sixth through ninth grade (Rierdan, Koff, Costos, & Stubbs, 1987b). The mode for sixth graders was the Self-Protective stage (Delta[1]), the mode for seventh and eighth graders was the next higher stage (Delta/3), and the mode for ninth graders was two stages above that, the Self-Aware stage (3/4). Collapsing these individual stages into three broad categories— preconformist (stages through Delta/3), conformist (Conformist and Self-Aware stages), and postconformist—the mode for sixth (70%), seventh (67%), and eighth (63%) graders was the preconformist level, whereas the mode for ninth graders (55%) was the conformist category. In the context of these grade-related increases in ego development, there were conspicuous individual differences. Within each grade, girls spanned at least four stages of ego development.

In both studies, the Beck Depression Inventory (BDI), short form, was used as the measure of depression (Beck & Beck, 1972). Although this measure has the weakness of any response-constraining objective measure, it also seems likely to transcend many of the limitations associated with

---

[1]The notation for ego levels used in this chapter corresponds to the notation of the first edition of the scoring manual for the WUSCT (Loevinger & Wessler, 1970; Redmore, Loevinger, & Tamashiro, 1978). The current edition of the scoring manual (Hy & Loevinger, 1996) introduced several changes. See the Appendix to the introductory chapter of this volume for a comparison between the previous and the current system.

such measures. It provides both a continuous measure of symptom severity (across 13 symptoms) and also cut-off scores for clinically validated categories. Scores from 0–4 reflect the absence of or minimal depressive symptoms, 5–7 reflect mild levels, 8–15 reflect moderate, and 16 and above reflect severe levels of depressive symptoms. Our research in other areas suggests that adolescents moderate to severe in depressive symptoms report a plethora of personal and interpersonal problems.Thus, high depressive symptom levels do not seem simply to measure one behavioral or psychological domain, but rather a way of being in the world that is organized around dysphoria.

Ego Development and Depression
in Adolescent Girls

Initial analyses of girls in sixth through ninth grades looked at the relationship between ego development and depression, as moderated by age. We hypothesized that overall relationships between lower levels of ego development and depression, if found in a group of girls with an age range of 4 years, would be accounted for by subgroups of youngsters. We expected that a preconformist level of functioning would be associated with depression only among older girls, for whom it represented immaturity and for whom it was unlikely to be congruent with age-graded life challenges; we expected preconformist levels to be unrelated to depression among younger girls, for whom this was the modal developmental level.

Results (Rierdan, Koff, Costos, & Stubbs, 1987a) showed that there was a significant relationship between level of ego development and depressive symptomatology in the sample of girls, overall, with lower stages of ego development associated with higher depression levels. Comparing girls in the broadly defined categories of preconformist and conformist levels of ego development, higher depression scores were more characteristic of preconformists (mean depressive score = 5.64) than conformists (4.03). The level of depressive symptoms, however, represented only minimal to mild depressive symptoms for both groups.

We then considered the relationship between ego development and depressive symptoms in the context of age. Preconformist girls were classified in terms of grade (grade was correlated .94 with age) and a one-way ANOVA assessed the relationship between grade and depression level. There was a significant effect. Depressive symptom scores for preconformist girls were 7.40 for sixth graders, 4.34 for seventh graders, 4.47 for eighth graders, and 7.95 for ninth graders. Post hoc analyses indicated, as expected, that ninth-grade preconformists, who were below the mode for ego development for their age, had higher levels of depressive symptoms than both seventh and eighth graders, for whom a preconformist level of ego functioning was modal. The problem was in the elevated scores on the sixth-grade girls. We were perplexed. Why were the sixth grade preconformist girls elevated in depressive symptom levels relative to their seventh and eighth grade peers? We could take little comfort in this difference being not-quite-statistically-significant at the .05 level. For some reason, the sixth-grade preconformists—at the modal level of ego development for age—looked almost as symptomatic as did the ninth-grade cohort at a delayed level of ego development. The model of Hauser (1976) and Noam et al. (1984), which explains maladjustment in terms of age–stage dysynchrony, that is, in terms of youngsters being lower in ego development than is normative for age and thus unable to cope with age-graded demands—did not offer an explanation, since the sixth graders were not low or dysynchronous in ego development relative to age.

We presented these results at a conference, started to write them for publication, but could never satisfy ourselves with explaining the depressive symptom levels of the sixth-grade preconformist girls. It did not make sense for their scores to be so high. And these scores were high—as a group, the mean score was almost in the moderate range of depressive symptomatology. We came back to these findings repeatedly over the years, and never felt satisfied that we understood them until we shifted our focus, looked at a different question related to pubertal development and depression, and then saw the connection between these two issues.

Puberty and Depression

In early adolescence, there is a significant increase in adolescent girls' depression. There has been considerable speculation about this, and it has been suggested that a normal developmental change—puberty, or most specifically, the onset of menstruation—may make girls vulnerable to depression. This explanation suffers from logical and empirical difficulties: Does it make sense, from a psychodynamic or evolutionary perspective, to assume that a developmental advance, one associated with reproductive maturity, would be inherently maladaptive? Does it make sense to attribute increases in prevalence of depression—characteristic, still, of a small percentage of early adolescent girls—to a developmental change experienced universally by healthy girls? The relationship is more complex than initially suggested.

The onset of menstruation, or menarche, is quintessentially a biopsychosocial event. Related to internal hormonal changes, menarche follows other more observable body changes—height and fat spurt, breast budding, the appearance of pubic hair. Yet, it is a unique developmental event. It is discrete and discontinuous; it occurs without precise predictability; it involves a tangible product: blood. Menarche precipitates and necessitates changes in body image, self-concept, family, and social status (Simmons & Blyth, 1987).

The mean age for menarche for White girls in the United States is 12.8 years (Faust, 1983). The normal age range is 10–16 years. Despite the large age range during which healthy girls may reach menarche, girls have definite preferences about when they want to reach menarche (Ruble & Brooks-Gunn, 1982). The preferred age for menarche seems to be between 12 and 13; if a girl differs from this, the preference is to be late. Very early menarche is perceived by girls as a deviation from a developmental "social clock" related to the timing of menarche—"off-time," not simply early, and highly undesirable.

Although it is likely that all girls experience menarche as a challenge as they attempt to assimilate the changes in body image, self-concept, family, and social status accompanying the onset of menstruation, it would seem especially challenging for early maturing girls. For these girls, menarche is often unexpected, frightening and confusing, and mistakenly related to soiling or disease or injury (Rierdan, Koff, & Flaherty, 1986). Unlike girls who mature between 12 and 13, early maturing girls are more likely to experience a loss of childhood than a leap to maturity with the onset of menstruation. They are, in their experience, socially deviant at a time when conformity is so important.

With a sample of sixth-, seventh-, and eighth-grade girls, some from the study reported earlier and some from the second study undertaken, we explored the hypothesis that timing of menarche, but not menarche per se, was related to elevated levels of depression. We hypothesized that postmenarcheal girls who matured very early would have higher levels of depression than did premenarcheal girls of the same age; we expected that postmenarcheal girls who had matured at an average age would be equivalent in depression to their premenarcheal peers.

Our results (Rierdan & Koff, 1991) supported this hypothesis. Postmenarcheal sixth-grade girls, who were within the youngest 10% of girls to reach menarche, had significantly higher depression scores (6.09) than did their premenarcheal peers (3.41). In contrast, postmenarcheal seventh-grade girls (30% of seventh graders) did not differ (5.89) from their premenarcheal peers (4.22), nor did postmenarcheal eighth graders (50% of the eighth graders) differ (4.02) from their premenarcheal peers (3.38). Very early menarcheal timing constituted a developmental challenge conducive to higher levels of depression, but menarche per se was not associated with increased depressive symptomatology.

At the same time that very early maturers, as a group, were more depressed than their on-time peers, there was variability within this group—not all had elevated depression scores. With this recognition came the clue to explaining the anomalous findings of the preconformist sixth graders reported earlier: Might the variability in depressive symptomatology within the group of very early maturing girls be accounted for in terms of their level of ego development? Might it be sixth graders at a preconformist level of ego development who had elevated depression levels when they were faced with the premature challenge of early menarche? We turned to investigate the hypothesis that ego development interacts with life challenges to affect levels of adjustment.

Ego Development as a Moderator of the Impact of Puberty Timing for Adolescent Girls' Depression. Our hypothesis (Rierdan & Koff, 1993) was that very early menarche would lead to elevated levels of depressive symptoms primarily for girls who were at lower levels of ego development. We reasoned that relative immaturity of impulse control, cognition, interpersonal stance, and preoccupations—even when modal for age—would make it difficult for girls to assimilate and master the biological, psychological, and social changes that very early timing of menarche presents. At the same time, we expected that the same level of ego functioning would be associated with minimal levels of depressive symptoms for girls not facing off-time developmental challenges or stress. We also reasoned that girls who were relatively advanced in ego development (above the mode for age) would be generally free of depressive symptoms not only in the absence of off-time challenges but also when experiencing very early menarche, by virtue of having a more mature capacity for coping and understanding that enables integration of the psychosocial changes precipitated and necessitated by their biological development. We viewed preconformist levels of ego functioning as a predisposing factor (a vulnerability) which, combined with the precipitating (risk) event of off-time maturing, would lead to maladjustment. We viewed conformist levels of ego functioning—advanced for age—as a protective factor enabling girls exposed to risk to remain adjusted. An interaction, then, was hypothesized between level of ego development and menarcheal timing. We did not expect ego development per se to be associated with level of depressive symptoms.

The results supported our hypotheses as we examined levels of depressive symptoms in a sample of 336 sixth-grade girls, over 75% of whom were preconformist. Controlling for age in ANCOVA, we found a significant interaction between level of ego development and menarcheal status. As predicted, those girls who were preconformist and confronted with a developmental challenge had relatively high levels of depressive symptoms—their mean score (8.25) was within the range of moderate depression. Girls who were conformist, that is, advanced for age, and experiencing the same developmental challenge were not any more depressed (2.74) than girls who were not exposed to very early menarche as a stressor. Within the latter group of girls, there was no difference between preconformist (3.39) and conformist (2.59) girls.

We explained the findings in terms of the themes and structures associated with preconformist and conformist stages of ego development. Because girls at preconformist stages of ego development are concerned with bodily feelings and issues of control, it is understandable that the experience of very early menarche could disrupt a sense of self. Furthermore, with a general immaturity of defenses, inflexible cognitive style, and dependent interpersonal style, preconformist girls would seem to be less able to adapt flexibly to the changes in body image, self, and social status that accompany very early menarche. With this difficulty renegotiating a new sense of self, depressive symptoms would likely ensue. Because a preconformist stage of ego development among sixth-grade girls does not in any way constitute "delayed" development (75% of the sample were functioning at this level), our findings suggest that girls at a level of ego development that is appropriate for their age may yet be unable to adapt well to biological events that are off-time chronologically and that present unusual demands for assimilation and adjustment. In contrast, we thought conformist girls were likely "protected" from depression by virtue of being less upset by a bodily change in the first place and by having the maturity of self-concept, interpersonal relationships, and cognitive style to permit restoration of well-being following a challenge. An advanced level of ego functioning relative to age seemed to be necessary to master successfully the challenges presented by early maturing.

To test this model further, we looked at the relationship between ego development, pubertal timing, and depressive symptoms in late maturing girls. Although girls report that late maturing is preferable to early maturing, it is nevertheless undesirable relative to maturing about the same time as peers. We assumed, therefore, that late maturing chronologically—though well within the normal age range for reaching menarche—would be a stressor for adolescent girls. Because the body experience which is challenging at this point is the failure to reach menarche when most of one's peers have, we could also clarify whether the psychological event of feeling socially deviant is a challenge in the absence of the biological changes associated specifically with the onset of menstruation.

Using the same methodological approach, we (Rierdan & Koff,

forthcoming) divided a sample of ninth grade girls according to two dimensions: level of ego development (preconformist, conformist) and level of pubertal development (premenarcheal, postmenarcheal). The developmental significance of these categorizations is different from the first analyses. Among ninth-grade girls, a preconformist level of ego functioning is immature and below the mode, whereas a conformist level of ego functioning is modal; a premenarcheal status is immature, whereas a postmenarcheal level is modal. The results were clear. The preconformist, premenarcheal girls—those immature in ego development and developmentally challenged, had unusually high levels of depressive symptoms; the mean score of 10.49 was well within the range of moderate depression. The other three groups of girls—preconformist girls at a normative stage of pubertal development (4.78), and conformist girls, whether immature (3.60) or modal (4.00) in pubertal development—were all significantly lower.

These results again illustrate that level of ego development is an important context for moderating the impact of a developmental stressor. Although a preconformist level of functioning is not inevitably associated with maladjustment—preconformist, on-time girls were not more depressed than conformist, on-time girls among either sixth or ninth graders—it does seem to constitute a vulnerability when the individual is confronted with a stressor, in this case, one that is developmentally related. Further, a conformist level does seem to protect against the possibly deleterious effects of a stressor. This study also clarifies that it may be the attainment of a conformist level of functioning—not an advanced level of functioning for age—that is key to coping with off-time pubertal development, the essential stress of which is the timing of the event, not the event per se.

EXTENSIONS AND IMPLICATIONS

The results presented are initial studies in the exploration of ego development as a predisposing or protective factor interacting with life stressors to lead to or avoid psychopathology. The results are consistent with Loevinger's contention that there is no necessary direct relationship between ego development and maladjustment, and at the same time validate the sense that a dimension of personality as inclusive as ego development must meaningfully be related to psychopathology. Because other studies (e.g., Kirshner, 1988) reported a relationship between ego development and duration of pathology and response to treatment, it may also be that ego development is a perpetuating factor for psychopathology, with maladjusted individuals at lower levels of ego development less likely to recover than similarly maladjusted individuals at higher levels of ego development.

The studies reported all focus on a biological event as a stressor, one age group, one gender, and one form of pathology, assessed with one psychometric instrument. Clearly, more work needs to fully examine all of these issues. Work currently underway with David Pillemer and Marylee Losardo examines the relationship between level of ego development, trauma, and posttraumatic stress disorder among a group of adults unlucky enough to be taken hostage in an armed robbery.

We must expand our frame of reference in other ways as we consider ego development and developmental psychopathology. First, it is important to determine if preconformist levels of ego development represent a generic vulnerability for all forms of psychopathology because of the lesser degree of differentiation and integration, or whether different preconformist stages involve vulnerabilities to different pathologies, as suggested by Loevinger (1968). Second, it is important to assess whether there are some forms of psychopathology likely to be associated with conformist or postconformist levels of ego development rather than preconformist levels because of the thematic sensitivities of higher stages in relation to particular life stressors. Third, it seems important to consider that different levels of ego development may be associated not only with different disorders but also with different forms of the same diagnosable disorder. Blatt and Berman (1990), for example, distinguished three forms of opiate addiction associated with different levels of ego development. Fourth, the relationship between level of ego development and comorbidity of disorders should be investigated. As the number of diagnoses proliferates, it becomes more common for individuals to receive multiple concurrent diagnoses. Thus far, these have been treated largely as if they were additive, or at best, interactive. It may be, however, that individuals bearing one or two or three diagnoses differ in level of ego development, with pathology appearing as less differentiated, that is, in terms of a greater number of concurrent diagnoses, for individuals at lower levels of ego development. This hypothesis is currently being explored in a large clinical sample of patients with single, dual, or multiple clinical diagnoses.

ACKNOWLEDGMENTS

Preparation of this chapter was supported by Grant DA08415 from the National Institute of Drug Abuse. The research reported was supported by Grant 16034 from the National Institute of Child Health and Human Development.

Solving the Ego Development–
Mental Health Riddle

Gil Noam
Harvard University

THE RIDDLE

Since the 1960s, the decade of the cognitive–developmental "revolution" in psychology, a riddle has intrigued, even plagued many developmental scholars and practitioners. In fact, researchers pursued many paths and were unable to "crack the code." The question: How are we to understand the relationship between social–cognitive development (i.e., self, ego, morality, and perspective-taking) and mental health, involving positive adaptation, a sense of well-being, and an absence of symptoms? The riddle: The stepwise progression from immature thought and impulsivity to complex, self-reflective, and tolerant forms of maturity consists of many components of mental health. And yet, many people at mature levels of development struggle with mental illness, neurosis, and dysfunctional adaptations to life. How is that possible?

Accepting the contradictory nature of the self, relationships, and the world at large are all hallmarks of complex development, and represent forms of positive adaptation which clinicians also tend to refer to as mental health. Thus, social–cognitive development from Piaget to Kohlberg and to Loevinger refers to evolving meaning structures and to better adaptations between the person and the world. Higher stages are better adaptations and better adaptations to the social world are also indicators of mental health. A person who is developmentally immature, for example, has fewer tools at his or her disposal with which to interpret the actions of others. As a consequence, he or she is more likely to interpret statements of others as hostile and rejecting. This lack of understanding of the inner workings of another person and the multifaceted nature of human

271

communication is a cognitive and developmental vulnerability clearly tied to adaptation. As a consequence, the likelihood of distorting ambiguous information and reacting in an aggressive and retaliatory manner is increased.

Conversely, having a more evolved understanding of what motivates people and of the contradictory nature of human thought, feeling, and action is generally more adaptive. It produces a greater repertoire of conflict resolution and protects the person from harm. Thus, more mature levels of meaning imply a more complex, accepting, and thus, more mentally balanced relationship between self and other.

But such a conclusion is understandably problematic to Jane Loevinger. Drawing on many clinical ideas from Jahoda, Erikson, Sullivan, Fromm, and others, she built the theory of ego development. She implied in 1968, that the evolution of the ego and mental health are orthogonal: two distinct constructs with no conceptual overlap. Supporting this argument, which has been repeated consistently in cognitive circles (e.g., Rogers & Kegan, 1991), is the unquestionable fact that symptoms and psychiatric syndromes exist at all levels and stages of ego development.

Thus, we have two perspectives with which to contend; both contribute to the riddle—ego development is, in part, a sequence of mental health capacities; the mental health dimensions are interwoven into the fabric of what the ego *is* and the direction in which it develops. Moving from impulsivity, manipulation, and retaliation to a psychological perspective and identity seeking position (transition from preconformist to conformist stages) is not only a gain in perspective and complexity, but also an achievement in adaptive capacity. The move from identifying with others to derive a sense of self to the developing of self as the constant, ambiguous, and contradictory process of interactions with others (transition from conformist to postconformist stages) is a step in mental health capacity: a move from overdependency or overdifferentiation to a relationship style that transcends submission and domination. From this point of view, to separate the concept of healthy adaptation and ego development into orthogonal entities or processes might be intellectually satisfying, yet contradicts the very definitions of the stages of ego development. This position is immediately apparent when we review Loevinger's coding system (Loevinger & Wessler, 1970), where we can trace the degree to which many mental health capacities and adaptive strengths and weaknesses are built into the stages of ego development.

And yet, ego development and healthy adaptation are also separate constructs. As Loevinger shows, mental health problems can exist at all levels of development, and strengths can exist also at early developmental positions. For that reason, it was logical to radicalize the separation between complexity levels and mental health and to make it a purely empirical question of how the two constructs relate.[1]

Suggesting an identity of ego development and mental health constructs flies in the face of our experience of symptoms and problems existing at all developmental levels. But declaring them separate is not supported, even with a superficial reading of ego development definitions and scoring terms, which include dimensions relevant for "mentally healthy" adaptations.

A line of research with clinical populations moved my associates and me sufficiently far to suggest a possible solution to the riddle. In addition, theoretical distinctions that expand our understanding of ego development and give us a new path to study the relationship of ego development and mental health are necessary. I argue two points in this chapter:

1. It is necessary to distinguish between the development of complexity (i.e., more differentiated meaning systems) and maturity (i.e., more integrated ways of understanding the world and applying these understandings in adaptive ways).

2. Because the ego development model combines complexity and maturity, we end up with two sets of findings: With development there is a decrease in mental health problems and conversely, delay in ego development puts people at risk of mental health problems. But another trend emerges as well: With an increase of developmental complexity can come an increase of more complex problems. This line of work is important for both psychopathology and "normal" development.

LOEVINGER'S PERSPECTIVE ON EGO DEVELOPMENT AND MENTAL HEALTH

Loevinger's position on the relationship between ego development and mental health seems at first easily captured. Although she wrote little about the subject, she was always interested in the question (personal communication). What she has contributed demonstrates a strong knowledge in developmental, personality and clinical thinking. As

---

[1]For this approach, a long tradition of judgment-action research has paved the way (e.g., Kohlberg & Candee, 1984). Cognitive-development of morality, for example, is about progression of thought about moral dilemmas and imperatives. Moral action involves very different behavioral and attitudinal systems which need to be studied separately. Kohlberg and his associates found a systematic relationship between judgment and action with persons at more mature levels being more likely to act on their moral ideas and principles.

mentioned, she stated emphatically (1968) that " . . . ego development is a dimension conceptually distinct from the health–illness dimension" (p. 170). But the clear separation is balanced by her acknowledgment that:

> Broadening the concept of mental health to include such positive aspects as competence, self-esteem, sense of being the agent of one's own destiny, and so on, is potentially diversionary and misleading. These are important and fascinating aspects of ego development, . . . but ego development is a dimension conceptually distinct from the health–illness dimension; these issues of competence, self-esteem, etc. arise or are phrased largely in terms most useful at the upper end of the ego development continuum; while direct relation between ego development and mental health, adjustment, or pathology is found only at the low end of the continuum. (p. 170)

The use of language in this quote invites ambiguity. "Issues of competence and self-esteem arise. . . at the upper end . . ." —Is this a statement suggesting that these issues are causally linked or possibly written into the "deep structure" of ego development? How else do they arise? And what is a direct relation at the earlier stage of ego development? The terms do not convincingly denote two distinct constructs, even if the author posits such a position.

The complexity of this association is further demonstrated as Loevinger revisited this problem in her 1976 book, *Ego Development*. In one section, she addressed clinicians, urging them to keep their patients' problems distinct from their ego levels. She explained that "[a] person of any ego level may become a patient, though there may be differences in the kind of pathology or presenting symptoms characteristic for different levels" (p. 427). This assertion, of course, reiterates that mental health and development are not the same. By illustrating mental health and development as conceptually distinct, Loevinger made a case for the existence of powerful empirical associations between the two phenomena.

But if the concepts of ego development and mental health are so distinct, why should there be any infiltration of one by the other? Is there a third construct, such as defense or coping style, underlying both ego development and symptom choice? I will elaborate further on the original formulation of ego development and will briefly review aspects of the ego development coding system (Loevinger & Wessler, 1970). This allows for a critical assessment as to whether ego development and mental health are indeed separated as postulated.

If we examine Loevinger's characteristics of higher stages we indeed find common indicators of mental health. For example, the more mature, postconformist stages are defined in terms of abilities to cope with and articulate ambiguity and complexity, adaptability and flexibility. Furthermore, self-fulfillment and self-expression become central aspirations often coexisting with emotional independence and a recognition and experience of multidimensionality of the self.

In contrast, among the characteristics of lower stages are found numerous indicators of psychopathology or maladaptation. These include a simple-mindedness, such as adherence to stereotypes and focusing on and understanding only superficial qualities, attributes, and so on. These early, preconformist stages of ego development are further defined by dependence on others to define self, submissive stance toward authorities, lack of conscience, and wish for autonomy but inability to handle it. Other attributes used to describe lower levels of ego development found in the coding manual include: egocentrism, self-interest, selfishness, opportunism, instrumental use of others seen solely as means to ends, impulsiveness, blaming others without accepting responsibility, helplessness, passivity, and many more negative and maladaptive patterns.

Of course, not all mental health issues are part and parcel of the developmental sequence. Symptoms and problems can emerge quite separately. For example, a biological manic depression or a posttraumatic stress reaction can have little connection to development and can produce symptoms at most points in life. But mental health issues, such as impulsivity, deception, manipulation, social anxiety, overdependence, overcontrol, and perfectionism are "written into" the ego development sequence and thus cannot be viewed as orthogonal, as distinctly separate constructs.

Rather than accepting these clear connections between development and the adaptive capacities involved in mental health, Loevinger explained that the similarities exist because the criteria for mental health established by Jahoda (1958) and others is inadequate. Loevinger explains that typical criteria most often used to define mental health apply only to individuals at higher stages of ego development. Therefore, these criteria cannot and do not indicate mental health in children who have not yet reached higher levels on the ego development continuum. Loevinger (1968) stated:

> Jahoda (1958), in her summary of the literature on positive mental health, acknowledges that all the specific characteristics are the ones of mature persons, that in general the traits are ones that develop with age. Now adjustment is not a systematic function of age, not at least in the first instance. There are well-adjusted and poorly adjusted people of all ages. Hence, the syndrome being described, which is unquestionably a systematic function of age, cannot be conceptually the same thing as adjustment. It may have some relation to conceptual distinction in order to determine exactly what the relations of maturity and adjustment are. (p. 163)

I agree with Loevinger's goals, but I believe her own theory does not provide a clear differentiation. Many of the clinical traditions influencing Jahoda's perspectives on positive mental health also influenced the telos of ego development. Loevinger (1976) emphasized that it is imperative to reconceptualize mental health and good adjustment; indicators must ". . . appl[y] irrespective of age in order to clarify the relation of maturity to psychic health" (p. 142).

This argument raises several questions. Is it possible to generate a single definition of mental health applying to all individuals regardless of age or developmental level? Just as Loevinger acknowledged that pathologies and their manifestations differ at different ego levels, so might mental health, good adjustment, and their manifestations differ at different points in development.

Since Loevinger's writing on this topic, it became a widely accepted idea that mental health and psychopathology need to be understood in developmental terms (see Cicchetti, 1984a, 1984b, 1990; Noam, 1988b, 1988c). Many conceptualizations of developmental psychopathology were introduced, the natural history of many disorders was traced, and longitudinal investigators followed at-risk children well into adulthood. Some of these researchers also used cognitive and constructivist theories and instruments (e.g., Hauser, Powers, & Noam, 1991). In 1968 and 1976, when Loevinger stated her position on the relationship between mental health and development, she cited only one study available to her, research conducted with 150 mental hospital inpatients. Today, we are fortunate to have access to much more ego development research with clinical populations, using larger samples as well as longitudinal analyses. Before addressing the research literature, especially the work of my associates and me at the Laboratory of Developmental Psychology and Developmental Psychopathology at Harvard, we conceptualize the possible relationships of ego development and positive adaptation–mental health.

THREE MODELS OF THE RELATIONSHIP OF
EGO DEVELOPMENT AND MENTAL HEALTH

Different conceptualizations of the association between ego development and mental health (or some combination) are underlying the work of most developmentalists building on Loevinger's model. We can construct three main types. On one extreme is the notion that development and mental health are, in fact, one and the same; individuals at lower stages of development are less "mentally healthy"; those at more mature stages enjoy greater mental health. This is especially the case when people remain in ego development positions

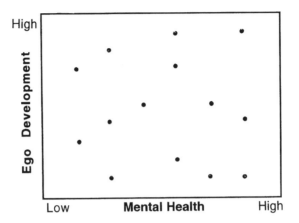

FIG. 16.1. Ego development and mental health as unrelated.

beyond their normative age *(age–stage dysynchrony)* Noam, 1988. As these categories are part and parcel of the ego development model, it is not possible to separate the two components. Against these positions one may raise a simple counterargument: Many people at earlier developmental positions live well-adjusted lives and many who have reached mature stages of ego development suffer from a variety of problems and psychiatric disorders.

The second view of the association between mental health and development is that the two are conceptually and empirically entirely distinct phenomena. Anyone can be afflicted with any form of psychopathology at any developmental position. The mechanisms underlying psychopathology and ego development are truly orthogonal. Such a model is shown in Fig. 16.1.

A less extreme position than the first two consists of a strong positive relationship between development and mental health such that people at higher stages of development are better adapted or better able to adapt and, therefore, are more apt to be mentally healthy. Or, mental health supports the maturation of the ego. This model is quite common in developmental research; a positive association between development and mental health was stated or implied by researchers in cognitive development (Piaget), moral development (Kohlberg), and is one Loevinger would also ascribe to as an empirical fact. However, this view implies that, although people at more mature developmental levels are not necessarily shielded from psychopathology or dysfunctional adaptations, there is greater probability of mental health. The associations can be charted either in continuous form as shown in Fig. 16.2 or in categorical form as shown in Fig. 16.3.

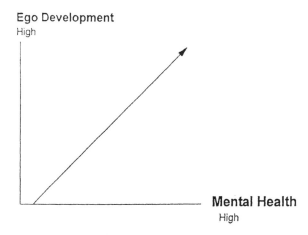

FIG. 16.2. Ego development and mental health as correlated.

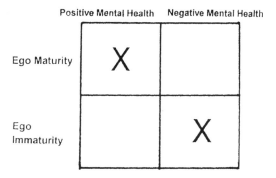

FIG. 16.3. Ego development and mental health.

What makes this general view on the relationship between development and mental health more complicated is the multitude of dimensions and factors underlying psychopathology and maladaptation. As mentioned earlier, some disorders such as schizophrenia are probably quite unrelated to ego development, whereas other problems such as antisocial behavior problems could be quite strongly related. What makes this empirical relationship more challenging is that ego development definitions have some overlap with typical psychological problem behaviors and protective abilities. For those disorders that might be connected to ego development, a fourth model can be introduced. This

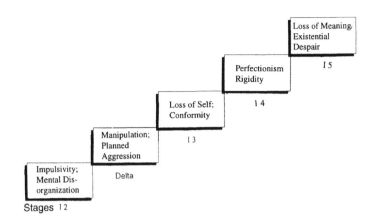

FIG. 16.4. Ego development: key vulnerabilities at each developmental position.
Note. The notation for ego levels used in this chapter corresponds to the notation of the first edition of the scoring manual for the WUSCT (Loevinger & Wessler, 1970; Redmore, Loevinger, & Tamashiro, 1978). The current edition of the scoring manual (Hy & Loevinger, 1996) introduced several changes. See the Appendix to the introductory chapter of this volume for a comparison between the previous and the current system.

model suggests key vulnerabilities, risks, and symptom combinations arising at each ego development position. Figure 16.4 shows in extremely abbreviated form what the interplay between vulnerabilities, developmental pathologies, and strengths might look like at each developmental stage.

These multiple possibilities make it apparent that systematic research into the nature of the connection between ego development, psychopathology, and mental health was essential for theoretical and practical reasons. We began a line of research hypothesizing that the nature of the relationship is, in fact, quite complex and that one model alone could not account for all developmental relationships. Instead, we searched for different patterns to solve the riddle.

Before describing the research it is important to summarize similarities and differences between Loevinger's and my positions. This is especially important since the topic is very complex and Loevinger's position is multifaceted.

1. Loevinger states that ego development and mental health are two distinct concepts and that her model is not a sequence of mental health capacities. I agree with her, that it would be beneficial to separate developmental complexity from the health–illness dimension. However, I do not view the ego development construct as accomplishing this goal. The ego development sequence has mental health dimensions woven into its fabric.

2. I radicalize Loevinger's goals to separate mental health and development by introducing (in greater depth later in the chapter) the

distinction between ego complexity and ego maturity. Complexity I define as sophistication of form, not integration, flexibility, or adaptive know-how, all of which refer to maturity. Loevinger combines maturity and complexity in her model, but we should not use the term ego maturity if we wish to keep development and mental health conceptually separate.

3. Loevinger and I agree that (a) delay of ego development, especially at the early stages, beyond early age, yields an increased probability of problems and the emergence of an antisocial stance and character; (b) each developmental position has specific strengths and weaknesses, which need to be further explicated; and(c)higher stages provide some added protection against mental problems, as compared to earlier stages. These areas of agreement are wide-ranging, and my research is a way to illuminate these common assumptions and to validate them empirically.

4. I am especially interested in a fourth possibility, in which ego development can give rise to more complex disorders and problems, rather than support mature adaptation. Again, to fully explore such a hypothesis, it is important to further differentiate ego complexity from maturity.

This comparison shows that areas of convergence are greater than those of divergence, but Loevinger would strongly defend against the position that complexity and maturity should be separate and that mental health and adaptive components are written into the stage descriptions. I return to these issues after I review our research.

EGO DEVELOPMENT AND MENTAL HEALTH: A LINE OF RESEARCH

Although our research involves a variety of models and methods, in the present chapter, I focus on the studies in which we utilized Loevinger's model and measure of ego development. Using psychological structure of meaning (as does Loevinger) rather than age as a marker for development is one of the benchmarks of my laboratory's approach to developmental psychopathology. A number of intriguing results emerged using this approach.

All of the research cited here, except where otherwise stated, was conducted with an inpatient, consecutive admission, longitudinal sample of adolescents admitted for psychiatric evaluation at a Harvard Medical School-affiliated psychiatric hospital. Data for this sample is being continually updated; thus, different sample sizes in various studies reflect particular data sets available for subsets of this group at given times. The adolescent group constitutes patients aged from 11 to 16 years. The patients are primarily White with a wide spread of social class (Hollingshead, 1957).

Patients present a wide variety of symptoms for which a full range of treatment services were available (e.g., individual therapy, group therapy, medication, etc.). In all of the studies, subjects with Wechsler Full Scale IQ levels below 85 have been eliminated from analyses.

Approximately 80% of the adolescents were found to be functioning at developmentally delayed preconformist positions. However, these developmentally delayed adolescents should not be viewed as a unitary group, as the three preconformist stages of ego development are marked by distinct meaning systems, interpersonal styles, and moral stances. This finding implies that a unitary view of adolescence should not be employed. Instead, we introduced in an earlier publication the term *adolescent worlds* (Noam, Powers, Kilkenny, & Beedy 1990). We introduced a developmental model accounting for differential adolescent conceptualizations of their important relationships with parents, peers, friends, and role models. This finding also suggests the possibility of subdividing disorders and symptoms from a developmental point of view.

Although this and other clinical samples were shown to be delayed in their ego development (e.g., Browning, 1986), some adolescents within these samples were functioning at more mature levels. This finding leads us to a discussion of how symptomatology differs at more mature and age-appropriate levels.

RELATIONSHIP BETWEEN EARLY STAGES OF EGO DEVELOPMENT AND EXTERNALIZING SYMPTOMATOLOGY

In a study of 140 male and female adolescent inpatients (Noam et al., 1984), the associations between ego development and specific groups of maladaptive behaviors were studied. We asked whether externalizing behaviors (e.g., aggression, delinquency) are significantly associated with immature ego development. This question is important both for exploring the relationship between social cognition and behavior, as well as to "developmentalize" the distinction between internalizing and externalizing behaviors and problems found throughout the adolescent research literature (e.g., Achenbach, 1982; Phillips & Zigler, 1964).

Using the Child Behavior Checklist (Achenbach & Edelbrock, 1987), it was found that both internalizing and externalizing symptom scales were significantly and negatively related to increases in ego development. When partialling out effects of age, gender, and socioeconomic (SES) background, ego level made a significant contribution to variance explained in externalizing scores, but not in internalizing scores.

This result was consistent with findings of other researchers, which suggested a relationship between early stages of ego development and externalizing symptoms. Powitzky (1975), for example, found that among less socialized young offenders (bank robbers, drug offenders) lower ego levels were more prevalent. Frank and Quinlan (1976) also found differences in ego stages when comparing delinquent and nondelinquent inner city adolescent females, with delinquents demonstrating lower ego levels. In a similar vein, Browning (1986) reported that although adolescent inpatients at lower stages of ego development frequently demonstrated externalizing symptoms, a corresponding relationship between internalizing symptoms and higher stages of ego development was not found.

This led to further research which refined our measurement of symptoms and diagnoses. Noam et al.'s 1984 study found that adolescents functioning at lower levels of ego development reported significantly more symptoms than did higher stage adolescents. Using this finding, it was hypothesized that differences might begin to emerge in the types of symptoms and diagnoses noted for adolescents at different ego levels. In another study of 320 adolescent psychiatric admissions (141 males and 179 females) Noam, Kilburn, and Ammen-Elkins (1989) found robust relationships between externalizing behaviors and lower ego levels, and internalizing symptoms with higher levels of ego development, using a self-report measure (Youth Self Report).

The relationship between symptomatology and ego level was further explored in Noam and Houlihan (1990), who studied a sample of 140 adolescents, 74 males and 66 females. Arranging diagnostic categories in order of severity from adjustment to psychotic disorders, a consistent pattern emerged. With the exception of affective disorders, as severity of diagnosis increased, so did the percentage of subjects at preconformist levels, whereas the percentage of subjects at conformist–postconformist stages decreased.

RELATIONSHIP BETWEEN EGO DEVELOPMENT, SYMPTOMS, AND DEFENSES

What the research was beginning to highlight were patterns of symptoms and syndromes that covaried with levels of ego development. The relationship of externalizing symptoms to preconformist levels of ego development was fairly robust. So, too, were the relationships linking symptom severity to lower ego levels. These findings led to the discussion regarding the relationship between symptom expression and ego development; that is, if symptom expression was moderated by ego level, ego level might also shed light on the mechanisms linking cognitive maturity to symptom expression. With that goal, my associate and I undertook studies examining the role of defenses in relation to ego level.

Supporting our finding, several studies using the Defense Mechanism Inventory (DMI; Ihilevich & Gleser, 1986) and Loevinger's measure in normal populations demonstrated a relationship between ego development and defenses. In a normative study of adolescents, Levit (1989) reported that turning against others (TAO), that is, responding to conflict through attacking an external source, was inversely related to ego development. Labouvie-Vief, Hakim-Larson, and Hobart (1987), in a study of nonclinical subjects aged 10–77 years, found that turning against others (TAO) and projection (PRO), or attribution of negative characteristics as justification for aggression, were associated with lower ego development. Turning against self (TAS), or responding to conflict by directing aggression inwards; reversal (REV), that is, responding neutrally or positively toward frustration; and principalization (PRN), or coping with conflict by separating affect from the source of conflict through, for example, rationalization or isolation of affect, were positively linked to ego development. Not all studies of defenses and ego development found similar relationships, however (e.g., Vailiant & McCullough, 1987).

In a later study (Recklitis & Noam, 1990) of 291 adolescent inpatients (122 males and 169 females), we examined the relationship between aggressive behavior, defenses, and ego development. Using criteria of clinical restraints of adolescents and staff reports, the link between externalizing behaviors (assaultive behaviors) and lower ego levels was clearly demonstrated. A pattern linking externalizing behaviors to defenses of TAO, PRO, and REV was also demonstrated. Turning against others and projection were negatively and significantly associated with ego development, whereas the more ideational and internalizing defenses of principalization, turning against self, and reversal were positively correlated with ego development. Partialling subjects into assaultive and nonassaultive groups revealed significant differences between groups in ego level scores in the expected direction. The only defense in which these groups differed, however, was PRN, or coping with conflict through intellectualization, rationalization, and isolation of affect. This suggests that the more psychosocially mature adolescents, those at conformist stages, were able to adopt a more cognitive approach to conflict resolution which serves as an inhibitor against impulsive action. Further work is necessary to ascertain whether the relationship between ego development and symptoms is mediated by a third set of variables, such as defenses. Our findings show such relationships exist, but ego development and symptoms have a distinct relationship.

RELATIONSHIP BETWEEN EGO DEVELOPMENT
AND INTERNALIZING SYMPTOMS

In a study of 277 inpatient adolescents, 124 males and 153 females (Noam, Paget, Valiant, Borst, & Bartok, 1994), we grouped diagnoses into categories of conduct, affective, and mixed conduct–affective disorders. Using this typology, conduct and mixed conduct–affective disorders were found to be more prevalent among preconformist stage adolescents. Affective disorders were more commonly associated with female gender and conformist ego level stages. The most important point in this research was that more complex forms of ego development were related to an increased presence of "pure depression" (in contrast to "comorbidity between aggression and depression").

In a line of research on suicidality, we also found a link between higher stages of ego development and increased rate of suicide (Borst, Noam, & Bartok, 1991; Borst & Noam, 1993). Previous research found that psychiatric disorders constitute one of the most important risk factors for adolescent suicidality. Retrospective studies of suicide completers found that 95% were suffering from a *DSM III–R* disorder (Shafii, Carrigan, Whittinghill, & Derrick, 1985). Depression was also noted among youthful suicide attempters (Pfeffer, Newcorn, Kaplan, Mizruchi, & Plutchik, 1989; Robbins & Alessi, 1985). Recent work also found a significant proportion of suicidal adolescents who were not depressed, but rather sought treatment for antisocial behavior conduct disorders (Apter, Bleich, Plutchik, Mendelsohn, & Tyano, 1988). Comorbidity of psychiatric disorder was found to enhance risk for suicidality (Brent et al., 1988; Kreitman, 1986). In a psychological autopsy of suicide completers, Shafii, Steltz-Lenarsky, Derrick, Beckner, & Whittinghill (1988) found that comorbidity, usually depression with substance abuse, conduct disorder, or other mental disorder, was present in 81% of victims. It was suggested that the comorbidity of conduct and affective disorders may be a potent precursor for suicidality (Blumenthal & Kupfer, 1988; Shaffer, 1974).

The complex nature of suicidality suggested a more complex model than the single link between developmental level and suicidal behaviors. Borst, Noam, and Bartok (1991) investigated the relationship of ego development, age, gender, and diagnosis to serious suicidal ideation and attempts among 219 inpatient adolescents, 96 males and 123 females. In addition to the established risk factors of gender and diagnosis (e.g., males tend to be more aggressive and females more depressed), it was found in a cross-sectional study that with increasing ego development adolescents became more prone to suicidal ideation and behaviors. Although suicidality was quite prevalent in the preconformist adolescents, it usually coexisted with externalizing problems and disorders. The depressed, unaggressive (to others) adolescent was typically at the Conformist level. We concluded that ego development could pose a risk factor in a vulnerable population, leading to an increase of depression and suicidality. Further longitudinal work is presently underway to build on these findings.

CAN WE USE EGO DEVELOPMENT
TO SUBDIVIDE SYMPTOMS AND DISORDERS?

Although suicidal behavior was not expected to be an exclusive phenomenon of the Conformist stage, we assumed and found a higher proportion of suicide attempters within that group. However, although suicidality was more prevalent among Conformist adolescents, the majority of adolescents studied were delayed in ego development, consistent with earlier findings about developmental delays among psychiatric adolescents (Noam et al., 1984). Hence, although 62% of conformist inpatients were found to be suicide attempters, the majority of attempters (79%) were at pre-conformist stages of ego development. These findings led us to propose two distinct profiles of suicidal adolescents— defiant and self-blaming. Defiant suicidal adolescents are explicitly angry, impulsive, concrete, and often see suicide as revenge. Self-blaming attempters are more often depressed, concerned with sociocentric perspectives, and view suicide in terms of loss and abandonment.

The use of distinct profiles of suicidality to explicate the relationship between ego level, defenses, and psychiatric symptoms was explored further in Noam and Borst (1994). A sample of 139 inpatient psychiatric females, aged 13–16, were divided into four groups based on dimensions of suicidality (suicidal–nonsuicidal) and stage of ego development (preconformist–conformist). Preconformist attempters were characterized by comorbidity of symptoms, both high internalizing and externalizing behaviors, or depressive and aggressive behaviors, as well as externalizing defenses, or projection, reversal. The conformist attempter showed primarily internalizing symptoms, that is, depressive, and scored highest on internalizing defenses, or principalization.

DO WE FIND A DECREASE OF SYMPTOMATOLOGY
WITH EGO DEVELOPMENT?

This same pattern was manifested in research conducted among adult psychiatric patients. Noam and Dill (1991) examined symptom severity and ego development in a sample of 86 adult outpatients with adverse symptoms. The sample consisted of 34 males and 52 females, aged 19–71, with a median age of 30. Subjects ranged in SES from 1–5, with approximately 10% of subjects evenly divided between the highest and lowest categories, and 36% in the middle category. Correlations between ego development levels and symptom severity scores were uniformly negative across all but two symptom scales (obsessive–compulsive and interpersonal sensitivity). These results indicated that symptomatology generally decreases as ego level increases. One other possible interpretation raised by this finding was that, although fewer symptoms might be associated with higher ego levels, this could be indicative of a movement toward more internalized symptomatology and pathology with higher stages of ego development. To study the relationship between reduction of symptomatology and ego development, we needed to follow the same subjects longitudinally.

A second longitudinal study further examined the relationship between defenses and symptomatology, this time among a small sample of adolescents, 21 males and 16 females, who were evaluated at admission to psychiatric hospital and re-evaluated 9 months later. Two "ego pathway" groups were defined in this study: progressors and nonprogressors. Progressors are subjects who progressed at least one-half stage in ego development during the 9-month period between evaluations. Nonprogressors are subjects who regressed or stayed at the same ego level during this period (Noam, Recklitis, & Paget, 1991). Although both groups showed significant reductions of symptoms in the 9 months, ego progressors showed greater reductions in internalizing symptoms and externalizing symptoms. Furthermore, although defenses remained virtually unchanged in the 9 months for nonprogressors, progressors demonstrated a decrease in the use of projection and reversal.

A RETURN TO THE EGO DEVELOPMENT–
MENTAL HEALTH RIDDLE

This line of research highlights the complex association among psychopathology, adaptation–maladaptation, and social, cognitive and interpersonal competence. It has great implications for enhancing our understanding of the relationship between development and mental health, helping us solve the riddle. This research challenges two of the three conceptualizations of the relationship between mental health and development presented earlier in the chapter, namely, mental health and ego development do not appear to be equivalent terms, nor do they seem conceptually entirely distinct.

Clearly, results do not support the contention that higher ego stages are ipso facto more adaptive. We find in some of our studies that better adaptation is related to maturation in ego development, but in others that higher stages are related to more internalizing disorders. Loevinger considers the existence of psychopathology at any stage as an indicator that mental health is orthogonal to ego development (Loevinger, 1968). Alternatively, we believe that this research emphasizes the complexity of the association between mental health and development we are just beginning to understand.

This complexity is clearly a function of the heterogeneity of the concepts of psychopathology as well as development. For example, with our present-day knowledge of schizophrenia and manic–depressive illness, we have to assume that biological factors are so strong, that the level of ego development would not play a large causal part.[2]

With certain types of delinquency we have to assume a very different relationship than with schizophrenia. Many dimensions that define early developmental stages of ego development (impulsivity, opportunism, self-protection, a drive toward immediate need-gratification, etc.) can influence an adolescent to 'choose' delinquent forms of adaptation. That does not mean that delinquency is entirely explained by ego development, nor that they are the same constructs. Many adolescents and adults who function at early developmental levels are not delinquents, but most delinquents do not function at mature developmental positions. The delinquent's difficulty with cognitively experiencing the world from another's point of view is implicit in a lack of empathy and guilt, typical for early developmental positions. This same lack of empathy and guilt are simultaneous indicators of conduct disorders and delinquency. However, not all forms of problems with empathy and guilt can be considered delinquent; there are many people who lack these human capacities without acting against social rules and laws. If we compare, for example, *Diagnostic and Statistical Manual of Mental Disorders*(4th ed. [DSM–IV]; American Psychiatric Association, 1994) criteria for conduct disorder, we find items corresponding directly to definitions of early ego development stages. If similar items define development and diagnoses, how can the constructs be entirely separate? In that case, it is not only that ego development and disorders end up being empirically correlated, but that they are conceptually overlapping, like two circles that share considerable

---

[2]They remain open and interesting questions, however, whether the level of development has something to do with the contents of the delusions and whether the process of recovery is aided by the skills inherent in development, such as growing ability for reflection. A number of case examples in the literature are suggestive of such a relationship (see Noam, Chandler, & LaLonde, 1995).

overlap. This complex overlap of constructs makes for a fascinating area of research, but suggests we should not make simple distinctions of orthogonality.

At mature levels, ego development and adaptation–maladaptation are also not entirely orthogonal. As mentioned earlier, a conception of psychopathology is integrated into the sequence in its converse, compared to early ego developmental levels: The higher stages read like definitions of psychological health. At the autonomous stage, for example, the person acknowledges and copes with conflict, transcends polarities, integrating complex ideas and relationships. Freed from oppressive demands from conscience, the person can act with tolerance and respect towards others and "cherishes personal ties among his most precious values" (Loevinger, 1976, p. 23). It is hard to envision such a person as stealing for personal gain or aggressively hurting another person. And even beyond negative symptom expression, the positive attributes are part of mentally healthy adaptation, as long as we do not define mental health only as the absence of symptoms. To reduce the health–illness dimension only to symptoms would be losing the developmental aspect of the active meaning-maker whose flexibility, innovation, and exploration are part of a vital adaptation to life (e.g., Noam & Fischer, 1996). How should we distinguish the person who functions well in love and work but feels chronically dissatisfied, from the risk-taker who feels alive, yet has problems with long-term commitment to a relationship? (See Noam, 1996, for a detailed discussion.)

EGO COMPLEXITY AND MATURITY
IN NORMATIVE DEVELOPMENT

This more complex view of developmental psychopathology and risk, which is beginning to take hold in other theory and research traditions (e.g., Cicchetti, 1991; Noam & Cicchetti, 1996), is equally important for a more complex view of normative development. Our line of research opened our view to a fundamental conceptual problem in developmental psychology. Developmental progression of social cognition (of which ego development is one example) consists of an unacknowledged combination of complexity of social understanding and maturity of adaptation. Complexity and quality of adaptation are not the same constructs and should not be intertwined in the way many theorists have done. The problems we face, however, are massive: If we reconstruct development of cognition, especially social cognition, without some ideal type of positive outcome (highest level), we might return to a rather positivistic, seemingly value-free position of description without prescription. But combining a view of positive adaptation with developmental complexity creates an illusion of a unitary process, which although theoretically concise, is frequently contradicted by reality. There are many people who are capable of developing complex understanding of themselves and others, but use these insights in the service of self-alienation, self-hate, and contempt for others. For them, the adaptive quality of development has to be questioned; the formal complexity of their thoughts and feelings does not. In the study of psychopathology, this neat combination of constructs, which should have been kept separate from the onset, breaks down. But I believe in this case psychopathology serves only as a magnifying glass for processes that need to be separated even for understanding nonpathological development. It will be a future task to create a developmental frame of the self and the ego that delineates complexity and allows for multiple pathways of maturity, adaptation, and alienation. At present, only the claim of such distinction exists, but not the detailed differentiation of constructs.

A NEW CONCEPTUALIZATION INFLUENCED
BY EGO DEVELOPMENT THEORY

In my redefinition of ego development in a theory of self (e.g., Noam, 1990, 1992), I recognize that each developmental advance in complexity produces the possibility for more complex and internalized self-destructive behavior, as well as for opportunities to transform vulnerabilities in order to create more mature adaptations. A new stage synthesis can be anything but integrative and holistic (Noam, Chandler, & LaLonde, 1995). Through continuous exchange between the organism and the environment, the person and the culture, the individual is challenged to establish increasingly more complex views about the self and others. These meaning systems are not purely related to thought, although their development is made possible by advances in the cognitive realm. At each new developmental position, typical affects, meanings, and motivations emerge. From a clinical perspective, each position brings out new strengths and opportunities to rework past vulnerabilities. But each new system of self complexity can also lead to new weaknesses or to more complex forms of old dysfunctions. Instead of outlining the developmental positions shown in a number of other publications (e.g. Noam, 1988d; Noam, Powers, Kilkenny, & Beedy, 1990), we refer the reader to Table 16.1. This table briefly describes the strengths and weaknesses inherent in three adolescent–developmental positions and what the implications are for clinical interventions. More detailed clinical implications of this work are discussed in Noam, 1992.[3]

---

[3]The idea that different stages involve different problems is in line with Loevinger's 1968 and 1976 perspective. We attempt to detail what problems are typically encountered at different stages of development and what interventions tend to be effective.

TABLE 16.1
Clinical–Developmental Interventions With Adolescents

| | *Self-Complexity Levels* | |
| *Subjective–Physical* | *Reciprocal–Instrumental* | *Mutual–Inclusive* |

Treatment focus

• Interventions that focus on cognitive and emotional disorganization, impulsivity, attention problems, lack of body control. • Focus on the constant need for physical presence of authority figures. • Supportive and be-havioral treatments in a structured environ-ment; interventions to change environment; e.g., classroom, family structure.	• Treatment focus on issues of fairness and support for behavior that takes other people into consideration. • Central role for peer learning, as struggles with authority figures are typical (e.g., AA, group interventions, community meetings. • Concrete activities with adult role models who work on skills and abilities, and fun tasks (e.g., coaches, mentors, Outward Bound Coordinators).	• "Interpersonal therapy" with focus on depression and low self-esteem emerging in closer relationships. • Special emphasis on one-on-one relationship. • Sharing of experiences to overcome loneliness.

Setting

• Usually structured environment (e.g., classroom) needed to contain serious impul-sivity, depression, and potential for short psychotic episodes. • Setting must provide strong limits and rules that foster the learning of consequences of self's actions; incentive must be provided to apply and internalize structure. • Predictable staff, teachers, or clinicians must be readily available.	• Containment needed for a long period of time, especially when antisocial trends are strong. • But despite seeming disinterest in individual therapy, one-to-one relationships are important to create trust, but need to entail mutually satisfying activities (e.g., eating, sports, walks). • Support to get needs met in a nondelinquent way.	• Individual treatment (often in conjunction with family treatment) to help express internalized feelings and, when necessary, short residential treatments (long, regressive hospital-izations to be avoided), but suicidality can make safe environment necessary.

Support

• Strong boundaries and limits with goal of internalizing external rules. Support with	• Support in experience of unfairness of rules and situations and with the world that	• Strong commitment in every aspect of person's experiences (e.g., clothes, sports,

(continued)

TABLE 16.1
(CONTINUED)

often enmeshed or abandoning family system, or disorganized school environment.	confronts externalizing stance ("others are at fault"). • Experience of nurturant relationship is critical as many patients have experienced trauma and neglect, but special attention must be given so that supportive stance will not be exploited. • Confrontations to address manipulations, but always in context of understanding the predicament.	peer group) even when it seems more like friends talking. • Encouragement of assertiveness needed. • Support of the expression of anger and frustration. • Help with tendency to have negative feelings "go underground" and to be so empathetic of others that the self's needs are not expressed.

Insight

• Work with emerging ability to review behaviors, feelings, and thoughts. • Begin to recognize that multiple feelings can co-exist about the same person or situation. • Learn about the fact that strategies are being used that are self-destructive.	• Emerging recognition that world can be influenced in productive ways and that rejections by others do not have to be addressed in terms of revenge and hostility. • Close relationships provide a possibility to begin to view the world through a sense of mutuality and community.	• Beginning reflection of what is occurring in the relationship as a pattern (e.g., "Every time I am silent, I feel ashamed."). • Framing regression and low self-esteem in terms of a lack of inner agency. • Explore the problems of expression of anger and the tendency to turn against the self.

Typical therapeutic binds

• Attempt by therapist, counselor, and teacher to interpret behavior in terms of symbolic meanings, when they are only understood in concrete and behavioral terms. • Feeding into split between "good family-bad peer world", "good therapist-bad parents" (or vice versa) often leads to a breakdown of the work.	• Person confuses the therapist "being on my side" with jointly breaking rules (e.g., smoking in office before age). • Fear of consequences can lead to a style of nondisclosure. • Difficulty in talking about problems emerging in the relationship and past hurts because a biographical and transference focus has not yet developed.	• Silences in the treatment (or other relationship) and feeling rejected by therapist require very taxing proofs of acceptance (e.g., midnight phone calls). • Danger of fluctuation of therapist (or teacher) between demand for too much insight and self-observation and underestimating the capacity to observe relationship patterns and feeling states.

Note. This table was adapted from Noam, 1992.

The model of separating self-complexity from maturity and adaptation provides a link to research on social competence, for not only does development depend on maturity and complexity, but also on capacity to function in an environment conducive to actualization of growth potentials.

So far, we showed that developmental complexity provides no guarantee that earlier problems become integrated into a new level of maturity. We further argued that new skill levels reflected in ego development (perspective taking, differentiating between different parts of the self, having a stronger sense of biography and trajectory into the future, etc.) can all be used in adaptive or maladaptive terms. A similar phenomenon is frequently seen in new developments and their application in the natural sciences. For example, few would argue the point that understanding nuclear physics constitutes scientific progress. However, the application of these insights to the creation and use of nuclear weaponry is far more controversial. Similarly, new capacities are not good just because we define them as developmental. Development has the great potential to create more insight, a greater ability for self-reflection, and more understanding and thus a more tolerant perspective of others. But the skills underlying these processes can also turn old hurts and new alienations into ever more complex forms. Reflective powers can be used to create more alternatives making the self less able to choose and act. Similarly, understanding how others function does not necessarily lead to more tolerance or empathy. This same reflective ability can be applied to think out complex ploys to hurt others and to take revenge. We could continue with many more examples, but the basic principles should be clear.

The idea may seem straightforward, and one imagines most interventions encompass this clinical–developmental idea. But this is not the case. Psychoanalysis views most forms of psychopathology as primitive, fixated, unevolved; and thus, developmental transformations of dysfunctions to higher forms in adulthood have not received the necessary attention. In the cognitive–developmental tradition, development has been viewed as leading to greater adaptation. Traditionally, most developmentalists thought maladaptation and dysfunction to be outside the purview of developmental psychology, thus leaving much of psychiatry unchallenged in the approach of creating entities rather than uncovering underlying developmental principles. With the establishment of developmental psychopathology and clinical–developmental psychology, new theoretical clinical and empirical bridges are now possible.

OUTLOOK

Further research into the relationship between ego development and symptomatology, as well as mental health, is underway. Three areas of investigation are especially important to strengthen our knowledge base:

1. To deal with the potential bias imposed by clinical populations, it is essential to draw on school and community-based at-risk children and adolescents. The available research with these populations suggests findings that parallel our clinical samples. We are pursuing systematic research with these populations.

2. Further longitudinal work with school and community samples will help clarify the relationships between increase in ego complexity and decrease in symptomatology versus increase in internalizing symptoms. What distinguishes these pathways? How do children and adolescents "exit" problem pathways and transfer to more adaptive ones? Our longitudinal study is presently exploring these questions by following at-risk children from early adolescence to early adulthood.

3. If we learn more about these naturally occurring transfers, we will deepen our knowledge of the ways in which interventions work. Much work with careful evaluations is needed to develop programs for prevention and intervention with clinical and nonclinical at-risk groups, taking account of developmental principles.

These research projects will provide us with further information about the relationship between ego development and mental health and the encouragement of developmentally sensitive protective factors, such as evolving forms of self-reflection, emotional maturity, and explorative capacities of meaningful relationships.

However, this new generation of research should not remain static in the application of measurement strategies. The SCT will continue to be an invaluable tool to detect broad developmental distinctions about moral development, interpersonal style, self-reflection, character, and personality development. Its success is based on the fact that we tend to generalize our thoughts and feelings and try to meld out of a magnitude of experiences a somewhat unified self or identity. But the ego or the self is far less unified than was traditionally posited. People do not develop moral sensitivities and interpersonal style solely out of a preprogrammed biological substrate. Participation in social relationships and opportunities to explore and challenge produces development. These opportunities are not necessarily available in areas relevant to all developmental domains and thus produce domain-specific ability and skill levels (e.g., Fischer, 1980; Gardner, 1993; Noam, 1993). Similarly, moving to more complex levels of development does not mean that all earlier forms of meaning-making have been integrated into the new, more complex structure. Dynamic development is multilayered and produces a great deal of fluctuation between different competency levels. Encapsulated aspects of the self (Noam, 1988a, 1988b, 1988c) are not only expressions of psychopathology, but of normative development. Research needs to address this reality by combining Loevinger's SCT with domain-specific measurement strategies, as well as qualitative biographical interviewing procedures. It will be essential to find differential associations between general ego development, domain-specific capacities, and symptomatology and mental health.

In the meantime, we made considerable progress in resolving the ego development–adaptation–mental health issue. We found:

1. Ego development and adaptation are not fully orthogonal constructs.

2. Within that reality, delay at early stages is a risk factor for externalizing disorders.

3. Maturation in ego development goes hand-in-hand with more adaptation, and longitudinally in a clinical population with a decrease in symptomatology.

4. Complex ego development can also be the context for more internalizing disorders and symptoms. This area is essential to pursue, as it provides the key to a truly developmental orientation in psychopathology, that is, that psychopathology is not only a sign of fixation, arrest, and delay, but can evolve into complex forms throughout development, not necessarily tied to childhood experiences.

5. Each developmental world needs its own specific forms of intervention and prevention. The lack of knowledge among clinicians of the ego development frame as well as other developmental theories deprives many patients at all ages of a wealth of knowledge that can have a major impact on treatment choice and intervention strategies.

Knowing about ego development is knowing about the client's frame of reference, abilities to make use of interpretations, and understandings of health and illness. In our efforts to achieve the goals of a clinical–developmental psychology that puts client and therapist as meaning-makers into center stage, our similarities with Jane Loevinger are far greater than the differences. We all greatly benefit from her profound insights, her dedication to a developmental focus in personality psychology, and her courage to take on many simplistic theory and research traditions.

Theory and research about psychopathology and mental health were never central in Loevinger's pursuits. But she provided important tools for all of our future explorations.

ACKNOWLEDGMENTS

I would like to thank Tracy Stempel for her insightful help in reviewing some of the literature, her excellent comments, and the editing of earlier drafts of this chapter. Dr. Gayle Valiant helped review the findings from our laboratory. Bracha Molad's, Amy Briggs', and Francie Fries' comments and support strengthened this chapter, as well. Thanks also to Michiel Westenberg for detailed comments. Support for the research came from the Alden Trust, the American Foundation for Suicide Prevention, the Milton Fund of Harvard University, and the Klingenstein Third Generation Foundation.

Organizational Levels of Self
and Other Schematization

Mardi Horowitz
Department of Psychiatry
University of California at San Francisco

Loevinger (1976) described stages of ego development and measured them empirically with her SCT. She defined stages in terms of impulse control, conscious preoccupations, and interpersonal behavioral patterns. An important ability acquired during development is the capacity to view others as separate people with whom one might cooperate and be interdependent. Before achieving this capacity, the individual might view others as objects to be manipulated. Such concepts helped me evolve my work.

This chapter aims to clarify how clinicians may formulate a case in treatment in terms of developmental level of person schematizations involving roles of relationship between self and others. The work presented here is based on person schemas theory, an effort to integrate relevant sectors of psychodynamic and cognitive science theories (Horowitz, 1988a, 1988b, 1991, 1997). One aspect stems from cognitive science theory of the functional properties of schemas. Another aspect stems from psychoanalytic concepts of multiple potential states of self-identity and relationships. Unconscious motives combine with social contexts to evoke person schemas. Those motives may range from a search for gratification of a passion to habitual defenses against social dangers and threats to self.

PERSON SCHEMAS THEORY

Schemas are viewed in cognitive science as inferred mental structures used to fill in information gaps. They function as ways to rapidly arrive at a mental interpretation of an external situation or event (Bartlett, 1932). These large-scale mental structures are based on active processes rather than on static storage of knowledge. Schematizing processes may be based on long lasting associational linkages between memory units in a network of interconnected information. Learning occurs not only by adding knowledge but by a functional change in linkage strengths. This increases or decreases the connectivity of meanings (Minsky, 1975; Norman & Rumelhart, 1975; Rumelhart & McClelland, 1986; Schank & Abelson, 1977; Stinson & Palmer, 1991).

Person schemas are inferred structures of mental meanings about self and other. These packages of information integrate past interpersonal experiences into generalized, flexible organizations of knowledge about self and relationships. Identities, identifications, affiliations, attachment bonds, and enduring "we" agencies or communions all involve person schematization. Person schemas theory is reviewed in *Person Schemas and Maladaptive Interpersonal Patterns* (Horowitz, 1991) and summarized briefly here.

Modern person schemas theory can be traced back to Freud's discovery of *transference phenomena*. To this, Jung added explorations of self-representation. Proponents of psychoanalytic object relations theory moved the field along (Fairbairn, 1954; Klein, 1948; Winnicott, 1957) as did self psychology (Kohut, 1971, 1977). The principles of modern psychodynamics retain these constructs: the importance of conflicts such as wish–fear dilemmas, the vital forces of unconscious passions, and the construct of often unconscious defensive maneuvers that can form character through repetitive use.

PROPERTIES OF PERSON SCHEMAS

Whole and organized schemas of self and other allow chunking, clustering, outlining, and formatting of information. Memory is laid out, generalized, and smoothed over to organize and connect knowledge for use in interpersonal contexts. These properties of knowledge schematization quicken the speed with which information is processed in relation to personal identity and relationship opportunities or dangers. This is particularly useful during interpersonal communication when verbal and nonverbal signals are transmitted at speeds and complexities that are often faster than conscious recognition processes can follow.

Person schemas add information to perception of interpersonal events and social frameworks by filling in gaps in registered stimuli (Markus, 1977; Piaget, 1954). This filling-in function may be motivated by the current motivational states of desire and fear as well as by the general cognitive aim to categorize and complete appraisal of events.

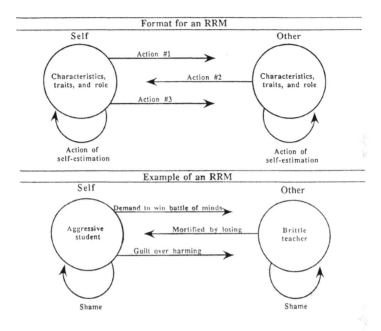

FIG. 17.1 A role relationship model.

The use of person schemas to quickly process and add information has an expense to pay. The information that is added may be wrong. Transference phenomena result from motives combined with inappropriate interpersonal appraisals. Regressive activation of earlier schemas of self and other are the source of the misappraisals.

ROLE RELATIONSHIP MODELS

Role relationship models provide one way to format contents of person schemas. Role relationship models contain roles, characteristics, and attributes of self and other. They also contain the scripts of aims, expected responses, and reactions to responses. The scripts define sequences of transaction, self appraisal, as well as the overall frame and value contexts of social conditions. A role relationship model format is illustrated in Fig. 17.1. Such formats place self-identity in the context of a relationship.

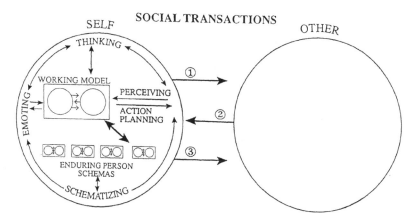

FIG. 17.2. A social frame and mental processes of appriasing the self and other.

WORKING MODELS OF IDENTITY
IN SOCIAL CONTEXTS

Person schemas allow a person to form working models of external social situations by combining the examination of what is occurring with the activation of enduring person schemas from a mental repertoire. Both the resultant working models and the activated, enduring schemas of self and other influence emotion, thinking, perceiving, and acting as is shown in Fig. 17.3. The circles within the context of a rectangle symbolize an actual social interchange.

Several role relationship models may exist for any specific attachment to another person, or for any past, present, or future view of self. It was helpful to format these into a configuration of role relationship models (RRMs) as shown in Fig. 17.3. The configuration of RRMs (RRMC) contain aspects of deep motivations, *desired* and *dreaded* RRMs. Defensive motivations are also contained, these are placed closer to the surface, in the upper one half of the RRMC. Problematic *compromise* RRMs have negative aspects and are contrasted with less negative defensive positions, called a *quasi-adaptive* compromise RRM. These quasi-adaptive compromise RRM may include the "ought to be" relationship discussed by Loevinger (1976, 1987b).

Configurations of role relationship models and multiple self schemas allow one to view personality as an evolving and flexible entity. A repertoire of self-identities contained in role relationship models can be considered a composite of possible states, transitions across states, and

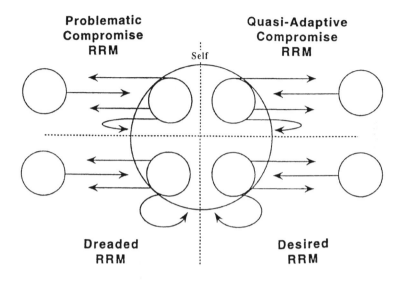

FIG. 17.3. A role relationship model cofiguration.

defense against entry into certain possible states. An inferred configuration of RRMs can also allow an analysis of how new memories, particularly stressful ones, may be integrated. The memory of traumatic loss, for example, has to be processed in relation to many RRMs if a mourning process is to be completed, and grief to end. In addition, drives such as sexuality or a desire for revenge become goals and intentions as the aims are given targets and endpoints.

DYNAMIC PROCESSING

Different person schemas organize the information processing of ideas and emotions, perceptions, and action plans about a given topic. This would lead to different anticipations of emotional states, and different styles of defensive coping with what is anticipated. For these reasons, in Fig. 17.2, a specific social situation in a specific state is being contemplated with a working model organized by primarily one role relationship model. Alternative RRMs could lead to a different working model of the same social transaction. If these alternative role relationship models were activated (rather than inhibited by defensive control processes), the current state of the person would shift, and the state of the social transaction could change. This is how some self-fulfilling prophecies occur.

STATE CYCLES

Each RRM, once triggered, may activate the next RRM. The result is a sequence of role relationship models and a cycle of states. Each response serves as a stimulus that triggers the activation of the next RRM in a sequence. For example, an individual may see a victim and rescue a helpless person. When reviewing the act, the individual may feel sadistic for hurting the other person in the act of rescue. If that happens, it triggers the next schematized step, in turn triggering the next RRM, which may contain meanings that lead to intentions toward acts that punish the self. Eventually, to expiate a chronic sense of guilt, the person may look for new victims in need of rescue and repeat the cycle. By rescuing others, the individual may again enjoy feeling powerful and superior, the superiority may lead to a guilty RRM, and so on.

CONFLICT MODELS

Role relationship model configurations (RRMC) can clarify enduring contradictions in beliefs about self and others. Character layers can be described and polarities of opposite traits identified. These RRMC may show wish–fear dilemmas.

Contradictory polarities of motives and identities often endure throughout life. But the individual may develop a more mature and integrated character in terms of supraordinate integration of the polarities. That is the central issue of this chapter: How can we describe integration or lack of integration of enduring contradictions in person schemas?

SUPRAORDINATE PERSON SCHEMAS

The function of supraordinate person schemas in containing contradictions can lead to mature character. Persons without containment of contradictions through supraordinate self and other schemas may be more prone to immaturity or more prone to continued, enduring and unresolved conflicts. A lack of capacity for integrating schemas into supraordinate forms could be a partial causation in the narcissistic, borderline, histrionic, and dissociate identity (formerly multiple personality) disorders (Horowitz, 1988a; Valliant, 1993).

THE EXPERIENCE OF "I"

Because subjective experiences may be organized by multiple self-concepts, the "I" of one state of mind is not necessarily the same as the "I" of an individual's next state of mind (Globus, 1980; Kernberg, 1976; Horowitz, 1979). In this respect, the "I" experience can seem transitory, even fragile. Such people may have more frequent depersonalization experiences, or states with a sense of chaotic and disintegrating identity. On the other hand, an "I" experience can feel solid and relatively enduring. A firm sense of "I" can lead to a continuous sense of identity.

Identity does not rest upon a single self view as, for example, "the surgeon who cares." On the contrary, an individual who is a surgeon has several potential "I" experiences, depending on which self-schemas are active. Social and biological factors will effect that "I" experience. As the individual remembers and compares different "I" experiences, a new "I" experience based on a larger supraordinate organization of subsidiary self-concepts may be developed. This new organization establishes continuity between subsidiary self-identities.

SUPRAORDINATE ROLE AND
RELATIONSHIP MODELS

There are developmental levels of schematizing capacity as suggested by Loevinger (1976) and Gedo and Goldberg (1973). There are degrees to which schematic containment of smaller order RRMs may have developed. Clinicians can even agree, to an extent, on a hierarchical classification of evaluated patients by categorizing them on a rough continuum of such supraordinate schemas. This categorization is shown in Table 17.1. It was applied to 52 cases by an evaluating clinician and a treating clinician. They agreed in their independent ratings at a correlation level of $r = .6$ using these categories (Horowitz, Marmar, Weiss, DeWitt, & Rosenbaum, 1984).

TABLE 17.1
Organization Level of Self and Object Schematization (OLSOS)

Mode	Description
Mode 5 Ideal of Normal Character	Such persons have a well-developed supraordinate self (a schema of several self schemas) and function from a relatively unitary position of self as agent and having values about long-standing issues. They have conflicts and negative moods and own these as "of the self." Conflicts are between various realistic pros and cons or limitations of real relationships. Conflicts tend to be consciously handled well through the use of well-modulated restraints, renunciations, sublimations, choices, wisdom, humor, or even

(continued)

TABLE 17.1
(CONTINUED)

	resignation. The person is able to achieve intersubjectivity or "we-ness" and to empathically know that another is separate with equivalent characteristics to his or her own, also experiencing wishes, fears, emotional reactions, conflicts, memories, and fantasies. When stressed or frustrated, the person can temper the bad with recognition of the good in a tolerant and wise manner.
Mode 4 Neurotic character	Such persons have self schemas of a realistic nature, but discrepancies exist between ideal, real, and other self schemas so that these persons experience contradictory aims of self as agent of action and self as critic that are not resolved in a reasonable time by rational choices. For example, they may see themselves continually as both intending to express some aim in behavior and opposing such expression on moral ground, with indecisive repetitive rumination on the theme or repetitive doing and undoing actions. Enduring, unresolved enactments of conflicts about sexuality, love, attention, responsibility, and power indicate this mode. These persons have stereotyped maladaptive patterns or defensive avoidance that are self-impairing. When frustrated, they may be irritable, submissive, passive-aggressive, and guilty.
Mode 3 Narcissistically vulnerable character	These persons are often able to maintain a cohesive and relatively realistic self schema, but there are states of exception; in these situations, they are vulnerable to a sense of self-improvement, a loss of a sense of self-cohesion, or to grandiosity, or to externalization and internalization of characteristics of self and other at an unrealistic level. For example, a person with enduring grandiose delusions confined to a sphere of creativity or sexuality might be assigned this mode, as would a person who consistently disowned personal aggressive behavior, although it was flagrantly obvious to others. Some others are viewed irrationally as if extensions of self (self-objects). There may be cycles of rage, shame, fear, and reconciliation upon frustration.
Mode 2 Borderline character	These persons are not able to stabilize self-cohesion that includes positive and negative self schemas in a supraordinate schema or schemas. Rather, they have various self schemas that are each only part of the actual self and various schemas of others that include only part of the actual behavior of others. Composites that are all-good may be dissociated from composites that are all-bad. When frustrated they may act suddenly, irrationally, and destructively, including self-mutilation.
Mode 1 Fragmented character	These persons have a self and other differentiation that is only partial and transitory. At times, they display or experience a significant level of confusion of self with other, or they regard self and other as merged or interchangeable. Parts of the bodily self may be disowned or dissociated. When frustrated, magical delusions and hallucinations may occur.

Note. Modes derived and revised from Gedo and Goldberg (1973) and Horowitz (1977, 1991).

PROGRESSION AND REGRESSION

There will be times when new realities do not accord with inner knowledge structures. Even recognition that one has acquired a new skill may evoke not only pleasure but also a mild, transient sense of nonagency until self-organization is modified into congruence with the change. This is reflected in such exclamations as "Was that me?" and "I could not believe I was able to do that!" With progression, new skills are integrated into self-organizing schemas.

Negative changes, as in the loss of mental or physical abilities, may evoke unpleasant emotions and regressions. A depersonalization experience may occur. If the train of thought modifying symbolic structures is interrupted by defensive maneuvers such as denial, progression may not occur. These defensive maneuvers prevent or avoid entry into dreaded states of mind, but may lead to and prolong a regression in sense of identity.

MASTERY OF DISCREPANCIES
AND AMBIVALENCE

Well-developed persons tend to have only transient states of depersonalization in response to discrepancies between actual and enduring schemas. Such persons have supraordinate structures that can eventually progress to contain contradictions. In persons without such capacity to contain discrepancies, states of self-depersonalization or regression will be more intense.

For example, consider a man who has achieved a reasonably advanced level of development and supraordinate self and other schemas. He has a well-developed self-organization and relational repertoire. He has supraordinate views containing various self-identities and role relationship models. He has a well-integrated and nested hierarchy from large scale information structures such as an overall self-organization to smaller scale ones such as self-identities embedded in role relationship models, and subsidiary body images, values, and procedural styles for each self-identity. Such components of self-organization are illustrated in Fig. 17.4.

His supraordinate schematic structure contains attributes of various possible roles of self in relationship with others. In states when his supraordinate self-organization is actively functional, he organizes thought with the knowledge that he can and does have different states of mind. He knows and anticipates that as he cycles through familiar states, he may behave in ways that seem contradictory. He knows that he is nice in some states of mind and nasty in others. He knows these character traits—being mean, being kind, or even being too selfishly mean, too altruistically kind.

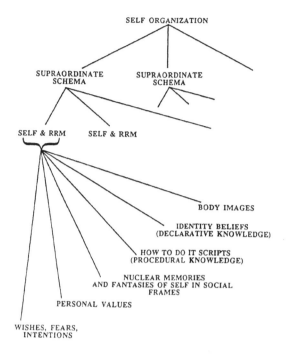

FIG. 17.4. A model of self-organization: supraordinate and subordinate schemas of self and other.

He also knows that in different states of mind he will see the same relationship between himself and another person differently. Sometimes he will see self and other as interdependent, cooperative, fairly giving and receiving. Sometimes he will experience the other as attempting to control and exploit him. Sometimes the other seems weak and dependent. He knows both his own and the other person's attitude can shift through varied states of mind, dependency can seem good or bad, caretaking can seem worthwhile or worthless.

This kind of man is able to soften and tolerate his own ambivalence and that of his valued companion. Frustrations do not lead to impulsive estrangement and hostility, the emotional responses are ameliorated by supraordinate schemas that retain active knowledge about mutuality and tenderness. Because of the operation of supraordinate schema his flow from one state mind to another is smooth and seamless rather than disjunctive. He is able to view the unfolding of interpersonal situations in light of various self and role relationship concepts. He knows his various possible patterns of mood and action and can modulate them.

Suppose this man is severely strained by a traumatic life change event. He may regress to activation of a less advanced self organization; one that envelops several self attributes, but is dissociated or unclear about other ones. In terms of thought processes, this can mean the simultaneous association of some self concepts, but the inability to associate to other self concepts.

The regression includes a loss of associative capacity. Recovery from that regression can lead to a progression, an advance in associative capacity and establishment of new associative linkages that build complexity, differentiation, and flexible meaning structures (Mandler, 1984).

During his regression, the man might be transiently unsure that he was even kindly whenever he was in a mean or guilty state of mind. He might have to undo his meanness in an extreme way lest he feel too guilty. He might shift abruptly into a flagrantly pseudo-kind state of mind. Then, he might react by feeling anxious that he was obsequious and unctuous. He might shift abruptly, back into a mean state. But he might rapidly progress from this regression because supraordinate schemas could be resumed.

Now, consider a man with similar schematic contents, yet with less supraordinate integrations of contradictions and discrepancies. He has had a more pathological development. That has made him vulnerable to a more turbulent regression when he is strained by stress or events. Under strain, he loses his capacity to link self- and other-concepts within even a transiently active supraordinate RRM.

The manifestation would be thinking and acting as if he (or another person) *only* had the attributes dominant in the immediately current state of mind. He would not acknowledge attributes manifested by either party in other states. His isolation, segregation, and dissociation of attributes into disparate clusters, without the ameliorating containment of supraordinate schemas, would result in states in which he reacted to another person quite differently. In his cycle of states he might exhibit explosive shifts in emotion and action. The segregated processes would be organized by different role relationship models, ones not actively contained within a supraordinate organization.

A regression in such a vulnerable person may reach a point in which relational concepts are split into all-good and all-bad sectors, as in borderline personality organization (Kernberg, 1967, 1976). There may be vulnerability to enter states of even greater extremity, tumultuous states organized only by chaotic fragments of self-identity, as in psychotic character structures. As Rosenfeld (1965) pointed out these experiences can be so very anguished that oscillation between all good and all bad views is preferable to the sense of falling apart. Stabilization at the irrationally dissociative all-good, all-bad level is defensive against a possible regression of identity into chaos. Yet, it is also the result of a deficiency, a pathological inability to schematize and stabilize a supraordinate organization of self and other relatedness.

SOCIAL CONTEXTS

Regressions may be precipitated by social stressors. The degree of psychological and social regression will depend in part on the schematic repertoire of the individual. Certain schemas, usually dormant, may be activated by the specific social events. Reemergence of a damaged or faulty self-concept, once problematic but then subordinated to the activity of a more competent one, may reoccur in situations of being abandoned, trapped, or helpless. Or the person may use irrationally defensive control processes to grandiosely compensate for criticism and threatened entry into states of feeling worthless, degraded, and inferior.

SOCIAL INSULTS

Kohut (1971, 1977) described regression during times of strain in people with narcissistic character structure. When threatened by insult or injury, realistic self-concepts are difficult for such persons to stabilize. States organized by defectively vulnerable self-concepts are anticipated. Grandiose schemas are defensively activated in the repertoire of such individuals. Manifestations of both deficiency (inability to stabilize states of mind organized by advanced, realistic self-concepts) and defensive operations (use of grandiose self-concepts to prevent the distress of states organized by defective ones) may occur, leading to irrational action choices.

In such regressive states of mind, other people are not modeled as fully independent centers of initiative. Instead, they are regarded as extensions of the self. Earlier terms point out this phenomenon, Jacobson's *archaic object images* (1964) and Fairbairn's (1954) *internal objects*.

Kohut (1971) called this mechanism of the use of others as *self-objects*. Regressive activation of self-object schemas can be described as inclusion of object concepts within the self rather than within the object. The role relationship models would have others mirroring ideal properties of the self or providing the self with idealized and essential supplementation.

TRANSFERENCE RECONSIDERED

Transference is the displacement of feelings originally experienced with significant childhood figures onto current figures. Because it is not possible for an adult to form a new relationship without utilization of some preexisting schema of self and some object, such "transfer" is always present. This is the essence of how schemas function. Labeling a phenomenon as a transference reaction is a judgment about the degree to which the activated organizing schemas are inappropriate to the real properties of the situation. In therapy transferences contrast with a more rational relationship called a *therapeutic alliance* (Greenson, 1965; Zetzel,1956). Both transference and therapeutic alliance are guided by self and relational schemas.

A therapeutic alliance RRM implies a tolerance for ambivalent feelings toward the clinician. If the patient has some supraordinate self and object schemas, these schemas can frame and conceptualize the relationship with the therapist. Early in treatment, preexisting role relationship models such as teacher–student views will be activated in a patient to organize a working model of a therapeutic alliance. Gradually changes will begin to include the attributes of what is really a new situation.

Transference elements may be present early in the therapeutic alliance. As the therapy progresses, the therapeutic alliance RRM may become more realistic by schematizing the actual qualities of both parties in a new kind of transactional pattern. The transference reactions of some patients early in therapy are sometimes less regressive than those experienced and communicated later in therapy. Sometimes the safety of an evolving therapeutic alliance permits a riskier regression, in the service of what Freud (1923) called "repeating, remembering, and working-through."

In *regressive transference reactions*, the patient organizes experience by self, object, and relationship schemas that were dormant, at least in relation to the therapist, during the states of mind that characterized earlier treatment sessions (Grotstein, 1981). Whether or not such activations of regressive transferences are useful to self-development depends on what then occurs in terms of new relationship experiences.

Therapeutic progress has been more frequently noted in patients said by clinicians to have "capacity for insight," "ability to establish a therapeutic alliance," or "a split between observing and experiencing self-reflective awareness" (Loewald, 1960; Stone, 1962; Zetzel, 1956). In patients without these characteristics, transference reactions may occur intensely but they only repeat inappropriate attitudes. Change is less likely. The change in a so-called "good insight" patient can be discussed in terms of how states of mind may be governed by supraordinate RRM.

RESCHEMATIZATION

Reschematization may be fostered by conscious confrontation with incompatible views of the same vividly experienced interpersonal situation. The presence of supraordinate RRM organizations allows a comparison of contradictory views. Interpretations by a therapist may help a patient look at contradictions between beliefs about what is happening. Realistic and less realistic concepts about the meaning of interpersonal feelings, attitudes, and actions can be considered together. In that sense, every clarification of an unrealistic self, object, and relationship belief can also strengthen more realistic beliefs. Supraordinate schemas may be forged by repetitions and enactments based on such confrontations.

New relationship experiences can provide a person with a growing coherence between previously isolated, split apart, and dissociated person schemas. Differentiation between reality and fantasy allows for a more realistic working model of present interpersonal situations. This more realistic working model builds new schemas.

The growing safety provided by realistic working models allows a patient in therapy to tolerate emotional and regressive experiences, including the recovery of awareness about relationships, memories, and fantasies of the past. Interpretations and reconstructions of the origin of person schemas may help a person to recast the past into a more realistic and continuous story line of personal history. Revised memories join with attitudes about the present and point toward a more adaptive future.

ON THE OTHER HAND, TRANSFERENCE REGRESSIONS MAY NOT BE HELPFUL

Progression is unlikely with patients who have low capacities for supraordinate organization of person schemas. Interpersonal beliefs tend to be segregated. When the patient is in a given state of mind, organized by a set of concepts, there is little parallel recognition of other self, object, and relationship concepts (Loewald, 1960; Stone, 1962).

The patient is the I, the therapist the "you," without the recognition of there being, simultaneously and potentially, another I and another you.

When the state of mind is organized by less realistic and more regressive concepts, and the therapist attempts to interpret both the transference- and alliance-based views, the patient selects one or the other, and does not compare them. Modification of one by the other, or linking one to the other, does not occur. The patient cannot engage in parallel processing of both views. In these situations, slower, more repetitive, more supportive, more tactful, and more varied therapy techniques are indicated (Horowitz, 1990).

EMPIRICAL FINDINGS

Such theory suggests different techniques with patients at lower levels of self and other schematization. This could be empirically tested. The organizational level of self and other schematization as shown in Table 17.1 was applied by evaluating clinicians to a group of bereaved individuals who sought brief psychotherapeutic treatment for pathological grief reactions after the death of a relative, either a parent or spouse. People who had lower levels of self and other schematization had more distress before treatment and in general did better with supportive rather than exploratory–interpretative approaches. We were able to categorize and reliably assess different supportive and expressive actions of therapists, and so we could quantitatively relate such therapist actions to changes in distress from periods before to periods after treatments (Horowitz et al., 1984).

Using a different scale on self and object capacities with a similar theoretical basis, these quantitative findings were replicated on another sample by a different investigative group (Piper, Azim, Joyce, & McCallum, 1991). Wallerstein (1986) reported similar findings in a qualitative interpretation of investigations of process and outcome.

The organizational level of self and other schematization as assessed by clinician evaluators using the categories shown in Table 17.1 was next related to the course of grief in 70 subjects. They were interviewed at 6 and 14 months after the death of a spouse or long-term domestic partner. These new subjects were drawn from notices, and were not seeking treatment for grief related psychiatric disorders. Bereaved subjects with higher levels of self and other schematization, at 6 months, had less psychiatric and physical symptoms reported on self-report batteries at 14 months after the loss ($r = -.33, p < .01$).

In this same sample, there were also two self-report measures relating to self and other schematization. One was a group of questions that assessed use of the deceased other as an extension of the self, as a kind of self-object as described earlier. The other was a measure of a sense of overall self-coherence. Both of these measures assessed at 6 months after loss also correlated with distress at 14 months. Use of the other as a self-object was higher in those subjects with prolonged distress ($r = .42, p < .01$), higher self-coherence ratings were correlated with less prolonged distress ($r = -.40, p < .01$). These data are in accord with the theoretical assertions that persons with lower levels of self and other schematization will find the reschematization process of mourning more difficult to accomplish (Horowitz, Bonanno, & Holen, 1993).

IMPLICATIONS FOR FUTURE RESEARCH
AND THEORY DEVELOPMENT

Future research could usefully, I think, apply different possibly converging measures to the same group of subjects. Ego development, as measured by the WUSCT of Loevinger, might overlap with scores on the OLSOS shown in Table 17.1. I would expect a medium level of correlation. The reason is that constructs have a moderate overlap; both theories are based on concepts about schematizations of self and relationships, including value schematizations.

The organizational levels of self and other schematization imply an association between optimum adjustment to life stressors at higher levels of capacity for supraordinate self-organization. However, this organization may not be the case in all populations. As the person becomes more capable of integrating contradictions, he or she may take on more challenging life tasks or assume more responsibility for groups of people. He or she may initiate changes in conservative values and practices. The results of initiative may engage the person in more stress and lead to health consequences. Persons at low levels of self and other schematization who are relatively conventional may, in contrast, maintain a good fit between their values and practices and those of the surrounding social network. The conventional person may have a high health adjustment because of low stress. Still, overall, I expect more resilience to change will be found in persons at the higher levels of self and other schematization. Thus, I predict at least a small correlation between this scale and adjustment as well as small negative correlations between it and distress. In particular, I would predict that depersonalization, loss of coherence of identity, and more intrusive and pathologically avoidant symptoms after stressful circumstances will occur in persons at lower levels of OLSOS and WUSCT when exposed to equivalent traumatic life events. One aspect of this prediction is that evidence will be found that it is possible with adult traumas to regress to earlier developmental stages even though the formation of higher level schematizations offers relative resilience.

Another prediction is that patients at relatively high SCT levels, such as at or above the *Conscientious stage*, as well as patients at higher levels (neurotic range) on OLSOS, will have better process-to-outcome correlations where process is insight into unconscious motives and contradictions in explorative psychotherapies. Persons at lower levels might have better outcomes where process is more supportive and educative.

We do not yet know what may account for a patient's increasing capacity for supraordinate organization. The advances I have witnessed in children around age 13, with an increment in the late 20s may be due to life experiences, neurotransmitter changes, gene expressions, or other increases in biological information processing capacity at the level of brain modular systems. Here I stand at the frontier of speculation.

A related question is when does development in these domains stop? I believe development in this domain of supraordinate schematization need never stop. Even with reduction in synaptic functions with aging of the brain, the brain–mind seems to make new schematic combinations. Self-identity can advance throughout the life cycle, even with the stressors attendant upon old age, biological decline, and social retirement. Very capable persons can develop new combinations that achieve higher levels of supraordinate organization late in life. I predict that Loevinger's hypothesis, that the SCT stabilizes in early adulthood, is incorrect, and that persons at lower levels can reach the highest levels later in life.

CONCLUSIONS

Every person has a repertoire of self-concepts and role relationship schemas. These can be formulated in terms of how they relate to the main states of mind experienced by the person. It is also desirable to formulate the functional capacity of a person for maintenance of supraordinate organization. Better theory and methods on person schema may advance the scientific study of character formation.

ACKNOWLEDGMENTS

This material was prepared while the author was a Fellow at the Center for Advanced Study in the Behavioral Sciences. The research upon which it was based was supported by the Program on Conscious and Unconscious Mental Processes of the John D. and Catherine T. MacArthur Foundation.

CHAPTER

18

Interpretive Communities
of Self and Psychotherapy

Polly Young-Eisendrath
Department of Psychiatry
University of Vermont Medical College

Carol Foltz
University of Pennsylvania

This chapter presents narratives of psychotherapy: the role of therapist, client, and change, ordered by stages of ego development. Its purpose is to open further inquiry into the relationship between ego development and conceptions of psychotherapy. In the context of contemporary philosophical considerations of subjectivity, the chapter reviews and summarizes some findings from an exploratory study to investigate the relationship between adults' ego development and their representations of psychotherapy. One hundred and fifteen subjects, 64 from student settings and 51 from patient settings, completed the Washington University Sentence Completion Test (WUSCT; Loevinger & Wessler, 1970) and the Reasoning About Psychotherapy (RAP) questionnaire constructed for the present study. Results suggested a positive relationship between ego development and conceptions of psychotherapy for the patient group after education was partialed out. Results were similar, but not as consistent, for the student group. These results, suggestive of the importance of ego development for clinical effectiveness, are used as a backdrop to a qualitative presentation of the subjects' representations of psychotherapy.

Since the 1980s, there has been a flurry of interest in self and subjectivity. In philosophy, psychoanalysis, and feminism, writers and practitioners have opened new inquiries into the experience of being an individual self. Roughly speaking, there are those who characterize the self as multiple, fragmented, discontinuous, dependent on momentary content (rather than process), and those who claim that the self is structured, coherent, more or less continuous, and dependent on development.

We are in the latter group. We see the self firmly grounded in narratives, but constrained by human of embodiment, and by cognitive, interpersonal, and moral development. The self is, then, not entirely individual, free, or governed merely by local demands. Its constraints are universal structures that both limit and engender meaning. Forms of development can be seen as interpretive contexts in which people construct selves in terms of life histories, emotional organizations, and type and degree of boundedness and mastery that might be counted as ideal.

As philosopher Charles Taylor (1989) puts it, "One is a self among other selves. A self can never be described without reference to those who surround it" (p. 35). Narratives of self are created and sustained in relationships, and psychotherapy is a unique kind of relationship in which the client's self is encountered and engendered. Therapists, both beginning and experienced, may recognize that a client's self should be respected in terms of the particular meaning it carries—such as gender, class, and ethnic meanings. Few therapists, however, recognize the possibility that there is an extensive developmental context that may underlie both the client's self and her or his fundamental beliefs about psychotherapy.

These are the premises we bring to this chapter in which we discuss the conclusions of an exploratory study conducted by Young-Eisendrath and some graduate students in human development at Bryn Mawr College. As far as we know, this study is the first study of its kind: an attempt to investigate the developmental differences that may underlie conceptions of psychotherapy among adults at different ego levels. A study by Dill and Noam (1990) demonstrated that this might be a promising topic. They found a significant relationship between peoples' ego development stage and the type of therapy they would select for themselves. Because no one else has studied developmental narratives of psychotherapy, the Bryn Mawr study is a first step, and was designed to be exploratory.

Results are presented here as a means of surveying the subjective context surrounding beliefs and attitudes about psychotherapy, a context that would generally have to be inferred by the therapist from signs and signals from the client. Therapists, especially beginners, may fail to account for the constraints of a client's self, and then impose ideas and interventions that make no sense to the client (e.g., insisting on talking about feelings) because they do not match the client's world.

In our view, ego development is a theory and method for making inferences about clients' selves. For clinicians, it provides a window through which various cues can be read in order to see more clearly into the client's world and especially into the context of meaning that defines the kind of "change" that can take place in psychotherapy.

This study measured the ego development of 115 adults and asked them to respond to open-ended questions such as, "What is psychotherapy?" and "What does a psychotherapist do?" After briefly summarizing our results, we discuss the different narratives of psychotherapy we discovered at each stage of ego development, narratives indicating the contribution of the client to the meaningful context of psychotherapy. First, we would like to make a distinction between persons and selves that leads directly into a discussion of ego development.

PERSONS, SELVES, AND NARRATIVE

Many theorists in psychology and philosophy define the self as a set of attitudes, beliefs, images, and actions that permit a person to sustain individual subjectivity across contexts of public and private life. The experience of being an individual subject includes coherence, continuity, agency, and emotional arousal. These conditions are sustained through conscious and unconscious attitudes, beliefs, images, and actions. In discussing subjectivity, the category of *self* is more elusive and abstract than that of *person*. (For an in-depth discussion of the implications of these distinctions for clinical work, see Young-Eisendrath, 1987; Young-Eisendrath & Hall, 1987, 1991).

Personhood can be universally identified by fairly reliable public criteria. Although we can identify person criteria in a public way, we cannot know in advance how any particular person may represent "self" without knowing about that person's interpretive community and level of development. The strong tension between person and self is often ignored in clinical discussions of psychotherapy. In general, client descriptions do not include any systematic account of cognitive, interpersonal, or moral development. Clients are described as "demographic" persons with particular problems and life situations. Although symptoms and defenses may be carefully delineated, the client's frame of reference on the world is rarely noted.

Harré (1989) urged us to see the significance of self-making in the development of a person: "Animate beings are fully human if they are in possession of a theory—a theory about themselves. It is a theory in terms of which a being orders, partitions, and reflects on its own experience and becomes capable of self-intervention and control." Harré further challenges psychological investigators to "look for conversational practices in which a theory of the appropriate kind could be acquired by an animate being who is . . . organized in a strong unitary fashion" (p. 404). Being so organized refers, of course, to coherence and continuity in the self. Harré called for a study of conversational practices that allow people to develop different self theories, the narratives that permit our self-recognition over time, space, and causality. (For a full discussion of the problems in psychology arising out of the confusion of person and self, see Harré, 1984).

EGO DEVELOPMENT AND SELF
IN PSYCHOTHERAPY

Loevinger (1979c) claimed that ego development is a master variable that "encompasses the complexity of moral judgement, the nature of interpersonal relations, and the framework within which one perceives oneself and others as people" (p. 3). We cannot help but see the model of ego development as a model of self development.

It also seems that ego development research is the type of research recommended by Harré (1984). In essence, studies of ego development are investigations of "conversational practices," progressively organizing a subject in a strong unitary fashion. The SCT for ego development is a measure of conversational practices that is, we believe, fairly exhaustive of types of subjectivity among adolescents and adults in our society. Each of the stages is a paradigm of meaning derived from people's actual narratives of self and other.

Contemporary clinical investigations of ego development demonstrated its usefulness for theories of developmental psychopathology (e.g., Hauser, 1993; Labouvie-Vief, DeVoe, & Bulka, 1989). Noam (1992) suggested that treatment modalities need to be sensitive to developmental differences among adult clients. Symptoms and defensive styles vary with ego development. In his review, Noam emphasized that higher levels of ego development may lead to a more integrated theory of self, but this kind of integration in no way guarantees greater psychological health. Advancement in ego development opens the way to greater vulnerabilities or greater resilience.

Dill and Noam (1990) investigated the specific relationship between the ego development stages of adult clients and their choices of treatment modality. Clients at higher stages of ego development were more likely to request psychodynamic insight therapy, whereas at lower stages, clients wanted more social and behavioral interventions and triage (referral).

In the study reported here, we specifically look at adults' narratives of psychotherapy, at their representations and beliefs as they might relate to ego development stages. If the self is a set of attitudes, beliefs, images, and actions, then different selves (different ego development stages) should imply different narratives of psychotherapy, its purposes and interventions. To leave the door open to respondents' own ideas, we asked four open-ended questions: What is psychotherapy? What does a psychotherapist do? What does a client do? Do you think that psychotherapy can change people? If yes, how? If no, why not?

REPRESENTATIONS OF PSYCHOTHERAPY

We wanted a sample that would include a range of ego development stages. In order to achieve this end, we invited graduate students (at the master's and doctoral levels) and outpatients, from two community mental health settings and one private practice setting, to participate. Because many of the graduate students were taking classes involving psychotherapy and related topics, analyses were conducted separately for the student group and the patient group (i.e., those subjects without such training) in order to examine whether training in psychotherapy contributed to conceptions of psychotherapy. One hundred and fifteen adult subjects participated (64 from student settings, 51 from patient settings). There were 54 female students and 10 male students ranging in age from 23 to 70 years with an average age of 42.06, $SD = 11.19$. There were 31 female patients and 20 male patients ranging in age from 16 to 77 years, with an average age of 38.13 years, $SD = 13.56$. The average educational level of the student group was a master's degree ($M = 4.08$, $SD = .51$, where 1 = less than a high school degree, 2 = high school degree, 3 = college graduate, 4 = master's, 5 = doctorate) and the average educational level of the patient group was some college ($M = 2.48$, $SD = 1.22$; note that there were some patients with graduate degrees). The student sample was primarily White (98%), whereas the patient sample was 65% White and 35% African American.

All subjects completed the WUSCT (Loevinger & Wessler, 1970) and the RAP questionnaire, constructed for the present study. The RAP questionnaire consists of the four open-ended questions and some demographic questions. Coding categories for each question were constructed with data from a pilot study ($N = 52$). First, logical categories of reasoning about psychotherapy were drafted from theory only, using moral, ego, and interpersonal development as a theoretical backdrop. We began with five rating levels: concrete help, problem solving, expressing feelings, processing feelings, and interpersonal discovery. For each RAP question, we developed relevant categories of response for these theoretical levels. Two raters scored each RAP protocol using our preliminary manual. After the protocols were scored and compromised, we looked at the results of our initial RAP scoring in light of the pilot subjects' SCT total protocol ratings. We made amendments to our manual based on actual responses from our pilot subjects, and discussed at length many issues involving technical jargon (e.g., the words *process* and *transference*). Although such jargon is in the popular domain as well as used in psychotherapy training, we made a list of more than 25 such words that were to be by-passed as specific indicators in favor of more developed themes. Raters were instructed to look at reasoning rather than terms. After detailed examination of the pilot study material, we composed the final RAP manual and validated it for accessibility by having two fresh raters score 25 of the pilot subjects and compromise the ratings. They had 70% to 80% agreement, depending on the question.

For each RAP question in the final manual, there are six possible response categories. Although the content varies across RAP questions, each set of six categories is based on an underlying developmental sequence ordered from *less* to *more complex*, from concrete to abstract, from less to more agency and personal responsibility, and from conceptions of psychotherapy that are linear or unidimensional to ones that are relational. Appendix A offers an example of the set of six categories for the RAP item, What does the psychotherapist do? It includes examples from both students and patients of exemplary responses in each category.

For each item, subjects receive a score ranging from 1 to 6. A total score was formed by summing the scores across the four RAP items. Percent agreement across coding categories for two raters ranged from 25% to 100%, with a mean percent agreement of 82.81 ($SD = 19.97$). Discrepancies were resolved by discussion.

The administration and scoring of the SCT conformed to Loevinger's (Loevinger & Wessler, 1970) standard rules. The percent agreement between any two raters ranged from 72% to 100%, with a mean percent agreement of 91.25 ($SD = 5.38$).

The distributions of subjects across the nine stages of ego development were the following: four subjects from patient settings and none from student settings were at the Impulsive stage, three patients and no students were at the Self-Protective stage, four patients and no students were at the Concrete Conformist,[1] seven patients and three students were at the Conformist stage, 12 patients and 12 students were at the Self-Aware stage, 15 patients and 30 students were at the Conscientious stage, four patients and 16 students were at the Individualistic stage, two patients and one student were at the Autonomous stage, and no patients and two students were at the Integrated stage. Although we have divided our sample, for purposes of analysis here, into groups representing the two kinds of settings in which data were collected—student (a college) and patient (clinic

---

[1]The Concrete Conformist has been eliminated from the most recent revision of Loevinger's scoring manual. However, we included this stage in the analyses because it existed in Loevinger's (1970) manual at the time this study was analyzed.

or private practice) settings—this division is complicated by the fact that some of the "students" had also been "patients" in psychotherapy, either before or at the time they completed the questionnaires. On the RAP, we asked the question "Have you ever been in psychotherapy?" and so we also examined the data according to "experience" (yes/no) in psychotherapy. This difference was not significantly related to ego development.

The modal stage for the entire sample was Conscientious, slightly higher than the modal stage obtained in a national probability sample of U.S. adults (Browning, 1987; Holt, 1980). Preliminary analyses suggested that age, gender, and marital status were not significantly related to subjects' ego development. Education level was significantly related to ego development for the patient group ($r = .67, p < .0001$) although not for the student group, and thus education was treated as a covariate in subsequent analyses for the patient group.

The correlations and partial correlations between ego stage and RAP item scores for both the patient and student groups are listed in Table 18.1. There is a significant relationship between ego development and

TABLE 18.1
Correlations Between Ego Stage and Reasoning About Psychotherapy Item Scores

	Ego Stage		
	Student (N = 64)	Patient (N = 32)	Patient, Education, Controlled[a]
RAPI	.18	.67***	.49*
RAP2	.55***	.71***	.51*
RAP3	.26*	.77***	.52**
RAP4	.04	.65***	.47*
RAP total	.42**	.80***	.62***

Notes. RAP1 refers to the item, What is psychotherapy? RAP2 refers to the item, What does the therapist do? RAP3 refers to the item, What does the client do? RAP4 refers to the item, Can therapy change people?
[a]These are partial correlations. Removing the effect of education from RAP scores via part correlations yielded results comparable to the partial correlations listed in the table. The results for students when education was partialed out did not effect the zero-order correlations.
*$p < .01$. **$p < .001$. ***$p < .0001$.

reasoning about psychotherapy across all content domains for the patient group, even when the effect of educational level is partialed out. These relationships were similar for the student group, except for the items "what is psychotherapy" and "can psychotherapy change people?" The smaller degree of variability in the student group may explain the attenuated correlations for these items. Although we can only speculate about this finding, there was a consistent relationship between ego development stage and conceptions of psychotherapy across RAP items in the patient group.

INTERPRETIVE COMMUNITIES
OF PSYCHOTHERAPY

The results of this exploratory study provide preliminary evidence that representations of psychotherapy are related to ego development in adults. After we analyzed the formal results of the study, we wanted to survey informally the types and range of themes in RAP responses expressed across subjects' ego development stages. Although all responses were carefully scored using the RAP manual, we now assembled them by stages of ego development of the subjects. In presenting these responses, organized by respondents' ego levels, our purpose is to acquaint the reader with the themes emerging in these narratives. Responses listed here are exemplary of those given, and they are presented for their heuristic value to encourage future study of developmental differences of therapeutic narratives, and to awaken clinicians' interest in the ways clients think about psychotherapy.

As we summarize the themes at each ego stage, remember that we are collapsing many responses in order to report themes that might be of interest to researchers and clinicians. Obviously, themes often overlapped across ego stages. When we formally scored the RAP, all responses were rated out of context of the total protocol and scored according to the categories listed in Appendix A. In summarizing the responses here, we note whether a particular response came from a patient (P) or a student (S) setting.

As becomes apparent, the overall context of meaning seems to shift from the idea of psychotherapy as a concrete provision, with the responsibility for success on the therapist (at the lower stages), to the idea that psychotherapy is an internal discovery process, with the responsibility for success primarily on the client.

Impulsive Stage (Patient-Only Settings). The few responses we collected from this stage are illustrative of concrete thinking about psychotherapy as a provision. In regard to psychotherapy, two subjects showed confusion between therapy and therapist: psychotherapy is a "doctor"— "a doctor who helps people." What does the psychotherapist do? "help," "talk to you," and "he listens to our problems." What the client does is "I don't know—maybe answer questions," "come for help" and "listen to what the doctor tells them to do, and take their medicine." Yes, therapy can change people, these respondents said, because "The change takes place when he talks to you and with treatments," and through "helping them." Clearly the resources for psychotherapy are provided by the doctor or helper and the client only needs to show up and cooperate. The passivity of the client is what is typically expected of a good patient in standard medical treatments.

Self-Protective Stage (Patient-Only Settings). The usual concreteness, simplicity, and guardedness of adults at this stage came through in a number of ways. Psychotherapy is "analiss" and "a listener and questioner," but what the therapist does is "cheat" and "they ask you questions." In response to the question about what the client does, one person said "not for me" and another, "try to find your problems while you talk about things that are troubling you," perhaps confusing the client and therapist's role. Does therapy change people? "Yes and no, non-chalant," and "yes, get you to talk about yourself, and find ways for you to solve some of your problems with his or her self." Although here again, we had few responses, those we got displayed both guardedness and the sense of therapy acting on, rather than with, the client.

Conformist Stage (From Both Settings). Talking about problems and trying to find solutions is the main way in which psychotherapy is described at the Conformist stage. Psychotherapy is "discussion with another person (P)"[2] or "dealing with emotional problems of people (S)" or "to tell the truth, I really have no idea (P)" which might be an expression of being unable to distinguish therapy from other kinds of talking (to friends or family) about problems. The therapist is usually portrayed as the agent of action (change): "He tells you what to do (P)," "talks to people—wants to help with your problems (P)" and "helps patient feel better about himself (S)." What does the client do? "listens to his doctor, and does what he asks them to do (P)," "he or she should participate wholeheartedly in each session (P)," "hopefully relate to the therapist to help self (S)" and "expose painful parts of him/herself—allow therapist to expose motivations for behavior (S)." Can people change? "I hope so (P)," "no, I don't think after a certain age, that you can actually change,

---

[2](P) indicates a response from a patient setting and (S) from a student setting.

however, you can be helped to handle a situation and accept things (P)" and "Yes, I haven't found out yet (P)." Occasionally we saw more apparently insight-oriented responses at the Conformist Stage, such as one that said "No" to whether psychotherapy can change people with the caveat "you can only help people understand themselves better (S)" and another subject who said what psychotherapy involves "on a one to one basis you get to talk about your problems and life with someone else in hopes to have a better understanding (P)."

Self-Aware Stage (From Both Settings). At this stage, concepts of change through relationship, process, and self-discovery emerge for the first time. Here are some typical responses from this stage to the question, What is psychotherapy? "A shared process of problem solving, the client offering the content, the therapist providing the tools (S)," "an interpersonal process in which the client is helped to change his thoughts, feelings, and behavior (S)," "a process whereby someone wanting to change asks for another's assistance in that process (S)," "a means of helping a person or persons to understand him/herself better and to improve his or her relationship via the transference relationship (S)" and "psychotherapy helps you to understand yourself better and helps place emotion in better perspective (P)."

From the Self-Aware perspective, the therapist "is a neutral person who would discuss and try to help solve problems that a person could not deal well with alone (P)," "he/she tries to make you more aware of what really goes on inside you (P)," "listens to the client, reflects back to him / her, points out patterns, summarizes, relates (S)," "helps people reorganize their feelings, thoughts, and behavior into a consistent and socially acceptable form (S)"—and "listen, intervene, structure, experience, feedback, act, be a mensch (Yiddish for human being) (S)." The image of the psychotherapist is more active of the two doing psychotherapy. What is the client doing? "Talk! Try to understand himself, be honest with the psychotherapist (P)," "works a great deal and if willing—listens a lot to help him or herself (P)," "explores his or her life with the therapist (P)" and "creates with the therapist an emotional relationship which allows him to re-experience and change (S)."

Do people change? Unanimously, the answer is yes, but the descriptions of how vary. "The vehicle for change is the relationship between the therapist and patient. The unique experience impacts on the patient and brings about change. Also, much of therapy is education which leads to shifts in attitude and behavior (S)." "A combination of timing, fairy dust, cognitive change, working through transference issues, experiencing difference (S)." "Through support and education, the client tries new behaviors and new ways of thinking (S)." "At least change their feelings about themselves and by understanding more, he/she can approach things differently (P)." "It can help people understand what they are and then if they are not happy they are better equipped to change to what they would rather be (P)." "It is largely a process of building not only self-esteem but the necessary intrapsychic structure to regulate the self-esteem (S)." Clearly at the Self-Aware Stage we see all the complexity and insight necessary to engage in psychodynamic psychotherapy, and in this therapy-educated sample, we witnessed the seeds of what would develop at later stages as the strong theme of self-discovery.

Conscientious Stage (From Both Settings). Here the meanings of self-discovery are mapped out. Although many of the Conscientious themes were touched upon by our Self-Aware respondents, we saw them flowering at this stage. From our large number of Conscientious responses, here are some that are fairly typical. What is psychotherapy? "A relationship through which people learn to recognize and accept all their feelings and to act on them in a spontaneous, but not impulsive, socially acceptable way (S)," "an opportunity for individuals to learn about themselves and to use this understanding to change their way of thinking and responding to life situations (S)," "a process in which a person comes to know the self better, accept one's strengths and weaknesses; deal with the cause(s) of psychological imbalance and deal with faulty relationships to improve them (P)" and "a process whereby the client learns to identify his/her patterns of behavior and their psychosocial origins; and explores possible options for change with the therapist (S)."

When describing the role of the therapist, respondents at this stage give voice to the idea of following the client's direction and facilitating a process, rather than solving problems. "The psychotherapist is a facilitator —a mirror to the patient. He/she is a supportive and confrontive individual with whom the patient forms a bond of trust (P)." The psychotherapist "facilitates patient–client awareness of own coping capacity (S)," "initiates the process, but knows enough to pull out when the client is moving on her/his own (S)," and "offers a holding environment—a safe, predictable, trusting setting in which the client can explore his feelings and options. This is done by being consistent and receptive (S)." The emphasis on enabling, facilitating, and holding is strong and new at this stage.

What does the client do? "The client/patient does most of the work. He/she is responsible for all the actual `change' that takes place. The patient must self-examine, determine what is valid for him/her, and take the steps to change or modify behavior (P)." This response touches on many of the themes at this stage. The client "must be motivated and committed to change. The client must feel free to share his feelings and thoughts and learn to look at them less defensively (S)," "is with the therapist as fully as possible, accepts the emotional connection, is committed to change, and takes in and works on the therapist's interventions (S)," and "the therapist's questions and responses are to be carefully considered; outside the therapist's office, the client should think about what transpired during the session, and try to apply it to his/her own life (P)" or simply "accept their involvement in their life (S)."

Again, overwhelmingly the answer to the change question is yes, but there are many qualifiers. People change "through the efforts of the client or patient, and this is only in small stages (S)," "through a thorough understanding of one's actions and their consequences (P)," "when the client or patient is open enough to be truly understood or appropriately 'guided,' and is willing to independently and persistently work to effect chosen changes (S)," and "the change takes place gradually as the client tries on new feelings and behavior for size—with the encouragement and support of the therapist—and working through these new behaviors with significant others who may offer resistance to the client's change. The bottom line is the client's decision to allow change to take place (S)." Indeed, the bottom line continues to be the client's responsibility at later stages of ego development.

Individualistic Stage (From Both Settings). At all the post-Conscientious stages, we see themes developed further that were introduced at the Conscientious stage. Sophistication and complexity enter into descriptions of psychotherapy: "A human relationship played out with particular rules designed to enable emotional growth on the part of the client or patient (probably resulting secondarily in the growth of the therapist) (S)" and "an interpersonal process whereby a person is helped to an increased awareness of his/her feelings, thoughts, and behavior. Through this process the therapist helps the individual begin to change in ways that are growth-producing and will eventuate in an increased ability to deal with all aspects of living in a more gratifying way (S)." The idea of an inherent growth process is first articulated at this stage.

What does a psychotherapist do? "Aids others (patients, clients) in recognizing the conflicts in their lives and hopefully ways to cope with the conflicts or change behavior causing or contributing to the conflict (P)," "allows the client to come to insights that lead to change that improves the client's quality of life (S)," and "is an enabler who lends his/her expertise to the therapeutic process in the hopes of improving the client's position (S)." "Role is that of objective observer. He/she attempts to have the patient reevaluate their position from a perspective they have not considered. He/she helps the patient see underlying currents, themes in the patient's actions (P)." The client, on the other hand, "takes responsibility for learning how to change (S)" and "should be active in psychotherapy (P)."

Autonomous and Integrated Stages (From Both Settings). At these final stages, from the few examples we have, we see additional themes of self-discovery and limitation described with a poetic or humorous twist. Psychotherapy is "A process which takes time. [It] involves learning how a person contributes to his/her own difficulties and helping that person to see alternatives. Changes are really quite small and often involve accepting conflict and using old demons to one's advantage (S)" and "A body of knowledge and a method of facilitating change. If done well, it's a kind of shamanism (S)."

What does the psychotherapist do? ". . . engages the client in dialogue in order to ascertain what the sources of the problems in a client's life might be, providing the client with objective reflection and insight based on professional knowledge and experience, and helping the client to face and deal with various aspects of his problems as these become apparent to him (P)." "The psychotherapist provides a secure, loving human relationship in which persons may grow and change and be liberated for new life (P)" and " . . . Essentially, the therapist and client go on an exploration together, and integrate their findings through their interaction (S)."

What does the client do? "The client works toward an increased understanding of the realities of himself or his life, both in the context of his interaction with the therapist and in his reflection and daily life experience outside the actual therapy sessions (P)" or more simply "The exact same thing as the therapist, but without the skill that comes with studying theories and methods, and without the same enthusiasm for uncertainty (S)."

Can therapy change people? "Yes, the change takes place through new self-knowledge and commitment to grow into new ways of being and doing (P)" or in more detail, "Yes and no, it depends on how you interpret change. If you mean basic altering of the personality structure, then I doubt it—if it means development to another (higher?) level of making meaning, then yes (S)."

IN PRACTICE

These therapeutic narratives illustrate how the selves of clients may constrain the interpretive possibilities of psychotherapy. Clearly the self of the therapist places limits on the paradigms or narratives that can be discovered or evoked. The self (not simply the psychopathology) of the client also limits these possibilities. Our study illustrates how widely the subjective meanings of psychotherapy vary.

Although there was overlap in the narratives of psychotherapy across ego stages, some major narrative themes still emerged. At preconformist stages of ego development, it seems that effective psychotherapy needs to provide concrete services and match the client's belief that the therapist does the greater part of the work, providing solutions and even direct help (e.g., medications or advice). At the Conformist and Self-Aware stages, talking about problems and finding solutions are the key to having a good relationship with a therapist. Popular cognitive, behavioral, and family therapies tend to focus on problem solving and downplay self-discovery. If the Self-Aware stage represents the modal stage of U.S. society, there is little doubt that therapies rooted in this narrative will appeal to a majority of clients and practitioners.

At the Conscientious stage and beyond, the narratives of psychoanalysis and other psychodynamic therapies emerge. Self-discovery and responsibility of the client for the change process are central features of most insight-oriented therapies. The characteristic demands of these therapies, such as the patient taking the lead or freely associating to thoughts or images, seem meaningful and reasonable at these stages, whereas they may seem arbitrary and imposed by the therapist at earlier stages.

Does this mean that the SCT should be administered to incoming clients? I do not think so. Rather, I believe clinicians need to listen for the interpretive community of the client's self, and recognize the limitations of their most-favored therapeutic tools. To secure a therapeutic alliance, the clinician needs to learn the language and assumptions of the client; in order to embrace the self of the client, the therapist has to enter the client's interpretive community. To be an effective psychotherapist, an agent of change, requires the capacity to tap underlying assumptions about treatment and to match them through practice or an appropriate referral.

ACKNOWLEDGMENTS

The study presented here was supported by a research grant awarded by Bryn Mawr college. I would like to thank graduate students from Bryn Mawr who helped conduct the study and code the data.

APPENDIX A

Scoring Manual for RAP Item
"What Does the Psychotherapist Do?"

1. Concrete provision: Talk, helps, solves problems, gives advice, or no response (e.g., don't know). "Talks to people—wants to help with your problems" and "He tells you what to do."

2. Support and problem solving: Listen, reflects, and supports, lends understanding and problem solving. "On a one to one basis you get to talk about your problems and life with someone else—in hopes to have a better understanding" and "listens, questions, interprets, all based on diagnosis and understanding of the client's needs."

3. Emphasis on therapist's skills: The therapist has special interpersonal skills (listening, supporting, interpreting) that help the client change. The therapist acts as a change agent or catalyst which motivates the client to change. The individual has no understanding of discovery or insight. "Aids others (patients, clients) in recognizing the conflicts in their lives and hopefully ways to cope with the conflicts or change behavior causing or contributing to the conflict" and "listens empathetically and offers interpretations."

4. Psychotherapy as a special relationship: The therapist provides a special kind of relationship or environment to discover, explore, and know self. "Listens, supports, nurtures, clarifies, focuses, reflects back, and provides opportunities for rehearsal for action; removes the trash from the landscape so the client can see for himself what he needs to do."

5. Emphasis on client's agency and insight: The therapist guides the process in which the client can become responsible, independent, or integrated individual. Insight is present. "The psychotherapist is a facilitator" and "initiates the above process (a way of learning about self and what makes one tick. A tool for growth. An ongoing, lifelong process), but knows enough to pull out when the client is moving on her or his own."

6. Complex: Complex elaboration of knowledge, skills, and process leading to client's growth and self-discovery. "The psychotherapist listens, gradually establishes her or himself as a trustworthy person in the eyes of the client and is then able to present to the client a picture of what the client has been saying in words and behavior about him or herself. The therapist's role is to help the client use his or her capacities to find "solutions" to the difficulties he or she is experiencing."

CHAPTER
19

Ego Development
and Counselor Development

L. DiAnne Borders
Department of Counseling and Educational Development
University of North Carolina at Greensboro

Once upon a time, at the beginning of a fall semester, there were two counseling students who came to learn the rules for doing therapy. The students dutifully practiced basic counseling skills, learned how to sit in an open and inviting posture, and memorized ethical guidelines. Despite good grades and positive feedback, the students approached the first practicum experience with much trepidation, fearful that the wrong response or movement would do irreparable harm to a client. The students gratefully turned to a supervisor, who provided support and encouragement, and who explained what the beginning counselor should do. The students sought to emulate this role model's actions, mannerisms, and theoretical approach. The students began to believe that they had learned the rules for doing therapy and diligently applied them to each client.

Over time, however, the students experienced some confusion, as a session or client did not follow the rules. One student viewed the offending clients as the problem; exceptions to the rules were mostly ignored as he or she employed the "right" interventions for a particular client category or counseling issue. For the other student, however, new rules and rules for the exceptions to rules provided only short-term relief. Confusion turned into turmoil as this student became aware of frustration, impatience, even negative feelings towards some clients, particularly in response to some clients' reluctance to change and their inability to get past that reluctance. A supervisor provided a calm affirmation that, yes, the rules often do not apply, and suggested that negative—as well as positive—responses to clients may provide valuable information about the client, the client's world, the counseling interaction, or the counselor. The student stopped thinking in terms of rules for therapy; he or she began to more closely listen to what was said and not said during a session and looked to his/her internal responses for clues about the client's unique needs and patterns.

With time, the counselor began to sense a rhythm and flow to the therapeutic process, and was less often surprised by unpredicted client behaviors. The counselor appreciated a client's efforts to survive and make sense of seemingly overwhelming circumstances, even those so different from the counselor's own experience. Therapy took on the flavor of a collaborative, creative endeavor designed to create change for a client. Now the counselor began to note how the unassertive client's passivity gave her power in the family—and the therapeutic relationship—and then discovered similar paradoxes in other clients and their families. The counselor also began to recognize how his or her own life changes had influenced his or her expectations of clients, even how therapeutic interactions provided insights into the counselor's own needs and issues at a particular time. The counselor began to anticipate that such changes would be a "rule" of therapy. The counselor accepted that he or she would not always know exactly how or why counseling worked or did not work. The counselor shared these observations and learnings with a supervisor, and solicited other perspectives and insights from the supervisor and colleagues.

COUNSELOR DEVELOPMENT

The evolutionary process of counselor growth, and the mechanisms by which students do or do not evolve, has been a central focus in counselor education since 1980. Our understanding of this process largely is due to publication of developmental models of supervision (e.g., Blocher, 1983; Loganbill, Hardy, & Delworth, 1982; Stoltenberg, 1981). Authors of these models describe sequential and hierarchial stages through which, ideally, counselors progress as they gradually acquire more advanced conceptual and behavioral skills and become more insightful about themselves, their clients, and the therapeutic process.

These models are primarily based in cognitive–developmental theories, particularly those of Hunt (Harvey, Hunt, & Schroder, 1961) and Loevinger (1976), and these theories are readily apparent in descriptions of counselors at various stages. In fact, changes across supervision stages often parallel progressions outlined in Hunt and Loevinger's theories. Counselors at early stages, for example, are characterized by concrete categorical thinking and dependency on the supervisor, whereas counselors at later stages evidence complex thinking and an acceptance of their strengths and weaknesses as a counselor. In essence, a mature, effective counselor, one at a high developmental stage, is one who embodies high levels of conceptual and ego functioning. As summarized by Blocher (1983),

This functioning includes the ability to take multiple perspectives in order to achieve empathic understanding with people who hold a variety of world views, value systems and personal constructs. It includes the ability to differentiate among and manipulate a wide range and large number of relevant facts and causal factors. Finally, it involves the ability to integrate and synthesize in creative or unusual ways large amounts of such information to arrive at an understanding of the psychological identity and life situation of a wide range of other human beings. Still further the counselor engages in this quest in active collaboration with the client, and in the hope of imparting some skill and understanding of the process to the client. (p. 28)

The parallel nature of counselor development stages and conceptual and ego levels also is evident in several assumptions underlying developmental models of supervision. First, it is assumed that one's general developmental level will create a ceiling effect on his or her growth as a counselor. Students will not be able to learn and perform counseling skills or express conceptual understandings of their clients that are beyond their general ego functioning level. As a result, a counselor's developmental level cannot be equated with his or her level of experience. A counselor with many years of experience may express simplistic and rigid perceptions of clients, whereas a relatively inexperienced counselor may describe complex client dynamics and understand mutuality in relationships. It is expected that counselors' conceptual and ego development levels will govern their rate of progress through the supervision stages, with higher level counselors being able to move more quickly toward supervision stages that equal their general levels of development.

Finally, it is assumed that supervised practica and internship experiences, in which counselors work with actual clients, provide ideal opportunities for encouraging conceptual and ego development. Such development hinges on the availability of an *optimal environment* (Stoltenberg, 1981) in supervision, one in which there is an appropriate balance of challenge and support, innovation and integration (Blocher, 1983). Given such an environment, the counselor feels secure enough to take risks and is able to achieve insights characteristic of the next developmental level.

This assumption is supported somewhat by earlier work in the area of deliberate psychological education (Mosher & Sprinthall, 1971). Those earlier educational programs were designed to stimulate the social, personal, ego, and moral development of various student populations, ranging from high school to college students. Such curricula typically included empathy training, study of various developmental theories, and experiential activities (e.g., tutoring or peer counseling), which required

BORDERS

students to apply their new knowledge in interactions with others. A number of studies demonstrated the efficacy of these programs, typically yielding increases in empathic skills, moral judgment, and (less frequently) ego development (e.g., Cognetta, 1977; Erickson, 1975, 1977; Hurt, 1977; Mosher & Sprinthall, 1971; Oja & Sprinthall, 1978; Rustad & Rogers, 1975). Given the similarities between deliberate psychological education programs and counselor education programs, it seems reasonable to expect developmental growth in counseling students, also.

Thus, high levels of conceptual and ego development are the desired outcomes of counselor training and supervised clinical experiences. Counselor effectiveness and growth will be stunted unless these outcomes are achieved.

RELEVANCE OF EGO DEVELOPMENT THEORY TO COUNSELOR DEVELOPMENT

Although Hunt's (Harvey et al., 1961) theory of conceptual systems certainly has relevance to counselor development, Loevinger's (1976) ego development theory more often has been cited as a promising theoretical framework because of its wider application to counselor growth and development (see also Cebik, 1985). The inclusiveness of ego theory, in which conceptual development has been integrated with character, moral, interpersonal, and self development, makes it a useful unifying umbrella for various aspects of counselor development. The cognitive and interpersonal styles characteristic of each ego level have particular relevance for counseling effectiveness. Cognitive style, for example, denotes a counselor's case conceptualization skills, indicating ability to avoid stereotypical and conventional client descriptions (e.g., sex roles), to identify underlying feelings and patterns of behavior, and to distinguish between process and outcome. Similarly, interpersonal styles are highly relevant to a counselor's ability to fully appreciate the dynamics at play in a client's family and other relationships, and how these dynamics may be played out in the counselor–client relationship. Traits of high ego levels, such as flexibility, tolerance for ambiguity, appreciation of individual differences, and acceptance of conflict as a natural part of relationships are critical qualities of effective counselors. Thus, Loevinger's theory of ego development has been the theoretical foundation for my research agenda in counselor supervision.

In general, my research questions have been focused on investigating the efficacy of ego development theory for counselor preparation programs and supervision experiences. One particular focus has been the interaction of ego development level and experience level, for, although there are a rather substantial number of empirical studies supporting developmental models of supervision (see Stoltenberg, McNeill, & Crethar, 1994; Worthington, 1987), almost all have ignored the theoretical bases of the models. Most researchers have operationalized developmental stage by grouping supervisees according to experience level (e.g., practicum, internship, postdegree counselor) rather than developmental level (e.g., conceptual or ego development level), thus ignoring the ceiling effect of developmental level described earlier. Thus, one goal of my research agenda has been to investigate the usefulness of Loevinger's ego development theory for explaining differences in supervisees beyond those attributed to experience level.

Colleagues and I have investigated the impact of counseling students' ego levels on their counseling-related cognitions (Borders, 1989; Borders, Fong, & Neimeyer, 1986), and on their acquisition of counseling skills and actual counseling performance (Borders & Fong, 1989). The reciprocal influence of counselor preparation and supervision activities on students' ego levels (Fong & Borders, 1996) is also being investigated.

STUDENTS' COUNSELING-RELATED COGNITIONS

For some time, writers have emphasized the need to more fully investigate counseling students' cognitions (e.g., Fuqua, Johnson, Anderson, & Newman, 1984; Mahon & Altmann, 1977). These writers highlighted the central role of cognitions in governing students' behaviors and, ultimately, their counseling effectiveness. In addition, authors of the developmental models of supervision (e.g., Loganbill et al., 1982; Stoltenberg, 1981), but particularly Blocher (1983), described desired changes in counseling-related cognitions across developmental stages. Getting inside a student's head, however, is no easy task, and few studies of students' cognitions have been published. Thus, in line with this interest in expanding our understanding of the nature and development of counseling students' cognitions, two of our studies were focused on the relationship between ego levels and counseling students' cognitions.

Perceptions of Clients

In the first such study (Borders et al., 1986), we focused on the relationship between counseling students' ego levels and their perceptions of clients, including the structural complexity (differentiation and integration) and content of these perceptions. Participants were 63 students enrolled in first practicum ($n = 27$), second practicum ($n = 10$), and internship ($n = 26$) experiences. Five levels of ego development were present in the group: Delta[1] ($n = 1$), Conformist (I–3; $n = 1$), Self-aware (I–3/4; $n = 16$),

Conscientious (I–4; $n = 39$), and Individualistic (I–4/5; $n = 6$).

As a measure of client perceptions, students completed a variation of the Repertory Grid Technique (Rep Grid; Fransella & Bannister, 1977; Neimeyer & Neimeyer, 1981), a technique based on Kelly's (1955) theory of personal constructs. Following the standardized Rep Grid procedure, students first listed eight current clients who fit specified criteria (e.g., the client who is or was your greatest success; the client who is or was the hardest for you to understand). Then, presented with a series of eight groupings of three clients each, students (a) described how two of the clients were similar (e.g., both are "straightforward"), (b) described how the third client was different from the other two along the same dimension (e.g., "manipulative"), (c) specified a positive or negative preference for each pole of the construct pair (e.g., straightforward [+] versus manipulative [-]), and then (d) rated each client separately on a Likert-type scale ranging from -3 to +3, using their own eight bipolar descriptions (construct pairs). Computer scoring of these ratings yields continuous scores of *cognitive differentiation*, a measure of the degree of complexity of the constructs, and *cognitive integration*, a measure of the sophistication of the hierarchial arrangement of the constructs and the degree of flexibility with which they are used. High differentiation combined with high integration is considered the most complex and flexible set of constructs (Landfield, 1977).

We also coded the Rep Grid client descriptions (construct pairs) for content using Duck's (1973) categories of (a) physical characteristics or factual information, (b) interactional style, (c) roles or habitual activities, and (d) psychological (personality and cognitive) characteristics. We hypothesized that students at higher ego levels would report more complex perceptions and perceptions characterized by more abstract content. Level of experience was included in the analyses as a possible interacting variable.

Results indicated that variations in the structural complexity of students' client perceptions were neither a function of the students' experience levels nor of their ego levels. In contrast to our hypotheses, students at high ego levels did not report more structurally complex and flexible client perceptions, as both ego development theory and developmental models of supervision would suggest.

Separate analyses (Friedman test, corrected for ties) were used to

---

[1]The notation for ego levels used in this chapter corresponds to the notation of the first edition of the scoring manual for the WUSCT (Loevinger & Wessler, 1970; Redmore, Loevinger, & Tamashiro, 1978). The current edition of the scoring manual (Hy & Loevinger, 1996) introduced several changes. See the Appendix to the introductory chapter of this volume for a comparison between the previous and the current system.

analyze relationships of the content of client perceptions with ego level and experience level. Content codes across experience levels were quite similar, suggesting that a student's client perceptions were not influenced by level of experience. There were, however, significant differences in the content of perceptions by ego level, and these differences seemed a logical manifestation of ego level as described by Loevinger. Students at the Self-Aware (I-3/4) ego level, for example, who are focused on feelings and internal states, used relatively more psychological descriptions than did other students. Individualistic (I-4/5) students, who value interpersonal relationships and have some understanding of the complexity of these relationships, used relatively more interactional descriptive statements.

Similar differences were found within ego levels in the wording of the constructs. Self-aware students, for example, used psychological descriptors (e.g., *unhappy–happy*) that were much less sophisticated than those used by Individualistic students (e.g., *feel responsible for self–feel responsible for others*). Interactional constructs also varied by ego level, ranging from *assertive–timid* (Self-Aware) to those based on counselor–client dynamics, such as *I was unable to express ideas I thought important; evoked similar defensive responses in me–one with whom I feel able to express anything I deem important* (Conscientious).

These results, although limited, offered the first empirical support for the efficacy of ego development theory in understanding differences in supervisees. We concluded that although experience level should not be ignored, it also should not be equated with counselor development level. We also noted that the restricted range of ego levels was a limitation of the study.

In-Session Cognitions

It seemed that ego level not only should influence students' post-hoc conceptualizations of their clients, but also their in-session cognitions, including the type of information they considered and how they processed this information. Thus, in a second study of counseling students' cognitions (Borders, 1989), I used an open-ended recall procedure (Dole et al., 1982) to obtain the full range of students' thought processes during an actual session. To control for possible effects of counseling experience, only students in first practicum were studied. A total of 27 student volunteers participated; they represented three ego levels: Self-Aware (I-3/4; $n = 8$), Conscientious (I-4; $n = 14$), and Individualistic (I-4/5; $n = 5$).

Following Dole et al.'s (1982) standardized recall procedure, students reviewed the videotape of a counseling session in the hour immediately following the session. (Students were allowed to select a client and session they believed was representative of their work.) The students were asked to relive the session by thinking aloud, using the present tense to describe what they were thinking and feeling during the session. They recorded their retrospections on audiotapes, which were then transcribed and collated with transcriptions of the counseling sessions. Each retrospection was then classified into categories along six mutually exclusive dimensions (Dole et al., 1982): (a) time (retrospection about *past, present, or future* events and feelings), (b) place (about *in-session* or *out-of-session* events and feelings), (c) focus (about the *client, counselor, client–counselor* interaction or relationship, or *supervisor*), (d) locus (about an *external,* observable characteristic or behavior, or an *internal,* inferred trait, opinion, or value), (e) orientation (from a *professional* or *personal* perspective), (f) mode (in cognitive, *neutral* or *planning,* or affective, *positive* or *negative,* terms).

Results revealed differences by ego level for the mode category only. Students at higher ego levels reported significantly fewer negative thoughts about their clients, tended to be less critical of themselves, and tended to report more objective retrospections overall.

Students at the Self-Aware (I–3/4) ego level reported feelings of frustration, impatience, and even anger about their clients; one commented on how the client was "making me look bad." Students at the Conscientious (I–4) ego level expressed concern about whether their verbal responses to clients sounded judgmental, although neither their thoughts nor responses had the judgmental tone found at the Self-Aware level. Students at the Individualistic (I–4/5) ego level evidenced a nonjudgmental, objective analysis of their internal reactions to clients and their own counseling performance. One wondered whether her strong verbal response to a client was "coming from my need or [the client's] need," suggesting some awareness of countertransference phenomena.

It should be noted that these differences paralleled changes across stages of developmental models of supervision despite the fact that the students were all at the same experience level (e.g., first practicum). It also should be noted, however, that some characteristics of early developmental stages were found at all ego levels (e.g., few planning statements, focus on present events vs. themes and patterns), and that some supervision issues characteristic of advanced developmental stages (e.g., theoretical identity, personal motivation, personal ethics) were not evident at any ego level. There also was a preoccupation with issues of competence. In sum, the first practicum supervisees' in-session cognitions reflected both their ego levels and their lack of experience. Again, a limitation of the study was the restricted range of ego levels.

STUDENTS' COUNSELING ABILITY

Thoughts are not automatically translated into action, so that one should not assume that students at higher ego levels could necessarily apply their more sophisticated thoughts in their actions with clients during a session. At the same time, however, ego theory would suggest that certain ego levels would be a prerequisite for learning and performing a skill. Two published studies (Carlozzi, Gaa, & Liberman, 1983; Zielinski, 1973) provided some preliminary support for the relationship of ego levels and counseling ability, although only one counseling skill, empathy, was considered in both studies. The impact of ego level on other basic skills and more advanced skills was not addressed. In a related study, Cummings and Murray (1989) found that ego levels did not significantly predict instructors' ratings and formal course grades of students in a counseling practicum. Actual counseling performance, however, was not rated. To expand on these findings, we conducted two studies focused on the impact of students' ego development levels on their skill acquisition and their effectiveness with actual clients.

Skill Acquisition

In the first study (Borders & Fong, 1989, Study 1), we rated pre–post audiotaped counseling sessions of 86 first semester students enrolled in an introductory skills class. Students scored at four levels of ego development: Conformist (I–3; $n = 3$), Self-Aware (I–3/4; $n = 4$), Conscientious (I–4; $n = 33$), and Individualistic (I–4/5; $n = 3$). Selected counselor responses were rated for effectiveness on a 4-point scale ranging from 1 (*damaging and ineffective communication*; e.g., ridiculing feelings, dominating conversation) to 4 *accurate and facilitative responding*; e.g., responding to underlying feelings, moving from vagueness to clarity) (Gazda, Asbury, Balzer, Childers, & Walters, 1984). At posttest, we also administered a videotaped counseling skills exam designed to measure verbal performance of eight counseling skills covered in the course (i.e., warmth, empathy, genuineness, concreteness, self-disclosure, advanced empathy, confrontation, and immediacy).

Results yielded no significant effect of ego development on counseling ability. Instead, the pretraining counseling rating was significantly related to the counseling skills exam scores, but not the posttraining counseling rating. There was a significant moderate correlation ($r = .24$, $p = .02$), however, between ego development level and students' pretraining counseling ability. Based on these results, we speculated that students at higher ego levels arrive with some interpersonal awareness that potentiates their counseling training but is not sufficient alone to predict training success.

Advanced Counseling Effectiveness

In the second study (Borders & Fong, 1989, Study 2), we rated audiotaped counseling sessions (working session of their choice) of 44 students enrolled in practicum or internship experiences. Five levels of ego development were present in the group: Delta ($n = 1$), Conformist (I–3; $n = 1$), Self-Aware (I–3/4; $n = 13$), Conscientious (I–4; $n = 26$), and Individualistic (I–4/5; $n = 3$). Audiotape ratings were completed using a measure of broader and more advanced aspects of counseling effectiveness, including therapist's warmth and emotional involvement with the client, attitudes that might intimidate or threaten the client, and attempts to examine the psychodynamics underlying a client's problems (Vanderbilt Psychotherapy Process Scale; O'Malley, Suh, & Strupp, 1983; Strupp, 1981; Suh, Strupp, & O'Malley, 1986). Training or experience level was controlled for in the data analyses.

Results indicated no significant relationship between ego development levels and ratings of counseling effectiveness, although we observed a pattern of increasing scores across both ego levels and experience levels. In addition, students with less experience who were at higher ego levels tended to score higher on counseling effectiveness than did students at lower ego levels. We observed that, due to numerous sources of error variance (e.g., different practicum and internship settings, clients, and supervisors), it was noteworthy to find that the relationship of ego level and counseling effectiveness approached significance.

CHANGES IN STUDENTS' EGO LEVELS

Studies published in this line of research (both ours and others) have been informative and, for the most part, supportive of at least an indirect link between students' ego development level and their counseling-related cognitions and counseling abilities. These studies, however, have been primarily descriptive (with only one brief pre–post study) and cross-sectional in nature. In addition, they have not addressed a critical issue related to developmental models of supervision. In essence, if the goal of counselor preparation programs is to stimulate functioning at higher levels of cognitive and ego development, do students evidence this growth?

We, along with others (e.g., Blocher, 1983; Borders & Fong, 1989; Lovell, 1990), had speculated that certain aspects of counselor education programs contain the necessary ingredients for stimulating students' conceptual and ego development, much like the earlier deliberate psychological education programs. During their clinical experiences, for example, students are challenged to integrate and synthesize large amounts of information about clients, deal with abstractions and process, understand multiple perspectives of an issue, achieve empathy with clients who evidence a wide range of emotions and behaviors, and interpret feedback from a variety of sources (e.g., client, environment, supervisor, etc.). We also had observed that students in the skills training study (Borders & Fong, 1989, Study 1) on average had lower ego levels than did the students in other studies who were further along in their counselor preparation programs. Thus, we began a longitudinal investigation of 33 counseling students, assessing ego levels before and after an introductory skills training class during the first semester, and then after their practicum and internship experiences, for a typical total period of about 3 years (Fong & Borders, 1996).

Our preliminary analysis of the data indicates that students' ego levels did not increase during their counselor preparation program. Over one half the students (all of whom scored at the Self-Aware [I–3/4] or Conscientious [I–4] levels) fluctuated back and forth between I–3/4 and I–4 across the four data collection points, typically ending at the pretraining level. Of those who changed ego levels from the pretraining to the final practicum or internship experience, four declined (all four moved from I–4 to I–3/4) and four increased (two from I–3/4 to I–4, one from I–3 to I–4, and one from I–4 to I–4/5). Overall, however, most students had not matured in terms of their ego development level during their counselor preparation program.

Although these results are disappointing for an ego development enthusiast, they perhaps should not be surprising. Loevinger (1976), for example, emphasized the amazing stability of ego development levels of adults, even in light of attempts to advance those levels. And at least two other researchers reported similar results with other professionals. Glickman and Tamashiro (1982) compared ego levels of first-year, fifth-year, and former teachers. They found that the first-year and fifth-year teachers scored significantly higher (primarily at the Self-Aware [I–3/4] level) than did the former teachers (primarily at the Conformist [I–3] level), but not significantly different from each other.

In addition, White (1985) found no significant changes overall in ego levels of students in a 6-month nurse practitioner training program (from entry to follow-up 15 months after training). White did note, however, that those at the Self-Aware level or below either stayed at the same level or moved up, whereas those at the Conscientious level or above either stayed at the same level or moved down in ego level. She concluded that "the changes that the training program achieved seem to have resulted in higher development only for those who were at ego levels which were responsive to the emphasis on autonomy and independence" (p. 571). In other words, it appeared that the instructional methods did not match the learning needs of students at the higher ego levels.

IMPLICATIONS FOR COUNSELOR EDUCATION AND SUPERVISION

One might conclude, based on these findings, that counselor educators, supervisors, and researchers now should focus on identifying interventions that do lead to desired changes in students' ego functioning. First, however, we probably should question whether this is a realistic or necessary goal.

We are reminded, for example, of Loevinger's (1976, 1980) caution that adult's ego levels are stubbornly stable and highly resistant to change efforts. Our longitudinal results (and those of White, 1985) certainly seem to corroborate this statement, although both studies covered relatively short time period. We also should recognize that a majority of the counseling students seem capable of effectively working with their clients. Across the samples of students from two university counselor education programs who have participated in our studies (and those in the Cummings and Murray, 1989 study), over 52% scored at the Conscientious (I–4) level, the modal level for graduate students (Swenson, 1980). This level, according to Swenson (1980), is an appropriate match for the typical client (Self-Aware, I–3/4). In fact, it is a perfect match based on Swenson's recommendation that the counselor be no more than one ego level higher than the client. To what extent, then, should counselor educators and supervisors accept and work with their students' ego levels rather than trying to increase the students' levels?

Such a question, of course, is based on the assumption that counselor educators and supervisors are functioning at an ego level that is at least one stage higher than their students' and thus are capable of stimulating their students' ego functioning. To date, such an assumption has not been validated empirically. To my knowledge, there are no published studies that include even such descriptive information regarding the ego levels of counselor educators and supervisors, nevertheless the impact of their levels on their preferred instructional and supervisory approaches and student outcomes. It may be that research along these lines is a key to explaining the lack of change in the ego levels of our counseling students (Fong & Borders, 1996) and White's (1985) nursing students. It also may be the key to any advancement in the effective application of ego development theory to counselor preparation and supervision.

SUMMARY AND CONCLUSIONS

Several conclusions seem warranted based on results of our research program on counselor supervision and related literature. First, Loevinger's ego development theory is a useful framework for understanding various aspects of counselor development, including counseling students' counseling-related cognitions and their effectiveness with clients. It appears that students' ego levels interact with or override their counseling experience in explaining these counseling-related variables. In short, students' ego levels appear to limit their ability to learn and then to think and behave with clients. Thus, the intuitive appeal of Loevinger's theory for counseling supervisors has some empirical support, although much additional work is warranted. For example, our studies were limited by the restricted range of ego levels of students admitted to counselor education programs. Although this limitation has some positive connotations, it presents major difficulties (e.g., lack of statistical power) for researchers. The use of nonparametric analyses, often necessary for measures of cognitive variables, presents similar limitations.

A second conclusion is that most counseling students (I-4) seem capable of working with the typical client (I-3/4), as they are within one stage, but higher, than their clients (cf. Swenson, 1980). "Most" and "typical," however, are not inclusive of all students and all clients. We are left with at least two choices. One is to help graduating counselors find work environments that are appropriate matches for their ego levels (cf. Swenson, 1980). A second, more personally appealing option is to begin to identify interventions (e.g., training and supervision approaches) that stimulate students' ego functioning, including expansion within an ego level (cf. horizontal decalage) and movement to a higher stage. Such work will depend on several factors, including counselor educators' and supervisors' abilities to assess students' ego levels and then engage students in activities that challenge them to think and behave at more advanced ego levels. If counselor educators and supervisors only teach the "rules" for doing therapy, or if students only learn the rules, counselors will be limited in their ability to help clients, and clients will have limited opportunities to grow in their own functioning.

ACKNOWLEDGMENTS

Appreciation is extended to Dr. Margaret L. Fong for her contributions to this chapter and the studies described herein.

POSTSCRIPT

CHAPTER

20

Completing a Life Sentence

Jane Loevinger
Stuckenberg Professor of Human Values
and Development, Emerita
Washington University in St. Louis

Many years ago, when our conception of ego development and its measurement by sentence completions were still news, I was occasionally asked to speak to graduate or even undergraduate students at various colleges and universities.

Certain questions were raised repeatedly by students. Many wanted me to tell how one could raise people's ego levels. My stock answer was that my enterprise was understanding and measuring, not intervening. Some student would reproach me (I particularly remember an earnest undergraduate), "Given the parlous state of the world, shouldn't you try to improve things?"

I cannot claim to be completely innocent of do-good impulses, sometimes tinged with self-righteousness. But I believed then, and still do, that the time-scale of world events precludes any influence from my empirical approach.

Currently my enterprise is being challenged from a different direction. Someone facile at programming has offered, if given enough data, to work out computerized scoring of the SCT. In fact, knowledgeable users of the SCT (Holt & Kaus) have tried it, but their apparent success was followed by failure of crossvalidation; so they concluded that it will not work (R. R. Holt, personal communication, 1995).

WHY DO WE HOLD OUT AGAINST THE
IRRESISTIBLE WAVE OF THE FUTURE?

Ego development as measured by the SCT is correlated with age, as every developmental sequence must be; with intelligence, as most individual differences are; and with SES, as many things are. When measuring ego development, those are confounded variables, and the scoring rule is that they should not influence the rating. A computerized scoring program would undoubtedly pick up signs of age, of intelligence, of SES in short— everything but ego level.

If all we want is the endgame, a Total Protocol Rating, we can just set up a regression equation with measures of age, intelligence, SES, and so on. No need to give the SCT. The purpose of the SCT measure of ego development was not just to arrive at some kind of score or prediction. It is a source of insight into personality development in general and of the individual subject.

Forays into original theorizing are not what I do. I lack the panache to be an original theorist, and the antennae to pick up airborne signals from people. I plod along as a pedestrian, going only where my data lead me. I have tried to make a virtue of that necessity, emphasizing the empirical grounding of my conception.

I am haunted still by the question of whether it would not have been wiser and more satisfying to have devoted a career to a more clearly useful endeavor, like curbing juvenile violence.

My somewhat macabre title reflects my experience that the wide interest in the SCT has acted as a confinement, constraining me to work on it. Publication of the revised SCT scoring manual (Hy & Loevinger, 1996) should signal my liberation.

The present volume, illustrating a variety of applications and implications of the conception of ego development, including but extending beyond use of the SCT, has vindicated some of my choices. One choice was to look beyond any short-term predictions to implications for a general view of personality. A second choice was to leave practical applications of the conception and its measurement to others more qualified and interested in the several areas, such as counseling, and its supervision.

Several issues raised by the essays herein remain to be dealt with, including the origin of the conception of ego development and its relation to cognitive development, or intelligence.

THE PROVENANCE OF MY CONCEPT
OF EGO DEVELOPMENT

As there is some question about the provenance of my concept of ego development, I may be forgiven for recounting its history. Following my graduation from the University of Minnesota, I stayed on to earn a masters in psychometrics. Minnesota was known as the bastion of Midwestern

Dust-Bowl Empiricism at that time. B. F. Skinner was its rising star, and one of my professors, Starke Hathaway, was working on the MMPI, the quintessential empirically-derived personality test. Psychoanalysis was dismissed with a wave of the hand, as no more worthy of serious scientific consideration than ESP.

The graduate students mocked psychoanalysis, assigning each other the roles of ego, superego, or id. I was always the superego, never the ego, and certainly not the id.

When one of the senior graduate students told me that he had been reading Freud, and Freud wasn't as bad as our professors said, I couldn't understand what had come over him. The only psychoanalyst in the community was a family friend, but it never occurred to me to ask him what "studying in Vienna" had been like.

In 1939, when I began doctoral work at the University of California at Berkeley, Jerzy Neyman (the statistician), Else Frenkel-Brunswik, and Erik Erikson arrived at about the same time. Luckily, I came to know all of them.

My advisor, Jean Macfarlane, knowing my Minnesota background, immediately enrolled me in the introductory seminar on psychoanalysis that Erikson was about to offer. I had read nothing by Freud prior to that time.

Erikson's seminar was the big event of the semester for the graduate students, most of whom were as naive about psychoanalysis as I was. Erikson was working on the ideas that became *Childhood and Society* (Erikson, 1950). The class was an exhilarating experience. I do not recall him ever mentioning the so-called structural hypothesis of ego, superego, and id. His lectures on the case histories were vivid and compelling. Any metatheoretical formulation would have been unnecessary, and uncharacteristic of his style.

The following semester, I was assigned to be research assistant to Erikson. At this time he was working on "configurations in play."

The previous year, working on Murray's study of personality at Harvard, he had asked the Harvard men to "make an exciting scene for a movie," using blocks and small toys. Most of them made automobile accidents. At Berkeley he was giving the same task to the preadolescent girls of the Berkeley Guidance Study. For them, an exciting scene regularly turned out to be someone intruding into a peaceful domestic scene.

I remember coming into his office when one of the girls had just left and he had not yet taken down her construction. I remarked that her construction was virtually a depiction of her body, as well as being a domestic scene. Erik frankly expressed his disappointment in me. Evidently he had been assured that I was so rigidly statistical in outlook that he did not need to worry about my getting caught up in interpretations.

If Macfarlane hoped I would infuse Erikson with a U.S. quantitative approach to his data, I failed her. I never saw any interest in quantification on his part. I doubt he would have approved of later attempts to turn his crises of normal psychosocial development into a developmental scale, nor, I think, would he have approved of turning identity achievement into a measurement scale.

The first of Freud's writings that I read were the Clark lectures (Freud, 1910)—I do not remember whether at the behest of Erikson or Egon Brunswik (to study for the German exam). I still consider those five lectures the best introduction to Freud's reasoning, and have assigned them to my own students for that purpose.

When asked to summarize Freud's argument in their own words, most students found the ubiquitous ego, superego, and id there. When I protested, they said, "But Prof. K. told us . . ." the purpose of the assignment was to show students the nature of analytic reasoning prior to those thought-stopping terms.

How fortunate I was to have been introduced to psychoanalysis by Erikson, rather than by psychology professors with only second-hand, superficial knowledge of analysis. Thus, I was doubly protected against the worst of psychoanalytic theorizing, first by Minnesota skepticism and training in scientific reasoning, and then by having been imprinted by Erikson's enthralling clinical presentations. I never had any patience with the concept of cathexis or "psychic energy."

For my dissertation, I reverted to my Minnesota mode, critically analyzing the psychometric concept of reliability (Loevinger, 1957). While working on my thesis, I taught statistical courses ordinarily covered by professors then on leave for war work and had a brief personal analysis. So ended my career preparation.

There followed a long domestic interlude, which took me first to Los Alamos, and then to St. Louis, after which for many years I had only a tenuous connection with academic psychology, and almost no contact with psychoanalysis, which was not flourishing in St. Louis then.

When I began to think about psychology again, I was aware that personal problems of mothers were an unexplored field. Drawing on my own experience, and propelled by two friends who suffered postpartum psychoses, I began to think about this relatively new field, accompanied by an informal group—chiefly Dr. Blanche Sweet, a Berkeley clinical graduate, and Kitty LaPerriere, a Washington University clinical student.

Again reverting to my Minnesota mode, I began by composing the Family Problems Scale (FPS; Loevinger, Sweet, Ossorio, & LaPerriere, 1962). It covered as many areas of family life as we could think of. Each item presented a choice between two opinions, each stated in sympathetic terms, such that the person holding the position would recognize it as her own. Here I was influenced by Frenkel-Brunswik and the work on the authoritarian personality that had been going on when I was at Berkeley (Adorno, Frenkel-Brunswik, Levinson, & Sanford, 1950). Our intent was to bypass the defenses of the respondents.

Lacking an academic appointment, I did not have the option of giving the test to my sophomore students. My first recourse was to mothers' groups, in churches, PTAs, and so on. This catch-as-catch-can sampling method was tedious, but in the long run, an advantage. By exploiting various resources of interested friends as well as our local contacts, we gradually accumulated data from a wide range of women.

Although our initial focus was mothers' problems, the pool of items was also seeded with items directed at various theories and ideas current in clinical discourse, such as punitiveness versus permissiveness, acceptance of the feminine role, and the psychoanalytic psychosexual stages. We always hoped to learn something about the personalities of women in general, and ultimately about all people.

After assembling the responses of a few hundred women, the items were intercorrelated and the correlations were analyzed by a factorial method—homogeneous keying (Loevinger, Gleser, & DuBois, 1953). Each statistically homogeneous cluster of items was examined to see what content it covered. None corresponded exactly to the supposed traits we had planted in the pool of items. There was no evidence of traits corresponding to the Freudian psychosexual stages. The concept of punitiveness–permissiveness had to be altered because of the inclusion of items such as "A father should be his son's best pal."

That cluster of items was renamed Authoritarian Family Ideology (AFI). It proved to be the most pervasive and robust cluster of items. For Dr. LaPerriere's dissertation, she administered the test postpartum in three St. Louis hospital's maternity wards, to samples of women varying in religion (Catholic, Protestant, and Jewish), in education (from part high school to college graduate), and in experience in childrearing, contrasting primiparous mothers with those having second or third children. AFI proved to be higher for younger women, did not vary significantly with religion, was lower with more education and with more experience in childrearing. When age was held constant statistically, the relation of AFI to education and experience in child-rearing remained significant.

These results suggested that AFI was a developmental variable. Dr. LaPerriere's faculty advisor, Professor Abel Ossorio, suggested that what we were measuring was *ego development*, a term I adopted despite LaPerriere's prescient warning that that term had been appropriated by psychoanalysts. Professor Ossorio also called my attention to the work of

Harry Stack Sullivan (1953) and to a paper on stages of interpersonal
integration by a group of psychologists in California studying delinquency
(Sullivan, M. Q. Grant, & J. D. Grant, 1957). Their conception of
interpersonal integration drew on ideas from Piaget, with whose work I
was completely unfamiliar, and from H. S. Sullivan.

To test the idea of AFI as a developmental variable we needed an
independent test applied to people who also took the Family Problems
Scale. That was the project of Dr. Elizabeth Nettles, who was interested
also in acceptance of women's role by adolescent girls, in connection with
their relations with their mother.

As the California group studying delinquency had used a sentence
completion test, that was a natural starting point. They had not published
a usable scoring manual, so we adopted a rough idea of their stages from
their article, and proceeded to improvise our own scoring system. We
began with their main stages, Impulsive (I–2), Conformist (I–3),
Conscientious (I–4), and Integrated (I–8).

Using the time-honored psychometric method of internal consistency,
from that point on the data drove the evolution of our manual, and with
the evolution of the manual, the description of the several stages, which
embody my conception of ego development.

During the time we were working on AFI, and it was leading to the
SCT for ego development, psychoanalysis—with which I was not then in
touch, was also changing.

The ego paradigm succeeded the original psychoanalytic drive
paradigm and partly superseded it (Loevinger, 1976, 1987b). I do not
understand how that shift could or should affect the use or evolution of
the SCT method, which has been data driven.

To me, the SCT method is intimately tied not to psychoanalytic theory
but to H. S. Sullivan's (1953) concept of the *self-system*. Sullivan proposed
self-system as an explicit alternative to the Freudian ego, superego, and id
formulation. The self-system is formed to protect the child from anxiety,
which would result from admitting observations or ideas inconsistent with
the person's current frame of reference. It is thus a cognitive dissonance
theory. When pressed to write about the self or ego, I compared it to the
immune system (Loevinger, 1987a), which has the similar function of
protecting the physical organism from foreign substances. The SCT is a
method of obtaining a sample of the ideas a person offers spontaneously.
Those ideas are assumed to provide clues to the person's frame of reference.
That is essentially what the ego stage is.

Some chapters herein point out, correctly, that I am unfamiliar with
many recent developments in psychoanalytic theory, including the work
of Winnicott. However, I do not see how those recent theoretical

contributions would affect the use of the SCT or its manual construction.

Understandably, I have continued to read major works of Erikson. I have also been interested in the writings of some other analytic theorists, including Hans Loewald (1980) and Mardi Horowitz (1979). I found their ideas compatible with my own thinking, but, even so, I have not found how they should affect the work with the SCT.

In any case, my conception of ego development did not precede its measurement by the SCT; rather, the stages of ego development that developed from our many studies with the SCT embody and shaped my conception of ego development.

The question of the relation of ego development to intelligence remains. That there is a correlation between the SCT and measures of intelligence is frequently observed. What does that import? Clearly one cannot expect a severely retarded person to advance to the highest ego level, but within any cohort fairly homogeneous with respect to intelligence, one can expect to find a range of character structures. In a small, unpublished study, I once found a range of ego levels in a group of "educable retarded" school children, including some at the Self-Aware level, although most were pre-Conformist.

Public figures, holding high office and being reasonably intelligent, on public record, range from those who will commit unethical acts for their own advantage or self-protection, to those who relinquish positions of power and profit rather than betray their own conscience.

Most of us in adult life, who have reached our plateau for ego development, are not prevented from reaching a higher level by intellectual limitations.

Measurement of intelligence has been part of psychology since about 1905. Early on there were those who suggested that all delinquency and criminality could be explained by intellectual deficit, but that idea was given up even before computer fraud came on line.

But in all the years of exploring intelligence and its implications, no one ever came to the idea of stages of character development like what is here called ego development. The stage-type conceptions of character in recent years have had various provenances, including studies of delinquency, interpersonal relations, moral judgment, and in our case, family problems.

The operative question is whether intelligence plays a larger part in the SCT measure than it does in ego development proper. It probably does, to some extent. Intelligence is more easily (indeed, inescapably) measured than are other elements, sources, and manifestations of ego level; so it is likely to dominate, partly as a methodological artifact. All personality tests are subject to such artifacts, usually due to intelligence.

CONCLUSION

It is gratifying, after years of wandering in the academic wilderness, to find that some active investigators have been reading what I have been writing. They permit me to hope that when my life sentence is completed, it will not be found devoid of meaning.

At the same time, it is disconcerting to find that some readers are reading my words with more earnest attention to detail and assumptions and implications than I paid in the writing.

References

Achenbach, T. M. (1982). *Developmental psychopathology* (2nd ed.). New York: Wiley.

Achenbach, T. M., & Edelbrock, C. (1987). *Manual for the Youth Self Report and Profile.* Burlington,VT: University of Vermont Department of Psychiatry.

Adams, G. R., & Shea, J. (1979). The relationship between identity status, locus of control and ego development. *Journal of Youth and Adolescence, 8,* 81–89.

Adorno, T. W., Frenkel-Brunswik, E., Levinson, D. J., & Sanford, R. N. (1950). *The authoritarian personality.* New York: Harper & Row.

Allen, J. P., Hauser, S. T., Bell, K. L., & O'Connor, T. G. (1994). Longitudinal assessment of autonomy and relatedness in adolescent-family interactions as predictors of adolescent ego development and self-esteem. *Child Development, 65,* 179–194.

Apter, A., Bleich, A., Plutchik, R., Mendelsohn, S., & Tyano, S. (1988). Suicidal behavior, depression, and conduct disorder in hospitalized adolescents. *Journal of the American Academy of Child Adolescent Psychiatry, 27,* 696–699.

Arlin, P. (1990). Wisdom: The art of problem finding. In R. J. Sternberg (Ed.), *Wisdom* (pp. 230–243). New York: Cambridge University Press.

Armon, C. (1984). Ideals of the good life and moral judgment: Ethical reasoning across the lifespan. In M. L. Commons, F. A. Richards, & C. Armon (Eds.), *Beyond formal operations: Late adolescent and adult cognitive development* (pp. 357–380). New York: Praeger.

Avery, R. R., & Ryan, R. M. (1988). Object relations and ego development: Comparison and correlates in middle childhood. *Journal of Personality, 56(3),* 547–569.

Bakhtin, M. M. (1981). *The dialogic imagination.* Austin: University of Texas Press.

Bakermans-Kranenburg, M., & Van IJzendoorn, M. (1993). A psychometric study of the Adult Attachment Interview: Reliability and discriminant validity. *Developmental Psychology, 29,* 870–897.

Baldwin, J. M. (1906). *Social and ethical interpretations in mental development.* New York: Macmillan.

Baron, R. M., & Kenny, D. A. (1986). The moderator–mediator variable distinction in social psychological research: Conceptual, strategic, and statistical considerations. *Journal of Personality and Social Psychology, 51,* 1173–1182.

Bartholomew, K. (1994). Assessment of individual differences in attachment. *Psychological Inquiry, 5,* 23–26.

Bartholomew, K., & Horowitz, L. M. (1991). Attachment styles among young adults: A test of a four-category model. *Journal of Personality and Social Psychology, 61,* 226–244.

Bartlett, F. C. (1932). *Remembering: A study in experiential and social psychology.* Cambridge, England: Cambridge University Press.

Basseches, M. (1989). Toward a constructive–developmental understanding of the dialectics of individuality and irrationality. In D. A. Kramer & M. J. Bopp (Eds.), *Transformation in clinical and developmental psychology.* New York: Springer-Verlag.

Baumeister, R. F. (1986). *Identity: Cultural change and the struggle for self.* New York: Oxford University Press.

Beck, A. T., & Beck, R. W. (1972). Screening depressed patients in family practice: A rapid technique. *Postgraduate Medicine, 52,* 81–85.

Belsky, J., & Cassidy, J. (1994). Attachment and close relationships: An individual difference perspective. *Psychological Inquiry, 5*, 27–30.

Bem, D. J., & Allen, A. (1974). On predicting some of the people some of the time: The search for cross-situational consistencies in behavior. *Psychological Review, 81*, 506–520.

Benjamin, J. (1988). *The bonds of love*. New York: Pantheon.

Benjamin, J. (1992). Recognition and destruction. In N. J. Skolnick & S. C. Warshaw (Eds.), *Relational perspectives in psychoanalysis*. Hillsdale, NJ: The Analytic Press.

Benjamin, J. (1994). The shadow of the other (subject): Intersubjectivity and feminist theory. *Constellations, 1*, 231–254.

Bergson, H. (1911). *Creative evolution* (A. Mitchell, trans.). New York: Holt.

Bernier, J. E. (1980). Training and supervising counselors: lessons learned from deliberate psychological education. *Personnel and Guidance Journal, 5*, 15–20.

Bernier, J. E., & Rustad, K. (1977). Psychology of counseling curriculum: A follow-up study. *Counseling Psychologist, 6*, 18–22.

Bertalanffy, L. von (1968). *General system theory*. New York: Braziller.

Blanck, G. (1976). An ambitious undertaking. *Contemporary Psychology, 21*, 801–803.

Blasi, A. (1976). Concept of development in personality theory. In J. Loevinger, *Ego development: Conceptions and theories* (pp. 29–53). San Francisco: Jossey-Bass.

Blasi, A. (1980). Bridging moral cognition and moral action: A critical review of the literature. *Psychological Bulletin, 88*, 1–45.

Blasi, A. (1982). Kognition, Erkenntnis und das Selbst [Knowledge in social cognition]. In W. Edelstein & M. Keller (Eds.), *Perspectivitat und Interpretation* (pp. 289–319). Frankfurt: Suhrkamp Verlag.

Blasi, A. (1984). Autonomie im Gehorsam: Die Entwicklung des Distanzierungsvermogens im socialisierten Handeln [Autonomy in obedience: The development of distancing in socialized action]. In W. Edelstein & J. Habermas (Eds.), *Soziale Interaktion und soziales Verstehen* (pp. 300–347). Frankfurt am Main: Suhrkamp.

Blasi, A. (1988). Identity and the development of the self. In D. K. Lapsley & F. C. Power (Eds.), *Self, ego, and identity: Integrative approaches* (pp. 226–242). New York: Springer-Verlag.

Blasi, A. (1993). The theory of ego development and the measure. *Psychological Inquiry, 4*, 17–19.

Blasi, A. (1995). Moral understanding and the moral personality. In W. Kurtines & J. Gewirtz (Eds.), *Moral development* (pp. 229–253). Boston, MA: Allyn & Bacon.

Blasi, A., & Milton, K. (1991). The development of the sense of self in adolescence. *Journal of Personality, 52*(2), 217–242.

Blatt, S. J., & Berman, W. H. (1990). Differentiation of personality types among opiate addicts. *Journal of Personality Assessment, 54*, 87–104.

Blocher, D. H. (1983). Toward a cognitive developmental approach to counseling supervision. *The Counseling Psychologist, 11*(1), 27–34.

Block, J. (1978). *The Q-sort method in personality assessment*. Palo Alto, CA: Consulting Psychologist Press.

Block, J. (1990). Ego resilience through time: Antecedents and ramifications. In *Resilience and psychological health*. Symposium of the Boston Psychoanalytic Society, Boston, MA.

Block, J. (1991). *Prototypes for the California Adult Q-Set*. Unpublished manuscript, Department of Psychology, University of California, Berkeley.

Block, J., Block, J. H., & Keyes, S. (1988). Longitudinally foretelling drug usage in adolescence: Early childhood personality and environmental precursors. *Child Development, 59*, 336–355.

Bloom, B.L. (1985). A factor analysis of self-report measures of family functioning. *Family Process, 24*, 225–239.

Blos, P. (1962). *On adolescence*. New York: Free Press.

Blumenthal, S. J., & Kupfer, D. J. (1988). Overview of early detection and treatment strategies for suicidal behavior in young people. *Journal of Youth and Adolescence*, 1–22.

for suicidal behavior in young people. *Journal of Youth and Adolescence*, 1–22.

Bond, M., Gardner, S. T., Christian, J., & Sigal, J. J. (1983). Empirical study of self-rated defense styles. *Archives of General Psychiatry, 40*, 333–338.

Borders, L. D. (1989). Developmental cognitions of first practicum supervisees. *Journal of Counseling Psychology, 36*, 163–169.

Borders, L. D., & Fong, M. L. (1989). Ego development and counseling ability during training. *Counselor Education and Supervision, 29*, 71–83.

Borders, L. D., Fong, M. L., & Neimeyer, G. J. (1986). Counseling students' level of ego development and perceptions of clients. *Counselor Education and Supervision, 26*, 36–49.

Borst, S. R., & Noam, G. G. (1993). Developmental psychopathology in suicidal and non-suicidal adolescent girls. *Journal of the American Academy of Child and Adolescent Psychiatry, 32*, 501–508.

Borst, S. R., Noam, G. G., & Bartok, J. A. (1991). Adolescent suicidality: A clinical-developmental approach. *Journal of the American Academy of Child and Adolescent Psychiatry, 30*, 796–803.

Boulding, K. E. (1956). Toward a general theory of growth. *General Systems, 1*, 66–75.

Boulding, K. E. (1978). *Ecodynamics, A new theory of societal evolution.* Beverly Hills, CA: Sage.

Boulding, K. E. (1986). The next thirty years in general systems. *General Systems, 29*, 3–5.

Bowlby, J. (1969). *Attachment and loss: Vol. 1. Attachment.* New York: Basic Books.

Bowlby, J. (1973). *Attachment and Loss: Vol. 2. Separation.* New York: Basic Books.

Bowlby, J. (1980). *Attachment and Loss, Vol. 3. Loss.* New York: Basic Books.

Bowlby, J. (1988). *A secure base: Parent-child attachment and healthy human development.* New York: Basic Books.

Bowlby, J. (1989). *The making and breaking of affectional bonds.* London: Routledge.

Brabeck, M. (1983). Moral judgment. *Developmental Review, 3*, 274–291.

Breger, L. (1974). *From instinct to identity: The development of personality.* Englewood Cliffs, NJ: Prentice-Hall.

Brenner, C. (1982). *The mind in conflict.* New York: International Universities Press.

Brent, D., Perper, J., Goldstein, C., Kolko, D., Allan, M., Allman, C., & Zelenak, J. (1988). Risk factors for adolescent suicide: A comparison of adolescent suicide victims with suicidal inpatients. *Archives of General Psychiatry, 45*, 581–588.

Bretherton, I. (1985). Attachment theory: Retrospect and prospect. In I. Bretherton & E. Waters (Eds.), *Growing points in attachment theory and research. Monographs of the Society for Research in Child Development, 50*(1-2, Serial No. 209), 3–35.

Bronfenbrenner, U. (1992). *Ecological systems theory. Six Theories of Child Development: Revised Formulations and Current Issues*, Ross Vasta. London: Jessica Kingsley Publishers.

Bronowski, J. (1972). New concepts in the evolution of complexity. (Part 2.) *The American Scholar, 42*, 110–122.

Broughton, J., & Zahaykevich, M. (1977). Review of the book *Ego development. Telos, 32*, 246–256.

Broughton, J., & Zahaykevich, M. (1988). Ego and ideology. In D. Lapsley & C. Power (Eds.), *Self, ego, and identity* (pp. 179–208). New York: Springer-Verlag.

Brown, L. (1989). *Narratives of relationship: The development of a care voice in girls ages seven to sixteen.* Unpublished doctoral dissertation, Harvard University Graduate School of Education.

Brown, L., Argyris, D., Attanucci, J., Bardige, B., Gilligan, C., Johnston, K., Miller, B., Osborne, D., Tappan, M., Ward, J., Wiggins, G., & Wilcox, D. (1988). *A guide to reading narratives of conflict and choice for self and moral voice.* Cambridge, MA: Harvard Project on Women's Psychology and Girls' Development.

Brown, L., & Gilligan, C. (1992). *Meeting at the crossroads: Women's psychology and girls' development.* Cambridge, MA: Harvard University Press.

Browning, D. L. (1983). Aspects of authoritarian attitudes in ego development. *Journal of Personality and Social Psychology, 45*, 137–144.

Browning, D. L. (1986). Psychiatric ward behavior and length of stay in adolescent and young adult in patients: A developmental approach to prediction. *Journal of Consulting and Clinical Psychology, 54,* 227–230.

Browning, D. L. (1987). Ego development, authoritarianism, and social status: An investigation of the incremental validity of Loevinger's Sentence Completion Test (short form). *Journal of Personality and Social Psychology, 53,* 113–118.

Browning, D. L., & Quinlan, D. M. (1985). Ego development and intelligence in a psychiatric population: Wechsler subtest scores. *Journal of Personality Assessment, 49*(3), 260–263.

Bruner, J. S. (1986). Actual minds, possible worlds. Cambridge, MA: Harvard University Press.

Bruner, J. S. (1990). Acts of mind. Cambridge, MA: Harvard University Press.

Buber, M. (1965). *The knowledge of man.* New York: Harper Collins.

Bursik, K. (1991). Adaptation to divorce and ego development in adult women. *Journal of Personality and Social Psychology, 60,* 300–306.

Bushe, G. R., & Gibbs, B. W. (1990). Predicting organization development consulting competence from the Myers-Briggs Type indicator and stage of ego development. *Journal of Applied Behavioral Science, 26,* 337–357.

Campos, J. J., Campos, R. G., & Barrett, K. C. (1989). Emergent themes in the study of emotional development and emotional regulation. *Developmental Psychology, 25,* 394–402.

Candee, D. (1974). Ego developmental aspects of the new left ideology. *Journal of Personality and Social Psychology, 30,* 620–630.

Cantor, N., & Zirkel, S. (1990). Personality, cognition, and purposive behavior. In L. Pervin (Ed.), *Handbook of personality theory and research* (pp. 135–164). New York: Guilford Press.

Carlozzi, A. F., Gaa, J. P., & Liberman, D. B. (1983). Empathy and ego development. *Journal of Counseling Psychology, 30,* 113–116.

Carlson, E. A., & Sroufe, L. A. (1995). Contribution of attachment theory to developmental psychopathology. In D. Cicchetti & D. J. Cohen (Eds.), *Handbook of developmental psychopathology* (pp. 581–617). New York: Wiley.

Carlson, V. K., & Westenberg, P. M. (in press). Cross-cultural research with the WUSCT. In J. Loevinger (Ed.), *Technical Foundations for measuring ego development.* Mahwah, NJ: Lawrence Erlbaum Associates.

Carroll, B. (1986). *Subject–object: Changes in structure between the ages of five and seven.* Doctoral dissertation, Harvard University.

Case, R. (1992). Neo-Piagetian theories of child development. In R. J. Sternberg & C. A. Berg (Eds.), *Intellectual development* (pp.161–196). New York: Cambridge University Press.

Cattell, R. B. (1971). *Abilities: Their structure, growth, and action.* Boston, MA: Houghton-Mifflin.

Cebik, R. J. (1985). Ego development theory and its implications for supervision. *Counselor Education and Supervision, 24,* 226–233.

Charme, S.T. (1984). *Meaning and myth in the study of lives: A Sartrean perspective.* Philadelphia: University of Pennsylvania Press.

Cicchetti, D. (1984a). *Developmental psychopathology.* Chicago, IL: University of Chicago Press.

Cicchetti, D. (1984b). The emergence of developmental psychopathology. *Child Development, 55,* 1–7.

Cicchetti, D. (1990). A historical perspective of developmental psychopathology. In A. M. J. Rolf, D. Cicchetti, K. Neuchterlein, & S. Weintraub (Ed.), *Risk and protective factors in the development of psychopathology* (pp. 2–28). New York: Cambridge University Press.

Cicchetti, D. (1991). Fractures in the crystal: Developmental psychopathology and the emergence of self. *Developmental Review, 11,* 271–287.

Clark, L. A., & Watson, D. (1991). General affective dispositions in physical and psychological health. In C. R. Snyder & D. R. Forsyth (Eds.), *Handbook of social and clinical psychology* (pp. 221–245). New York: Pergamon Press.

Cognetta, P. (1977). Deliberate psychological education: A high school cross-age teaching model. *The Counseling Psychologist, 6*(4), 22-25.

Cohler, B. J. (1982). Personal narrative and the life course. In P. Baltes & O. G. Brim, Jr. (Eds.), *Life span development and Behavior* (Vol. 4, pp. 205–241). New York: Academic Press.

Cohn, L. D. (1991). Sex differences in the course of personality development: A meta-analysis. *Psychological Bulletin, 109,* 252–266.

Colby, A., & Kohlberg, L. (1987). *The measurement of moral judgment* (Vols. 1-2). New York: Cambridge University Press.

Cooper, C. R., Grotevant, H. D., & Condon, S. M. (1983). Individuality and connectedness in the family as a context for adolescent identity formation and role-taking skill. In H. D. Grotevant & C. R. Cooper (Eds.), *Adolescent development in the family.* San Francisco: Jossey-Bass.

Costa, P. T., & McCrae, R. R. (1992). *Revised NEO Personality Inventory (NEO-PI-R) and NEO Five-Factor Inventory (NEO-FFI) Professional Manual.* Odessa, FL: Psychological Assessment Resources.

Costa, P. T., & McCrae, R. R. (1993). Ego development and trait models of personality. *Psychological Inquiry, 4,* 20–23.

Crittenden, P. M. (1992). Treatment of anxious attachment in infancy and early childhood. *Development and Psychopathology, 4*(2), 209–241.

Crowell, J., & Waters, E. (1994). Bowlby's theory grown up: The role of attachment in adult love relationships. *Psychological Inquiry, 5,* 31–33.

Cummings, A. L., & Murray, H. G. (1989). Ego development and its relation to teacher education. *Teaching and Teacher Education, 5,* 21–32.

Damon, W., & Hart, D. (1988). *Self-understanding in childhood and adolescence.* New York: Cambridge University Press.

Digman, J. M. (1990). Personality structure: Emergence of the five-factor model. In M. R. Rosenzweig & L. W. Porter (Eds.), *Annual review of psychology* (Vol. 41, pp. 417–440). Palo Alto, CA: Annual Reviews, Inc.

Dill, D. L., & Noam, G. G. (1990). Ego development and treatment requests. *Psychiatry, 53,* 85-91.

Dixon, J. W. (1986). *The relation of social perspective stages to Kegan's stages of ego development.* Doctoral dissertation, The University of Toledo.

Dole, A. A., et al. (1982). Six dimensions of retrospections by therapists and counselors: A manual for research. JSAS: *Catalog of Selected Documents in Psychology, 12,* 23. (Ms. No. 2454)

Duck, S. W. (1973). *Personal relationships and personal constructs: A study of friendship formation.* New York: Wiley.

Ekstrom, R. B., French, J. W., Harman, H. H., & Dermen, D. (1976). *Manual for the Kit of Factor-Referenced Cognitive Tests.* Princeton, NJ: Educational Testing Service.

Elder, G., Nguyen, T., & Caspi, A. (1985). Linking family hardship to children's lives. *Child Development, 56,* 361–375.

Epstein, S. (1994). Integration of the cognitive and the psychodynamic unconscious. *American Psychologist, 49,* 709–724.

Erickson, V. L. (1975). Deliberate psychological education for women: From Iphigenia to Antigone. *Counselor Education and Supervision, 14,* 297–309.

Erickson, V. L. (1977). Deliberate psychological education for women: A curriculum follow-up study. *The Counseling Psychologist, 6*(4), 25–29.

Erikson, E. H. (1950). *Childhood and society.* New York: Norton.

Erikson, E. H. (1959). Identity and the life cycle: Selected papers. *Psychological Issues, 1*(1), 5–165.

Erikson, E. H. (1964). *Insight and responsibility.* New York: Norton.

Erikson, E. H. (1984). *The life cycle completed.* New York: Norton.

Fairbairn, W. R. D. (1952). *Psychoanalytic studies of the personality.* London: Routledge & Kegan Paul.

Fairbairn, W. R. D. (1954). *An object relations theory of the personality.* New York: Basic Books.

Faust, M. S. (1983). Alternative constructions of adolescent growth. In J. Brooks-Gunn, &

A. C. Petersen (Eds.), *Girls at puberty* (pp. 105–125). New York: Plenum.

Feldman, S., & Elliot, G. (Eds.). (1990). *At the threshold: The developing adolescent*. Cambridge, MA: Harvard University Press.

Fischer, K. W. (1980). A theory of cognitive development: The control and construction of hierarchies of skills. *Psychological Review, 87*, 477–531.

Fischer, K. W., & Ayoub, C. (1994). Affective splitting and dissociation in normal and maltreated children: Developmental pathways for self in relationships. In D. Cicchetti & S. L. Toth (Eds.), *Rochester Symposium on Developmental Psychopathology: Vol. 5. Disorders and dysfunctions of the self* (pp. 147–222). Rochester, NY: Rochester University Press.

Fisher, S., & Greenberg, R. P. (1996). *Freud scientifically reappraised: Testing the theories and therapy*. New York: Wiley.

Fiske, D. W. (1974). The limits of the conventional science of personality. *Journal of Personality, 42*, 1–11.

Fiske, S. T., & Taylor, S. E. (1984). *Social cognition*. Reading, MA: Addison-Wesley.

Fong, M. L., & Borders, L. D. (1996). *Students' cognitive development during a counselor education program: A longitudinal study*. Unpublished manuscript.

Frank, S. J., & Quinlan, D. M. (1976). Ego development and adjustment patterns in adolescence. *Journal of Abnormal Psychology, 85*, 505–510.

Fransella, F., & Bannister, D. (1977). *A manual for Repertory Grid Technique*. New York: Academic.

Freud, S. (1910). *The origin and development of psycho-analysis*.

Freud, S. (1921). Group psychology and the analysis of the ego. In J. Strachey (Ed. and Trans.), *The standard edition of the complete psychological works of Sigmund Freud* (Vol. 18). London: Hogarth Press. (Original work published 1961)

Freud, S. (1923). The ego and the id. In J. Strachey (Ed. and Trans.), *The standard edition of the complete psychological works of Sigmund Freud* (Vol. 18). London: Hogarth Press.

Funder, D. C., & Colvin, C. R. (1991). Explorations in behavioral consistency: Properties of persons, situations, and behaviors. *Journal of Personality and Social Psychology, 60*, 773-794.

Fuqua, D. R., Johnson, A. W., Anderson, M. W., & Newman, J. L. (1984). Cognitive methods in counselor training. *Counselor Education and Supervision, 24*, 85–95.

Gardner, H. (1993). *Multiple intelligences: The theory in practice*. New York: Basic Books.

Garner, D. (1981). Body image in anorexia nervosa. *Canadian Journal of Psychiatry, 26*, 224–227.

Gazda, G. M., Asbury, F. R., Balzer, F. J., Childers, W. C., & Walters, R. P. (1984). *Human relations development* (3rd ed.). Boston: Allyn & Bacon.

Gedo, J., & Goldberg, A. (1973). *Models of the mind*. Chicago: University of Chicago Press.

George, C., Kaplan, N., & Main, M. (1985). *The attachment interview for adults*. Unpublished manuscript. University of California, Berkeley, Department of Psychology.

Gerard, R. W., Kluckhohn, C., & Rapoport, A. (1956). Biological and cultural evolution: Some analogies and explorations. *Behavioral Science, 1*, 6–34.

Gergen, K. J., & Gergen, M. M. (1988). Narrative and the self as relationship. *Advances in Experimental Social Psychology, 21*, 17–54.

Gfellner, B. M. (1986). Changes in ego and moral development in adolescents: A longitudinal study. *Journal of Youth and Adolescence, 15*, 147–163.

Gilligan, C. (1982/1993). *In a different voice*. Cambridge, MA: Harvard University Press.

Gilligan, C., & Attanucci, J. (1988). Two moral orientations: Gender differences and similarities. *Merrill Palmer Quarterly, 34*(3), 223-237.

Gilligan, C., Brown, L., & Rogers, A. (1990). Psyche embedded: A place for body, relationships, and culture in personality theory. In A. Rabin, R. Zucker, R. Emmons, & S. Frank (Eds.), *Studying persons and lives*. New York: Springer.

Ginsburg, S. D., & Orlofsky, J. (1981). Ego identity status, ego development and locus of control in college women. *Journal of Youth and Adolescence, 20*, 297–307.

Gjerde, P. F. (1995). Alternative pathways to chronic depressive symptoms in young adults: Gender differences in developmental trajectories. *Child Development, 66*, 1277–1300.

Glass, G. V., McGaw, B., & Smith, M. L. (1981). *Meta-analysis in social research*. London: Sage.

Gleick, J. (1987). *Chaos: Making a new science*. New York: Viking.

Glickman, C. D., & Tamashiro, R. T. (1982). A comparison of first-year, fifth-year, and former teachers on efficacy, ego development, and problem solving. *Psychology in the Schools, 19,* 558–562.

Globus, G. (1980). On "I": the conceptual foundations of responsibility. *American Journal of Psychiatry, 137,* 417–422.

Gold, S. N. (1980). Relations between level of ego development and adjustment patterns in adolescents. *Journal of Personality Assessment, 44,* 630–638.

Gough, H.G. (1987). *California Psychological Inventory — Administrator's Guide*. Palo Alto, CA: Consulting Psychologists Press.

Gould, S. J. (1977). *Ontogeny and phylogeny*. Cambridge, MA: Harvard University Press.

Greenberg-Lake Analysis Group (1991). *Shortchanging girls, shortchanging America: A nationwide poll to assess self esteem, educational experiences, interest in math and science, and career aspirations of girls and boys ages 9–15*. Washington, DC: American Association of University Women.

Greenberg, J. R., & Mitchell, S. A. (1983). *Object relations in psychoanalytic theory*. Cambridge, MA: Harvard University Press.

Greenson, R. (1965). The working alliance and the transference neuroses. *Psychoanalytic Quarterly, 34,* 155–181.

Grice, H. P. (1975). Logic and conversation. In D. Davidson & G. Harman (Eds.), *The logic of grammar* (pp. 64–153). Encino, CA: Dickinson.

Grotstein, J. (1981). *Splitting and projective identification*. New York: Jason Aronson.

Haan, N. (1977). *Coping and defending: Processes of self-environment organization*. New York: Academic Press.

Habermas, J. (1979). *Communication and the evolution of society*. Boston: Beacon Press.

Hanson, N. R. (1958). *Patterns of discovery*. Cambridge, England: Cambridge University Press.

Harré, R. (1984). *Personal being: A theory for individual psychology*. Cambridge,MA: Harvard University Press.

Harré, R. (1989). The "self" as a theoretical concept. In M. Krausz (Ed.), *Relativism: Interpretation and confrontation*. Indiana: Notre Dame University Press.

Hart, D. (1988). The adolescent self-concept in social context. In D. K. Lapsley & F. C. Power (Eds.), *Self, ego, and identity: Integrative approaches* (pp. 71–90). New York: Springer-Verlag.

Harter, S. (1983). Developmental perspectives on the self-system. In P. H. Mussen (Ed.), *Handbook of child psychology: Vol. 4. Socialization, personality, and social development* (pp. 275–386). New York: Wiley.

Harter, S. (1986). Cognitive-developmental processes n the integration of concepts about emotions and the self. *Social Cognition, 4,* 119–151.

Hartmann, E. (1939). *Ego psychology and the problem of adaptation*. New York: International University Press.

Harvey, O. J., Hunt, D. E., & Schroder, H. M. (1961). *Conceptual systems and personality organization*. New York: Wiley.

Hauser, S. T. (1976). Loevinger's model and measure of ego development: a critical review. *Psychological Bulletin, 33,* 928–955.

Hauser, S. T. (1978). Ego development and interpersonal style in adolescence. *Journal of Youth and Adolescence, 7,* 333–352

Hauser, S. T. (1993). Loevinger's model and measure of ego development: A critical review II. *Psychological Inquiry, 4,* 23–30.

Hauser, S. T., & Allen, J. P. (1991). *Antecedents of young adult ego development: The contributions of adolescent and parent ego development*. Paper presented at the biennial meeting of the Society for Research in Child Development, Seattle, WA.

Hauser, S. T., & Daffner, K. (1980). Ego functions and development: Emirical research and clinical relevance. *McLean Hospital Journal, 5,* 87–109.

Hauser, S. T., & Huffman, L. (Eds.). (1994). Affective processes in adolescence. *Special Issue of Journal of Research on Adolescence, 4*.

Hauser, S. T., & Levine, H. (1993). Relatedness and autonomy in adolescence: Links with ego development and family interactions. *Adolescent psychiatry*. Chicago: University of Chicago Press.

Hauser, S. T., Powers, S. I., & Noam, G. (1991). *Adolescents and their families: Paths of ego development*. New York: The Free Press.

Hauser, S. T., Powers, S., Noam, G., Jacobson, A., Weiss, B., & Follansbee, D. (1984). Familial contexts of adolescent ego development. *Child Development, 55*, 195–213.

Hauser, S. T., & Safyer, A. W. (1994). Ego development and adolescent emotions. *Journal of Research on Adolescence, 4*(4), 487–502.

Hauser, S. T., & Safyer, A. F. (1995). The contributions of ego psychology to developmental psychopathology. In D. Cicchetti & D. J. Cohen (Eds.) *Handbook of developmental psychopathology* (pp. 555–580). New York: Wiley.

Hauser, S. T., & Smith, H. F. (1991). The development and experience of affect in adolescence. *Journal of the American Psychoanalytic Association, 39* , 131–165.

Hazan, C., & Shaver, P. (1987). Romantic love conceptualized as an attachment process. *Journal of Personality and Social Psychology, 52*, 511–524.

Hazan, C., & Shaver, P. (1994). Attachment as an organizational framework for research on close relationships. *Psychological Inquiry, 5*, 1–22.

Heath, D. H. (1965). *Explorations of maturity: Studies of mature and immature college men*. East Norwalk, CT: Appleton & Lange.

Heath, D. H. (1991). *Fulfilling lives: Paths to maturity and success*. San Francisco: Jossey-Bass.

Hedges, L.V., & Oklin, I. (1985). *Statistical methods for meta-analysis*. New York: Academic Press.

Helson, R. (1967). Personality characteristics and developmental history of creative college women. *General Psychology Monographs, 76*, 205–265.

Helson, R., Mitchell, V., & Hart, B. (1985). Lives of women who became autonomous. *Journal of Personality, 53*, 257–285.

Helson, R., & Roberts, B. (1994). Ego development and personality change in adulthood. *Journal of Personality and Social Psychology, 66*, 911–920.

Helson, R., & Wink, P. (1987). Two conceptions of maturity examined in the findings of a longitudinal study. *Journal of Personality and Social Psychology, 53*, 531–541.

Henderson, A. F., & Kegan, R. (1989). Learning, knowing, and the self. In K. Field, B. Cohler, & G. Wool (Eds.), *Motive and meaning: psychoanalytic perspectives on learning and education*. New York: International Universities Press.

Hermans, H. J. M., & Kempen, H. J. G. (1993). *The dialogical self: Meaning as movement*. New York: Academic Press.

Hewer, A. (1982). *Structural-developmental assessment*. Unpublished manuscript, Harvard University.

Hollingshead, A. B. (1957). *Two factor index of social position*. Unpublished rep., New Haven, CT.

Holt, R. R. (1971). *Assessing personality*. New York: Harcourt Brace Jovanovich.

Holt, R. R. (1980). Loevinger's measure of ego development: reliability and national norms for male and female short forms. *Journal of Personality and Social Psychology, 39*, 909–920.

Holt, R. R. (1989). *Freud reappraised: A fresh look at psychoanalytic theory*. New York: Guilford.

Holton, G. (1973). *Thematic origins of scientific thought: Kepler to Einstein*. Cambridge, MA: Harvard University Press.

Horowitz, M. J. (1977). Cognitive and interactive aspects of splitting. *American Journal of Psychiatry, 134*, 549–553.

Horowitz, M. J. (1979). *States of mind*. New York: Plenum.

Horowitz, M. J. (1988a). *Introduction to psychodynamics: A new synthesis*. New York: Basic Books.

Horowitz, M. J. (Ed.). (1988b). *Psychodynamics and cognition*. Chicago: University of Chicago Press.

Horowitz, M. J. (1990a). A model of mourning: Change in schemas of self and other. *Journal* of the American Psychoanalytic Association, 38, 297–324.

Horowitz, M. J. (1990b). Nuances of technique in dynamic psychotherapy. Northvale, NJ: Aronson.

Horowitz, M. J. (1991). The development of person schemas. In M. J. Horowitz (Ed.), Person schemas and maladaptive interpersonal patterns. Chicago: University of Chicago Press.

Horowitz, M. J. (1997). Formulation 2, a basis for planning psychotherapy. Washington, DC: American Psychiatric Press.

Horowitz, M. J., Bonanno, G., & Holen, A. (1993). Pathological grief: Diagnosis and explanation. Psychosomatic Medicine, 55, 260–273.

Horowitz, M. J., Marmar, C., Weiss, D., DeWitt, K., & Rosenbaum, R. (1984). Brief psychotherapy of bereavement reactions: The relationship of process to outcome. Archives of General Psychiatry, 41, 438–448.

Howard, G. S. (1991). Culture tales: A narrative approach to thinking, cross-cultural psychology, and psychotherapy. American Psychologist, 46, 187–197.

Hurt, B. L. (1977). Psychological education for teacher education students: A cognitive-developmental curriculum. The Counseling Psychologist, 6(4), 57–60.

Hy, L. X., & Loevinger, J. (1989). Measuring ego development: Supplementary manual and exercises for Form 81 of the Washington University Sentence Completion Test. Unpublished manuscript, Department of Psychology, Washington University.

Hy, L. X., & Loevinger, J, (1996). Measuring ego development (Rev. ed.). Mahwah, NJ: Lawrence Erlbaum Associates.

Ihilevich, D., & Gleser, G. C. (1986). Defense mechanisms. Owosso, MI: DMI Associates.

Jackson, D. N., & Paunonen, S. V. (1980). Personality structure and assessment. In M. R. Rosenzweig & L. W. Porter (Eds.), Annual review of psychology (Vol. 31, pp. 503–552). Palo Alto, CA: Annual Reviews, Inc.

Jacobson, A. M., Hauser, S. T., Powers, S. I., & Noam, G. G. (1981). Ego development in diabetics: A longitudinal study. In A. Laron & A. Galatzer (Eds.), Psychological aspects of diabetes in children and adolescents. Basel: Karger.

Jacobson, A. M., Hauser, S. T., et al. (1982). Ego development in diabetics: A longitudinal study. Pediatric and Adolescent Endocrinology, 10, 1–8.

Jacobson, E. (1964). The self and the object world. New York: International Universities Press.

Jahoda, M. (1958). Current concepts of positive mental health. New York: Basic Books.

James, W. (1892/1963). Psychology. Greenwich, CT: Fawcett.

Joffe, P., & Naditch, M. P. (1977). Paper and pencil measures of coping and defense processes. In N. Haan (Ed.), Coping and defending: Processes of self-environment organization (pp. 280–294). New York: Academic Press.

John, O. P. (1990). The "Big Five" factor taxonomy: Dimensions of personality in the natural language and in questionnaires. In L. Pervin (Ed.), Handbook of personality theory and research (pp. 66–100). New York: Guilford Press.

John, O. P., Pals, J. L., & Westenberg, P. M. (in press). Personality prototypes and ego development: Conceptual similarities and relations in adult women. Journal of Personality and social Psychology.

Jöreskog, K. G., & Sörbom, D. (1993). LISREL 8 user's reference guide. Chicago, IL: Scientific Software International.

Josselson, R. (1980). Ego development in Adolescence. In J. Adelson (Ed.), Handbook of adolescent psychology. New York: Wiley.

Josselson, R. (1992). The space between us: Exploring the dimensions of human relationships. San Francisco: Jossey-Bass.

Josselson, R. (1996). Revising herself. New York: Oxford University Press.

Jung, C. G. (1963). Memories, dreams, and reflections. New York: Pantheon Books.

Kane, S. R. (1994). Shared meaning in young children's peer relationships: The development of practical social-cognitive know-how. Paper presented at the annual meeting of the Jean Piaget Society, Chicago, IL.

Kane, S. R., Raya, P. A., & Ayoub, C. C. (1997). Pair play therapy with toddlers and preschoolers. In R. L. Selman, C. L. Watts, & L. H. Schultz (Eds.), *Fostering friendship: Pair therapy for treatment and prevention* (pp. 185–206). Hawthorne, NY: Aldine de Gruyter.

Kapfhammer, H. P., Neumeier, R., & Scherer, J. (1993). Ich-Entwicklung im Übergang von Jugend und jungen Erwachsenenalter: Eine empirische Vergleichstudie bei Psychiatrischen Patienten und gesunden Kontrollprobanden [Ego development in the transition from youth and young adulthood: An empirical comparison study of patients and healthy controls]. *Praxis der Kinderpsychologie und Kinderpsychiatrie, 42,*106–113.

Kauffman, S. A. (1993). The sciences of complexity and "Origins of order." *Annals of Earth,11*(3),19–26.

Kegan, R. (1976). *Ego and truth.* Doctoral dissertation, Harvard University, Cambridge, MA.

Kegan, R. (1982). *The evolving self: Problem and process in human development.* Cambridge, MA: Harvard University Press.

Kegan, R. (1985). The loss of Pete's dragon: transformation in the development of the self during the years five to seven. In R. Leahy (Ed.), *The development of the self.* New York: Academic Press.

Kegan, R. (1986). The child behind the mask: Sociopathy as developmental delay. In W.H. Reid, J. W. Bonner III, D. Dorr, & J. I. Walker (Eds.), *Unmasking the psychopath.* New York: Norton.

Kegan, R. (1994). *In over our heads.* Cambridge, MA: Harvard University Press.

Kegan, R., Broderick, M., & Popp, N. (1992). *A developmental framework for assessing youth in programmatic interventions.* Unpublished report for U.S. Dept. of Labor and Public Private Ventures, Philadelphia.

Kegan, R., & Lahey, L. (1983). Adult leadership and adult development. In B. Kellerman (Ed.), *Leadership multidisciplinary perspectives.* Englewood Cliffs, NJ: Prentice-Hall.

Kegan, R., Noam, G., & Rogers, L. (1982). The psychology of emotions. In D. Cicchetti & P. Pogge-Hesse (Eds.), *Emotional development.* San Francisco: Jossey-Bass.

Kelly, G. A. (1955). *The psychology of personal constructs* (Vols. 1-2). New York: Norton.

Kernberg, O. (1967). *Borderline conditions and pathologic narcissism.* New York: Jason Aronson.

Kernberg, O. (1975). *Borderline conditions and pathological narcissism.* New York: Jason Aronson.

Kernberg, O. (1976). *Object relations theory and clinical psychoanalysis.* New York: Jason Aronson.

Kernberg, O. (1984). *Severe personality disorders.* New Haven, CT: Yale University Press.

Kirshner, L. A. (1988). Implications of Loevinger's theory of ego development for time-limited psychotherapy. *Psychotherapy, 25,* 220–226.

Klein, J. (1987). *Our need for others and its roots in infancy.* New York: Tavistock.

Klein, M. (1948). *Contributions to psychoanalysis.* London: Hogarth Press.

Kobak, R. (1994). Adult attachment: A personality or relationship construct? *Psychological Inquiry, 5,* 42–44.

Kobak, R., Allen, J. P., & Hauser, S. T. (1993). *Ego psychology revisited: Implications from attachment theory and research.* Manuscript submitted for publication.

Kohlberg, L. (1958). *The development of modes of thinking and choice in the years 10 to 16.* Unpublished doctoral dissertation, University of Chicago, IL.

Kohlberg, L. (1969). Stage and sequence: The cognitive-developmental approach to socialization. In D. A. Goslin (Ed.), *Handbook of socialization theory and research* (pp. 347–480). Chicago: Rand McNally.

Kohlberg, L. (1973). Continuities in childhood and adult moral development revisited. In P. B. Baltes & K. W. Schaie (Eds.), *Lifespan developmental psychology: Personality and socialization* (pp. 179–203). New York: Academic Press.

Kohlberg, L. (1979). *The meaning and measurement of moral development. The Heinz Werner Lecture Series, Vol. 13.* Worcester, MA: Clark University Press.

Kohlberg, L. (1983). Loevinger as an example of a quasi-structural approach to ego development. In J. Snarey, L. Kohlberg, & G. Noam (Eds.), *Ego development in perspective. Developmental*

Review, 3, 303–338.

Kohlberg, L. (1984). *Essays on moral development. Vol. 2. The psychology of moral development.* San Francisco, CA: Harper & Row.

Kohlberg, L. (1986). A current statement on some theoretical issues. In S. Modgil & C. Modgil (Eds.), *Kohlberg: Consensus and controversy* (pp. 485–546). Brighton, England: Falmer.

Kohlberg, L., Boyd, D., & Levine, C. (1990). The return of Stage 6: Its principle and moral point of view. In T. Wren (Ed.), *The moral domain* (pp. 151–181). Cambridge, MA: MIT Press.

Kohlberg, L., & Candee, D. (1984). The relation of moral judgment to moral action. In W. Kurtines &. G. Kurtines J. (Eds.), *Morality, moral behavior, and moral development.* New York: Wiley.

Kohlberg, L., Levine, C., & Hewer, A. (1983). *Moral stages: A current formulation and a response to critics.* New York: Karger.

Kohlberg, L., & Kramer, R. (1969). Continuities and discontinuities in childhood and adult moral development. *Human Development, 12,* 93–120.

Kohut, H. (1971). *The analysis of the self.* New York: International Universities press.

Kohut, H. (1977). *The restoration of the self.* New York: International Universities Press.

Krebs, D., & Hesteren, F. V. (1994). The development of altruism: Toward an integrative model. *Developmental Review, 14,* 103–158.

Kreitman, N. (1986). The clinical assessment and management of the suicidal patient. In A. Roy (Ed.), *Suicide* (pp. 181–195). Baltimore, MD: Williams & Wilkins.

Kuhn, T. S. (1970). *The structure of scientific revolutions* (2nd ed.) IL: University of Chicago Press.

Labouvie-Vief, G. (1982). Dynamic development and mature autonomy: A theoretical prologue. *Human Development, 25,* 161–191.

Labouvie-Vief, G. (1993). Ego processes in adulthood: A comment on Jane Loevinger. *Psychological Inquiry, 4,* 34–37.

Labouvie-Vief, G. (1994). *Psyche and eros: Mind and gender in the life course.* New York: Cambridge University Press.

Labouvie-Vief, G., Chiodo, L. M., Goguen, L. A., Diehl, M., & Orwoll, L. (1995). Representations of self across the life span. *Psychology and Aging, 10,* 404–415.

Labouvie-Vief, G., DeVoe, M., & Bulka, D. (1989). Speaking about feelings: Conceptions of emotion across the life span. *Psychology and Aging, 4*(4), 425–437.

Labouvie-Vief, G., Hakim-Larson, J., & Hobart, C. J. (1987). Age, ego, and the life-span development of coping and defense processes. *Psychology and aging, 2*(3), 286–293.

Lahey, L. L. (1986). *Males' and females' construction of conflict in work and love.* Doctoral dissertation, Harvard University.

Lahey, L. L., Souvaine, E., Kegan, R., Goodman, R., & Felix, S. (1988). *A guide to the subject object interview: Its administration and interpretation.* Unpublished manual, Laboratory of Human Development, Harvard University, Cambridge, MA.

Landfield, A. W. (1977). *Personal construct systems in psychotherapy.* Chicago: Rand McNally.

Langer, J. (1969). *Theories of development.* New York: Holt, Rinehart & Winston.

Lasser, V., & Snarey, J. (1989). Ego development and perceptions of parent behavior in adolescent girls. *Journal of Adolescent Research, 4*(3), 319–355.

Leadbeater, B. J. (1989). Relational processes in dialogue: The problem of intersubjectivity. *New Ideas in Psychology, 7*(2), 173–184.

Lee, L., & Snarey, J. (1988). The relationship between ego and moral development. In D. Lapsley & C. Power (Eds.), *Self, ego, and identity* (pp. 151–178). New York: Springer-Verlag.

Levinger, G. (1994). Attachment therapy as a paradigm for studying close relationships. *Psychological Inquiry, 5,* 45–47.

Levit, D. B. (1989). *A developmental study of ego defenses in adolescence.* Unpublished doctoral dissertation, Boston University, Boston, MA.

Levitt, M. Z., & Selman, R. L. (1996). The personal meaning of risky behavior: A developmental perspective on friendship and fighting in early adolescence. In G. G. Noam &

K. Fischer (Eds.), *Development and vulnerabilities in close relationships* (pp. 201–233). Hillsdale, NJ: Lawrence Erlbaum Associates.

Lewis, M., & Brooks-Gunn, J. (1979). *Social cognition and the acquisition of self.* New York: Plenum.

Lifton, R. J. (1986). *The Nazi doctors: Medical killing and the psychology of genocide.* New York: Basic Books.

Locke, D. C., & Zimmerman, N. A. (1987). Effects of peer-counseling training on psychological maturity of Black students. *Journal of College Student Personnel, 28,* 525–532.

Loeb, A. J. (Ed.). (1996). *The wit and wisdom of Mark Twain.* New York: Barnes & Noble.

Loevinger, J. (1947). A Systematic approach to the construction and evaluation of tests of ability. *Psychological Monographs, 61* (Whole No. 285).

Loevinger, J. (1957). Objective tests as instruments of psychological theory. *Psychological Reports, 3,* 635–694.

Loevinger, J. (1962). Measuring personality patterns of women. *Genetic Psychology Monographs, 65,* 53–136.

Loevinger, J. (1966a). The meaning and measurement of ego development. *American Psychologist, 21,* 195–206.

Loevinger, J. (1966b). Three principles for a psychoanalytic psychology. *Journal of Abnormal Psychology, 71,* 432–443.

Loevinger, J. (1968). The relation of adjustment to ego development. In S. B. Sells (Ed.), *The definition and measurement of mental health* (pp. 161-180). Washington, DC: U.S. Department of Health, Education, and Welfare.

Loevinger, J. (1969). Theories of ego development. In L. Breger (Ed.), *Clinical-cognitive psychology: Models and integrations.* Englewood Cliffs, NJ: Prentice-Hall.

Loevinger, J. (1976). *Ego development: Conceptions and theories.* Jossey Bass: San Francisco.

Loevinger, J. (1979a). Construct validity of the Sentence Completion Test of Ego Development. *Applied Psychological Measurement, 3*(3), 281–311.

Loevinger, J. (1979b). *Scientific ways in the study of ego development.* Worcester, MA: Clark University Press.

Loevinger, J. (1979c). The idea of the ego. *Counseling Psychologist, 8*(2), 3–5.

Loevinger, J. (1979d). Theory and data in the measurement of ego development. Worcester: MA: Clark University Press.

Loevinger, J. (1980). Some thoughts on ego development and counseling. *Personnel and Guidance Journal, 58,* 389–390.

Loevinger, J. (1983). On ego development and the structure of personality. *Developmental Review, 3,* 339-350.

Loevinger, J. (1984). On the self and predicting behavior. In R. A. Zucker, J. Aronoff, & A. Rabin (Eds.), *Personality and the prediction of behavior* (pp. 43–68). New York: Academic Press.

Loevinger, J. (1985). Revision of the Sentence Completion Test for Ego Development. *Journal of Personality and Social Psychology, 48*(2), 420–427.

Loevinger, J. (1986). On Kohlberg's contributions to ego development. In S. Modgil & C. Modgils (Eds.), *Lawrence Kohlberg: Consensus and controversy.* London: The Falmer Press.

Loevinger, J. (1987a). The concept of self or ego. In P. Young-Eisendrath & J. Hall (Eds.), *The book of the self: Person, pretext, and process* (pp. 88-94). New York: New York University Press.

Loevinger, J. (1987b). *Paradigms of personality.* New York: Freeman.

Loevinger, J. (1993a). Measurement of personality: True or false. *Psychological Inquiry, 4*(1), 1-16.

Loevinger, J. (1993b). Ego development: Questions of method and theory. *Psychological Inquiry, 4,* 56–63.

Loevinger, J. (1994). Has psychology lost its conscience? *Journal of Personality Assessment, 62,* 28.

Loevinger, J., & Blasi, A. (1991). Development of the self as subject. In J. Strauss & G. R. Goethals (Eds.), *The self* (pp. 150–167). New York: Springer-Verlag.

Loevinger, J. (in press). *Technical foundations for measuring ego development*. Mahwah, NJ: Lawrence Erlbaum Associates.

Loevinger, J., Cohn, L. D., Bonneville, L. P., Redmore, C. D., Streich, D. D., & Sargent, M. (1985). Ego development in college. *Journal of Personality and Social Psychology, 48*, 947–962.

Loevinger, J., Gleser, G. C., & DuBois P. H. (1953). Maximizing the discriminating power of a multiple-score test. *Psychometrika, 18*, 309–317.

Loevinger, J., & Hy, L. X. (1989). *Measuring ego development: Supplementary manual and exercises for Form 81 of the Washington University Sentence Completion Test*. Unpublished manuscript, Psychology Department, Washington University, St. Louis, MO.

Loevinger, J., & Knoll, E. (1983). Personality: Stages, traits, and the self. *Annual Review of Psychology, 34*, 195–222.

Loevinger, J., Sweet, B., Ossorio, A. G., & LaPerriere K. (1962). Measuring personality patterns of women. *Genetic Psychology Monographs, 65*, 53–36.

Loevinger, J., & Wessler, R. (1970). *Measuring ego development: Construction and use of a Sentence Completion Test, Vol. 1*. San Francisco: Jossey-Bass.

Loevinger, J., Wessler, R., & Redmore, C. (1970). *Measuring ego development: Scoring manual for women and girls*. San Fransisco: Jossey-Bass.

Loewald, H. W. (1960). The therapeutic action of psychoanalysis. *International Journal of Psychoanalysis, 41*, 16–26.

Loewald, H. W. (1980). *Papers on psychoanalysis*. New Haven, CT: Yale University Press.

Loganbill, C., Hardy, E., & Delworth, U. (1982). Supervision: A conceptual model. *The Counseling Psychologist, 10*(1), 3–42.

Lovell, C. W. (1990, November). *Cognitive development (Perry scheme) in students of counseling: The national sample (1990)*. Paper presented at the annual meeting of the Southern Association for Counselor Education and Supervision, Norfolk, VA.

MacIntyre, A. (1984). *After virtue*. Notre Dame, IN: University of Notre Dame Press.

Magnusson, D., & Endler, N.S. (Eds.). (1977). *Personality at the cross-roads: Current issues in interactional psychology*. New York: Wiley.

Mahler, M. S., Pine, F., & Bergman, A. (1975). *The psychological birth of the human infant*. New York: Basic Books.

Mahon, B. R., & Altmann, H. S. (1977). Skill training: Cautions and recommendations. *Counselor Education and Supervision, 17*, 42–50.

Main, M. (1990). Cross-cultural studies of attachment organization: Recent studies changing methodologies, and the concept of conditional strategies. *Human Development, 33*(1), 48–61.

Main, M., & Goldwyn, R. (1984). Predicting rejection of her infant from representation of her own experience: Implications for the abused-abusing generational cycle. *Monograph of International Journal of Child Abuse and Neglect, 8*, 203–217.

Main, M., & Goldwyn, R. (1991). *Adult attachment rating and classification system, Version 5.0*. Unpublished manuscript. Berkeley: University of California.

Main, M., & Goldwyn, R. (1994). *Adult attachment rating and classification system, Version 6.0*. Unpublished manuscript. Berkeley: University of California.

Main, M., & Goldwyn, R. (in press). Interview-based adult attachment classifications: Related to infant-mother and infant-father attachment. *Developmental Psychology*.

Main, M., & Hesse, E. (1990). Parents' unresolved traumatic experiences are related to infant disorganized attachment status: Is frightened and/or frustrating parental behavior the linking mechanism? In M.T. Greenberg, D. Cicchetti, & E. M. Cummings (Eds.), *Attachment in the preschool years: Theory, research, & intervention* (pp. 161–184). Chicago: University of Chicago Press.

Main, M., Kaplan, N., & Cassidy, J. (1985). Security in infancy, childhood, and adulthood: A move to the level of representation. In I. Bretherton & E. Waters (Eds.), *Growing points in Attachment Theory and Research* (pp. 66–104). Monographs of the Society for Research in Child Development (Serial No. 209).

Mandler, G. (1984). *Mind and Body.* New York: Norton.

Marcia, J. E. (1966). Development and validation of ego identity status. *Journal of Personality and Social Psychology, 3,* 551–558.

Marcia, J. E. (1993). The ego identity status approach to ego identity. In J. E. Marcia, A. S. Waterman, D. R. Matteson, S. L. Archer, & J. L. Orlofsky (Eds.), *Ego identity: A handbook for psychosocial research.* New York: Springer-Verlag.

Markus, H. (1977). Self-schemata and processing information about the self. *Journal of Personality and Social Psychology, 35,* 63–78.

McAdams, D. P. (1980). A thematic coding system for the intimacy motive. *Journal of Research in Personality, 14,* 413–432.

McAdams, D. P. (1985). *Power, intimacy, and the life story: Personological inquiries into identity.* New York: Guilford Press.

McAdams, D. P. (1990). Unity and purpose in human lives: The emergence of identity as a life story. In A. I. Rabin, R. A. Zucker, R. A. Emmons, & S. Frank (Eds.), *Studying persons and lives* (pp. 148–200). New York: Springer.

McAdams, D. P. (1992). The five factor model in personality: A critical appraisal. *Journal of Personality, 60,* 329–361.

McAdams, D. P. (1993). *The stories we live by: Personal myths and the making of the self.* New York: William Morrow.

McAdams, D. P. (1994a). Can personality change? Levels of stability and growth in personality across the life span. In T. F. Heatherton & J. L. Weinberger (Eds.), *Can personality change?* (pp. 299–314). Washington DC: American Psychological Association Press.

McAdams, D. P. (1994b). *The person: An introduction to personality psychology* (2nd ed.). Fort Worth, TX: Harcourt Brace.

McAdams, D. P. (1995). What do we know when we know a person? *Journal of Personality, 63,* 363–396.

McAdams, D. P. (1996). Narrating the self in adulthood. In J. Birren, G. Kenyon, J. E. Ruth, J. J. F. Shroots, & J. Svendson (Eds.), *Aging and biography: Explorations in adult development* (pp. 131–148). New York: Springer.

McAdams, D. P., Booth, L., & Selvik, R. (1981). Religious identity among students at a private college: Social motives, ego stage, and development. *Merrill-Palmer Quarterly, 27,* 219–239.

McAdams, D. P., Ruetzel, K., & Foley, J.M. (1986). Complexity and generativity at midlife: Relations among social motives, ego development, and adults' plans for the future. *Journal of Personality and Social Psychology, 50,* 800–807.

McCrae, R. R., & Costa, P. T. (1980). Openness to experience and ego level in Loevinger's sentence completion test: Dispositional contributions to developmental models of personality. *Journal of Personality and Social Psychology, 39,* 1179–1190.

McCrae, R. R., & Costa, P. T. (1983). Psychological maturity and subjective well-being: Toward a new synthesis. *Developmental Psychology, 19,* 243–248.

McCrae, R. R., & Costa, P. T. (1990). Personality continuity and the changes of adult life. In R. R. McCrae & P. T. Costa, Jr. (Eds.), *Personality in adulthood.* New York: Guilford Press.

McCrae, R. R., & Costa, P. T. (1996). Toward a new generation of personality theories: Theoretical contexts for the five-factor model. In J. S. Wiggins (Ed.), *The five-factor model of personality* (pp. 51–87). New York: Guilford Press.

Mead, G. H. (1934). *Mind, self, and society.* Chicago: University of Chicago Press.

Miller, J. B. (1976). *Toward a new psychology of women.* Boston: Beacon Press.

Miller, J. B. (1987). *What do we mean by relationships?* (Work in Progress, No. 22). Wellesley, MA: Stone Center Working Paper Series.

Miller, J. B. (1988). *Connections, disconnections and violations* (Work in Progress, No. 33). Wellesley, MA: Stone Center Working Papers Series.

Miller, J. G. (1978). *Living systems.* New York: McGraw-Hill.

Minsky, M. (1975). A framework for representing knowledge. In P. H. Winston (Ed.), *The psychology of computer vision*. New York: McGraw-Hill.

Mischel, W. (1968). *Personality and assessment*. New York: Wiley.

Mischel, W. (1973). Toward a cognitive social-learning reconceptualization of personality. *Psychological Review, 80*, 252–283.

Mischel, W. (1977). On the future of personality measurement. *American Psychologist, 32*, 246-254.

Mitchell, S. A. (1988). *Relational concepts in psychoanalysis*. Cambridge, MA: Harvard University Press.

Mosher, R. L., & Sprinthall, N. A. (1971). Psychological education: A means to promote personal development during adolescence. *The Counseling Psychologist, 2*(4), 3–82.

Murray, H. A. (1938). *Explorations in personality*. New York: Oxford University Press.

Neimeyer, G. J., & Neimeyer, R. A. (1981). Personal construct perspectives on cognitive assessment. In T. Merluzzi, C. Glass, & M. Genest (Eds.), *Cognitive assessment*. New York: Guilford Press.

Neugarten, B. (1979). Time, age, and the life cycle. *American Journal of Psychiatry, 136*, 887–894.

Nichols, K. E. (1981). *Moral and ego development in early adolescents: a longitudinal study of deliberate moral and psychological educational intervention*. Unpublished doctoral dissertation, Utah State University, Logan, UT.

Noam, G. G. (1988a). A constructivist approach to developmental psychology. In E. Nannis & P. Cowan (Ed.), *Developmental psychopathology and its treatment* (pp. 91–122). San Francisco:Jossey-Bass.

Noam, G. G. (1988b). The self, adult development, and the theory of biography and transformation. In D. K. Lapsley & F. C. Power (Eds.), *Self, ego, and identity: Integrative approaches* (pp. 3–29). New York: Springer Verlag.

Noam, G. G. (1988c). Self-complexity and self-integration: Theory and therapy in clinical-developmental psychology. *Journal of Moral Education, 17*, 230–245.

Noam, G. G. (1988d). The structural theory of biography and transformation: Foundation for clinical-developmental therapy. In S. Shirk (Ed.), *Cognitive-developmental approaches to child therapy* (pp. 213–317). New York: Plenum Press.

Noam, G. G. (1990). Beyond Freud and Piaget: Biographical worlds - interpersonal self. In T. E. Wren (Ed.), *The moral domain* (pp. 360–399). Cambridge, MA: MIT Press.

Noam, G. G. (1992). Development as the aim of clinical intervention. *Development and Psychopathology, 4*, 679–696.

Noam, G. G. (1993). Ego development: True or false? *Psychological Inquiry, 4*, 43–48.

Noam, G. G. (1996). Reconceptualizing maturity: The search for deeper meaning. In G. G. Noam, & K. W. Fischer (Ed.), *Development and vulnerabilities in close relationships*. Hillsdale, NJ: Lawrence Erlbaum Associates.

Noam, G. G., & Borst, S. (1994). Developing meaning, losing meaning: Understanding suicidal behavior in the young. *New Directions for Child Development, 64*, 39–54.

Noam, G. G., Chandler, M., & LaLonde, C. (1995). Clinical-development psychology: Constructivism and social cognition in the study of psychological dysfunctions. In D. Cicchetti & Cohen D. J. (Eds.), *Handbook of developmental psychology* (Vol. I, pp. 424–464).

Noam, G. G., & Cicchetti, D. (1996). Cognition and attachment: A response to Bretherton and Edelstein. *Human Development*.

Noam, G. G., & Dill, D. L. (1991). Adult development and symptomatology. *Psychiatry, 54*, 208–217.

Noam, G. G., & Fischer, K. (Eds.). (1996). *Development and vulnerabilities in close relationships*. Mahwah, NJ: Lawrence Erlbaum Associates.

Noam, G. G., Hauser, S. T., Santostefano, S., Garrison, W., Jacobson, A. M., Powers, S. I., & Mead, M. (1984). Ego development and psychopathology: A study of hospitalized adolescents. *Child Development, 55*, 198–194.

Noam, G. G., & Houlihan, J. (1990). Developmental dimensions of DSM-III diagnoses in adolescent psychiatric patients. *American Journal of Orthopsychiatry, 60*(3), 371–378.

Noam, G. G., & Kegan, R. (1982). Social cognition and psychodynamics: Toward a clinical developmental psychology. In W. Edelstein & M. Keller (Eds.), *Perspektivat und interpretation*. Frankfurt: Suhrkamp Verlag.

Noam, G. G., Kilburn, D., & Ammen-Elkins, G. (1989). *Adolescent development and psychiatric symptomatology*. Unpublished McLean Hospital Report, Belmont, MA.

Noam, G. G., Paget, K., Valiant, G., Borst, S., & Bartok, J. (1994). Conduct and affective disorders in developmental perspective: A systematic study of adolescent psychopathology. *Development and Psychopathology, 6,* 519–532.

Noam, G. G., Powers, S. I., Kilkenny, R., & Beedy, J. (1990). The interpersonal self in life-span developmental perspective: Theory, measurement, and longitudinal case analyses. In P. B. Baltes, D. L. Featherman, & R. M. Lerner (Eds.), *Life-span development and behavior* (Vol. 10, pp. 59–104). Hillsdale, NJ: Lawrence Erlbaum Associates.

Noam, G. G., Recklitis, C., & Paget, K. (1991). Pathways of ego development: Contributions to maladaptation and adjustment. *Development and Psychopathology, 3,* 311–321.

Norman, D. A., & Rumelhart, D. E. (1975). *Explorations in Cognition*. San Fransisco: Freeman.

Ogilvie, D. M. (1987). The undesired self: A neglected variable in personality research. *Journal of Personality and Social Psychology, 52,* 379–385.

Ogilvie, D. M., & Clark, M. D. (1992). The best and worst of it: Age and sex differences in self-discrepancy research. In R. P. Lipka & T. M. Brinthaupt (Eds.), *Self-perspectives across the life span* (pp. 186–222). Albany, NY: State University of New York Press.

Oja, S. N., & Sprinthall, N. A. (1978). Psychological and moral development for teachers: Can you teach old dogs? *Character Potential: A Record of Research, 8,* 218–225.

O'Malley, S. S., Suh, C. S., & Strupp, H. H. (1983). The Vanderbilt Psychotherapy Process Scale: A report on the scale development and a process-outcome study. *Journal of Consulting and Clinical Psychology, 51,* 581–586.

Ostrove, J., & John, O. P. (1994, August). *Personality types: Relations to traits, identity status, and life outcomes*. Paper presented at the meeting of the American Psychological Association. Los Angeles, CA.

Pascual-Leone, J. (1984). Attentional, dialectic, and mental effort: Toward an organismic theory of life stages. In M. L. Commons, F. A. Richards, & C. Armon (Eds.), *Beyond formal operations: Late adolescent and adult cognitive development* (pp. 182–215). New York: Praeger.

Pepper, S. C. (1942). *World hypotheses; a study in evidence*. Berkeley: University of California Press.

Petersen, A. (1988). Adolescent development. *Annual Review of Psychology, 39,* 583–607.

Pfeffer, C. R., Newcorn, J., Kaplan, G., Mizruchi, M. S., & Plutchik, R. (1989). Subtypes of suicidal and assaultive behaviors in adolescent psychiatric patients: A research note. *Journal of Child Psychology and Psychiatry and Allied Disciplines, 30,* 151–163.

Phillips, L., & Zigler, E. (1964). Role orientation, the action-thought dimension, and outcome in psychiatric disorder. *Journal of Abnormal and Social Psychology, 68,* 381–389.

Piaget, J. (1952). *The origins of intelligence in children*. New York: International Universities Press.

Piaget, J. (1954). *The construction of reality in the child*. New York: Basic Books.

Piaget, J. (1965). *The moral judgment of the child* (M. Gabain, Trans.). New York: Free Press.

Piaget, J. (1970). *Structuralism*. New York: Basic Books.

Piaget, J. (1981). *Intelligence and affectivity: Their relationship during child development* (T. A. Brown & C. E. Kaegi, Trans.). Palo Alto, CA: Annual Reviews.

Piaget, J. (1985). *The equilibration of cognitive structures: The central problem of intellectual development*. Chicago: University of Chicago Press.

Piaget, J., & Inhelder, B. (1969). *The psychology of the child* (Helen Weaver, Trans.). New York: Basic Books.

Picano, J. (1984). *Ego development and adaptation in adult women*. Unpublished doctoral dissertation, California School of Professional Psychology, Berkeley.

Piper, W. E., Azim, H, Joyce, A., & McCallum, M. (1991). Transference Interpretations, Therapeutic alliance, and outcome in short-term individual psychotherapy. *Archives of General Psychiatry, 48,* 946-953.

Polkinghorne, D. (1988). *Narrative knowing and the human sciences.* Albany, NY: SUNY Press.

Powitzky, R. J. (1975). *Ego levels and types of federal offenses.* Doctoral thesis, University of Texas at Dallas.

Prager, K. J., & Bailey, J. M. (1985). Androgyny, ego development, and psychosocial crisis resolution. *Sex Roles, 13,* 525-536.

Rapoport, A. (1978). General systems theory: A bridge between two cultures. Third Annual Ludwig von Bertalanffy Memorial Lecture. *General Systems, 23,* 149-156.

Recklitis, C. J., & Noam, G. G. (1990, August). *Aggression in adolescent psychopathology: Developmental and personality dimensions.* Poster presented at the American Psychological Association meeting, Boston, MA.

Redmore, C. D., & Loevinger, J. (1979). Ego development in adolescence: Longitudinal studies. *Journal of Youth and Adolescence, 8,* 1-20.

Redmore, C. D., Loevinger, J., & Tamashiro, R. (1978). *Measuring ego development: Scoring manual for men and boys.* Unpublished manuscript, Psychology Department, Washington University, St. Louis, MO.

Rest, J. R. (1979). *Development in judging moral issues.* Minneapolis: University of Minnesota.

Rest, J. R., & Narvaez, D. (1994). *Moral development in the professions: psychology and applied ethics.* Hillsdale, NJ: Lawrence Erlbaum Associates.

Riegel, K. F. (1973). Dialectic operations: The final period of cognitive development. *Human Development, 16,* 346-370.

Rierdan, J., & Koff, E. (1991). Depressive symptomatology among very early maturing girls. *Journal of Youth and Adolescence, 20,* 415-425.

Rierdan, J., & Koff, E. (1993). Developmental variables in relation to depressive symptoms in adolescent girls. *Development and Psychopathology, 5,* 485-496.

Rierdan, J., & Koff, E. (forthcoming). *Ego development, late pubertal development, and depression in adolescent girls.*

Rierdan, J., Koff, E., Costos, D., & Stubbs, M. L. (1987a, April). *Depression and ego development in adolescent girls.* Poster presented at the Biennial Meeting of the Society for Research in Child Development, Baltimore, MD.

Rierdan, J., Koff, E., Costos, D., & Stubbs, M. L. (1987b, April). *Ego development and pubertal status in adolescent girls.* Poster presented at the Biennial Meeting of the Society for Research in Child Development, Baltimore, MD.

Rierdan, J., Koff, E., & Flaherty, J. (1986). Conceptions and misconceptions of menstruation. *Women and Health, 10,* 33-45.

Robbins, D. R., & Alessi, N. E. (1985). Depressive symptoms and suicidal behavior in adolescents. *American Journal of Psychiatry, 142,* 588-592.

Robins, R. W., John O. P., & Caspi, A. (in press). The typological approach to studying personality. In R. B. Cairns, J. Kagan, & L. Bergman (Eds.), *The individual in developmental research: Essays in honor of Marian Radke-Yarrow.* Beverly Hills, CA: Sage.

Robins, R. W., John, O. P., Caspi, A., Moffitt, T. E., & Stouthamer-Loeber, M. (1996). Resilient, overcontrolled, and undercontrolled boys: Three replicable personality types? *Journal of Personality and Social Psychology, 70,* 157-171.

Rogers, A. (1987a). *Gender differences in moral thinking: A validity study of two moral orientations.* Unpublished doctoral dissertation, Washington University.

Rogers, A. (1987b). *Manual for rating moral orientations: The care orientation.* Unpublished manuscript. St. Louis, MO: Washington University.

Rogers, A. (1987c). *Manual for rating moral orientations: The justice orientation.* Unpublished manuscript. Washington University, St. Louis, MO.

Rogers, A. (1988). *A method for identifying a fugue of developmental themes in sentence com-*

pletions. Cambridge, MA: Harvard Project on Women's Psychology and Girls' Development.

Rogers, A., Brown, L., & Tappan, M. (1993). Interpreting loss in ego developent in girls: Regression or resistance? In R. Josselson & A. Lieblich (Eds.), *The narrative study of lives* (Vol. 2). Newbury Park, CA: Sage.

Rogers, L., & Kegan, R. (1991). Mental growth and mental health as distinct concepts in the study of developmental psychopathology: Theory, research, and clinical implications. In D. Keating & H. Rosen (Eds.), *Constructivist descriptions on developmental psychopathology* (pp. 103–147). Hillsdale, NJ: Lawrence Erlbaum Associates.

Rogosa, D. (1983). Demonstrating the reliability of the difference score in the measurement of change. *Journal of Educational Measurement, 20,* 335–343.

Rosenfeld, H. (1965). *Psychotic states.* New York: International Universities Press.

Rosznafsky, J. (1981). The relationship of level of ego development to Q-sort personality ratings. *Journal of Personality and Social Psychology, 41,* 99-120.

Rothbard, J. C., & Shaver, P. R. (1994). Continuity of attachment across the life span. In M. B. Sperling & W. H. Berman (Eds.), *Attachment in adults.* New York: The Guilford Press.

Ruble, D. N., & Brooks-Gunn, J. (1982). The experience of menarche. *Child Development, 53,* 1557–1566.

Rumelhart, D. E., & McClelland, J. C. (1986). *Parallel distributive processing: Explorations in the microstructure of cognition.* Cambridge, MA: MIT Press.

Rustad, K., & Rogers, C. (1975). Promoting psychological growth in a high school class. *Counselor Education and Supervision, 14,* 277–285.

Rutter, M. (1986). The developmental psychopathology of depression: Issues and perspectives. In M. Rutter, C. E. Izard, & P. B. Read (Eds.), *Depression in young people: Clinical and developmental perspectives* (pp. 3-30). New York: Guilford Press.

Rutter, M. (1990). Psychosocial resilience and protective mechanisms. In J. Rolf, A. S. Master, D. Cicchetti, K. H. Nuechterlein, & S. Weintraub (Eds.), *Risk and protective factors in the development of psychopathology* (pp. 181–214). New York: Cambridge University Press.

Sagi, A., van IJzendoorn, M., Scharf, M., Koren-Karie, N., Joels, T., & Mayseless, O. (1994). Stability and discriminant validity of the Adult Attachment Interview: A psychometric study of young Israeli adults. *Developmental Psychology, 30,* 771–777.

Sampson, E. (1993). *Celebrating the other: A dialogic account of human nature.* Boulder, CO: Westview.

Sasaki, M. (1981). Measuring ego development of female adolescents by sentence completions. *The Japanese Journal of Educational Psychology, 29*(2), 147–151.

Schank, R., & Abelson., R. (1977). *Scripts, plans, goals and understanding.* Hillsdale, NJ: Lawrence Erlbaum Associates.

Schultz, L. H. (1993). *Manual for scoring Young Adult Close Peer Relationship Interviews with the Developmental Relationship Scales.* Unpublished manuscript, Harvard University.

Schultz, L. H., Hauser, S. T., Selman, R. L., & Allen, J. P. (in preparation). *Construct validation of a measure of young adult close peer relationships: Relation to adolescent ego development, attachment representations, and gender.*

Schweder, R. A. (1975). How relevant is an individual difference theory of personality? *Journal of Personality, 43,* 455–484.

Schweder, R. (1977). Likeness and likelihood in everyday thought: Magical thinking in judgments about personality. *Current Anthropology, 18,* 637–658.

Scott, J. P. (1979). Critical periods in organizational processes. In F. Falkner & J. M. Tanner (Eds.), *Human growth* (Vol. 3). New York: Plenum.

Sechrest, L. (1976). Personality. In M. R. Rosenzweig & L. W. Porter (Eds.), *Annual review of psychology.* Palo Alto, CA: Annual Reviews, Inc.

Selman, R. L. (1980). *The growth of interpersonal understanding: Developmental and clinical analyses.* New York: Academic Press.

Selman, R. L. (1993). Analysis of personality development: Which analysis when? *Psychological Inquiry, 4,* 49–52.

Selman, R. L., & Schultz, L. H. (1990). *Making a friend in youth: Developmental theory and pair therapy.* Chicago: University of Chicago Press.

Selman, R. L., Schultz, L. H., Nakkula, M., Barr, D., Watts, C., & Richmond, J. R. (1992). Friendship and fighting: A developmental approach to the study of risk and prevention. *Development and Psychopathology, 4,* 529–558.

Shaffer, D. (1974). Suicide in childhood and early adolescence. *Journal of Child Psychology and Psychiatry, 15,* 275–291.

Shafii, M., Carrigan, S., Whittinghill, J. R., & Derrick, A. (1985). Psychological autopsy of completed suicide in children and adolescents. *American Journal of Psychiatry, 142,* 1061–1064.

Shafii, M., Steltz-Lenarsky, J., Derrick, A. M., Beckner, C., & Whittinghill, J. R. (1988). Comorbidity of mental disorders in the post-mortem diagnosis of completed suicide in children and adolescents. *Journal of Affective Disorders, 15*(3), 227–233.

Siegler, R. S. (1995). How does change occur: a microgenetic study of number conservation. *Cognitive Psychology, 28,* 225–273.

Silverman, W. K., La Greca, A. M., & Wasserstein, S. (1995). What do children worry about? Worries and their relation to anxiety. *Child Development, 66,* 671–686.

Simmons, R. G., & Blyth, D. A. (1987). *Moving into adolescence: The impact of pubertal change and social context.* Hawthorne, NY: Aldine de Gruyter.

Simon, H. A. (1965). The architecture of complexity. *General Systems, 10,* 63–76.

Sinnott, J. (1993) Use of complex thought and resolving intragroup conflicts: A means to conscious adult development in the workplace. In J. Demick & P. M. Miller (Eds.), *Development in the workplace.* Hillsdale, NJ: Lawrence Erlbaum Associates.

Skolnick, N. J., & Warshaw, S. C. (Eds.). (1992). *Relational perspectives in psychoanalysis.* Hillsdale, NJ: The Analytic Press.

Slaughter, D. T. (1983). Early intervention and its effects on maternal and child development. *Monographs of the Society for Research in Child Development, 48*(4, Serial No. 202).

Slomowitz, A. M. (1981). *The relationships of graduate training in psychotherapy, moral development, and ego development.* Unpublished doctoral dissertation, Adelphi University.

Smith, L. B., & Thelen, E. (Eds.). (1993). *A dynamic systems approach to development; applications.* Cambridge: MIT Press.

Snarey, J. (1995). In a communitarian voice. In W. Kurtines & J. Gewirtz (Eds.), *Moral development* (pp. 109–139). Boston, MA: Allyn & Bacon.

Snarey, J., & Blasi, J. (1980). Ego development among adult kibbutzniks. *Genetic Psychology Monographs, 102,* 117–157.

Snarey, J., Friedman, K., & Blasi, J. (1986). Sex role strain among kibbutz adolescents and adults: A developmental perspective. *Journal of Youth and Adolescence, 15*(3), 223–242.

Snarey, J., Kohlberg, L., & Noam, G. (1983). Ego development in perspective: Structural stage, functional phase, and cultural age-period models. *Developmental Review, 3,* 303–338.

Snarey, J., & Lydens, L. (1990). Worker equality and adult development: The kibbutz as a developmental model. *Psychology and Aging, 5*(1), 86–93.

Souvaine, E., Lahey, L., Kegan, R. (1990). Life after formal operations. In C. N. Alexander & E. J. Langer (Eds.), *Higher stages of human development.* New York: Oxford University Press.

Spencer, H. (1896). *Principles of sociology.* New York: Appleton.

Spengler, O. (1926). *The decline of the west* (C. F. Atkinson, Trans.). New York: Knopf.

Sperling, M. B., & Berman, W. H. (Eds.). (1994). *Attachment in adults* (pp. 31–71). New York: Guilford Press.

Sprinthall, N. A. (1994). Counseling and social role taking: Promoting moral and ego development. In J. R. Rest & D. Narvaez (Eds.), *Moral development in the professions: Psychology and applied ethics.* Hillsdale, NJ: Lawrence Erlbaum Associates.

Sprinthall, N. A., Reiman, A. J., & Thies-Sprinthall, L. (1993). Roletaking and reflection. *Learning and Individual Differences, 5*(4), 283–299.

Starrett, R. H. (1983). The conceptual communality between impulsiveness as a personality trait and as an ego development stage. *Personality and Individual Differences, 4,* 265–274.

Stern, D. (1985). *The interpersonal world of the infant: A view from psychoanalysis and development psychology.* New York: Basic Books.

Stinson, C., & Palmer, S. (1991). Parallel distributed processing models of person schemas and psychopathologies. In M. J. Horowitz (Ed.), *Person schemas and maladaptive interpersonal patterns.* Chicago: University of Chicago Press.

Stolorow, R., & Atwood, G. E. (1992). *Contexts of being: The intersubjective foundations of psychological life.* Hillsdale, NJ: The Analytic Press.

Stoltenberg, C. (1981). Approaching supervision from a developmental perspective: The counselor complexity model. *Journal of Counseling Psychology, 28,* 59–65.

Stoltenberg, C. D., McNeill, B. W., & Crethar, H. C. (1994). Changes in supervision as counselors and therapists gain experience: A review. *Professional Psychology, 25,* 416–449.

Stone, L. (1962). *The psychoanalytic situation.* New York: International Universities Press.

Strupp, H. H. (1981). *Vanderbilt Psychotherapy Process Scales (VPPS): Rater manual* (rev. ed.). Unpublished manuscript, Vanderbilt University, Nashville.

Suh, C. S., Strupp, H. H., & O'Malley, S. S. (1986). The Vanderbilt process measures: The Psychotherapy Process Scale (VPPS) and the Negative Indicators Scale (VNIS). In L. S. Greenberg & W. M. Pinshof (Eds.), *The psychotherapeutic process: A research handbook* (pp. 285-323). New York: Guilford Press.

Sullivan, C., Grant, M. Q., & Grant, J. D. (1957). The development of interpersonal maturity: Applications to delinquency. *Psychiatry, 20,* 373–385.

Sullivan, H. S. (1953). *The interpersonal theory of psychiatry.* New York: W. W. Norton.

Sullivan, H. S. (1962). *Schizophrenia as a human process.* New York: W. W. Norton.

Swenson, C. H. (1980). Ego development and a general model for counseling and psychotherapy. *Personnel and Guidance Journal, 58,* 382–388.

Taylor, C. (1989). *Sources of the self: The making of modern identity.* Cambridge, MA: Harvard University Press.

Tellegen, A. (1988). The analysis of consistency in personality. *Journal of Personality, 56*(3), 621–663.

Thelen, E., & Smith, L. B. (1994). *A dynamic systems approach to the development of cognition and action.* Cambridge, MA: MIT Press.

Thorne, A. (1993). On contextualizing Loevinger's stages of ego development. *Psychological Inquiry, 4,* 53–55.

Toynbee, A. J. (1946). *A study of history: Vol. 1.* (Abridged by D. C. Somervell). New York: Oxford University Press.

Vaillant, G. E. (1977). *Adaptation to life.* Boston: Little, Brown.

Vaillant, G. E. (1987). The Washington University Sentence Completion Test compares with other measures of adult ego development. *American Journal of Psychiatry, 144,*1189–1194.

Vaillant, G. E. (1993). *The wisdom of the ego.* Cambridge, MA: Harvard University Press.

Vaillant, G. E., & McCullough, L. (1987). The Washington University sentence completion test compared with other measures of adult ego development. *American Journal of Psychiatry, 144,* 1189–1194.

Van IJzendoorn, M. H. (1995a). Adult attachment representations, parental responsiveness, and infant attachment: A meta-analysis on the predictive validity of the adult attachment interview. *Psychological Bulletin, 113,* 387–403.

Van IJzendoorn, M. H. (1995b). Of the way we are: On temperament, attachment and the transmission gap: A rejoinder to Fox. *Psychological Bulletin, 117,* 411–415.

Villegas, E. (1988). *Judgments of responsibility.* Doctoral dissertation, Harvard University.

Walker, S. (1995). *College age drinking.* Doctoral dissertation, Harvard University.

Wallerstein, R. S. (1986). *Forty two lives in treatment.* New York: Guilford Press.

Wallerstein, R. S. (1988). One psychoanalysis or many? *International Journal of Psycho-Analysis, 69*, 5–22.

Weiss, R. (1982). Attachment in adult life. In C. M. Parkes & J. Stevenson-Hinde (Eds.), *The place of attachment in human behavior.* New York: Tavistock.

Weiss, R. (1994). Is the attachment system of adults a development of Bowlby's attachment system of childhood? *Psychological Inquiry, 5*, 65–67.

Wells, H. K. (1972). Alienation and dialectical logic. *Kansas Journal of Sociology, 3*(1).

Werner, H. (1957). The concept of development from a comparative and organismic point of view. In D. Harris (Ed.), *The concept of development.* MN: University of Minnesota Press.

Werner, H. (1961). *Comparative psychology of mental development.* New York: Science Editions. (Originally published 1948)

Werner, H. (1964). *Comparative psychology of mental development.* New York: International Universities Press. (Originally published 1940)

Westen, D. (1989). Are "primitive" object relations really preoedipal? *American Journal of Orthopsychiatry, 59*(3), 331–345.

Westen, D. (1990a). Psychoanalytic approaches to personality. In L. Pervin (Ed.), *Handbook of personality: Theory and research* (pp. 21–65). New York: Guilford Press.

Westen, D. (1990b). Toward a revised theory of borderline object relations: Implications of empirical research. *International Journal of Psycho-Analysis, 71*, 661–693.

Westen, D. (1991). Social cognition and object relations. *Psychological Bulletin, 109*, 429–455.

Westen, D. (1996). *Is Freud really dead? Toward a psychodynamically informed psychological science.* Unpublished manuscript, Harvard Medical School.

Westenberg, P. M., & Block, J. (1993). Ego development and individual differences in personality. *Journal of Personality and Social Psychology, 65*, 792–800.

Westenberg, P. M., Jonckheer, J., & Treffers, Ph. D. A. (in press). *Handleiding bij de Curium Zin Aanvul Lijst: Een Nederlandse Bewerking van de Washington University Sentence Completion Test for Ego Development* [Manual for the Curium Sentence Completion Test: A Dutch Adaptation of the Washington University Sentence Completion Test for Ego Development]. Lisse, The Netherlands: Swets Test Services.

Westenberg, P. M., Treffers, Ph. D. A., & Drews, M. J. (in press). A new version of the WUSCT: A sentence completion test for children and youths (SCT-Y). In J. Loevinger (Ed.), *Technical foundations for measuring ego development.* Mahwah, NJ: Lawrence Erlbaum Associates.

White, K. M., Speisman, J. C., Costos, D., & Smith, A. (1987). Relationship maturity: A conceptual and empirical approach. *Human Development, 18*, 221–234.

White, M. S. (1985). Ego development in adult women. *Journal of Personality 53*, 561–574.

White, R. W. (1959). Motivation reconsidered: The concept of competence. *Psychological Review, 66*, 296–333.

White, R. W. (1960). Competence and the psychosexual stages of development. In M. R. Jones (Ed.), *Nebraska Symposium on Motivation* (Vol. 8, pp. 97–141). Omaha: University of Nebraska Press.

White, R.W. (Ed.). (1964). *The study of lives.* New York: Prentice-Hall.

Whitmont, E. C. (1969). *The symbolic quest: Basic concepts of analytical psychology.* Princeton, NJ: Princeton University Press.

Winnicott, D. W. (1957). *Mother and child.* New York: Basic Books.

Winter, D. G. (1973). *The power motive.* New York: The Free Press.

Wohlwill, J. F. (1973). *The study of behavioral development.* New York: Academic Press.

Worthington, E. L., Jr. (1987). Changes in supervision as counselors and supervisors gain experience: A review. *Professional Psychology, 18*, 189–208.

York, K. & John, O. P. (1992). The four faces of Eve: A typological analysis of women's personality at midlife. *Journal of Personality and Social Psychology, 63,* 494–508.

Young-Eisendrath, P. (1987). Mental structures and personal relations: Psychodynamic theory in social work. In R. Dorfman (Ed.), *Paradigms of clinical social work.* New York: Bruner-Mazel.

Young-Eisendrath, P., & Hall, J. (1987). *The book of the self: Person, pretext, process.* New York: New York University Press.

Young-Eisendrath, P., & Hall, J. (1991). *Jung's self psychology: A constructivist perspective.* New York: Guilford Press.

Zetzel, E. (1956). Current concepts of transference. *International Journal of Psychoanalysis, 37,* 369–376.

Zielinski, C. E. (1973). Stage of ego development as a correlate of ability in discrimination and communication of empathic understanding. *Dissertation Abstracts International, 34,* 1635A.

Zucker, R. A., Aronoff, J., & Rabin, A. I. (Eds.). (1984). *Personality and the prediction of Behavior.* New York: Academic Press.

Author Index

W

Walker, S., 55, 374
Wallerstein, R. S., 59, 311, 374, 375
Walters, R. P., 339, 360
Ward, J., 147, 152, 156, 357
Warshaw, S. C., 237, 373
Wasserstein, S., 111, 373
Waters, E., 210, 359
Watson, D., 234, 358
Watts, C., 183, 186, 373
Weiss, B., 191, 212, 362
Weiss, D., 303, 311, 363
Weiss, R., 192, 203, 375
Wells, H. K., 40, 375
Werner, H., 42, 79, 254, 258, 375
Wessler, R., 22, 90, 91, 92, 93, 111,
    114, 133, 142, 172, 181, 205, 207,
    219, 206, 220, 226, 272, 274, 319,
    367
Westen, D., 62, 63, 66, 68, 90, 375
Westenberg, P. M., 91, 92, 94, 110,
    115, 116, 117, 118, 119, 122, 123,
    125, 127, 128, 130, 363, 375
White, K. M., 189, 375
White, M. S., 115, 116, 117, 118, 143,
    209, 240, 341, 342, 375

White, R. W., 21, 27, 375
Whitmont, E. C., 220, 375
Whittinghill, J. R., 284, 373
Wiggins, G., 147, 152, 156, 357
Wilcox, D., 147, 152, 156, 357
Wink, P., 116, 117, 119, 142, 209, 222,
    259, 362
Winnicott, D. W., 298, 375
Winter, D. G., 28, 375
Wohlwill, J. F., 256, 375
Worthington, E. L., Jr., 335, 375

Y

York, K., 113, 114, 121, 122, 123,
    127, 130, 375
Young-Eisendrath, P., 317, 375

Z

Zahaykevicyh, M., 164, 357
Zelenak, J., 284, 357
Zetzel, E., 309, 376
Zielinski, C. E., 339, 376
Zigler, E., 281, 370
Zimmerman, N. A., 141, 366
Zucker, R. A., 206, 376

Subject Index

ego development and, 28
predicting, 28, 29

C

Care orientation, 172-177
see Justice and care
Character development
see Interpersonal development
Cognition
ego development and, 13-24
Cognitive complexity
ego development and, 7-9
style, 17
Cognitive grasp, 15
Cognitive-developmentalism, 13-25, 221
compensatory transformations, 14
environmenntal interaction, 14
equilibration, 20
impulse control, 15
Kohlberg, 13, 14, 16
Loevinger's theory and, 15, 19, 20, 23-25
mental strategies, 14
personality, 14, 15
Piaget and, 13-17
universal development, 14
see Taxonomy and ontogeny
Competence
ego and, 119, 120, 222
Conflict
social conventions and, 6
Consistency (or holism) 4, 41, 55-58
Construct validity
adolescence/adulthood, 5, 6
age and gender, 5, 6
ego development and, 5, 6
scoring categories, 6
Counseling
see Psychotherapy
Counselor development, 331-341
cognition/perceptions, 335-338
counseling ability/skill/
effectiveness, 339, 340

developmental models of
supervision, 332, 333, 342, 343
horozontal decalage, 343
moral development, 334
relevance to ego development, 9, 333-335, 340-342
rules application, 331, 332

D

Depression
adolescent girls, 262-264
adolescents and, 284, 285
Beck Depression Inventory
(BDI), 262-269
ego development and, 8
Development
dialectic of personal growth, 19
internal differentiation, 19
motivation for mastery, 20, 21
reversal of active to passive
voice, 19
trans-stage theory, 19
Developmental domains, 153, 154
see Developmental psychopathology
Developmental psychopathology, 253-257
ego development and, 257-261
exposure to risk factors, 255
vulnerabilities, 149, 154, 159, 255
see Mental healath
Divorce, 143
Dutch scoring manual (SCT), 6, 89-112
adjustments in ego level descriptions, 96
and U.S. scoring categories, 89, 90, 94-96
cross-national value of, 109-112
expectations of, 91
Loevinger's model applied, 89
statistical/conceptual analyses, 94-96
subsequent studies, 92

I

Identity
  assimilation, 241, 243
  seeking, 272
  study (mother-daughter), 244-248
  ego development and, 29, 164, 180
  life story and, 33-36
  consolidation of, 37
  from traits to identity, 38
  I-Me quality of, 32-35
  intersubjectivity, 244-249
  schemas, 303
  self-schemata, 34
  status research, 244-248
  see Ego; Ethics; Schemas
Impulse control, 118, 146, 206, 257, 272, 287
Infant
  attachment and, 209, 210
  emotional resonance, 241
  intersubjectivity, 241-243
  maternal subjectivity, 243
  see mother-child systems
Intelligence, 3
  ego level and, 9
Interpersonal action, 185-188
Interpersonal development, 181-202
  autonomy/intimacy processes, 185, 186, 187, 189, 190
  Close Peer Relationship Interview and Developmental Relationship Scale, 182, 189-192
  longitudinal studies, 192-201
    interpersonal meaning, 197, 198
    interpersonal negotiation, 195, 196
    interpersonal understanding, 184, 185, 198, 199
  personal meaning, 186, 187
  social-cognitive process, 182
  tripartite model, 183-187
Interpersonal relations, 207, 257
Intersubjectivity, 237-243, 249
Intimacy, 116

J

Justice orientation, 172-177

K

Kibbutz, 172, 173, 177

L

Life-span, 168, 170, 174, 178, 180
  attachment, 203, 204
  ego development, 243, 244
  maturity, 225-231
  see Attachment; Schemas theory; Ego development
Loevinger's theory
  and moral development, 41-44
  and cognitive development, 41-44
  and sociocognitive development, 41-44
  and ego development, 41-44

M

Mastery
  cognition and, 19-22
  impulse control, 22, 24
  personality and, 22
Maturity, 133, 140-143, 224
  complexity vs. maturity, 273
  mature/immature models, 222, 224, 271
  mental health and, 271, 277, 280
  see Age trends in personality development
Meaning, 24
  vs. significance, 17, 18
Mental health, 271-295
  adaptation/maladaptation, 271-273, 275, 286-294
  aggression, 61, 272, 283, 284, 287
  convergence/divergence, 280
  complexity vs. maturity, 273
  conflict resolution, 272
  delinquency, 287

depression, 284, 285
ego development and, 8, 9, 117-
120, 272, 276-283
externalizing/internalizing
behaviors, 281-285, 289
identity, 272
immaturity, 271
interventions, 289
suicidality, 284, 285
symptoms, 282-286, 293
vulnerabilities, 272, 279, 289
Youth Self Report, 282
Micro-validation procedure, 3
Moral development, 6, 163-180
Moral Judgment Interview (MJI),
167, 173, 177, 179, 180
moral primacy, 166, 170, 178
see Ethics in ego development
Morality, internalized, 62
Mother-child system, 238-249
connection/autonomy, 242
goals and values, 245
infant in, 241, 242
intersubjectivity, 239-249
maternal subjectivity, 243
separation-individuation, 240-243
subject-subject relations, 238
see Attachment, Ego development
Mutuality, 241, 243

N

Nurturance
ego level and, 116
see Family, Mother-child system

O

Object constancy, 17
Object relations theory, 17, 63, 237,
238
Operations, operational, 14

P

Personality, adult, 114

basic personality types, 121-127
conflicted, 122-127
individuated, 122-127
traditional 122-127
beliefs and values, 114, 115
California Adult Q-Set (CAQ),
114, 122-131
cognitive complexity and
creativity, 115, 116
cognitive vs. interpersonal
functioning, 114, 116
ego development and, 3, 6, 20
gender roles, 117
impulse control, 118
measurement issues, 127-130
Mills Longitudinal Study, 122-131
openness to values scale, 114
psychological well being, 117-120
SCT and CAQ compared, 127-130
self-awareness, 116
theory of, 258
types and stages, 122-127
see Age trends in personality;
Ego development; Taxonomy to
ontogeny; Gender
Personality development, 3, 35-38
conscientious stage, 37
concept of trait, 36
ego and, 35
individual differences, 3
life stories in, 36
polar variables, 3
quantitative vs. qualitative
differences, 3
types, 6
Piaget
epistemic subject, 16
equilibration, 14, 18-20, 42
framework, 4
on structure of logic, 18
preoperational thinking, 42
Psychoanalytic theory, 59-69
Five Factor Model, 61
Freud's classical models, 61, 62
Loevinger/Freud models
compared, 64-66

50242378R00221

Made in the USA
Lexington, KY
26 August 2019